I0881432

TRANSFORMING THE SOUTH

MAKING THE MODERN SOUTH

David Goldfield, Series Editor

TRANSFORMING THE SOUTH

Federal Development in the Tennessee Valley, 1915–1960

MATTHEW L. DOWNS

Louisiana State University Press
Baton Rouge

Published by Louisiana State University Press
Copyright © 2014 by Louisiana State University Press
All rights reserved
Manufactured in the United States of America
First printing

Designer: Barbara Neely Bourgoyne
Typefaces: Anodyne and Cinta, display; Whitman, text
Printer and binder: Maple Press, Inc.

Portions of chapters 3, 4, and 5 first appeared, in different form, in the author's essay "'From Nothin' to Somethin'': The Tennessee Valley Authority and Federal-Local Cooperation in the Sunbelt South, 1940–1960," in *Nation within a Nation: The American South and the Federal Government*, ed. Glenn Feldman (Gainesville: University Press of Florida, 2014). Reprinted with permission of the University Press of Florida.

Library of Congress Cataloging-in-Publication Data are available at the Library of Congress.

ISBN 978-0-8071-5714-5 (cloth: alk. paper) — ISBN 978-0-8071-5715-2 (pdf) —
ISBN 978-0-8071-5716-9 (epub) — ISBN 978-0-8071-5717-6 (mobi)

The paper in this book meets the guidelines for permanence and durability of the Committee on Production Guidelines for Book Longevity of the Council on Library Resources. ♾

For Sarah and Graham

CONTENTS

TRANSFORMING THE SOUTH

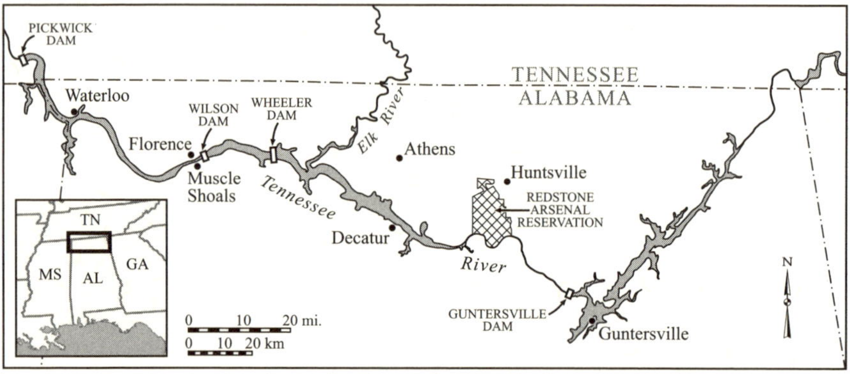

North Alabama's Tennessee Valley. Drawn by Mary Lee Eggart.

INTRODUCTION

BRISK MEN, ENERGETIC OF MOVEMENT AND SPEECH

Between 1915 and 1960, the communities situated in Alabama's Tennessee River Valley experienced a remarkable economic transformation, a change mirroring that of the larger South in spirit but outpacing it in scope and intensity. Like much of the post-Reconstruction "New South," Alabama's northernmost counties were dominated by profit-oriented agriculture, centered largely on the cultivation of corn and cotton. This monoculture depleted the soil of valuable nutrients, drove newly emancipated slaves and marginal farm families into dependent relationships with larger landholders, and precluded the diversification and modernization of the region's economy. Only Huntsville, and to a lesser degree Florence and Decatur, provided an industrial alternative, but low-wage, low-skill textile work did little to address rampant poverty and underdevelopment. Yet while farmers and mill workers struggled to survive, some community leaders enunciated an alternative path, promising growth and prosperity should the region encourage economic development and support diversified industrialization. Their vision of a modernized southern economy, when combined with increased interest from the federal government, sparked the transformation of the region. The resulting change was slow and uneven, marked by numerous social and political conflicts, but by 1960, the once-agricultural region evidenced a growing industrial economy, most notably in the aerospace and defense hub of Huntsville. This is the story of that transformation, and particularly of the local, regional, and national leaders who enacted that vision of a new South.

The modernized economy of cities like Huntsville, marked by federal and private investment, has become synonymous with growth in the South and Southwest in the late twentieth century, helping to demarcate a region colloquially called the "Sunbelt." Geographically, the Sunbelt stretched from the Carolinas to California, encompassing a number of "modern" economies, including military and defense installations, technology hubs, large-scale commercial farms, oil and gas refineries, and tourism and retail centers, many of which were encouraged or even funded by the federal government. As one northern journalist noted, by the latter half of the twentieth century, the Sunbelt had gained "enormous economic importance . . . changing the pleasant little backwaters and half-grown cities into an industrial and financial colossus."[1] Such growth did not happen quickly or spontaneously; in fact, a number of factors combined to draw those "pleasant backwaters" into the modern era. And, while some of the impetus for the modernization of the Sunbelt economy did emerge from Washington, D.C., community leaders throughout the region played a crucial role in encouraging and directing federal attention and investment. Thus, the history of the Sunbelt must be a history of the complicated relationship between the federal government and the towns and communities of the region itself, and no area better exemplifies the development of such a relationship than the Tennessee Valley.

In fact, the Tennessee Valley provides a near-perfect microcosm for the study of southern economic modernization in the twentieth century since few, if any, regions of the United States experienced such a long, intensive (and ongoing) period of federal attention and investment. Across North Alabama, civic leaders and regional development organizations worked to ensure that the growing relationship between Washington, D.C., and Florence, Huntsville, Decatur, and other valley communities continued. Civic leaders kept in constant contact with their congressmen and developed close connections with government officials and business owners. Local developers built roads, schools, hospitals, and parks, hoping to prove to investors that their communities were prepared for economic expansion. They organized municipal and regional groups with the sole responsibility of recruiting industry. Federal money poured into the South in the twentieth century, but southerners took the lead in directing the flow. In the Tennessee Valley and across the region, southerners modernized their own economy, and in doing so, played a crucial role in the creation of the Sunbelt.

As the valley boomed, however, prosperity failed to erase inherent inequalities, and just as the history of the Tennessee Valley illuminates the ways in which Sunbelt communities encouraged growth, it also shows just how complicated and fraught that growth could be for those unable or unwilling to participate in the modernization of the regional economy. Development brought dislocation, driving people from the land, taxing municipal infrastructures, and challenging southern mores and traditions. In some cases, the government called attention to southern shortcomings, forcing recipients of public funds to follow federal regulations and requiring political and social change as a precursor to further development. At other times, the community leaders joined with representatives of the government to privilege the prospect of growth over needed reforms. Many southerners, unwilling to wait on the federal government to respond, took advantage of the economic dislocations that came with rapid growth in the South to call for greater change. In the Tennessee Valley, African Americans demanded full inclusion, workers called for better wages and conditions, women worked to participate more fully in the growing prosperity, and conservationists decried the environmental consequences of unregulated industrialization. At the same time, myriad dislocations accompanied development. Thus, the history of the modernization of the Tennessee Valley perfectly captures the rise of the Sunbelt—the emergence of an industrial and commercial economy, marked by active cooperation (and contestation) between local, regional, and federal developers and accompanied by major changes in the everyday lives of southerners.

In his short story "Boom Town," Thomas Wolfe captures the sense of dislocation and alienation felt by his protagonist, John Hawke, in the face of the first hints of the rapid modernization that marked the emergence of the Sunbelt economy. Hawke returns to his childhood hometown, Altamont, on the eve of the Great Depression, only to find that it has been changed dramatically by a fever of real estate speculation and rapid economic development: "It was fantastic: within the town, along any of its streets, the property was being sold by the inch, the foot—thousands of dollars were being paid for each front foot of earth along these streets, and when the supply of streets were paved or a house had been built upon them, the land was being sold by the inch, the foot, for hundreds and thousands of dollars."[2] A "beautiful green hill," surmounted by a "glorious" old wooden hotel, once evoked the slow pace and genteel culture of the small southern town; now, the hill was "leveled . . . to an ugly mound of clay" and covered with "stores and garages and office buildings and parking spaces," and even a new hotel, a "gigantic biscuit-cutter" called the Ritz-Altamont.[3]

Wolfe's most biting critique, however, is reserved for the developers themselves, Hawke's former neighbors and classmates now caught up in the hysteria. One friend greets Hawke with a sneer for his "two-thousand-dollar-a-year school-teacher" life and inquiries into the availability of his mother's home. "Rufe" Mears, another childhood acquaintance, emerges as the mastermind behind Altamont's new culture. Hawke last knew Mears as a "black sheep," possessed by a "dark and corrupt energy" that led to get-rich-quick schemes, but also illegal gambling, cocaine addiction, and physical and mental "disintegration" that ended with a stint in the state insane asylum. Now, Mears was a development guru, a leading voice in the speculative ventures overtaking the town: "He had become . . . the high priest and prophet of this insanity of waste."[4]

For Wolfe, the mania for development that wrenched Altamont mirrored cries for progress across his New South. The author stressed the tragic nature of such ideals, as even Hawke's mother gave herself over to the frenzy. Standing in a cemetery, literally atop the town's buried past, she looked on the promise of a "great city" at Altamont, the "fortunate, good, and happy life" that would result from rapid prosperity. Hawke, seeing beyond the dreams to the reality of a town that had "passed from their possession" into bonds and mortgages in far-flung northern banks, lamented the loss: "It seemed to him that they were ruined: it seemed that even when they laughed and shouted and smote one another on the back, the knowledge of their ruin was in them—and they did not care, they were drunk and mad and amorous of death."[5]

Wolfe was not alone in viewing the rage for economic development as an alien force in southern society. Just as Hawke decried his former friends as they sold off their homes for profit, southerners feared that, in attracting industry and commerce to the former Confederacy, developers were mortgaging the values and culture that made the region unique and opening the South to a specifically nonsouthern way of life. Wolfe's account of immoral, even insane developers perfectly embodied his feelings of nostalgia and loss for a changing way of life, but in such an exaggeration the author overstates his case. Across the region, southerners did embrace the possibility of economic development, sometimes devolving into a form of the speculative madness of Wolfe's Altamont, but the impetus for development was neither as alien nor as haphazard as Wolfe's story suggests. Instead, southern leaders worked persistently and methodically to improve their community's and their region's economic foundations. In doing so, they played a crucial role in the creation of the modern southern economy.

Wolfe's "drunk" and "mad" boosters, his denuded hills, his greedy speculators, and his larger lament for the loss of an idyllic way of life all implied that the desire for rampant development was abnormal for the South. As such, Wolfe's protest recalls one of the first major reactions to industrialization in the South, the revolt of the Nashville "Agrarians." In 1930, a group of writers, academics, and intellectuals at Vanderbilt University calling themselves "Twelve Southerners" published a collection of essays entitled *I'll Take My Stand.* Afraid that industrialization, and particularly the pursuit of investment for industrial growth and development in communities across the region, might lead to a loss of regional identity, the authors praised an agrarian and rural lifestyle as the source of a uniquely southern way of life directly opposed to that of "northern" urban, industrial areas. In the introduction to the collection, Donald Davidson asked readers to "look very critically at the advantages of becoming a 'new South' which will be only an undistinguished replica of the usual industrial community."[6]

Like Wolfe, Davidson held particular ire for the younger generation of southerners who seemed to value the promise of economic growth from industrial development over the longstanding culture of the region. He warned that "younger Southerners, who are being converted frequently to the industrial gospel, must come back to the support of the Southern tradition," and he held out particular scorn for local chambers of commerce, which were "always trying to import some foreign industry that cannot be assimilated to the life-pattern of the community."[7] Beneath Davidson's romantic rhetoric was the belief that any desire for development, regardless of its source, was "foreign" to the South, and that southerners who sought such development acted on a specifically unsouthern impulse.

Other southerners echoed the Agrarians' concerns. In 1941, in *The Mind of the South,* Wilbur J. Cash agreed that calls for industrialization shaded toward the "unsouthern," calling some developers a "Yankeeizing party" and "fuzzy-witted fellows, without any clear understanding of what it was they were proposing."[8] Yet Cash also admitted that other boosters viewed development as a means to a particularly southern end, and in crafting an argument by which southerners might support development, Cash paved the way for a new reckoning of economic development. If pursued on the South's terms, he argued, "Progress stood quite accurately for a sort of new charge at Gettysburg, which should finally and incontestably win for [the South] the right to be itself for which, in the last analysis, it had always fought."[9] Thus Cash perceived a role for southerners in industrial development on the eve of the defense boom of World War II, in which the region experienced an influx of federal and private investment.

Southerners were certainly capable of introducing new ideas and new methods with the aim of preserving older traditions. As the preeminent southernist C. Vann Woodward remarked, those who had come to embrace "Progress" accepted "a new philosophy and a way of life and a new scale of values."[10] Woodward's developers were "new men," distinct from the plantation leadership with a different vision for the future of southern politics, the southern economy, and the southern social structure. Yet to argue that economic development was "new" or "unique" to the South is to miss the central fact of economic change after the Civil War: southerners may have looked beyond agriculture, but they refused to look beyond southern beliefs and values, particularly the racial and class lines firmly asserted after Redemption. In fact, as James Cobb suggested, the architects of this New South came to understand that economic development and social inequality could be mutually reinforcing, and "preserving social and political stability actually became part of the development effort."[11]

Efforts to bring industry to the South, then, were not so divorced from the region's character, and after the Civil War, southern civic and business leaders escalated their attempts to improve the local and regional economy by attracting industries, new and old. During Reconstruction, northern businessmen entered the South as veterans, philanthropists, occupiers, investors, and, in the eyes of many southerners, as "carpetbaggers." There, they found civic leaders in cities like Atlanta and Nashville eager to put northern capital to work in developing the southern economy, building railroads, investing in commercial districts where merchants could buy and sell southern crops, and founding mines and mills to turn raw materials into usable resources. Over the course of the 1880s, wages, capital, and the value of "cheap iron, cheap cloth, cheap coal, cheap lumber, turpentine, sugar, and tobacco products" doubled.[12]

The reality of northern investment in southern manufacturing, and particularly in industry that emerged in the South between Reconstruction and World War II, has led some scholars to call the region a "colonial economy." And as economic historian Gavin Wright has astutely noted, while the description of a colonial New South might be overwrought, southerners lacked the "technology, . . . industrial standards, specifications, [and] techniques" to create a uniquely southern program of industrialization. Instead, the money and know-how to create an economy based on manufacturing had to come from outside the region. When those skeptical of industrialization called the process "northern" and "unsouthern," they were essentially correct.[13] Many critics, including some in favor of industrialization, also noted the problems inherent in a program of development funded and enacted by outsiders. Southern communities attracted only the most rudimentary of industries, those able to use cheap and unskilled southern laborers to process the region's raw materials, and while southerners received paychecks, they found that white-collar positions, corporate profits, and the processed materials all left the South. As one novelist quipped, the southerner "performs the labor, gets the tuberculosis, [and] reaps the desolation and hardships, while the Northern or Eastern capitalist gets the profits."[14] Much of the ire of those angry at the northern presence was directed at the southerners who attracted outside investment, those "short-visioned Southerners who not only permit but seek this method of destroying themselves."[15]

The civic leaders who brought new businesses to the New South were largely born before the Civil War, though some were too young to serve and others "sat out the war or profited from the business opportunities it offered"; most were self-made men who left the antebellum farms and fields of their fathers for the opportunities that came in growing southern cities. They adopted a Whiggish political ideology that rejected regional separation in favor of national economic growth, entering into what the quintessential New Southerner, Henry Grady, called the "framework of the nation."[16] By the 1880s, these "New Men" of the New South had come to adopt an ideology that stressed development, growth, and prosperity; they had become "boosters" of retail, commerce, and manufacturing. Mark Twain concisely captured the spirit of these "new" southerners, calling them "Brisk men, energetic of movement and speech; the dollar their god, how to get it their religion."[17]

The most prominent boosters were newspaper writers and editors whose calls for development reached a national audience. Richard H. Edmonds and Daniel Augustus Tompkins of Baltimore's *Manufacturer's Record* and Henry Watterson of the *Louisville Courier-Journal* became spokesmen for a business-oriented South, but none gained the renown of the editor of the *Atlanta Constitution*, Henry Grady.[18] Atlanta's rapid growth after its destruction during the Civil War proved a microcosm of the New South. Efforts in the "Gateway City" centered on the chamber of commerce, an organization founded to protest railroad rate discrimination. By the 1890s and early 1900s, the chamber actively promoted the possibilities for business investment in the city, advertising in journals, publishing brochures and books, and attracting conferences and conventions. The organization encouraged Atlanta's municipal government to sponsor tax concessions and infrastructure improvement, and chamber members held subscription drives to sponsor localized industrial growth.[19] In 1881, and again in 1887 and 1896, the city sponsored expansive industrial expositions, selling national and international business leaders on the possibilities inherent in the city and the South.[20]

Grady captured the ethos of Atlanta's and the New South's civic leadership. Speaking to a collection of investors in New York City in 1886, the newspaperman described a South fundamentally different from the antebellum plantation society of the Confederacy. Grady's South had come to accept its defeat in the Civil War, and as such, considered itself part of the nation as a whole, "full-statured and equal among the people of the earth," and "emancipated" with "her honest purpose . . . crossed, and her brave armies beaten."[21] The South was defeated but not humbled, and had "nothing for which to apologize"; instead, Grady's South was firmly dedicated to a new and prosperous future.[22] Southerners themselves would lead the effort to remake the southern economy: "We shall see how the people of this section . . . met new and adverse conditions with unquailing courage. . . . How at last, controlling with their own hands their local affairs, they began, in ragged and torn battalions, that march of restoration and development that has challenged universal admiration."[23]

On the eve of the First World War, southern cities had the framework necessary for concentrated economic development. In urban centers like Atlanta, Nashville, and Birmingham, civic leaders used promotional techniques and generous concessions to attract industrial investment and encourage business growth.[24] The industries that located there were rudimentary and extractive, mining coal, manufacturing steel and textiles, and processing tobacco and lumber, and they did little to move the southern economy beyond the low-wage, low-skill industries that consistently failed to reinvest profits in the improvement of the South. In fact, New South industry largely reinforced the inequalities that left wealthy white men in positions of power in southern society. Yet, like Grady, boosters continued in their quest for a modern, prosperous economy, and the defense effort for the Great War provided a new opportunity for investment. With the increased demand for cloth to produce uniforms, lumber and steel for armaments, and munitions for the front, southerners pursued lucrative government contracts; as a columnist for the *Manufacturer's Record* noted, southerners proved themselves "born booster[s], and the mood is contagious."[25]

This history traces the "contagion" of economic development in the South as it matured in the middle of the twentieth century, specifically focusing on the efforts of organizations and individuals in one geographic location, the Tennessee River Valley. Over the course of the twentieth century, the federal government lavished millions of dollars on the region in an attempt to encourage economic growth in an area that had long stagnated due to a heavy reliance on cotton cultivation and extractive, low-wage industry. The process began at Muscle Shoals during the World War I defense effort, as the promise of a government dam and fertilizer plant inspired local leaders, Tennessee Valley farmers, and national politicians to begin a dialogue on the importance of economic growth. As Congress debated the relative merits of private ownership and continued government operation, Nebraska's progressive Republican senator, George Norris, laid the foundation for a regional planning authority centered in the Tennessee Valley. Yet at the local level, residents organized for industrial and commercial growth. Inspired by federal investment, they prepared to work with the government when beneficial, and insisted that prosperity meet the perceived needs of the community and region. Throughout the 1920s, groups argued over the future of the regional economy, and in the process, gave rise to a plan of development which foreshadowed the later Sunbelt economy.

The fight over Muscle Shoals convinced some of the need for greater regional cooperation, and beginning in 1933 the Tennessee Valley Authority provided federal leadership for such a program, overseeing the preservation and utilization of the Tennessee River watershed's natural and human resources. Led by the idealistic Arthur E. Morgan, the New Deal agency tried to address the valley's economic problems by training and employing workers, instructing farmers in intelligent agricultural practices, and taming floods with newly constructed dams. Very quickly, however, Morgan found that even the benefits of his program brought serious complications. TVA reservoirs flooded thousands of acres along the river, covering fertile bottomlands ideal for cultivation and displacing thousands of residents. Many of those who relocated moved into valley towns and cities, where they abandoned agriculture for wage labor. In Florence, Decatur, and other towns across the valley, community leaders used TVA's emergence to ask for federal assistance in attracting new industry. One member of TVA's governing board of directors, David E. Lilienthal, sympathized with their demands. By the late 1930s, philosophical differences between Lilienthal and A. E. Morgan exploded into a power struggle for leadership. Ultimately victorious, Lilienthal led TVA into World War II and into cooperation with the private sector in an unprecedented manner. By the 1950s, the authority was a leading force in encouraging valley leaders to adopt directed industrial growth as the most effective path to prosperity, particularly in Decatur, where civic boosters led by newspaper editor Barrett Shelton mobilized the city to action. As in Florence and Muscle Shoals, federal investment gave this southern town a completely new character.

More than any other Tennessee Valley city, however, Huntsville embraced the booster ethos with a civic leadership dedicated to building a prosperous economy on a foundation of federal investment. The small mill town changed overnight when the U.S. Army located an ordnance plant on riverfront farmland. The city's population boomed, wages rose, and community leaders scrambled to prepare Huntsville for such rapid growth. Federal money was never certain; when World War II came to a close, the government decommissioned its arsenals, threatening the city's newfound success. Cold War missile and space programs revitalized the city, and by the 1960s Huntsville perfectly captured the spirit of the Sunbelt, with active government facilities, an array of defense contractors, and a rapidly growing suburban middle class. No longer a sleepy southern cotton-processing center, Huntsville emerged as a regional nexus of high-paying, high-tech jobs, forcing the surrounding community to work ceaselessly to keep up with the economic, political, and social consequences of rampant growth.

The economic development of the South was the result of decades of cooperation and conflict as residents, civic leaders, state officials, and federal politicians determined the economic future of a rapidly changing region. Much of the impulse for change came not from above, but from within southern communities eager for prosperity. Farmers, failing to turn a profit on rented fields, looked to limited industrialization as a means of economic salvation. Local businessmen, hurt by falling profits and failing business, called for economic development as a means of community revitalization. Government funding was an important aspect of southern development, but it did not force change on its own. Instead, federal investment provided the means by which locals created (or attempted to create) the prosperity they sought. In order to understand how an economically stagnant South entered the booming national economy, historians must see economic modernization as a dialogue in which southerners worked to attract and direct federal funds, even as government leaders struggled to retain control of the process. In the Tennessee Valley and across the South, development was a long and complicated process, and southerners deserve a share of the credit, as well as a share of the blame, that accompanied the emergence of the Sunbelt. In North Alabama, regional economic development began at Muscle Shoals, where the World War I defense effort spurred residents to look to the federal government for much-needed investments. The fight over the resulting dam and nitrate plants was the first in a long struggle by Tennessee Valley leaders to industrialize their dying agricultural economy.

ONE

A LIVING MONUMENT TO THAT BROAD PRINCIPLE OF DEMOCRACY 1915–1924

In June 1921, industrialist Henry Ford arrived unannounced in Muscle Shoals, Alabama, and toured the site of Wilson Dam and two government-owned nitrate-producing plants, inactive since their completion during World War I. Ford tried to downplay the visit, saying that he hoped to use hydroelectric power in his own factories in Michigan, but the *Florence Times* ran the story on the front page, and the region buzzed with the possibility that, given Ford's interest, "Florence may expect to become a great manufacturing center, and a big city, at a much earlier date than has been anticipated."[1] The next month, Ford submitted an offer to lease the dam and purchase the nitrate plants outright. He promised to make hydroelectric power cheaply available to the farmers of the area, agreed to use the nitrate plants to make high-grade fertilizer at the lowest possible price, and began to enunciate plans for the region's industrialization.[2] Ford offered salvation for the struggling farmers of North Alabama and promised rapid growth for the region's boosters. Already nationally known as a successful businessman, Ford was turning his substantial fortune and organizational wizardry to the solution of the stalled government development at Muscle Shoals.[3]

By November, no longer trying to hide his intentions, Ford boasted of the economic potential of the Muscle Shoals properties. He claimed that he would employ a million men in the South by bringing in industries that would develop the region. He called for a "dozen dams" on the Tennessee River and noted that, with each additional unit of horsepower produced, he could hire one extra man in his factories. He promised that his nitrate plants would produce enough fertilizer to improve the entire cotton belt and run farms more efficiently, allowing farmers to work an average of only twenty days per year. Freed from the farms, this new industrial working class would spend the rest of the year in a factory near home, working for a wage.[4] In December, Ford, his friend Thomas Edison, and his son, Edsel, arrived in North Alabama and toured the facilities. The party was fêted with impromptu parades, glowing praise, and even an "old-fashioned southern barbecue" at a local residence. After the whirlwind visit, Ford left a message for the people of the Tennessee Valley: "[If] the Ford organization takes over the Muscle Shoals development the country roundabout will experience a great wave of prosperity."[5]

Henry Ford did not succeed in creating the "great wave of prosperity" that he promised. Facing overwhelming opposition in Congress and localized pressure in the Tennessee Valley, the automotive magnate exited the debate over the properties with little to show for his campaign. Yet Ford's attempt to lease the site was profoundly important in the long economic development of the valley. His intervention encouraged an interest in industrial growth and development in North Alabama that outgrew the facilities at Muscle Shoals. Businessmen and farmers, local and state leaders, and national politicians debated the merits of development against the realities of declining agriculture and decided that industrial investment alone might save the regional economy. The spirit that emerged in the heyday of Ford's plans spurred the emergence of a modern development ethos in North Alabama, and in the fight for Muscle Shoals the valley took the first step in the economic transition from cotton belt to Sunbelt.

The shallow, rapid shoals on the Tennessee River near Florence, Alabama, long challenged developers at the local, state, and federal levels; one commenter called the shoals "an obstructive fist thrust up by God or Devil."[6] Throughout the nineteenth century, scientists, engineers, and politicians devised a number of plans to overcome the hazard, ranging from dams to raise the water level to a canal bypassing the shoals completely.[7] By the turn of the twentieth century, a private corporation, the Muscle Shoals Hydro-Electric Power Company (MSHEPC), had purchased the land around the shoals and planned to construct a hydroelectric dam at the site, generating power that would operate a nitrate-producing facility located nearby. In 1912, Alabama Traction, Light, and Power, a holding company that included the statewide utility, Alabama Power, bought out MSHEPC, taking control of a number of sites along the Tennessee River along with the property at Muscle Shoals. J. W. Worthington, a Sheffield banker who helped found MSHEPC, became vice-president of the power group at Alabama Traction, Light, and Power and immediately began lobbying Congress for the rights to build a dam at Muscle Shoals.[8]

Worthington's campaign attracted the attention of many Alabamians who hoped that support from the federal government might provide additional motivation for the power group's designs for the region. In Florence, the Commercial Club asked Senator John H. Bankhead Sr. to back the plan, hoping that the improvements would bring new business to the city's fledgling industrial prospects.[9] Bankhead's Senate colleague Oscar Underwood concurred, noting that the people were "entitled" to cheap electricity for factories and homes.[10] Tennessee Representative Richard Austin recounted the "splendid manufacturing cities" that would be built in the region, should improvements on the river proceed, and promised that "thousands" would be employed.[11] Yet, despite the ardor of its supporters across the valley and its congressional allies, Alabama Traction, Light, and Power failed to convince the federal government of the soundness of investing money in the North Alabama project. Discussions stalled until 1916, when the coming war made hydroelectric development along the Tennessee a reality.

On June 3, 1916, President Woodrow Wilson signed the National Defense Act, which gave him the power to investigate the production of nitrates by water power, select a site for a dam that could be used to power a nitrate plant, and operate any plants built as a result of the act.[12] As the title suggested, the legislation was a wartime measure, designed to give the nation the means to produce additional munitions for World War I, then raging in Europe. The United States imported most of its nitrates from Chile, and the possibility of being cut off from the main ingredient in munitions scared Army and Navy officials. As the British blockaded Europe, and as German U-boats harassed American and Allied shipping, Wilson came to appreciate the importance of domestic production, particularly the manufacture of weaponry and munitions needed for national security. As hostilities continued in Europe, Worthington and his congressional supporters saw an opportunity to promote the development of Muscle Shoals.

With the potential improvement on the table, a group of Alabama and Tennessee businessmen met in Nashville and published a comprehensive report, *America's Gibraltar, Muscle Shoals*, advertising the Tri-Cities (Florence, Muscle

Shoals, and Sheffield) as the perfect site for the government waterpower and nitrate facilities. Calling itself the "Muscle Shoals Association," the group looked beyond national defense to the project's peacetime potential, suggesting that the same plant that built bombs could use nitrates to make cheap and abundant fertilizer for southern farmers.[13] The brief listed the benefits that would accrue from a site on the Tennessee River. The development would free the country from its dependence on foreign-produced nitrates, and the site was conveniently located in the midst of the country's neediest agricultural population. In "the heart of rural America," Muscle Shoals would allow for cheap and quick distribution of fertilizer to those who needed it most.[14] In choosing North Alabama as the site for the operation, the government would, in effect, make Muscle Shoals "the source of an economic influence that shall be felt from coast to coast, lightening in a measure the burdens of the people, bringing the greatest good to the greatest number, and making this enterprise a living monument to that broad principle of democracy."[15]

For the citizens of the Muscle Shoals District, an official decision was little more than a formality. Even as the people of North Alabama planned for a prosperous future, differences began to emerge. For the business leadership of Florence, the largest town in the region, investment at nearby Muscle Shoals meant a boost in economic activity, particularly in the growth of local industry. In 1910, Florence counted just under nine thousand residents in a town surrounded by over 100,000 acres of farmland sown in cereals and cotton. Agriculture dominated the region, so much so that the 1910 census failed to account for any notable manufacturing in the area.[16] Not surprisingly, city leaders hoped interest in Muscle Shoals would bring in new and diverse economic activity for the city and its surrounding region.

Even before an official announcement, excitement built as Florence experienced a sudden burst in real estate activity. Frontage on the downtown streets sold quickly to businessmen looking to set up shop by the time construction began.[17] Mass meetings encouraged land owners to offer acreage at the potential sites for reasonable rates, subscriptions poured in to the chamber of commerce, and city leaders paid government experts to attest to the benefits that would come from cheaper fertilizer produced at Muscle Shoals.[18] In the minds of area businessmen, government plants were only the tip of the iceberg.

Local leaders moved to take control of the situation, hoping to use the development as a springboard to further growth. In August 1916, President R. T.

Simpson of the Florence Commercial Club planned a meeting to mobilize the citizenry and predicted that his city would "awake from her Rip Van Winkle sleep" and "spring into the rank of metropolitan cities." For Simpson and many of his fellow citizens, the federal project promised a new era of economic development. As long as the population of Florence and its surroundings worked to promote their city and region, they would hear "the song of machinery, the busy hum of industry."[19] Anticipating increased activity, the city's chamber of commerce moved into a new space that provided more display room for the city's resources and manufactured products and, soon after, began contacting companies interested in relocating to the Tri-Cities area, including a furniture manufacturer and a limestone processor.[20] With Congress on the verge of choosing the site at Muscle Shoals, Florence's civic leaders looked to use the incoming payrolls and positive press to incite an even larger influx of business. Their efforts met with some success, and by 1920, Florence boasted twenty-six industries with 744 wage earners (the surrounding county had nine additional manufacturers and 12 additional workers).[21]

The hope for a more "metropolitan" Florence reflects a larger sentiment that swept through the South in the 1920s and 1930s, one that historian Blaine Brownell called the "urban ethos." This spirit of civic growth and development was most apparent in the "urban" South, cities such as Nashville, Atlanta, and Birmingham. Yet as the pronouncements of R. T. Simpson and the valley's other "civic-commercial elite" suggest, even the Tri-Cities area counted its share of urban boosters. In particular, Florence's chamber of commerce became a leading voice in "promoting urban unity, growth, and commercial civic priorities" in a concentrated effort to grow their city.[22] As Brownell also suggests, civic leaders embraced rural improvements, so long as those improvements complemented urban growth plans and goals.[23] In the case of Muscle Shoals, the promise of investment at the nitrate plants and hydroelectric generation suggested a larger boost in the regional economy, bound to improve business in city and country alike.

On October 1, 1917, Bankhead and Underwood informed Worthington that, as long as the site could be obtained for a reasonable price, a hydroelectric dam and nitrate plant would be located at Muscle Shoals (a second plant would soon follow). Four days later, the *Florence Times* announced the good news. From the outset, Bankhead echoed the hopes of locals and suggested that the selection of Muscle Shoals had larger implications.[24] The facilities promised to bring in thousands of construction workers and retain many to operate the production lines, and the dam would produce enough power to run the nitrate plants and fuel factories, homes, and farms. As the Tennessee River became navigable, planners believed that the channel would open the valley to goods from the North and West at much cheaper rates. Most significantly for Bankhead and his farming constituency, the end of the war in Europe would allow the transition from munitions to fertilizer.

While the "civic-commercial elites" of Florence saw the economic benefits of industrialization, the farm communities that surrounded Muscle Shoals counted on the expected output of the nitrate plants, specifically the peacetime production of (what they hoped would be) cheap and widely available plant fertilizer. With cheaper plant food, farmers hoped to increase crop yields, resulting in higher and higher financial returns; as such, investment at Muscle Shoals would lead to a revitalization of farming as a viable way of life. Like many farmers, the people of the Tennessee Valley focused heavily on corn and cotton, crops that might turn a profit in good years but which depleted the soil and, as a result, forced farmers to use more fertilizer to maintain productivity. This was particularly apparent as the market for southern cotton collapsed after the war.[25]

Besides a brief period of peak cotton prices from 1916 to 1919, the postwar years were difficult for most southern farmers. The combination of wartime demand and smaller plantings led to high cotton prices during the war, but beginning in 1920, cotton prices dropped steeply, from 35 cents a pound in 1919 to 14 cents.[26] While declining profits hurt all farmers, economic straits were particularly profound for the region's tenant farmers and sharecroppers, a group that had increased dramatically in size since the late nineteenth century. For the Tennessee Valley as a whole, stretching through Tennessee, Alabama, Mississippi, and into Kentucky, from 1880 to 1930, the population grew by two-thirds, but the number of farms doubled and the number of tenants and sharecroppers tripled.[27] Conditions were just as bad on the fields surrounding Muscle Shoals.

In the decades surrounding the turn of the century, nearly 60 percent of farms in the western Tennessee Valley were worked by tenants. Though ownership rates in the valley were generally higher than those in the Black Belt, many in the large minority considered "owners" were little better off than those working the fields for rent of a share of the crop. In fact, the typical valley farm shrank between 1880 and 1930, from a maximum of 139 acres at the outset to a low of 55 on the eve of the New Deal. Shrinking farms were symptomatic of a much larger problem: as the number of total farms rose, the number of farms worked by tenants rose, and the number of farms worked by owners saw only sluggish increases before dropping during the onset of the Depression (see table 1). When combined, shrinking farms and a growing population of tenants meant that the farmers of North Alabama struggled to make a living on the land. As contemporary agricultural studies showed, smaller farms meant smaller investments, a lower likelihood of mechanization or electrification, less chance of additional processing or diversification, and, thus, smaller profits. As one agriculturalist noted, surveying southern farms: "The farm unit . . . is too small to function efficiently."[28]

TABLE 1. Farm Size and Rates of Ownership and Tenancy in the Western Counties of Alabama's Tennessee Valley, 1880–1930

Year	*Total Farms*	*Farms Worked by Owners*	*Farms Worked by Tenants*	*Average Farm Size (in Acres)*
1880	12,317	6,105 (50%)	6,221 (50%)	139
1890	11,419	6,121 (55%)	5,289 (45%)	133
1900	15,447	5,373 (35%)	8,004 (57%)	89
1910	19,576	8,161 (41%)	11,379 (58%)	77
1920	22,273	9,270 (41%)	12,911 (58%)	65
1930	24,697	5,663 (23%)	17,126 (69%)	55

TABLE 2. Farm Production and Fertilizer Usage in the Western Counties of Alabama's Tennessee Valley, 1880–1930

Year	*Total Acreage in Production*	*Average Yield, Corn (in Bushels/Acre)*	*Average Yield, Cotton (in Bales/Acre)*	*Amount Spent on Fertilizer*
1880	563,071	15.94	.34	$22,009
1890	577,892	16.16	.20	$41,947
1900	627,595	14.11	.32	$73,160
1910	767,161	15.50	.29	$255,115
1920	837,040	15.58	.38	$986,129
1930	789,182	17.18	.46	$1,838,510

While landholdings and labor numbers speak to a serious change in the nature of farming, the problem facing Tennessee Valley farmers also revolved around production, and specifically the efforts that farmers made to keep land productive and yields high. Corn and cotton sapped the soil of nutrients, making it increasingly difficult to turn a profit from the same patch of soil year after year. Farmers refused to abandon these crops and instead sought to increase the acreage dedicated to their growth. Between 1880 and 1930, valley farmers significantly increased the amount of acreage in production. Even with the increase, though, farmers could not maintain crop yields without chemical assistance. Hence, one of the most telling statistics for valley agriculture, and one particularly relevant to the ongoing discussion on the necessity of Muscle Shoals, was the amount of fertilizer applied to southern farms. In 1880, farmers in the western Tennessee Valley reported paying $22,000 for fertilizer; by 1930, the amount had skyrocketed to nearly $2 million. But even as farmers paid more for the chemicals that kept the soil productive, crop yields remained static. In fact, despite more land in production and widespread use of fertilizer, yields for corn and cotton in 1930 were only slightly more than the average per-acre yields from fifty years earlier (see table 2).[29]

In sum, farmers were no more likely to work their own land in 1920 than they had been some four decades earlier. Instead, they witnessed thousands more acres brought into production in an attempt to wring profits out of declining soil. They saw large landholders carve up fields in an attempt to remain solvent (even if most farmers had little chance of purchasing the land being put up for sale). And most galling, they found themselves paying more and more for fertilizer in the futile hope of increasing productivity. Unsurprisingly, farmers in Muscle Shoals and throughout the region turned to the possibilities inherent in fertilizer production and industrial development at Muscle Shoals as they sought a solution for the growing agricultural crisis.

Valley farmers were aware of the myriad problems of a one-crop system, and across the state, the Alabama Cooperative Extension Service used local agents to try and persuade farmers to change their practices. As early as 1915, the agent assigned to Limestone County, Fred Stewart, was specifically ordered not to encourage farmers to grow cotton; instead, throughout the late 1910s and 1920s, he and other agents pressured farmers to raise hogs and purebred cattle, to grow soybeans and other legumes on increasingly infertile land, and to convert some of their former cotton acreage to pastures of hay and oats, decreasing the production of cotton and providing home-grown feed for livestock.[30] A number of farmers took this advice. In 1916, Stewart described a "young, intelligent" farmer named J. H. Peebles who converted several hundred acres of cotton monoculture to clover, oats, seed corn, and pasture land. Peebles also boasted a flock of sheep, a "nice herd" of hogs, and a Hereford bull. He told Stewart that the agent had "helped him wonderfully in getting his method of farming changed," though Peebles's neighbors believed that "if [Stewart] would ask him to stick his hand in the fire . . . he would do it."[31]

Unfortunately, Stewart and his fellow agents were unable to change the culture of farming in the valley. Instead, as Colbert County agent W. I. Abernathy noted, "As a general thing the farmers depend upon cotton wholly as a money crop. This coupled with a fair price causes a number of farmers to go cotton crazy."[32] Agents continued working to improve agriculture but found it difficult to convince most farmers to abandon monoculture, even as the price of cotton plummeted. By 1931, agents in the valley began adding a standard paragraph in their annual reports blaming "poor soils, eroded lands, improper use of fertilizers . . . [and] the farmer's dependence on cotton for his sole cash income" for the persistence of poverty.[33] And, as agricultural historians have noted, even the most proactive extension agents failed to reach all of those suffering on southern farms. Agents tended to prescribe solutions and methods beyond the means of small owners, sharecroppers, and tenant farmers.[34] Faced with already scant resources, few marginal farmers would abandon cotton, even given low prices, for other crops that might require additional investment in new seed, equipment, and know-how. Most sharecroppers and many tenant farmers lacked the authority to make such decisions.

Given the impossibility of weaning the South off of cotton, most extension agents simply sought to encourage more intelligent cotton farming, particularly in the use of fertilizer. As early as 1916, agents reported that high fertilizer prices and the "scarcity" of good product limited usage among most farmers.[35] Agents suggested collective purchasing, saving by buying in bulk, and mixing fertilizer at home, avoiding a more expensive ready-mixed option. In 1920, Stewart noted that cooperative buying and home-mixing "amounted to a saving of thousands of dollars" for Limestone County farmers. Yet these programs, too, depended on disposable income and personal choice. Some owners had the financial ability to contribute to a cooperative purchase, and some made the decision to follow the agents' prescribed mixing formula, but even then, many farmers simply could not afford enough fertilizer to restore the soil. As the Lauderdale County agent noted in 1923, "generally speaking crop fertilization has meant simply some sort of goods, usually that which was cheapest per hundred pounds and which could be bought most easily on a credit, and this used promiscuously on any or all crops alike at a rate of one hundred fifty pounds average," seventy-five pounds less than recommended.[36] Given the unwillingness or inability of most farmers to abandon cotton monoculture, and given the necessity of more and cheaper fertilizer, production at Muscle Shoals seemed an easy and essential solution.

Three months before the official decision on Muscle Shoals, Tuscaloosa farmer Thomas H. Maxwell introduced a resolution at the State Farmer's Union convention to "give us nitrates quickly, no matter where the plant for its manufacture should be located." Senator Bankhead praised Maxwell's spirit: "The farmers need the relief. . . . [S]omething should be done for the men whose labor must feed and clothe the nation."[37] Another farmer advised Bankhead to make a public statement about reducing the price of fertilizers. Having recently learned that Muscle Shoals would get the development, Bankhead replied optimistically that, when the plant was finished, southern farmers would have all the nitrates they needed at half the current price.[38] The need for assistance for the struggling farmers of the Tennessee Valley, combined with the peacetime promise of fertilizer production, helped make the case for development at Muscle Shoals. Senator Thomas Heflin later made this fact clear, arguing that the plants would "supply the farmers with fertilizer[,] . . . increase the productivity of the soil [and] deliver the farmers from the clutches of the fertilizer trust."[39]

In October 1917, with the United States officially at war, construction started on the nitrate plants, and the government began preparations for the site of the hydroelectric dam. In Florence, leaders prepared to accommodate the thousands of workers expected in the city, seeing the influx as the first stage in the valley's coming boom. In a region with few alternatives to farming, the government plants provided a real opportunity for those in Muscle Shoals and across the South who could no longer make a living in agriculture. People flooded into the Tri-Cities looking for work, and while many found employment in the construction force of 2,000 working on the plants and the dam, others added to the growing population of the unemployed that taxed the city's infrastructure.[40] Florence's chamber of commerce divided its time between consulting with interested companies and finding housing for the expanding population.[41] As construction picked up, arriving migrants taxed regional services, and the situation worsened.[42] By April 1918, finding a home had become almost impossible, with many families in the area around the construction site already boarding out-of-town workers. When combined with the nature of expedited, sometimes dangerous, defense work, the housing crisis led to massive turnover; the facility eventually hired 60,000 workers to staff 20,000 positions.[43] Hoping to address such instability, the government encouraged home building through low-interest loans, and Florence began construction on hundreds of houses scattered throughout the town, hoping that workers would assimilate into the community. In adjusting to meet the needs of the industry, civic leadership saw an opportunity to "build a city" around what they hoped would be permanent plants.[44] North Alabama's citizenry realized that federal development created jobs. As the government poured money into the plants and the dam, thousands of southerners (both lifelong and recent arrivals) reaped the benefits with wages that returned money to the community. Across the region, municipalities hoped that their struggles would be rewarded with increased retail sales, additional tax revenue, and the promise of further industrial development and agricultural prosperity.

The Air Nitrates Company, a subsidiary of American Cyanamid operating on a government contract to construct one of the nitrate plants, also turned to the African American community. In newspaper advertisements seeking black workers, the company promised that the plant provided "one of the most wonderful opportunities ever offered to the workingmen of the negro race."[45] In addition to a non-farm wage, recruits enjoyed entertainment (including a "negro orchestra") and access to schools and medical care for their families.[46] One community leader praised the plant's managers as helping demonstrate that "the Negro has within him the very best qualities that go to make up the highest type of manhood." Another called the plant "the best chance for advancement, in every way, that the American negro has ever had."[47] In hindsight, the company's motives are painfully clear. Like many New South employers, the ANC undoubtedly understood that segregation, when combined with widespread tenancy and sharecropping, meant lower wages and fewer alternatives for black southerners. Willing to work for less and with fewer options than their white counterparts, black laborers could provide the much-needed labor at a fraction of the cost, and at peak operation African American workers made up a third of the workforce.[48]

As historian Victoria Ott notes, the plants provided a real economic alternative for Muscle Shoals's African American population, even if their pay and benefits paled in comparison with those for whites in other occupations.[49] Expanding employment opportunities, however, did not translate into a better life in the Jim Crow South. As the tone of the advertisement clearly suggested, black laborers faced segregation both at work and at home as the companies constructing the plants enforced southern racial legislation. Florence's leaders built segregated facilities for workers and expected incoming companies to adhere to local laws and customs.[50] Black workers faced the racism of fellow white workers, brutality from plant security forces, and wartime "work-or-fight" laws that led many to look to national organizations for assistance.[51] Even as the Muscle Shoals project opened the door to better jobs and higher wages, it furthered the social inequalities faced by black southerners.

By 1920, as construction proceeded on the hydroelectric dam, Alabama's congressional delegation found continued appropriations difficult to obtain, particularly in the face of a postwar recession and serious opposition from a resurgent and fiscally conservative Republican Party. The platform of the 1920 Democratic Convention sought to defend the $70 million facility from attacks by Republican leaders, trying "covertly to destroy the great nitrogen plant at Muscle Shoals."[52] In the spring of 1921, fiscal conservatives in Congress began fighting back. Led by Wisconsin Republican Irvine Lenroot, they pointed to the Muscle Shoals project as unwarranted pork, arguing that supporters of the project were using the farmers as an excuse to pump millions of dollars into Muscle Shoals.[53] In early March, opponents were able to defeat a $10 million appropriation for the project. Worthington promised that the "setback" was "temporary" and that the next session of Congress would surely restore the flow of funds to the construction site. The Florence Chamber of Commerce promised to stay in constant communication with Alabama's congressional delegation.[54] Yet without the means to continue, the War Department placed construction of Wilson Dam on "standby" condition. The workforce at the dam dropped from 2,000 to 500, and then to the bare minimum needed to perform basic maintenance. The Wilson Dam Club held a "Farewell Dance" to wish its former members well as they left for homes or work in other parts of the country.[55] On April 30, 1921, work on the dam halted.

Alabamians learned a valuable lesson from their experience during the initial excitement over the plants and the ensuing letdown as government appropriations stalled. Hoping for some kind of relief from the depressing farm conditions, many believed that peacetime production at the nitrate plants would bring cheap, widely available fertilizer to the region, allowing for the profitable cultivation of cash crops. In the towns and cities of North Alabama, leaders foresaw larger economic growth, centered on an industrial revitalization that was bound to accompany the influx of jobs at the nitrate plants and the cheap, government-produced power at the hydroelectric dam. However, just as the plants began production, federal funds evaporated. Valley residents, and particularly Florence's business community, realized that they could not rely solely on the government for economic development. Throughout the 1920s, as Congress and a number of private bidders fought over plans for Muscle Shoals, local leaders began a campaign to bring industries to the valley to provide the jobs and income needed to overcome economic straits. In doing so, the civic-commercial elites of Florence and the surrounding towns began to practice the means of development that would eventually result in a more modern regional economy.

In 1921, with Congress increasingly reluctant to fund the project at Muscle Shoals, War Department officials began a search for a private company that might be willing to lease the facilities. Secretary of War John Weeks told a trade magazine that he planned to ask Congress for the $30 million needed to complete Wilson Dam, but only if some commercial organization would "show faith enough in Muscle Shoals to agree to take over the project after it shall have been completed."[56] At the beginning of April the chief engineer of the Army, Lansing Beach, contacted J. W. Worthington, looking for advice on potential investors. Worthington suggested that Beach call on automobile manufacturer Henry Ford. Within days, Ford stated his interest, and by July the industrialist had placed a formal bid for the facilities at Muscle Shoals, backed by generalized promises that addressed both those who hoped the project would inspire industrial development and those who hoped production would be directed toward agricultural uses.

Between 1921 and 1924, Ford's offer for Muscle Shoals dominated discussions over the future of the plants. As Congress debated the merits of Ford's terms, the public took sides. In North Alabama, support for Ford resulted in mass meetings, numerous editorials praising the Detroit manufacturer, and a renewed real estate boom that taxed the surrounding countryside. His grand pronouncements went largely unquestioned as residents rushed to support his claims. Most took for granted his ability to build a successful business, and given the dire condition of the regional economy and the growing disappointment over the stalled project, Ford seemed an economic savior. The Ford offer sat in Congress for just over three years, but it had a profound effect on the direction of development in the Tennessee Valley. While Ford stressed his willingness to utilize the nitrate plants and dam for the benefit of agriculture, his status as a manufacturer lent credence to the possibility that Muscle Shoals might mean more than cheap fertilizer and rural electrification. Ford promised new industries to the valley, creating employment opportunities for struggling farmers and non-farmers alike. Many Alabamians, including most of the state's congressional delegation, became ardent supporters of private development of the projects at Muscle Shoals, even as Nebraska Senator George Norris forcefully made the case for government operation. In the end, Ford's bid failed in the face of congressional opposition, but he left a lasting legacy for the economic development of the Tennessee Valley, and the overwhelming popularity he enjoyed in the region demonstrated a clear willingness on the part of residents to consider alternatives to their old economy.

As his biographers have noted, the early 1920s were perhaps the height of Henry Ford's national popularity. The Ford Motor Company found itself in the forefront of Jazz Age economic prosperity, yet Ford crafted a public image that stressed humanitarianism over financial profit. He portrayed himself as "the greatest of manufacturers, the fairest and most liberal of employers, a practical philanthropist who has brought hope and sunshine into millions of homes."[57] His Midas-like reputation brought numerous offers from across the country: Nebraska invited Ford to improve the state's waterpower resources, Michigan asked for help to organize the state railroad system, and in 1922, the *Wall Street Journal* suggested, "Why Not Ford for President?"[58] Ford actively cultivated his image as a "constructive pioneer," and many of his maxims were inspired by Muscle Shoals.[59] In his view, hydroelectric power could "increase and cheapen production so that all of us may have more of this world's goods." It could run machines, "liberate man from brute burdens, and release his energies to the building of his intellectual and spiritual powers for conquests in the fields of thought and higher action."[60] As Ford engaged in a contest with a private utility that many perceived to be a profit-driven trust, his rhetoric was especially potent. In North Alabama, and across the country, his supporters believed he was an industrialist with a heart, a magnate who would disavow profiteering in favor of community responsibility.

But Henry Ford's philanthropic image was carefully constructed. The manufacturer's public persona masked a willingness to use any means necessary to keep his factory running smoothly. Even as Ford's five-dollar-day plan earned him praise as "the best friend the working man ever had," the manufacturer hired "evaluators" to ensure that workers' home lives fit with his desire for a subservient workforce. When laborers signed new contracts accepting the higher pay, they gave explicit consent to have his "sociological department" investigate their "qualifications."[61] Ford hired former boxer Harry Bennett to head his "service department," gathering informants among the line workers and using physical force to prevent workers from unionizing or protesting.[62] Thus, through industrial espionage and personal intimidation, Ford kept overt opposition, and particularly labor organization, at a minimum. As the industrialist stressed the humanitarian aspects of his plan for Muscle Shoals, many of his supporters chose to disregard such faults and focus solely on his promised philanthropy. They failed to ask what Ford saw in Muscle Shoals that was worth years of legislative conflict and harried negotiations. Instead, Ford's carefully constructed reputation convinced many valley residents that he offered a solution to their economic difficulties.

Within weeks of submitting his bid to Congress, Ford enjoyed a remarkable boost of popularity among the people of the Muscle Shoals district. Just as the project began to stagnate, Ford had come to the rescue. A crowd gathered at the Florence courthouse overwhelmingly voted to support the Ford offer, calling for local officials to take word to Washington that "Mr. Ford should have Muscle Shoals." Relating public support, the *Florence Times* went so far as to suggest that the industrialist had a "deadly aversion to profiteering," a statement clearly at odds with both the general nature of Ford's work and his specific interest in the project.[63] Farm Bureau President J. R. Howard approved the offer, especially Ford's promise to produce fertilizer at an 8 percent profit. Concerned citizens even created their own Alabama–Muscle Shoals Association, charging membership dues to help fund delegations to Washington to lobby Congress, and giving each member a "Ford Button" to express their loyalties.[64] People came to support the Ford offer for a number of reasons, many of which reflected their own feelings about the future of the regional economy.

For those who had hoped that Muscle Shoals would provide some benefit for southern agriculture, Ford's offer promised cheap, reliable, high-grade fertilizer to farmers across the district. In June 1922, the House Committee on Military Affairs recommended the McKenzie Bill to lease the project to Henry Ford. Chairman John C. McKenzie, who crafted the bill, recommended full acceptance of Ford's offer, stating that the only other alternative, government operation, would require so many levels of bureaucracy that it would drive the price of fertilizer to new heights.[65] William B. Bankhead, an Alabama congressman, made the case particularly plain, outlining his "personal confidence in Henry Ford" and stating that Ford would cut fertilizer bills in Alabama and the rest of the country "half in two."[66] Ford included the major national farmers' groups in his proposal, agreeing to allow them to sit on a board to oversee fertilizer sales. In return, the American Farm Bureau began circulating pamphlets in Congress stressing its support for the Ford offer.[67] Writing for the *New York Times*, William Jennings Bryan warned that, should Congress fail to give Ford the nitrate plants, the farmers of the country would make it a "paramount issue" in the next presidential campaign, and they would be joined by consumers, who would realize that affordable fertilizer would result in cheaper farm products.[68]

The potential for a Ford plant at Muscle Shoals inspired hyperbole. In the *Florence Times*, reporter Littell McClung called Nitrate Plant 2 the "most valuable manufacturing establishment ever built in any part of the world." Ignoring the cost of the plant, which was a sore spot with many of Ford's opponents in Congress, and the amount of power it would use from Wilson Dam, which rankled many supporters of private utilities, McClung praised the "wealth-creating power of its output." The operation of the nitrate plant would increase crop yields, and as farmers produced more and more crops, goods would become cheaper. More fertilizer also meant larger quantities of cotton, which would then increase agricultural revenues and allow farmers to climb out of oppressive mortgages.[69] McClung echoed the hopes of many North Alabama farmers who still believed that, if fertilizer costs could be reduced, agriculture would once again become a viable livelihood.

Despite his fame as a manufacturer, Ford had a history of prescribing solutions to the declining agricultural economy. In fact, the manufacturer experimented on a number of occasions, both before and after Muscle Shoals, with communities that combined small farming and light industry. Describing plans for such a program in Michigan's Upper Peninsula, Ford promised to "fit agriculture and industry together so that the farmer may also be an industrialist and the industrialist may also be a farmer."[70] In hindsight, then, it is perhaps unsurprising that a would-be farm reformer might view the combination of a depressed agricultural economy, facilities for producing fertilizer, and a source of cheap power as the perfect opportunity to remake southern farming. Yet his pronouncements, exaggerated and grandiose as they were, envisioned not just a new way of farming, but a completely new economy for the region. Ford encouraged listeners, and especially those civic and business leaders invested in an industrial and commercial future for the Tennessee Valley, to imagine productive fields alongside humming factories and bustling commerce.

As his bid suggests, Ford understood the importance of placating agricultural interests, and he specifically promised to produce fertilizer for valley farmers. However, the nation's preeminent industrialist did not ignore the potential for manufacturing in the Tennessee Valley. As Congress debated his offer, he began to outline his vision for the future of Muscle Shoals. In August, Ford prophesized that he could build a city of 100,000 in the area, all employed in factories powered by the Tennessee River.[71] Ford did not limit himself to the area directly surrounding his plants, and soon suggested that he could transform the entire valley into an industrial center. He foresaw a seventy-five-mile-long metropolis, stretching from Muscle Shoals to Decatur, made up of cities and towns interspersed with small tracts of farmland, where families would live in small communities and retain the "benefits" of rural life while still receiving an industrial paycheck.[72] His vision was, as his biographers noted, a "memorable object lesson" in the coexistence of agriculture and industry.[73] Ford's plan suggested to civic leaders and farmers alike that industrial development did not preclude agricultural prosperity—in fact, economic growth sparked by the operation of the plants and dams at Muscle Shoals might benefit everyone. This vision, realistic or not, provided space for the region's civic-commercial leaders and agriculturalists to see a bright future in his offer.

In January 1922, Mrs. Charles H. Durham, the chair of the Women of the Twentieth Century Club, wrote to her congressman with resolutions in support of the Ford offer. Noting the "distressing conditions of employment" in the region, Durham called for Tennessee Democrat Lawrence D. Tyson to support Ford's offer, which would bring relief by creating jobs and putting the inactive plants to use.[74] Durham did not ask for Tyson to support Ford for fertilizer or for rural electrification. Instead, she saw the offer as an opportunity for increased employment, a concern that had been growing in the Shoals District since dam construction slowed and cotton prices fell. She was not alone. C. C. Bailey wrote to the editor of the *Florence Times*, detailing his support for this "man of vision": "In Ford's own words he will need a million men. The houses, the schools, the churches, manufacturing enterprises, mercantile lines, shops and every conceivable thing imaginable will be in full force." Bailey called Ford's plan a "God-sent opportunity to enable our farmers and employees all over Alabama to stop making cotton that is bringing us to absolute want."[75]

Some compared Ford's Muscle Shoals to Birmingham, which exploded in population with the advent of the city's iron and steel industry; Ford seemed to recognize similar potential in the Tri-Cities.[76] In Huntsville, a chamber of commerce publication promised that the Tennessee Valley would blossom just as Niagara Falls had, using cheap hydroelectricity to power factories. Huntsville's leaders hoped that power generation at Muscle Shoals might give the surrounding towns and cities "commercial advantages which will make this location second to none as a center of these rapidly growing electric furnace industries."[77] Yet it was Florence where city leaders fully embraced the industrial possibilities Ford might bring to Muscle Shoals. The city's business community had been an early supporter of using the nitrate plants as a base for the expansion of the regional economy, and Ford's offer and pronouncements seemed to vindicate hopes for the city. According to one correspondent, Florence entered a "state of suspended animation" as "boosters, barbers, chambermaids and hardened newspaper men" all looked to the boom that would attend Ford. Sloss-Sheffield Steel and Iron purchased land in Florence, hoping to operate on Wilson Dam power, and city leaders expected railroads to run new lines to the city.[78] Locals built on Ford's already inflated predictions. Florence would get its own small dam, creating a harbor for the city that would be able to serve the entire Shoals district. Three "transcontinental" highways would crisscross the district. Ford would immediately hire five thousand workers to operate the nitrate plants, and spend $50 million in new factories and industries, paying "excellent wages" to a million men. As Littell McClung bragged, "[Ford] will be on the Tennessee River and starting industrial development such as even Detroit and Chicago have not seen."[79]

The enthusiasm surrounding Ford not only motivated supporters to envision development, it also forced the region to consider the consequences of growth. Just as real estate speculation increased in Florence after the news of the initial appropriation for Muscle Shoals, rumors of Ford's industrial-agricultural Eden sparked a second, larger real estate boom that threatened the regional infrastructure. "Prospectors, investors and adventurers" flocked to the Tri-Cities, buying up available land and marking off lots as small as could be sold—the "quaint and peaceful old towns of Northern Alabama" were unrecognizable.[80] The new Weeden Heights subdivision was typical of the boom towns that sprang up around the dam site. Owners advertised lots "within a few hundred feet" of the Wilson Dam reservation, and the "very finest drinking water" carried by privately built water lines. Future residents would never be forced to drive home through the "usual unsightly sections commonly associated with the exits from a city" since "there are no negroes living in that section of the city." The lots themselves measured 7,500 square feet (less than one-fifth of an acre) and sold for $450–500 each at a time when neighboring farmland averaged less than $40 per acre.[81]

The Florence Chamber of Commerce struggled to rein in buyers and sellers alike. Leaders suggested various strategies, including committees to oversee transactions, welcome parties to advise newcomers interested in purchasing land, a concerted effort to personally convince major landholders to keep land valuations reasonable, and a "progressive movement" to draw up specific zoning limits.[82] There was little the city could do. During the last half of 1921, more than $1,000,000 worth of property changed hands in the town of Sheffield alone.[83] Realty companies used Ford as bait, promising that his lease of the facilities would insure a wave of construction that would bring numerous plants to the area, giving every property owner in Florence "new inspiration" and "new hope." Even as property values inflated to ridiculous levels, realty companies assured potential buyers that "it would be impossible to conceive of a better and more favorable time" for existing landowners to add on or for first-time buyers to purchase land in the city.[84]

Muscle Shoals exemplified the land booms of the 1920s. South Florida witnessed a similar rush as a mixture of climate, the arrival of the affordable automobile, and economic prosperity led thousands to the Sunshine State. Miami's population more than doubled from 30,000 in 1920 to 75,000 in 1925, and may have surpassed 150,000 in the succeeding months. As in Muscle Shoals, buyers chose lots from maps in realty and investment offices hundreds of miles away from the actual property. The bubble burst when a series of hurricanes hit the state. As Frederick Lewis Allen noted, "many of the millions sunk in developments had been sunk for good and all . . . and the lesson of the economic falsity of a scheme of land values based upon grandiose plans, preposterous expectations, and hot air had been taught in a long agony of deflation."[85] Muscle Shoals added to that lesson.

Ford hysteria swept the Tennessee Valley, but the manufacturer's bid was not the only offer for Muscle Shoals before Congress. The Alabama Power Company also showed a strong interest in the properties, and during the 1920s the utility fought to recover control of the development of the Tennessee River and add the hydroelectric power from Wilson Dam to its statewide network. In January 1924, Alabama Power and a group of southern power companies officially proposed a lease of the hydroelectric dam, promising to give the government enough power to run the nitrate plants at no charge and agreeing to federal regulation of power rates from the dam. The bid allowed the government to retain control of the nitrate plants, to dispose of as Congress and the president saw fit.[86] Alabama Power's offer was restrained in comparison with the Ford offer, yet the utility drew immediate animosity from the region.

Such opposition is somewhat surprising, given the general support for private investment on behalf of many in the federal government, which sought a workable lease for Muscle Shoals, and among civic leaders and the general public, who had no qualms about supporting Ford's private offer. Yet Alabama Power found itself in a very different situation from Ford's. In fact, the utility's woes began much earlier, with the official decision to locate the development at Muscle Shoals. J. W. Worthington, Alabama Power's former vice-president, had done much to get Congress to act on behalf of development at Muscle Shoals, and the government responded by taking charge of the project. Frank Washburn, at one time the utility's president, was now at American Cyanamid, encouraging the government to use some of its patents to manufacture nitrates at the planned facilities. Even worse, in choosing to locate the facility at Muscle Shoals, the government demanded the exact site the utility had acquired with MSHEPC in 1912. Threatened with the possibility of a seizure by eminent domain, Alabama Power "donated" the land to the government for one dollar in exchange for the government's assurance that it would consider Alabama Power for the surplus power created at the dam. As Alabama Power's president, James Mitchell, noted in his letter offering the site: "I judge . . . that you are fully aware of what the Company has done in preparation for the ultimate development of this water power."[87] As Tom Martin later recalled in his personal history of Alabama Power, "The gift at Muscle Shoals in a time of national crisis is something the Company remembers with pride no matter how it came to be used against us, and against what we still deem the philosophy and best interest or our country."[88]

In the spirit of national defense, the private utility also turned over its plans and blueprints for the dam, effectively giving the government both the site and the means for development. The company also agreed to take responsibility for maintaining the transmission lines at the plant, and it even constructed extra generators at the existing Gorgas Steam Plant on the Black Warrior River, running lines to Muscle Shoals to help with construction needs. In the end, however, Alabama Power's hard work to develop Muscle Shoals seemed wasted. To make matters worse, in a 1921 magazine article, the company printed a copy of the one-dollar check it had received for its land at Muscle Shoals, and the government responded by fining the company $500 for printing the uncashed check.[89]

In a matter of months, the company had lost a major water power development and was increasingly becoming a pariah in Congress. When his son told him that he had accepted a retainer to serve as attorney for the company, John Bankhead Sr. let him know his true feelings: "They are arbitrary and dictatorial in their demands and are raising a howl everywhere they go." He told John Jr. that an official connection to the company would be a "mistake."[90] When, in November 1921, the utility signed a temporary contract to produce power at the site, Alabama Power's opponents saw more sinister motives.[91] Alabama Governor Thomas Kilby relayed the "wrath of the people" at Alabama Power's apparent attempt to "frustrate" Ford's bid. In Gadsden, where Alabama Power formed, the chamber of commerce favored Ford's offer as "far better for Alabama, and the entire country."[92] In a set of resolutions from Florence's chamber of commerce, Rotary Club, and the Exchange Club, members denounced Alabama Power as foreign owned and suggested that, should the utility add the Tennessee River to its network, it would drive rates upward. The organizations instead praised Ford, whose "mammoth plan of industrial development . . . grips the imagination and thrills the enthusiasm of every American citizen."[93]

The utility's woes in North Alabama and in Washington, D.C., stemmed in part from a growing distrust of private utilities. In the years after World War I, private power companies became concentrated in larger utilities holding companies, even as the number of municipal companies declined.[94] Utilities "trusts" were particularly galling to Progressive politicians, in that the companies' seemingly monopolistic practices had a direct impact on consumers.

And, given the nature of the debate over development at Muscle Shoals over the disposition of valuable natural resources, the perceived threat of a "trust" gobbling up water power without concern for the public interest was too great to ignore.[95] These antipathies were embodied in the work of Progressive conservationists such as Gifford Pinchot, chief forester for the U.S. Forest Service and later Progressive governor of Pennsylvania, and Morris Cooke, an engineer who worked on public power proposals under Pinchot's guidance. Pinchot and Cooke believed that "government must take an active part in providing electric service to rural areas," and as Cooke argued, government protection of power-producing resources "spells cheap power for the farm."[96] Allowing profit-based utilities control over such valuable resources would, in the eyes of their opponents, deprive the public of real prosperity.

For many Alabamians, Alabama Power was emblematic of a utility trust. The utility's holding company, Alabama Traction, Light and Power Company, had been incorporated in Canada in 1912, and was financed in part by an English investment house, Sperling and Company.[97] Though the company was rooted in Gadsden and committed to electrifying the state and region, the company became a "foreign presence" to its opponents. The utility's continued growth threatened an already shaky image. In September 1924, Alabama Power's Tom Martin incorporated a new holding company, Southeastern Power and Light Company, under Maine incorporation laws, and he headquartered the company at the utility's old New York office. Alabama Power expanded into the southern part of the state, purchasing Georgia Power, Mississippi Power, and northern Florida's Gulf Power. Such growth was not uncommon; by 1929, utility combinations collected 635 electric properties in the Southeast, where three utility companies controlled 70 percent of the region's electric output.[98] Yet this wave of consolidation did not sit well with Alabamians interested in regional growth and improvement. A speech to Congress by Representative Edward Almon in 1922 typified attacks on Alabama Power. Almon described the utility's holding company as a "trust" seeking to drive up the cost of electricity and, at Muscle Shoals, the cost of fertilizer. To allow Alabama Power to operate the facility would be to give a monopoly an unwarranted "gift" of millions in federal investments.[99] Almon and the utility's other detractors had little problem tying the company's growth to the actions of a profit-driven corporation, and the utility found itself increasingly on the defensive, highlighting its work for state and regional economic growth and development.

Ironically, the state utility was working toward many of the same regional goals as valley leaders, a fact made clear as Alabama Power sought to defend itself against the stream of bad publicity coming out of North Alabama. Rebutting claims that the "foreign-owned" utility sought to send profits out of the state, Alabama Power's representatives called attention to its many acts of public service. In an address to supporters of Ford's offer, Alabama Power's Captain William Lay reminded them that the utility was "an institution of which all Alabama should feel proud."[100] He argued, correctly, that the utility had always intended to improve the site at Muscle Shoals. Lay also pointed to his own history of bringing economic development to the state, having sponsored a public subscription drive in Gadsden in 1902 to bring a steel and wire company to the city.[101]

In fact, like the civic leadership in Florence, Alabama Power was actively seeking industry for the state. In 1922, the utility formed a New Industries Division under T. D. "Tom" Johnson to recruit new companies for Alabama. While the campaign was an attempt to buttress power sales by adding new consumers, the division also hoped to wean the state from its addiction to cotton monoculture. As Johnson would later stress, the New Industries Division provided tangible evidence that the utility cared about the economic future of the state.[102] Some state newspapers took up the utility's cause. In January 1924, the *Montgomery Advertiser* ran a political cartoon equating a rejection of the power companies' offer for Muscle Shoals with a man shooting himself in the face. An accompanying article stated that the lease to Alabama Power and other utilities would "insure the building of many industrial enterprises at other cities than those in the immediate neighborhood of the Muscle Shoals district."[103]

Criticisms at Muscle Shoals also drove the utility to increase efforts to provide rural service, including several new lines reaching homes, businesses, and farms in the Tennessee Valley. Alabama Power's first "rural" line, in fact one of the very first "rural" power lines in the country, went up in 1920 in Madison County, serving ten farms and a cotton gin. The utility encouraged new rural customers to electrify home and farm, echoing language used much later by the Tennessee Valley Authority, and worked closely with researchers at Alabama Polytechnic Institute in Auburn, Alabama, to make electricity as profitable as possible for farm communities. As Alabama Power's Tom Martin promised, "we want to make agriculture a business rather than a mode of living."[104]

The distrust directed toward Alabama Power also fit with the larger political culture of the state, and opposing the state utility became a subtler protest against the vested economic interests of the state's political elite. V. O. Key believed that the state exhibited a progressive-conservative "cleavage," a holdover from the Populist revolt of the 1890s, which persisted in the ongoing power struggle between the "big mules," a coalition of Birmingham industrialists and Black Belt planters, and what later political scientists would call the "branch heads," the farmers and workers who seemed to exist only to make the big mules wealthier. North Alabama, a one-time Populist stronghold and a center of progressive opposition to the continued reign of the big mules, sought to prevent the wholesale surrender of its natural wealth to Alabama Power, whose investors and owners were the epitome of the conservative elites.[105]

Key's analysis also speaks to the importance of lobbying groups in the state, and here again the support for Ford and opposition to the state utility fit with the larger power structure of Alabama politics. Alabama's Democratic factions proved fairly illusory, emerging around idiosyncratic politicians in any given election. As such, candidates needed proven vote-getting machines, organized at the community level, in order to mobilize the masses. In Alabama, two of the most important such groups were the State Agricultural Extension Service and the Alabama Farm Bureau Federation, both of which were particularly effective in mobilizing the farm vote. At Muscle Shoals, the Farm Bureau effectively pressured congressional representatives to support the Ford offer (and later, the offer of American Cyanamid) while engendering opposition to Alabama Power.[106]

For most Alabamians, then, Ford and Alabama Power represented two distinct possibilities, a fact made clear in early 1922 when Alabama's League of Women Voters held a public debate in Birmingham, headlined by Tuscaloosa Congressman W. B. Oliver and William Logan Martin Jr., a former judge, an attorney for Alabama Power Company, and the younger brother of the utility's president. Logan Martin took the podium first, refuting attacks on the utility. He cited a number of impressive accomplishments: Alabama's electric rates dropped substantially in the past decade thanks to a growing power grid, and Martin's company was instrumental in developing a number of hydroelectric sites on the state's rivers.[107] He promised that the utility would direct its interest in statewide power development to the problem of Muscle Shoals, though the outcome would benefit the entire region. Martin spoke plainly: "If this Company takes [Muscle Shoals] it will bring to your doors and offer to the world an unlimited supply of power. . . . We will use this great resource for the people that they may enjoy what is theirs against monopoly." Ford would assume control of the facilities and parcel the output only to the surrounding farms and towns, while Alabama Power would make "this great resource" available to the entire South.[108]

Like the entire Alabama congressional delegation, Oliver gave his support to Ford after realizing the widespread acclaim for the auto manufacturer by the state's farming interests, and in his address he portrayed Alabama Power as hostile to Ford's bid and, therefore, hostile to southern farmers. He charged the company with monopolistic tendencies: "They never had any other dream than to gobble up all the power sites of Alabama they could get." Ford, however, sought to direct the power of the Tennessee River to the surrounding communities, the towns and fields of North Alabama feeling the pinch of a declining farm economy. Oliver argued that, via the hydroelectric dam and nitrate plants at Muscle Shoals, Alabamians could repay the "debt" the country owed to agriculture. Calling the plants "an opportunity for Alabama that may never come again," he spoke directly to farmers, promising that their "appeal shall not be heard in vain."[109]

As both Martin and Oliver surely realized, the nature of the project had implications reaching far beyond Muscle Shoals. Faced with a declining farm economy, the region needed help, and the facilities sitting unused provided a foundation for future growth. And, despite their differences, the men shared some key assumptions about the direction of that growth. First, they accepted the notion that any development at the nitrate plants and dam would be privately funded. With a government unwilling to invest additional millions, private capital was essential to restart the plants and operate the dam. Second, the development would be industrial in nature, though the benefits would help both city dweller and farmer alike. Alabama Power and Ford stressed their industrial abilities in "selling" the possibilities of Muscle Shoals, and even agriculturalists touted limited industrialization in the service of cheaper fertilizer and electricity. Finally, because Muscle Shoals began as a government project, and because the site was Congress's to grant, both Alabama Power and Ford crafted offers that focused on the widespread benefits of the site, in terms of associated development, electric power, and fertilizer, available to more than just the few thousand people living near the plants and dam. Both sides hoped to "sell" the possibility of regional economic growth to the federal government. In what amounted to Alabama's first great debate on the merits and means of industrial development, the basic themes of the region's growth were clearly evident.

The strongest opposition to private bids for the facility emerged in Washington, D.C., where a bloc of Progressive Republican congressmen, led by Nebraska Senator George Norris, hoped to retain public ownership and operation of the nitrate plants and dam. Alongside his colleagues, Norris argued that government control was the only possible way to ensure that the country's natural resources were used efficiently and that the government saw returns on its investment. Norris claimed that he "stumbled" into the debate over Muscle Shoals when Alabama's Oscar Underwood funneled Ford's bid into Norris's Senate Agriculture Committee.[110] In fact, Norris's leadership of government-backed development at Muscle Shoals came relatively easily, thanks in part to the continuing influence of the conservation movement.

Since the turn of the century, conservationists looked to the federal government to provide the funds for multipurpose river development. Many of Alabama's Democratic congressmen, including Senator John H. Bankhead Sr., had proven reluctant allies of the movement, preferring government assistance for the development of local resources, with Muscle Shoals a prime example, over the potential stalemate of partisan politics.[111] Norris drew heavily on the rhetoric of early conservationists, including several government-backed studies, in calling for publicly funded waterways development on the nation's riparian resources. However, the senator stood at the forefront of a new brand of conservationism, which held that "proper resource use and fair resource distribution could relieve rural poverty and raise rural incomes."[112] Development at Muscle Shoals, closely overseen by a disinterested federal government, would rebalance the scales, encouraging the region to participate more fully in the national economy.

Norris found a perfect opportunity to practice his beliefs on the proper utilization of natural resources in 1913 when, as a member of the Public Lands Committee, he oversaw the development of Yosemite's Hetch Hetchy Valley near San Francisco. One of California's Democratic representatives, John E. Raker, introduced legislation allowing the city to create a municipally owned reservoir in the valley with a dam to provide hydroelectric power for the growing city. Raker then added controversial provisions into the reservoir bill allowing the city to distribute power. Even though the dam would bring drastic environmental changes to Yosemite National Park, Norris heartily supported the Hetch Hetchy legislation, which he called the "highest act of conservation." Foreshadowing his later fight for publicly funded hydroelectric power from Wilson Dam, Norris promised, "Pass [the Raker legislation] and you put into the hands of the people a power God intended should do some good to man."[113] In supporting Raker, Norris won the enmity of numerous West Coast private power companies, particularly Pacific Gas and Electric, which wanted to protect its distribution rights in the region. Norris would later explicitly connect his perception of Pacific Gas with the work of Alabama Power, both of which were, in his estimation, "fattening [themselves] and tightening [their] strangle hold" on consumers.[114] By 1922, Norris had specific experience in the utilization of natural resources, and he consistently enunciated his belief that the federal government held a certain responsibility to protect the rights of the people to access the nation's physical wealth.

In fact, the debate over Hetch Hetchy's relevance to the fight for Muscle Shoals goes beyond conflict with utilities to speak to the environmental consequences of hydroelectric projects. As with the Hetch Hetchy, damming the Tennessee River interrupted its natural flow, turning shallow rapids into a relatively deep and placid lake, better suited for commercial (and recreational) traffic and more manageable in terms of hydroelectric output. In both cases, the desire to facilitate economic growth and development outweighed the long-term environmental impact of the project. In California, John Muir blasted the transformation of Hetch Hetchy, suggesting that the plan had as much to do with timber companies, eager for the lumber cleared from soon-to-be flooded land, as with demand for water or power.[115] But in Alabama no Muir arose to note the implications of the dam at Muscle Shoals, and no public discussion considered the long-term impact of such stark changes. Instead, the debate revolved around the control of and the best uses for the transformed river.

Regardless of how he "stumbled" into the debate at Muscle Shoals, Norris found the question of development on the Tennessee River the perfect opportunity to advance his conservationist beliefs, and he argued that a full utilization of its resources required a much broader investment than Ford's or even Alabama Power's comparatively narrow goals for the region. Power development and fertilizer production would certainly improve the southern economy, but only a comprehensive project embracing flood control, navigation, soil protection, and hydroelectricity would effectively marshal the resources of the Tennessee River watershed.[116] Norris also couched his argument in terms of fiscal solvency. Any decision concerning the plants and dam, he argued, must take into account the amount of money invested in the project. He equated privatization with selling U.S. battleships, planes, or the guns and munitions in forts and arsenals for scrap metal.[117]

Despite the aura of humanitarianism that had grown around Ford, Norris warned that his motives might not be as selfless as many believed. The senator enunciated a major concern with Ford's bid: the vagueness of his offer, particularly in regard to his plans for power consumption and fertilizer production. Many of Ford's opponents feared he might gain control of the plants and turn them toward his own manufacturing interests, including the production of parts for his automotive plants.[118] In April 1922, Norris submitted a bill for government operation that mirrored many of the features of the Ford bid, including a farmers' board to oversee fertilizer production; however, Norris's legislation specifically called for the broader development of the Tennessee Valley for hydroelectric generation, flood control, and general electrification. "Conserving" the resources for the benefit of the region's inhabitants, Norris laid the foundation for government-sponsored development in the valley. As the debate dragged on for nearly a decade, he became the leading voice for the federal government's development of Muscle Shoals, and his work toward that end foreshadowed a much larger role for the government in the development of the South. Yet the public, enamored with Ford, cared little for Norris's grand vision. The senator was burned in effigy, criticized in the local press, and even sent death threats. In his autobiography, he recalled a tense visit to Muscle Shoals, where he had to be escorted by an armed guard for his own protection.[119]

Despite local unpopularity, Norris's opposition proved potent enough to ensure Ford's (and Alabama Power's) defeat.[120] Afraid that a lease to any private concern might waste an important national resource, Norris used his influence in the Senate to consistently block legislation supporting both Ford's and Alabama Power's bid. He believed that the government could provide farmers with much needed fertilizer and could electrify communities throughout the valley, all while ensuring that the benefits of the dam and plants spread to as many as possible. Even as support for Ford built in the House of Representatives and across the Tennessee Valley, Norris's Senate Agricultural Committee rejected every private lease for the plants. After Ford's withdrawal, Norris continued to dominate the Senate, forcing Alabamians to compromise in order to have the plants operated. In the decade leading up to the creation of the Tennessee Valley Authority in 1933, Norris pushed two bills through Congress and saw a number of compromises emerge from the House, even though it was dominated by the supporters of private leasing. In Ford's defeat, Alabama's delegation learned to blend their desires for fertilizer production and plant utilization with legislation that acknowledged the possibility of public ownership. If North Alabamians wanted government-funded economic development, they would have to work with federal officials, even those with radically different plans for their region.

In May 1924, syndicated columnist John Temple Graves uttered words many Alabamians feared: "The battle royal [*sic*] for the lease of Muscle Shoals is ended, and Henry Ford has lost." Relating information gathered from Ford's assistants, Graves told readers that the manufacturer had decided that his resources and money would be better spent elsewhere.[121] Worthington, who first elicited Ford's interest in the development at Muscle Shoals, lost hope. In a letter to Congressman Lister Hill, the booster confessed his bewilderment, admitting, "I don't know really what turn to take for the best."[122] In October, Ford gave an interview with *Collier's Magazine* and expressed his own frustration with the situation: "A simple affair of business which should have been decided by anyone within a week has become a complicated political affair. We are not in politics and we are in business . . . we have passed Muscle Shoals. Productive business cannot wait on politics."[123] Frustrated with the fight, he withdrew his bid. Lister Hill perhaps best interpreted Ford's defeat: "[He] is tired of all the long delay, and of the bitter politics, and . . . he has doubtless found some other way to do the things he wanted to do at Muscle Shoals."[124]

Yet Ford's impact on the Tennessee Valley had consequences beyond his failed bid for Muscle Shoals. In promising development that would both revitalize agriculture and provide an industrial alternative, he captured the attention of the people of North Alabama. For those determined to carve out a life in cotton and cornfields, the operation of Muscle Shoals meant electrified farms and rejuvenated soil. For Florence's civic-commercial elite, Ford's investment was the spark that would touch off a wave of further development in towns and cities across the South. After 1924, the people of the Tennessee Valley might debate the source of further investment, and they might grumble over the changes inherent in economic growth, but they would not argue the merits of industrial development.

Ford's play for Muscle Shoals also raised important questions for developers and boosters. The people of the Tennessee Valley learned that depending on federal investment could be problematic; while the government might have the funds and wherewithal to begin a project, party politics and political realities could easily cause a halt to or even abandonment of that project. And if federal development was an unsure prospect, private investment was hardly better. For all of Ford's lofty promises, and for all of Alabama Power's plans, each depended on government approval, and each had specific goals for the facilities that did not always fit the perceived needs of the valley. As much as Ford's most ardent supporters may have hoped otherwise, both he and Alabama Power expected to turn a profit at Muscle Shoals, a concern that trumped aid for the region's farmers and associated economic development.

Perhaps the only sure consequence of the initial investment in North Alabama and the ensuing debate over Muscle Shoals was the emergence of a powerful and vocal group of local businessmen and community leaders, determined to use the initial public investment in development at Muscle Shoals to improve the economy of the region. Largely centered in Florence, they were early supporters of Ford, and his reputation and lofty promises fit their expectations for long-term growth and development in the region. However, their first loyalty was to the Tennessee Valley, and as Ford withdrew, boosters sought any path to growth that seemed feasible, whether that meant cooperation with the federal government, a private concern, or some combination of the two. And, as continued investment seemed both uncertain and increasingly contested, these civic and commercial elites worked to balance the question of Muscle Shoals with local development and industrial growth. In this, they began to adopt the methods and mindset of modern boosters, and they presaged the growth of a Sunbelt economy, spurred by federal and private investment and active boosters in the valley.

TWO

MUSCLE SHOALS SIGNIFIES POWER 1924–1933

Months after excoriating Alabama Power for working to undermine Henry Ford's bid for the facilities at Muscle Shoals, the *Florence Times* ran a surprising editorial. The paper praised the utility for its "evidences of good faith and cooperation toward working together in harmony." As the local electric company, the paper noted, Alabama Power undoubtedly benefited as the region grew and expanded its economic opportunities, and the *Times* promised that "the people of this section will join with them in the endeavor to bring about the complete development of this section. . . . The hatchet has been buried."[1] The reversal was remarkably abrupt and relatively unexpected. The *Times* had been one of the most vocal critics of the utility company, even before Henry Ford's offer went public, and the paper had voiced the sentiments of thousands in the Muscle Shoals District who feared that Congress would approve Alabama Power's bid and allow the utility to begin transmitting power to surrounding states without producing fertilizer or reserving enough electricity for regional industrial growth.

In retrospect, the paper's shift is understandable. In 1924, when Henry Ford withdrew his bid for Muscle Shoals, the project was endangered and Alabama Power was the only major bidder left for the facilities. To the city's leadership, concerned as they were for the continued growth and prosperity of the area, the private utility seemed the only entity willing to operate the plants and dam at Muscle Shoals. Florence's transformation was short-lived, and as other bids rose to prominence, the city's leaders transferred their allegiance away from the utility. However, the ease with which Florence's citizenry flocked to Alabama Power speaks to the similarity of their visions for the valley. Both hoped to put Alabamians to work in new factories, drawn to the region by water power from the Tennessee River. Alabama Power stressed regional development, and while Tri-Cities leaders feared the utility might ignore North Alabama in favor of statewide profits, they considered it an acceptable compromise if it meant the reactivation of Muscle Shoals.

Henry Ford was a unifying force, with an appeal that enchanted both farmers, who hoped to use the plants as a means of remaining in agriculture, and community leaders, who hoped the industrialist would create a localized economic renaissance for town and farm alike. Without Ford, the future of Muscle Shoals was less certain. Farmers refused to surrender fertilizer production at the nitrate plants, but in Florence at least, some citizens refocused their attention on the need for operation regardless of which party turned the wheels—economic expediency made for strange bedfellows. As other bids emerged to produce fertilizer and restart the nitrate plants, city leaders again rejected a perceived power monopoly in favor of local development. Tri-Cities leaders would compromise if, in the end, the utilization of Muscle Shoals could be turned to community development. As George Norris and the forces of government operation entered the political ascendancy in the late 1920s, they found an unlikely audience in the towns of North Alabama, interested above all in a new, prosperous southern economy.

This second stage of the debate over Muscle Shoals, beginning with Ford's withdrawal in 1924 and ending with the creation of the Tennessee Valley Authority (TVA) in 1933, was marked by the transition from widespread calls for private ownership to a general acceptance of operation by the federal government. The TVA, as envisioned in 1933, went beyond power production at Wilson Dam and the production of chemicals for fertilizer at Muscle Shoals; it encompassed the larger economic revitalization of the valley through labor training, education, improved health, land management, flood control, and industrial development. Undoubtedly, the key figure in the emergence of government support for federally funded, region-wide improvement was George Norris, the Nebraska Republican senator whose work for the public conservation of natural resources encompassed Wilson Dam and the accompanying nitrate plants. Norris dominated the U.S. Senate in the late 1920s, but he did not single-handedly give Muscle Shoals to the federal government. Instead, he found Alabamians in the halls of Congress, on the streets of Florence, and in the fields of the Tennessee Valley willing to work with him to operate the facilities. Florence's leaders finally turned to government operation, ready to direct Norris's interest in resource development to fit with their own nascent program of community growth. Farmers were more hesitant to support Norris's crusade, but as the senator proved willing to discuss dedicating the plants to fertilizer production, farmers found themselves tentatively optimistic, knowing that their needs would finally be met. Alabama's congressmen were the hardest group to convince, but by the late 1920s, they, too, found themselves working with the government to activate Muscle Shoals.

Equally important, the late 1920s saw the business community of Florence begin a determined effort to encourage economic development independent of the stalled facilities at Muscle Shoals. Concerned that continued bickering over the fate of the government site would leave the region in economic limbo, local leaders empowered the chamber of commerce to recruit, entice, and locate industry in the city. While Alabamians at home and in Washington inched toward compromise with the forces of government operation, Florence's businessmen tried to insulate the city from the vagaries of federal investment. This combination of public and private development, in which local leaders cooperated closely with both the government and the private sector to bring growth, foreshadowed later efforts to combine federal defense investments with commercial and industrial expansion. In this way, the debate over Muscle Shoals introduced the Tennessee Valley to the kind of economic development that would come to define the modern, Sunbelt economy.

In 1925, Florence's leadership cautiously began to cooperate with Alabama Power in the development of the city. Disappointed with the failure of the Ford offer and increasingly unwilling to rely on the government to move more quickly, the city looked to the utility to help boost its economic fortunes. In January, Alabama Power purchased a municipal utility, the old Sheffield Company, officially adding the Tri-Cities to its distribution network. In a statement on the occasion, Tom Martin promised to develop the region's resources, to make power widely available, and to begin working immediately for industrial development.[2] In March 1925, Alabama Power met with the Florence Chamber of Commerce and promised an "unlimited amount" of power to meet the demands of industries that might want to locate in the city. By June, the city had three definite prospects (a fiber mill, a knitting mill, and a cotton mill), and its leaders looked to purchase and list factory sites as incentives, even encouraging citizens to donate their own land and invest in stock in the companies.[3] The utility undoubtedly gained the city's confidence with its fledgling New Industries Division. In 1924, division head Tom Johnson realized his first success with Opelika's Pepperell Manufacturing, the first of a series of New England cotton mills approached by the utility. The next year, Alabama Power won three more industries, all cotton mills located in North Alabama.[4] Johnson provided concrete evidence that his utility company would actively work to improve the economy of its customers.

Yet Alabama Power did more than just talk with interested industries—the utility also created a foundation for further growth. As Florence prepared to advertise itself to the business world, the utility donated $2,500 to the chamber of commerce to help offset the cost of a Boston engineering firm's study of the region's available resources. Completed in November, the survey described Florence as suitable for twenty-four kinds of industries (mostly raw-material processing, though the list also included some chemical and metallurgical manufacturers) and noted the importance of Florence's access to electricity, water, and its employable population. Power, however, was the key. As one chamber of commerce official stressed, "MUSCLE SHOALS signifies Power. . . . [For] Florence to profit by Muscle Shoals [it] must create a power market."[5] Electric service made the city attractive to prospective industries, and the utility encouraged the city to think more broadly about economic growth. When combined with the declining fortunes of the region's agricultural economy and the stalled work at Muscle Shoals, Alabama Power's efforts spurred a business community gearing toward diversified development.

As Alabama Power worked to build support in Florence, the Coolidge administration sought to end the confusion surrounding Muscle Shoals. In March 1925, the president appointed a five-man commission to determine the best method for utilizing the properties at Muscle Shoals and appointed John C. McKenzie, the chair of the House Military Affairs Committee who had introduced legislation to accept Ford's offer, to head the committee.[6] For the supporters of private operation, the "Coolidge Commission" seemed a clear indication that a private lease would be the only acceptable solution for the plants. In a letter to Alabama Senator Oscar Underwood, the longtime lobbyist for the development of Tennessee Valley, J. W. Worthington, noted that a strong resolution from the commission would allow him to find a definite leasing plan among some "promising" candidates.[7]

The president himself was a strong supporter of private operation at Muscle

Shoals, and on numerous occasions he emphasized the importance of finding a profitable lease for the plants. In June 1924, at a meeting of the Business Organization of the Government, Coolidge called for "fair returns" on any government investment in public improvements, stating, "I am for economy. After that I am for more economy. . . . [That] is my conception of serving all the people."[8] His support for privatization reached every aspect of American enterprise, including agriculture. In the president's view, the nation's farm population shared his concern about public aid. Farmers "do not wish to have meddling on the part of the Government or to be placed under the inevitable restrictions . . . which would result from permitting the Government to operate in the agricultural markets." Instead, government leaders should encourage a "more intimate relation . . . between agriculture and the other business activities of the Nation."[9]

Muscle Shoals provided an ideal opportunity to practice government economy in agricultural relief and, as historian John D. Hicks noted, mirroring the president's famous aphorism, Coolidge believed that "the business of government . . . was to help business in every possible way."[10] In his third annual Message to Congress, Coolidge described the project at Muscle Shoals as primarily a nitrate-producing facility, and he argued that the government should dispose of it accordingly. In fact, the site was the perfect example of "the almost utter incapacity of the National Government to deal directly with an industrial and commercial problem. . . . We have expended vast fortunes, we have taxed everybody, but we are unable to secure results, which benefit anybody." The only apparent solution was transfer to the private sector.[11] A successful lease would remove, in his eyes, a substantial drain on the federal budget, thus meeting Coolidge's goal of government economy, and the activated plants would produce fertilizer for local farmers, providing a private solution to the region's farm problems.

In the midst of the Coolidge commission's discussions over the future of Muscle Shoals, Alabama Power restated its interest in the project. In a letter to Chairman McKenzie, Tom Martin emphasized the utility's ability to put the facilities to use, and he added that Alabama Power had completed preliminary work in fertilizer production and could quickly begin making the product. Martin planned to combine with Tennessee Electric Power Company and Memphis Power and Light to run the power plant and join with experienced fertilizer producers to create a second corporation to operate the fertilizer plants. Martin made clear that his role in the development of the Tennessee

Valley centered on power and warned that the region would never get industry until a permanent power solution could be reached.[12] In November 1925, when the Coolidge commission officially recommended a private lease, the power companies' bid was one of the first submitted.[13]

Coolidge knew that his committee's findings would incite a flurry of bidding, and in a December 1925 message to Congress, the president called for a "small joint committee" of congressmen from both houses to vet incoming bids, reasserting his call for private operation for fertilizer production with power a secondary concern.[14] In March, Congress approved the committee, which included three members each from the Senate Agricultural Committee (including Alabama's Thomas Heflin) and the House Military Affairs Committee.[15] The group received ten offers for the power and nitrate project, but those from the power companies, Union Carbide, and the agro-chemical American Cyanamid Company appeared the strongest contenders.[16] In mid-April 1926, Senator Charles S. Deneen of Illinois read the committee's majority report. Four of the six members backed the offer of the southern power companies, including Alabama Power.[17] The bid met the public demand for fertilizer, promised regional economic development, and highlighted the hydroelectric potential from the dam; it could now boast the backing of the Joint Congressional Committee, which was instructed by the president to find a workable solution and have it quickly enacted.

Despite its promising position, the power companies' offer faced some serious obstacles. Representative Frank James of Michigan refused to vote for the utilities and issued a minority report, calling the offer "a power proposition disguised as a fertilizer proposal."[18] In its offer, he argued, Alabama Power was simply trying to monopolize power from Wilson Dam while investing as little money as possible in fertilizer research.[19] The other minority vote belonged to Heflin, who supported the bid of American Cyanamid, more amenable to fertilizer-hungry farmers. The senator sent a telegram to the people of the Tennessee Valley, encouraging them to fight the offer of Alabama Power. He found an audience predisposed to oppose the private utilities. At a mass meeting in Florence, the assembled citizens called on Heflin to "protect our happiness and our future prosperity" by remembering the farmers and their need for fertilizer.[20] With an alternative possibility for the operation of the plants and dam at Muscle Shoals, Florence quickly retreated from its willingness to cooperate with Alabama Power.

Once again, the private utility found itself portrayed as an enemy. The *Flor-*

ence Times, sensing a worsening sentiment toward the utility, began listing the faults in the power bid, going so far as to suggest that government ownership might prove to be the only alternative to "being made the victims of a shrewd, voracious and domineering organization."[21] This hardly seemed the same utility that had done so much to prepare Florence for industrial development. Alabama Power found fighting its negative image difficult, especially with the waves of support for American Cyanamid's bid coming from farmers' organizations and civic groups. O. G. Thurlow, the president of the power companies' fertilizer wing, the Muscle Shoals Fertilizer Company, wrote a lengthy letter to President Sam Thompson of the American Farm Bureau pleading his case and directly comparing the two bids. He characterized his company's offer as another step in the utilities' continuing efforts to improve the region and noted the irony in the public criticism of Alabama Power for attempting to use Muscle Shoals for its own gain when the nitrate companies would also profit from production at the facility.[22]

The bid by the American Cyanamid Company became the darling of most southerners, thanks in part to the work of the farmers' organizations, which saw it as the greatest hope for more widely available, more affordable fertilizer. In the eyes of its supporters, the nitrate company would also be more likely use extra power to support industry in the Shoals area and, by cheapening fertilizer, provide a greater overall return to the region's farmers.[23] Alabama's delegation extolled the benefits of the Cyanamid bid in Washington. On the Senate floor, Heflin used farmer support for the bid to back his own claim that the company would best utilize the facilities.[24] Senator Oscar Underwood also praised the Cyanamid bid, stating that it would better fulfill the original intent of the National Defense Act by focusing on nitrate production and using hydroelectricity to power the plants.[25] Representative Edward Almon stated his support for American Cyanamid while criticizing the bid of the power companies. He noted that the Joint Committee's recommendation came under "widespread protest and disapproval" with hollow claims and flimsy guarantees for fertilizer, and in a moment of high praise, suggested that the Cyanamid offer resembled the bid by Henry Ford.[26] J. W. Worthington lobbied hard for the bid, and he felt sure of a victory over the hated utilities: "The pig is pinched and he is squealing—we have stuck him in a sore sport and he is bleeding, and I am going to do my best to bleed him to death—I will never stanch a drop."[27] With Worthington's help and growing congressional support for the Cyanamid bid, momentum shifted away from the power companies.

In January 1927, the support for the fertilizer company culminated in a bill, named for Illinois Republican Martin Madden, which called for the acceptance of the lease of the Muscle Shoals properties to American Cyanamid. After receiving the bill, the Military Affairs Committee drew up a list of requirements for a successful bid, and in a blow to the hopes of private operation, the committee decided that none of the bids met the necessary requirements. The committee called for revised bids and stated that, if no satisfactory bids were found, it would consider government operation.[28] The Madden Bill was by no means the last call for the private operation of the Muscle Shoals facilities; however, it was the last real legislative chance for a private company to control the project.[29] After March 1927, supporters of private operation began including clauses for conditional government operation in their bills to lease the plants and dam.

As supporters of private operation battled over the merits of individual bids, George Norris continued to praise the merits of public ownership. He charged the utility companies with creating a power trust that served to inflate costs across the country, and suggested that Alabama Power's bid for the facilities at Muscle Shoals was a poorly disguised attempt to add the Tennessee Valley to a national monopoly.[30] Instead, government ownership and operation meant an equitable distribution of the benefits of water and power incompatible with pure profit-seeking. Norris's ardor led him to eloquence: "If we should properly develop this project, we would tap this lightning that man has called electricity and convert its destructive and ruthless forces into a friendly power that would turn the countless wheels of toil all through the South and bring happiness and comfort to thousands of humble homes."[31] Government development promised a prosperity that reached every citizen, but only if the private power and fertilizer companies could be prevented from turning the investment at Muscle Shoals into a profit-driven enterprise.

By 1927, the government had reached yet another stalemate on the fate of Muscle Shoals. The House Military Affairs Committee rejected all promising bids, and the Senate continued to debate almost exclusively the merits of Norris's plans for government operation. The wait was frustrating, but the people of the Tri-Cities had learned not to rest on the hopes of a solution to the problem of Muscle Shoals. Early in 1926, the Sheffield-Tuscumbia Chamber of

Commerce announced that a campaign to raise $100,000 in municipal bonds to attract the King Company, a metal brackets manufacturer, had reached a "safe margin" and that the company was ready to set up shop in the region, eventually planning to hire 300 to 400 men and drawing on iron from the Sheffield furnace for production. The news led the *Florence Times* to praise the developers who had spent thousands in the area to pave streets and sidewalks and perform other improvements without waiting on word of a decision on Muscle Shoals. While some had "crawled in under a log," others had learned that "it does not take action by Congress or any other outside assistance to make progress worth while in local affairs." The federal government was not a "Santa Claus" who would "leave prosperity in their stocking some night while they are dreaming."[32] Washington's plans for economic progress served to encourage local entrepreneurship and economic leadership, even when it failed to produce real results.

In April 1926, inspired by the success of its neighbors, the Florence Chamber of Commerce held a mass meeting to encourage citizens to contribute money for a new underwear mill. Leaders promised that, with adequate public subscriptions, the Gardiner-Warring Company of Utica, New York, would assuredly choose Florence for a proposed $300,000 facility. As an added encouragement, the paper listed the most prominent donors, Thomas McLemore and Benjamin Armstead Rogers Jr., owners of a local department store, who added $10,000 to the drive (undoubtedly with expectations of a substantial increase in customers).[33] By February 1927, the Florence Industrial Corporation, which was formed by a local realty group to build and manage the factory site, boasted $55,000 in stock. Members pleaded for the final $10,000 to locate the plant: "The day ground is broken to build a mill of which the district will be proud, PAYROLLS made possible by YOUR SUBSCRIPTIONS to the Florence Industrial Corporation stock begin at once." As the group promised, "The industry of Florence supply the pay-rolls, and do more to build up the community than any other factor. . . . When we have located this industry, a good going concern, others will follow." Gardiner-Warring began construction later that year and was one of the city's few industries to survive the Great Depression.[34]

Civic organizations like the chamber of commerce and the Florence Industrial Corporation led the region's efforts to attract industry to North Alabama. Across the river from Florence, local realtors founded the Muscle Shoals Commercial Club on $30,000 in donations to lead the development of the entire district. The club addressed national issues, particularly working to fight the power companies' bid for Muscle Shoals, but its main task was to improve the economy of the Tri-Cities, building off the efforts of the individual chambers of commerce. The club made the final arrangements for financing the location of the Super Tool Company of Detroit and the Sorg Engine Manufacturing Company of Owosso, Michigan, at a dinner the next month and later signed a contract with Bliss Refrigerating. The Commercial Club promised to invest $140,000 toward the location of Super Tool, with a $60,000 public subscription. Local support would also help with Sorg and Bliss. Combined, the three plants projected a workforce of 1,500 skilled laborers—a welcome boon with employment down at the government projects.[35]

By all measures, the Muscle Shoals Commercial Club was a success, and it bridged the gap between federal and local development in several ways. The club was led by Tri-Cities developers for the improvement of the Muscle Shoals District. The group relied on public subscriptions in order to encourage companies to make the initial investment in the region, offsetting some of the cost of relocation while also giving the public a personal and financial stake in North Alabama's economic well-being. Tellingly, the club addressed the politics of the nitrate plants and dam, promising to help fight the bid from Alabama Power, but the political quagmire surrounding Muscle Shoals remained a secondary concern. The overarching goal was community improvement. If Congress would not act to assist the people of the Tennessee Valley, the people could just as easily help themselves.

In some ways, the business and civic leaders of the Tri-Cities resembled their New South booster predecessors, particularly those involved in the textile boom of the late nineteenth and early twentieth centuries. In the 1880s, communities in the Carolina Piedmont conducted "cotton mill campaigns" to attract the textile industry to the South. Drawn by expanding transportation networks, increased capital, abundant cotton, and cheap labor, northern investors and local entrepreneurs joined forces to introduce industry to the region. Upcountry towns, long overshadowed by coastal cities, witnessed a rapid influx of people. In Greensboro, North Carolina, for instance, the population rose from less than 500 in 1870 to over 10,000 in 1900. In Greenville, South Carolina, the population rose from 1,500 in 1860 to over 10,000 at the turn of the century. Locals saw the location of a mill as "progress," the watchword of Henry Grady's New South, and in communities across the Piedmont, towns clamored to bring a mill south or locate a new business in the region. As historians have noted, "Mill building became synonymous with town building and served as an index to community prosperity."[36] Such growth continued through World War I, so that by the 1920s, Gaston County, North Carolina, promised to "Organize a mill a week."[37]

In the Tennessee Valley, the once-agricultural town of Huntsville witnessed its own textile boom, becoming one of the largest mill cities in Alabama by the early 1920s. As in the Piedmont, Huntsville's growth came from private investments, largely made by northerners interested in taking advantage of cheap labor and a business-friendly environment. When the Dallas Manufacturing Company decided to locate in the city in 1892, for instance, investors from Pennsylvania and Rhode Island provided the bulk of the financing, and Huntsville provided free water, fifty acres of land, and a lengthy tax exemption.[38] Supporting public aid campaigns, financial concessions, and infrastructure improvements, civic leaders in Huntsville, Florence, and in towns across the South hoped to attract outside industries to the region.[39] They looked to state governments for aid in building roads and parks, funding utility expansion and supporting services, including educational and healthcare facilities. Alabama's Governor Bibb Graves, a quintessential southern Progressive, passed just such an improvement package during his tenure in Montgomery in the late 1920s.[40]

But the nature of the debate over Muscle Shoals added a complicating factor to the campaign for development, and in North Alabama these "business progressives" began to look beyond state and local assistance to the federal government. A solution to Muscle Shoals would allow the region to realize its economic potential, and even though locals refused to "wait" on such a solution, they understood that the federal government would play the deciding role in the outcome. As they looked to federal officials for help in creating an environment for economic growth, Tri-Cities leaders anticipated the outlook of the Sunbelt, even as they reflected the lingering effects of New South boosterism.

In October 1927, the *Florence Times* voiced an opinion quickly gaining popularity among many congressmen. The paper called government operation "more than a possibility" and suggested that even those opposed to Norris's plans for the properties would vote for temporary government operation, just to activate the plants.[41] The idea of a compromise gained traction, and in December 1927 Norris once again made his case for government operation. He led with an argument for the power possibilities at Muscle Shoals but carefully tied it to the larger development of the river. He called for government surveys of the Tennessee River, laying out a series of storage dams that would regulate the flow of the Tennessee, thereby increasing the hydroelectric potential. Such a massive project could only be reliably completed by the government, Norris argued, because private power companies would consume the benefits in their search for profits, demanding "tribute" for "the millionaires in Wall Street."[42] He blamed the inactivity at the plants and dam on southerners and their elected representatives: "The South itself refused the cup of happiness and contentment that was extended by a friendly hand." If the government had control, "[it] would develop a system of electrical distribution the benefits of which would ultimately reach every factory in the South, every home and every municipality between the Potomac and the Gulf, the Mississippi and the Atlantic."[43] On March 6, 1928, Norris's bill passed the Senate and awaited the results of debate in the House.[44]

Discussions of power production led to another potential compromise; both sides feared that the electric trust, headed by Alabama Power, would exploit the facilities for their own interests. The utility already received current from Wilson Dam and, as Congress deliberated, Alabama Power looked to use the extra power to extend their service in North Alabama. In the city of Athens, supporters of the private utility circulated a petition to sell the municipal power plant to Alabama Power in return for promises of cheap electricity. The *Florence Times* begged the city to consider the economic losses that would accrue from monthly payments to the utility. Senator Hugo Black praised Athens as one of the few cities not yet under Alabama Power's umbrella and expressed his concern that the government might sell its surplus power to the utility, making "free" cities like Athens centers of profit for the power trust.[45] Norris promised that, if his resolution passed, Athens could build a transmission line to Muscle Shoals, taking power directly from Wilson Dam. He accused Alabama Power's lawyers of combining personal profit and corporate propaganda, and he promised to send evidence to the Federal Trade Commission for possible investigation.[46] Both Black and Norris feared the power trust, and their opposition to Alabama Power created useful ties in the coming debate.

In the House, Military Affairs Committee Chairman John M. Morin submitted a committee report that would serve as an amendment to Norris's government operation bill. He called for the creation of a "Muscle Shoals Corporation" to produce fertilizer and sell surplus power at the best possible price. Where Norris built his bill around power and waterways development, Morin's compromise stressed fertilizer, calling for low-cost production at a minimum profit that would be returned to the government for its initial investment. Morin freely admitted that government operation was a last resort and claimed that government ownership would keep the plants in working order until a private company could lease them.[47] Several committee members dissented, including Alabama's Lister Hill, whose minority report explicitly refused government operation.[48] However, others in the Alabama delegation were prepared to deal with Norris in return for a final decision.

In House debates on the Norris Bill, Alabama's Edward Almon announced his support, calling the legislation the perfect farm relief measure. He explained that the government was already "in business" at Muscle Shoals and emphasized that the bill under discussion ensured that farmers would get the fertilizer they needed.[49] In Florence, the *Times* backed Norris as well, stating that the "advantages of government operation are so manifest that the only cause for refusal by Congress to accept it will be interpreted as being due to the activities of the lobby of the power trust which has so vigorously and so persistently fought government operation"; government operation was evidently preferable to Alabama Power.[50] With increasing pressure at home and in Washington, even Hill fell in line with his colleagues. In response to a letter from an economist with the National Lumber Manufacturer's Association calling for Hill to protect private enterprise, Hill responded that, while he did not support the measure, it was the "best bill that we can possibly get passed" and would finally put the plants to work. As long as the bill provided for the production of cheap fertilizers, Hill would vote for it regardless of other reservations.[51]

In late May, the compromise passed the Senate over a filibuster by Tennessee's Kenneth D. McKellar, who opposed the government construction of a dam at Cove Creek, near Knoxville. Both Heflin and Hugo Black fought for the bill—Black spent the night in an anteroom while Heflin slept on a cot on the floor of the Senate to be ready when the bill came up for a vote. The compromise passed the House and went to Coolidge for his approval.[52] The bill's proponents were not optimistic. Coolidge had consistently rejected government operation of Muscle Shoals, and while he called for domestically produced fertilizer to aid American farmers, he always couched production at Muscle Shoals in terms of an acceptable lease to a private corporation. While the bill sat on the president's desk, Norris promised that it "will do no injury to any legitimate business" and would benefit the region. He stated his case clearly, writing that "it would be an economic sin to permit [the Muscle

Shoals facilities] to be constructed and operated by private parties for profit," but his appeal fell flat. On May 29, 1928, the Morin-Norris compromise died by pocket veto.[53]

Ironically, as proponents of development at Muscle Shoals struggled to overcome presidential opposition, plans for the nation's other great hydroelectric project came to fruition. In December 1928, Congress passed legislation approving the construction of Boulder Dam (later renamed Hoover Dam) on the Colorado River on the border of California and Nevada. As at Muscle Shoals, officials planned the project in the hopes of encouraging agricultural and industrial development, in Boulder's case for the Imperial Valley.[54] While fiscal conservatism created initial opposition for Boulder (and Muscle Shoals), a series of disastrous floods in the Midwest combined with growing distaste for the actions of private utilities to bring Congress around to support.[55] At Muscle Shoals, the issue of nitrate production and the history of private bids for the facility kept opposition to government operation viable. By the late 1920s, as federal planners formally began work on the Colorado River, Congress continued to bicker over the status of the Tennessee River Valley.[56]

Coolidge's rejection of the Norris-Morin compromise changed the nature of the debate among Alabama's congressmen. They had abandoned their insistence on private operation to accept a bill that called for temporary government operation with the possibility of permanent public ownership. When that failed, the legislators faced a tough decision: support government operation and get legislation passed in the Senate or back private operation and hope the incoming Republican president would approve it. The state of the nitrate plants made the choice much harder. When national correspondent Robert Talley visited the facilities in November 1928, he found dust collecting on the equipment. Calling the project "a city of the dead," he pointed to dark furnaces and cold smokestacks. Talley found a "large glass jar" on a dusty shelf filled with "five pounds of a white substance that looks and feels like damp salt." The unused ammonium nitrate, manufactured during the brief period of operation during World War I, symbolized the sheer waste of the plants' potential. Talley described the vacant lots and empty streets amid the cotton fields of the Tri-Cities, waiting on a prosperity that seemed increasingly distant. In his estimation, the people of the area cared little who took control of the plant: "All they want is to have the plants operated."[57] The congressional delegation agreed. Between 1929 and 1932, Alabama's congressmen backed any measure likely to succeed, as long as it fit two requirements: aid to the rural population in the form of fertilizer and the rejection of the (loosely defined) trusts that sought to use Muscle Shoals for their own profits.

In the immediate aftermath of the veto, Hugo Black threw his support to government operation, explaining his position in a July 1928 speech before a crowd of 2,500 in Florence. The complicated nature of his argument illuminates the conflicted mood of his colleagues in the Tennessee Valley's delegation. Black began by acknowledging that many people were hesitant to support government operation, citing the United States' traditional encouragement of private industry. In many cases, Black agreed with the merit of that view. He admitted that he had wholeheartedly supported the Ford offer, which "would have meant great things to the development and industries of the South," and had initially backed the offer of American Cyanamid. Yet the failure of private-operation legislation caused Black to rethink his stance. While the private sector should be protected, some specific industries required a different economic outlook. He argued that the power industry carried the constant threat of monopoly, and in its original legislation, the Wilson administration recognized this threat and planned for government operation. In the same spirit, Norris called for government operation, but was denied by Coolidge in a "tragedy" for the farmers living a "measly existence for lack of funds." Black reluctantly admitted that the political situation indicated that government operation was the only way for the farmers of the Tennessee Valley to receive cheap fertilizer and for the people and industries of the area to enjoy the electric current that he believed would bring future prosperity.[58]

Lister Hill was more vocal in his support of the American Cyanamid offer, telling one Sheffield resident that the company would preserve the properties for national defense while still giving fertilizer to farmers and looking toward long-term river development (the bill called for the construction of two more dams on the Tennessee, the unnamed Dam 3 and Cove Creek).[59] But Hill also admitted that he had supported the original Norris Bill, which had been "emasculated" by the fertilizer trust, and had even backed Democratic New York Governor Al Smith's public-oriented waterpower policy.[60] Heflin best stated the position of Alabama's delegation: "I want to put that machinery to work; I want the power used to bless and benefit the people in that vicinity."[61] Alabama's representatives were willing to compromise. As long as Muscle Shoals gave assistance to the rural populations struggling to survive, Black, Hill, Heflin, and Almon would fall in line.

Once again, valley leaders received a lesson in the vagaries of economic development. The potential for growth at Muscle Shoals was clear and, for over a decade, locals and their representatives pushed for a disposition of the facilities that might ensure the long-term economic health of the region. But because of federal ownership, the final responsibility for a decision rested in Washington, D.C., where politicians could not agree on the best path for the development. As Alabama's congressmen navigated Senate channels dominated by Norris and a presidency controlled by fiscal conservatives, they found compromise nearly impossible. Locals quickly learned that, while the government's support in sparking growth might be beneficial (the plants did, after all, start out as a federal project), the long-term prospects for sustaining such development were dim. Instead, government investment would need to serve as a springboard for local action. Muscle Shoals legislation continued to wind its way through Congress, but the people of the valley had to take the initiative.

In an effort to stave off discouragement after Coolidge's veto, Florence's leaders encouraged citizens to forget about the operation of the plants in the "distant future" and focus on the foreseeable by working to attract small industries.[62] The *Florence Times* quoted the U.S. Chamber of Commerce on considerations for communities planning industrial expansion. The city needed to look to specific commodities that the region could economically produce and distribute, then locate factories with experienced managers to produce them for the market.[63] Leaders called for a "definite and determined" industrial campaign that would build up the community by systematically bringing in businesses that met local needs. They praised diversity, calling for more wage-based industries to balance North Alabama's existing agricultural economy.[64] City leaders evoked a region prepared to go ahead with its own development. Even as congressional leaders pushed for any bill with a chance of passing muster, the Tri-Cities planned for industrial development.

The stock market crash only served to underline the region's need for industry. By 1930, Lauderdale County's population had increased by 1,500 to over 41,000 inhabitants, but it lost four industries and only added 100 workers. The surrounding counties lost 130 workers and twenty-six industries.[65] The *Florence Times* downplayed the growing depression as a "natural" readjustment of the nation's wealth that would continue the decline in regional buying power. With its "basic advantages" untouched, all the area needed was confidence to continue its growth.[66] In rural areas, economic depression was an ongoing concern; in the words of writer Rick Bragg, it was a "creeping thing. . . . It did not make the rows any longer for a farmer plowing a mule, or change the diet of a family already eating cornbread and beans seven days a week."[67] In fact, the increasingly desperate condition of farmers motivated Alabama's congressional delegation to keep Muscle Shoals dedicated to the production of cheap fertilizer. As the region's urban leadership learned, however, the Crash lessened the prospects for growth. In early 1930, city leaders advised locals that outside industries would no longer be willing to move or expand to a new area, though they remained optimistic, suggesting that when the economy returned to normal the surviving businesses would be sounder for the experience. Leaders told citizens to keep the region's appeal visible. As long as the area maintained available factory sites, industries would recognize the "progressive" nature of Muscle Shoals and plan for a future there.[68]

The Great Depression also gave congressional discussions of the fate of Muscle Shoals an added urgency. In April 1930, with Congress nearing adjournment, Hill argued for Norris's legislation authorizing government ownership and operation. Compared with an unpassable House substitute that would replace the bill with a call for private operation, Norris's bill was an "easy choice." The legislation kept the dam out of the hands of Alabama Power and, while Norris's fertilizer provisions were not as strong as Hill might have liked, they guaranteed fertilizer for farmers at a limited profit.[69] Sensing the possibility of compromise, Norris proposed government operation of the power facilities and private operation of the nitrate properties. The bill died but, when Congress reconvened in 1931, Norris's compromise was resurrected, with growing support from those most concerned with the plants' operation.[70]

In fact, the supporters of Norris's bill were less concerned about the threat of congressional stonewalling than they were with the attitude of President Herbert Hoover. During the 1928 presidential campaign, Hoover had hinted at the possibility of allowing government operation at Muscle Shoals, but few felt certain he would honor that promise. On February 20, the House passed the compromise, followed by the Senate three days later. The *Florence Times*, ever optimistic, believed that Hoover would hold true to his word and approve it, even if it was not exactly what he wanted.[71] Alabama's Governor Benjamin M. Miller sent a telegram to the president, stressing the opportunity for private investment in the plants, which would in turn employ men and boost farm yields, helping to ameliorate the effects of depression and drought. When Hoover responded, asking if anyone would lease the plants under the conditions imposed by Congress, Miller responded in the affirmative. The need in the Cotton Belt for cheap fertilizer was great, and "at least one outstanding Alabama industrialist" expressed interest in the plants. Miller promised that Hoover would win the praise of those companies that feared government operation of the nitrate plants, and assured him that the business community would formulate a lease quickly.[72]

After several suspenseful days, Hoover vetoed the Muscle Shoals bill. In an accompanying statement, the former engineer analyzed the power possibilities and claimed that the government could not operate the power plant more cheaply than the power companies and still find the funds to construct more dams along the river. As suggested in his telegram to Governor Miller, Hoover also feared that the conditions for leasing the fertilizer plants were too restrictive, forcing potential businesses to make impractical guarantees. His main concern, however, was the creation of a government corporation to operate the hydroelectric generators and sell surplus power. In the Senate, Black and Norris were outraged. The Alabamian derided the "great engineer" for his failure to aid the people of the South. He argued that additional dams would boost the power potential of the site, causing electric rates to fall. Black tied Hoover to the trusts, comparing him to the agents of "special privilege and greed" that would not "give to the plain, average, everyday citizen the crumbs that fall from their tables."[73] He promised that the fertilizer plants could turn a profit, making them attractive to most businessmen. Finally, Black stressed his own credentials as a proponent of private industry in general but charged that a real change was needed: "Mr. President, the time is coming in this Nation when something must be done in order to curb the growing power of those who themselves seek to destroy the private initiative and competitive business system upon which the Nation has been built."[74] In a direct challenge to the Republican leadership, Black predicted that the coming Democratic Congress would have a new Muscle Shoals bill within a week of meeting. Norris concurred, telling Hoover he "ought to know better."[75] In the House, Almon described Hoover's statement as misinformed, and like Black, wondered why the president would go against his own promise to allow government operation at Muscle Shoals. On March 4, Norris marshaled a majority of forty-nine senators to override the veto but fell short of the requisite two-thirds vote, and his bill died.[76]

In his veto message, Hoover recommended that the states of Alabama and Tennessee appoint a joint commission to accept and review private bids for the Muscle Shoals plants. The interstate commission, which included Florence businessman W. F. McFarland, attracted a number of bids, seemingly demonstrating continued corporate interest in Muscle Shoals. The commission's report, released in November 1931, called for a private lease of both the power and nitrate facilities with the project dedicated to the revitalization of southern agriculture.[77] The task of enacting the report fell to the House Military Affairs Committee, particularly the subcommittee led by Alabama's Lister Hill. The committee charged Hill to craft legislation that would give "liberal" leasing provisions and a lengthy eighteen-month period to obtain a working bid, but with an alternate provision for government operation if no lease proved acceptable. Hill rose to the challenge, writing a bill that would "forge the first link in the chain of development and open up the industrial empire of the Tennessee Valley destined to become a greater Ruhr."[78]

The "Hill Bill" emphasized the importance of Muscle Shoals to the development of southern agriculture, explicitly dedicating the nitrate plants to the immediate production of fertilizer at minimal profit. The bill also allowed for further appropriations for government developments on the Tennessee Valley that would increase the power capabilities at Wilson Dam and work toward flood control and navigation on the Tennessee River, specifically suggesting the construction of a dam at Cove Creek, a site near Knoxville, Tennessee. Finally, the bill provided for government operation only if the board could not approve a lease after eighteen months, and only to ensure that the plants actively produced fertilizer.[79]

The Hill Bill was the final attempt by legislators to deal the dam and nitrate plants to an interested company. Hill's legislation mirrored earlier attempts to lease the facilities to Ford and to American Cyanamid, with clauses dedicated to fertilizer production, profit limits, and public oversight. The legislation effectively committed the plants to southern agriculture, and Hill used nearly half of the bill to describe specific fertilizer requirements. Power companies were barred specifically from participating, a nod to the general animosity toward the "power trust" and Alabama Power, still under contract for power from the dam. The *Florence Times*, more concerned about regional economic development, called the bill a "triumph" for Hill, a "bill of rights" for the people, and a "bill of justice" for industries planning to return the benefits of the plants to agriculture. Hill told his colleagues that the bill would free the farmers from the international nitrate "cartel," but also hinted at the industrial possibilities of the Shoals, suggesting that the plants would employ a population of thousands in Alabama and Tennessee, and serve as the "entering wedge for the development of the Valley."[80] On May 5, 1932, the House passed the Hill Bill, which went to the Senate to face Norris and his plans for government operation of the plants.

Norris's government operation bill passed the Senate in December, one month after the Hoover's commission's report recommended a bill for private operation of the plants. Since 1922, Norris's leadership in the Senate ensured that the upper house remained a solid obstacle to private lease, and the Hill Bill faced nearly impossible odds. The *Florence Times* called on Hugo Black to "fight . . . the best fight of his life" against Norris and his "radical Senate group" in support of private operation.[81] Alabama's junior senator, John H. Bankhead Jr., admitted the coming difficulties to one concerned Florence voter, and he outlined his strategy for combating Norris's legislation. Bankhead planned first to vote provisions into the Norris Bill that would substitute private operation, and then to mobilize Democratic senators around the revised legislation. While he supported the Hill Bill's provisions, he knew it would never pass the Senate, and he wanted something "workable" for valley farmers.[82] Bankhead introduced an amendment in the Senate Agricultural Committee that would substitute similar terms as found in the Hill Bill in place of Norris's clauses for government operation, but the addition died before debate or voting took place. In the summer of 1932, the presidential contest between Hoover and Franklin D. Roosevelt changed the nature of the discussion over development at Muscle Shoals.

Roosevelt came to national politics with a proven record of supporting the public development of hydroelectric power. As governor of New York, he had wholeheartedly supported the public development of state waterways, and the Democratic National Committee made waterpower an issue, stressing Roosevelt's belief that it belonged to the American public as a "fundamental principle." The Democratic Party *Campaign Book* instructed speakers to highlight planned legislation that would turn water power into energy and deliver it to the public at the lowest possible cost, allowing cities to erect their own power stations and distribution systems if private companies kept rates unreasonable.[83] The party platform, backed by Roosevelt's past support for public power, gave hope to those interested in the government operation of the facilities at Muscle Shoals. Weeks before the election, Roosevelt visited Knoxville, Tennessee, and spoke of the vast natural resources of the region. Near the site of the proposed Cove Creek Dam, he made his views clear:

"It is important to develop these sites for the small man, the consumer of electricity."[84] Roosevelt's ideas for the region mirrored those of Norris in that they envisioned the larger development of the Tennessee Valley. Where the Alabama delegation demanded fertilizer, Roosevelt stressed regional revitalization and power.

In January 1933, the president-elect stepped off a Southern Railway train at the Sheffield station platform alongside a number of congressmen and state officials. Roosevelt was the first president to visit the region in almost a hundred years, and the gathered "throngs" roared at the realization that "he was virtually promising them the operation of Muscle Shoals in the near future." Roosevelt rode along a parade route leading to the nitrate plant accompanied by Governor Miller, Senators Bankhead and Black, and Representatives Almon and Hill. After touring the plants, Roosevelt proclaimed them ready to operate and left for photo opportunities at Wilson Dam. The *Florence Times* gushed: "It was the greatest day that this District and the Tennessee Valley have ever seen. It was the most portentous and impressive event that this District has ever known. . . . [It] marks the beginning of the carrying through of [Roosevelt's] policies of development of great national projects, of which Muscle Shoals is a decade ahead of all others."[85]

Senator Black was similarly optimistic. He reminded the paper of his prediction that the election of a Democratic president would bring the operation of the Muscle Shoals plants within six days of the inauguration.[86] Roosevelt was more circumspect in his promises. In his speech at the Sheffield station, he told listeners that his trip was an opportunity to make an informed decision about the facility, and he called for his congressional contingent to help him "get something practical done." Later at Florence, he described the plant as a "nation-wide project" and expressed his hope that he would soon return to "find all of the great power possibilities of this Valley being used to its utmost."[87]

Back in Washington, the president-elect began working on a definite plan. The congressmen who had accompanied Roosevelt to the valley hinted at his mindset. They described his view as river-wide development "more gigantic and on a scale far greater than that now proposed in legislation pending before the national legislature." Roosevelt's plans included operating the nitrate plants, building a series of hydroelectric dams to produce power and control annual flooding, and opening a larger river channel to boost regional trade.

Implementation would require millions of dollars in federal funds, but the projects would employ 200,000 men and give work to thousands more as the valley's industrial possibilities emerged. Frank Walsh, the Roosevelt-appointed chair of the Power Authority of the State of New York, promised that Roosevelt would "widen opportunities and promote the comfort of millions of families in their homes throughout the South."[88] The president-elect promised that the project would "herald the birth of a new America, from which unemployment would be completely lifted." The scope of his plans for the Tennessee Valley went beyond even the broadest development envisioned by many of the proponents of government operation. Norris freely admitted that Roosevelt's vision dwarfed his own plans, suggesting that the "gracious and gratifying" revitalization of the Tennessee Valley would make power cheap enough that "people won't even stop to turn it off in the daytime." Conceiving of the Tennessee River watershed as a regional unit, Roosevelt brought Norris's ideas to their fullest conclusion.[89]

On the steps of the Capitol, Franklin Roosevelt gave an inaugural address that rallied the American people to confront the Great Depression. He exhorted listeners to let go of the fear and terror that accompanied economic disaster and to look to a new generation of political leaders who would prove better stewards of the country's bountiful resources. Roosevelt made no specific references to his comprehensive plan of development for the Tennessee Valley, but his goals were clearly in mind as he promised to put Americans to work, using the government to direct the projects that would utilize natural resources. Even as the Depression caused Americans to realize their interdependence, Roosevelt prepared to mobilize the population. As if speaking directly to the people of the valley, he promised: "I assume unhesitatingly the leadership of this great army of our people dedicated to a disciplined attack upon our common problems."[90] Here was a leader to force action on stale legislation and bring prosperity after more than a decade of failed promises.

In the House, Hill abandoned private leasing and introduced legislation creating the "Muscle Shoals Corporation," a government organization that would operate the nitrate plants and oversee the development of the Tennessee River for "national defense, agricultural conservation, fertilizer production, navigation, flood control, power distribution, reforestation, industrial development, and unemployment relief."[91] His bill allowed the corporation to sell surplus power and specifically addressed the production of fertilizer at the plants, calling for the government to make any necessary changes to the facility to ensure that plant food became readily available.[92] Under Hill's legislation, the corporation acted much like a private company, producing and selling both power and fertilizer. In particular, Hill wanted to ensure that government operation would preserve the use of the plants for fertilizer production. He even made provision for contracts with private fertilizer companies if the government corporation could not meet farmers' demands.[93]

In the Senate, Norris produced his own government operation bill. His Muscle Shoals Corporation operated much like Hill's, though with some important exceptions. Where Hill had been willing to work within the private sphere on fertilizer sale and power distribution (Hill's corporation would lease existing transmission lines), Norris demanded unhampered public operation of both power and fertilizer facilities. Skeptical of the capabilities of the plants at Muscle Shoals, Norris's legislation called for experimentation with the existing equipment and production techniques in order to determine whether fertilizer could be made for reasonable prices. He felt Hill's legislation exceedingly reckless, and argued it required the proposed government agency to use outdated processes and build new facilities to fulfill fertilizer guarantees that might prove unrealistic. Norris believed that his corporation needed the authority to build its own transmission lines to set cheap rates and make power more widely available.[94] Hill's bill exhibited the continuing influence of the valley's demand for agricultural revitalization and the predilection among many legislators to include aspects of private operation in the final decision. Buoyed by support from Roosevelt, Norris put forward his strongest plan for government operation, using public funds to develop an entire region with as little reliance on (or cooperation with) private industry as possible.

In April, Roosevelt sent an impassioned message to Congress, suggesting the creation of a government corporation called the Tennessee Valley Authority (TVA). The project at Muscle Shoals made up only a small part of the larger potential inherent in the valley, he argued, and those who focused simply on fertilizer or power excluded many of the other goals he envisioned for the region's development. TVA would be "a corporation clothed with the power of Government but possessed of the flexibility and initiative of a private industry."[95] Roosevelt gave a brief background of his own experience and mentioned Norris as his inspiration for regional development based in the Tennessee Valley.[96] Norris's bill fit squarely in the mold created by the president, and Hill's followed the basic outlines, though its differences on fertilizer production and power facilities provided ample room for debate. Within days of Roosevelt's message, the Hill Bill passed the House. When it reached the Senate, though, Norris substituted his own bill, which the body quickly adopted. The bill came back to the House, where the differences between the two bills became points of real contention, particularly Hill's restrictions on government construction of transmission lines. Roosevelt once again intervened, holding a conference with House and Senate leaders, resulting in a compromise bill that went before both houses. On May 16 and 17, the bill passed the Senate and House, and on May 18, Roosevelt signed the bill into law, creating the Tennessee Valley Authority.[97]

From the outset, the TVA Act called for the maintenance and operation of the facilities at Muscle Shoals for national defense, "agricultural and industrial development," navigation, and flood control. A three-man board of directors governed authority actions. Incorporating Hill's desire for fertilizer, the legislation called for the board to work with commercial producers to help acquire and develop fertilizers. The board also worked to educate farmers about new products and cooperate in experiments and demonstration farms. TVA could sell surplus power to government and private entities and build transmission lines, but only where towns were not already being supplied under reasonable rates. The government would issue bonds to help defray the cost of building new dams and facilities, and the act specifically called for the construction of a dam at Cove Creek. It also provided the authority with the right of eminent domain, an important clause that allowed TVA to condemn land, relocate roads, highways, electric plants, "and any and all other properties, enterprises, and projects whose removal may be necessary" in the cause of greater development.[98] The program envisioned in the TVA Act encompassed a remarkable array of projects: flood control, navigation, power production, land reclamation, reforestation, agricultural instruction in land use and soil revitalization, industrial development, and job creation. The legislation certainly exceeded the original plan for development along the Tennessee River, the National Defense Act of 1916 that called for a single hydroelectric dam and nitrate facilities. In its immensity, the TVA Act also surpassed the imagination of the people of Muscle Shoals, promising a bright future in the midst of a deep depression.

Hardly an innovation of the New Deal, the Tennessee Valley Authority embodied the give and take of the decade-and-a-half discussion over the future of development in the Tennessee Valley, centered on the nitrate plants and hydroelectric dam at Muscle Shoals. In its earliest manifestation, the North Alabama project looked to use federal funds to produce nitrates, making munitions during wartime and fertilizers for southern farmers in times of peace. The dam provided power for the plants, drawing on the Tennessee River and opening navigation possibilities at the rocky shoals that gave the region its name. In the final act, the properties served much the same purpose. Wilson Dam powered the Muscle Shoals nitrate plants, which produced ammonium nitrate for use as plant food. This was central to the demands of Alabamians who called for the revitalization of southern farming, and when Roosevelt promised a renewed commitment to agriculture, he echoed Tennessee Valley desires for assistance to farmers struggling to make a profit. As enacted, TVA envisioned a larger agricultural program than fertilizer distribution and, in its first decade, it truly worked to improve the soil of the South, to teach farmers advanced farming techniques like terracing and crop rotation, and to improve the home lives of southern tenants and sharecroppers. Yet even in its breadth, TVA's farm program grew out of the debate over the purpose of the government project at Muscle Shoals, and the arguments of Hill, Heflin, and Underwood were clearly present in the final legislation.

In the region's cities and towns, leading citizens expressed a different vision for development at Muscle Shoals. Impatient with an endless congressional debate over the plants, the business community began its own program of growth, hoping to bring in industries that would raise employment and encourage regional commerce. Leaders formed a civic organization geared toward development and used a number of techniques to attract industries, eventually employing a few thousand workers. Roosevelt also wanted to create jobs in the valley, and in particular saw the cheap power produced at Wilson as an important resource for attracting industry. TVA operated the plants, and the construction of additional dams put local men to work on a large scale. Initially, the authority shied away from direct industrial development, instead focusing on conserving the region's resources in hopes that local business might grow to meet its perceived potential. As the years passed, however, the agency gravitated toward industrial attraction, working with groups like

Florence's chamber of commerce in order to advance the cause of economic development. In that transition, TVA embodied the booster ethos that came to mark the economic growth of the modern South and again demonstrated the complicated nature of the interaction between the federal government and the people and communities it wanted to help.

THREE

WE ARE TRYING TO MAKE A DIFFERENT TYPE OF CITIZEN OUT OF THEM, 1933–1938

In 1935, Waterloo was a "sprawling country town" situated on the northern bank of the Tennessee River in the northwest corner of Alabama. The small town was fairly typical of southern agricultural communities in the early twentieth century. Its economy revolved around farming, mostly cotton, in the fertile bottomland occasionally flooded by the river. Some farmers owned their land, but many agricultural workers were tenants renting land to cultivate their crops, sharecroppers farming for a portion of the harvest, or laborers working for a wage. The upland soil was poor, especially in comparison to the rich bottomland, so only small gardens and subsistence plots proved viable in the hills above the river. There, hardwood forests supplied lumber mills, employing a number of people as operators and cutters, though by the 1930s, indiscriminate cutting had begun to deplete timber stocks.[1] The town had a number of churches and a few schools for black and white students, and ministers and teachers rounded out the non-farm workers in the community.[2] Waterloo's economy relied heavily on its natural resources as residents exported cotton and timber in return for the wages and income that drove the city's businesses and services. A highway connection to nearby Florence provided access to wider markets and healthcare when necessary, but the town clearly saw itself as a self-contained community, relying on its resources, both natural and human, to create a way of life along the Tennessee River.

In 1935, officials from the TVA began interviewing residents in preparation for a land acquisition campaign associated with the planned construction of

Pickwick Dam and Reservoir. Though the dam would be located across the state line in Tennessee, the reservoir would largely affect Alabama's Lauderdale and Colbert counties. Since rising water levels would subsume Waterloo's low-lying farms and most of the town itself, TVA's Reservoir Property Management Division, which conducted interviews with every family affected by the agency's reservoir program, made a special effort in Waterloo. Workers took a broad sampling of residents, including those not directly affected by the rising water level, and their findings, taken between 1935 and 1937, provide a concise view of the promise and problems associated with TVA's program in the valley.

From the outset, Waterloo residents had mixed feelings about the economic future of their community. When informed of the coming changes, some remained optimistic about the possibility of staying employed or finding a new job. W. E. Haynes, a sawmill operator, believed he could find work somewhere else "without sacrifice."[3] One of Waterloo's mail carriers understood that the flooding would effectively end his route, but he was sure that he would receive another.[4] The county school superintendent saw the change as an opportunity to shuffle system resources, removing an abandoned school from the flood zone to use as either a school for black students or as a teacher's residence in town.[5] An English teacher, William Wilson, voiced the views of the town's optimists most succinctly. Waterloo, he claimed, would be able to "readjust and sustain itself" if the town's citizens "open[ed] their minds to new ideas" like diversified farming and raising livestock.[6]

At the end of his interview, Wilson explained that his view "differs from that of most of the citizens of the town." In fact, many in Waterloo dreaded TVA's arrival. They knew that flood waters would cover the town's most productive farmland, leaving the most successful farmers and their tenants, sharecroppers, and laborers out of work. The town's stores would close without a viable market for goods, and the population would face unemployment, relocation, or outmigration. One farmer told TVA officials that he would love to stay on the land, but would not be able to do so at his current location. A Presbyterian minister confided that he would probably be transferred elsewhere, since most of his congregation would be forced to leave the community, and he frankly told TVA officials that the agency should purchase the town site and bring in industries to revitalize the area economy.[7]

Many agreed that TVA should play an active role in supporting Waterloo's continued existence. Realizing that agriculture would no longer be profitable in the community, a number of the town's citizens called on the government agency to bring in industry and provide at least part-time work for former full-time farmers. One resident told her interviewer that she was "very dissatisfied" with TVA policy and called for industrialization to put men (including her own sons) to work. A lifelong farmer confessed that he was hesitant to leave the land, but would if "other work is available . . . in the future."[8] Landowner Ben Lee would not be able to stay on his property since he would lose too much tillable land, though officials noted that he had enough of his own resources to relocate satisfactorily. His case worker gave a frank assessment of Lee's attitude toward the authority: "[He] is one of the Waterloo residents whose [actions] would be valuable in the readjustment of the community. Mr. Lee, however, is very pessimistic concerning the future of the town, and it would be difficult to convince him that it is possible for the citizens to readjust the community with their own resources."[9]

The situation at Waterloo posed a real challenge for TVA. As TVA Board member Harcourt A. Morgan told President Franklin D. Roosevelt, despite TVA's "extraordinary effort" to help people readjust, the situation at Waterloo had become "unsatisfactory." TVA planned to work with "responsible farmers" and, within a couple of years, have programs in place to make new land available for the agricultural economy. TVA contacted a number of local and national farmers groups, including the U.S. Department of Agriculture and the State Extension Service at Alabama Polytechnic Institute (later Auburn University), to work with people of the community. TVA officials predicted that the town would soon enjoy improved transportation, industrial and commercial development, and employment in recreation that would bring paychecks back to the region. Despite government assurances, the real test would lie with the residents themselves. Morgan warned, "The success of all these efforts . . . will depend largely upon the adaptability and cooperative spirit of the people in Waterloo."[10]

Two years later, Harcourt Morgan's realistic assessment of the changed community replaced his earlier cautious confidence. TVA flooded Waterloo in 1938, and by 1940 the town's optimists had gone silent. TVA purchased twenty-two houses, a church, a cotton gin, a sawmill, and a small shop, together making up 20 percent of the town. The population declined from 576 in 1935 to 475 in 1940, and 60 percent of the remaining heads of family in the town were unemployed.[11] In 1930, Waterloo boasted 236 farms with 17,785 acres of cultivated land, but by 1940, much of that land was under water or in government hands.[12] Out of a sample of 100 families, the number employed in agriculture dropped from 63 to 6, and the removal of the town's only cotton gin made cotton cultivation much less profitable. The fertile bottomlands disappeared, and farming failed to take hold in the upland hills. The timber industry was anemic, as unrestrained cutting had depleted nearly all of the useable lumber; only seven heads of family claimed full-time employment in timber.[13] The main highway connection to Florence was flooded, and a newly constructed replacement road bypassed Waterloo by several miles.[14] Retail sales fell by 50 percent, and merchants lowered prices to attract business, leading many to travel to Florence to sell products that once found a local market. Where before, Waterloo drew business from the entire western portion of Lauderdale County and parts of Tennessee's Hardin and Wayne counties, by 1940 the trade area shrank to six square miles.[15] Property values dropped over 50 percent, and the number of residents on government relief jumped from 8 percent to 36 percent. The school population increased, thanks to the consolidation of a number of outlying schools, and attendance became more regular because fewer students left class to work in the fields.[16] The city found itself unable to maintain its city hall, and the municipal government resorted to occasional meetings at the Waterloo barber shop.[17]

Despite the disheartening statistics, the TVA report found the unquantifiable changes the most profound. Officials commented on the "all-pervading pessimism and defeatist attitude of the people in the area."[18] Over a span of five years, Waterloo residents witnessed the destruction of their way of life. For all of the promises of TVA and its plans for intelligent resource use, farmers watched Pickwick Reservoir cover their community's most valuable resource—the land itself. Those with means left for other areas, but many could not afford to relocate. Families struggled to grow crops in the hills, cut retail prices to keep their stores afloat, or turned to the government for assistance. Their pessimism was hardly surprising, but the situation at Waterloo gave TVA a clear example of the challenges inherent in their program for the valley. As residents turned to the future, they looked to TVA to replace the lives and livelihoods they lost as such profound changes came to the region.

As the Tennessee Valley Authority began to implement its program in Waterloo and throughout the Tennessee River watershed in the mid-1930s, it struggled to define its mission. President Franklin D. Roosevelt and the authority's legislative "father," Senator George Norris, clearly intended the agency as a broad-reaching solution to the region's economic stagnation, and planners based their solution largely on the utilization of the region's natural resources in a balanced program of industrial and agricultural development. The federal government mobilized its resources to work with farmers, community leaders, and businessmen in order to diversify an economy founded on the cultivation and rudimentary processing of cash crops. Dams along the Tennessee River provided a navigable channel to carry goods to market, controlled seasonal flooding to prevent damage to homes and businesses, and electrified homes, farms, and industries. The program was ambitious, and its broad goals left much room for debate and dissention over the direction of economic development. As residents watched the valley transform, they questioned the continued feasibility of farming. As in Waterloo, new reservoirs covered the best farmland and, encouraged by agency officials, many residents moved to towns and cities, looking for industrial jobs. TVA began its program with an attempt to control local resources and revitalize the regional economy but, as the valley's transformation progressed, the agency forced residents to reconsider a future tied to the land.

From its inception, TVA relied heavily on the cooperation of residents to pursue its wide-ranging goals. Therefore, the relationship between the TVA Board in Knoxville, Tennessee, and local leaders in cities like Decatur and Florence was an important factor in the relative success or failure of the agency's work. And, as Waterloo's experience also shows, valley residents imagined community development in ways that sometimes differed drastically from those of government officials. As TVA built dams and flooded land, worked with farm agencies and local businesses, and cooperated with cities to bring improvements, residents pursued their own vision of the future, demanding immediate relief in the face of TVA's long-range goals. In Decatur, the largest city in North Alabama in 1930, the work of *Decatur Daily* editor Barrett Shelton helped to push TVA in a new direction. Shelton's vision of the region's economic future resembled that of TVA Board member David E. Lilienthal, who shifted the authority's mission from a diverse range of social and economic goals to directed industrial development, building closer ties with local leaders whose desire to bring in jobs and share in the coming defense boom fit his own goals for the federal agency.

The Tennessee Valley of the early 1930s looked much as it had at the outset of the debate over Muscle Shoals. Even after serious efforts by civic leaders to bring in business, diversified industry had yet to take root in any meaningful way and, despite the ongoing agricultural depression, residents remained overwhelmingly dependent on profit-driven farming. While extension agents had sporadic success in encouraging the cultivation of legumes and pastures and convincing some farmers to raise cattle and hogs, most farmers determined to make a living in corn or cotton. In fact, in 1930, over 90 percent of all cropland in the counties of the western Tennessee Valley was planted in either corn or cotton. As the region sank further into depression, the percentage of farms worked by tenants jumped from 60 percent in 1920 to 75 percent in 1930, while average farm size shrank to just over 50 acres.[19] County agents tried to remain optimistic, promising that the low price for cotton would drive farmers to feed crops and pasture; in 1932, Limestone County's G. B. Phillips hoped that the "better thinking classes of farmers and tenants realize the fact that they must adapt themselves to existing conditions and produce ample foods and feed other than the one cash crop cotton."[20] Few adapted, and by 1933, southerners remained irrevocably tied to the land.

President Roosevelt and TVA's leaders understood the valley's central economic problem: cash-crop agriculture brought diminishing returns, even as it overshadowed any economic alternative to farms of cotton and corn. And initially, the excitement that accompanied a solution to the decades-long question of Muscle Shoals and the beginning of a New Deal reform program targeting the people of the South brought a shared acceptance that the authority's program would mean a major transformation in the lives of the people of the Tennessee Valley. Even as engineers reshaped the environment of North Alabama, planners pictured a new, more profitable, better-educated, and community-oriented society. This vision was eminently idealistic and optimistic in its overall goals and in its expectations for success and, at first, few within TVA's leadership or across the valley questioned its necessity. As the agency's leaders began to translate their ideas into a workable solution, however, they divided sharply over the region's economic future. In the end, that division opened the door for civic leaders and like-minded administrators in Knoxville and Washington, D.C., to pursue economic development in the Tennessee Valley.

The Tennessee Valley Authority's first chairman, Arthur E. Morgan, interpreted the broad provisions of the TVA Act as a mandate for reconstructing the region's economy, forcibly weaning southern farmers off cash-crop monoculture. Yet, instead of simply diversifying farms, Morgan believed he might remake the way of life in the South, convincing most southerners to grow only what their community needed, manufacture only what their community might use, and live mutually dependent, economically sustainable lives. A. E. Morgan had some practice in such reforms. Before joining the TVA, he served as president of Antioch College, just outside of Dayton, Ohio. At Antioch, he worked to create what one scholar called an "educational utopia," where students balanced study with work in local farms and factories. The school was an early example of the community he hoped to build in the Tennessee Valley, improving society through education and agricultural and small-scale industrial labor while returning the benefits of employment to the larger community.[21] Morgan's planned community at Norris Dam (built in 1933 at the Cove Creek site near Knoxville, Tennessee) proved the culmination of his grand ideals, but early on, the chairman made his vision for the valley perfectly clear.

On May 26, 1933, A. E. Morgan visited Muscle Shoals and promised that TVA's first decision would address the future of the nitrate plants. Even as he planned for the renovation of the plants, however, Morgan insisted on exploring the larger consequences of utilizing the facility. TVA hoped to bring economic development by growing small, localized industries that would allow farmers to work on their farms in the summer and in factories during winter. In his own didactic style, Morgan promised to "develop the social side of the people and raise the standard of living generally." He wanted TVA to "teach the American people in the rural communities how to live."[22]

As he helped to shape the initial policies of the agency, Morgan called for a new social and economic order for the Tennessee Valley. He argued that urban centers were becoming overpopulated, and predicted that, given the national effects of the Great Depression, many city dwellers would soon return to the countryside looking for jobs. TVA would teach southerners, both long-time rural residents and new arrivals, to abandon profit-driven, self-serving individualism in favor of small, self-sufficient, mutualistic communities. In Morgan's estimation, the culture of the people was integral to the project's success, and to change the economic base of the valley was to change its inherent culture. He hoped TVA would "distribute the sense of social responsibility among the people."[23] As his son, Ernst, recalled, Morgan realized that "technical engineering and physical engineering without human engineering" precluded real change. TVA provided an opportunity for him to prove this maxim; Morgan understood that "[y]ou need a lot more than just dams and dredging to [make] a culture."[24]

Morgan believed that cotton monoculture represented the worst aspects of a "rugged individualism," which hampered cooperation among the region's producers. This overriding sense of self-reliance led southerners to seek profit regardless of personal, environmental, or economic consequences. Morgan argued that this resulted in a lack of resource control, a population "stranded . . . in poverty and despair," soil erosion, and wasted horsepower.[25] He told farmers in East Tennessee to stop competing with each other to cultivate crops in hilly land. Instead, farmers should wait on power to reach their farms, so that they could create "a little factory in the barn by plugging into [the] wall."[26] Home-based industries, powered by rural electrification, would produce the goods needed in communities, provide an employment outlet for overtaxed farmland, and bring income into the region. To this end, Morgan encouraged the production and sale of handicrafts, community self-help, and "the restoration of lost folkways."[27] He believed that TVA could teach the valley to work as a community, meeting each other's needs while creating a foundation of needed skills and financial stability that would allow the region to participate in the national economy. More than any other board member, A. E. Morgan truly saw TVA as a regional experiment, and he believed that the valley could come to represent the power of the federal government to better lives through careful organization, comprehensive planning, diversified agriculture and industry, and the intelligent use of natural resources.

The president's vision for TVA fit largely with Morgan's, at least initially. In his fourth "fireside chat," Roosevelt drew on Biblical allusions to illustrate his desire for a new American economy. The "edifice of recovery" created by his New Deal would "no longer be a temple of money changers or of beggars, but rather a temple dedicated to and maintained for a greater social justice, a greater welfare for America."[28] Stemming from his own work in New York and his initial support for George Norris's TVA bill, Roosevelt called for the unified development of the valley in order to create that new economy. Like A. E. Morgan, he wanted to empower the community to better itself. Remembering an early meeting with Roosevelt, Morgan noted his concern for the southern people: "[He] spent most of our time together talking . . . about the quality of life of the people of the Tennessee Valley."[29] At a November 1934 press conference, Roosevelt made his views blatantly clear: "Now for the T.V.A. I can put it this way: Power is really a secondary matter. What we are doing there is taking a watershed with about three and a half million people in it, almost all of them rural, and we are trying to make a different type of citizen out of them, not what they would be under their present conditions."[30]

Roosevelt had high expectations for the Tennessee Valley. He, too, saw the federal agency as a tool, using careful planning, intelligent resource utilization, hydroelectric power, and community development to remake the southern collective consciousness.[31] And, like Morgan, Roosevelt believed that the federal government had the power to change southerners for the better, creating entirely "different" citizens. No longer single-mindedly pursuing cash crops with little regard for the economic well-being of their region, southerners would work together to diversify their communities, farm more intelligently and efficiently, and turn to small-scale industry to provide jobs for unprofitable farmers and goods and services for those still able to work the land.

Beyond the general shape of the new southern economy, Morgan's and the president's plans diverged. The chairman portrayed the new southerner as communalistic, and he consistently spoke of his vision for the valley in terms of cooperation. He hoped to encourage self-subsistence on farms and in towns all along the Tennessee River. Local crops fed farmers and workers alike, just as small-scale local industry produced for regional demand. The president, however, tied the region's economic recovery to purchasing power—his southerners were just more considerate capitalists. Concerned with a solution to the nationwide economic crisis, Roosevelt preferred to empower workers and farmers as consumers. He stressed wages, which allowed southerners to purchase needed goods on the national market.[32] For the president, revitalized farms and factories were primarily sources of jobs and wages, not the foundation of a communal economy as Morgan envisioned it. Even though both men proved idealistic in their goals for the depressed South, they did not agree on the nature of economic progress. In the heady days of TVA's creation, this difference proved relatively minor —unemployment relief, flood control, and power generation came first. As the authority began to implement its program in the valley, however, Roosevelt proved more amenable to a different future for the region, particularly the pragmatic program, centered on cheap power, envisioned by board member David E. Lilienthal.

Lilienthal later recalled his disbelief at being offered a position on the TVA Board: he was younger than either A. E. Morgan or the third board member, University of Tennessee agriculturalist Harcourt A. Morgan; he was midwestern (not southern); and he had no real engineering experience. Yet Roosevelt saw specific advantages in Lilienthal's background. The Indiana lawyer had an intricate knowledge of public utilities law and a familiarity with the workings of the electric business that proved useful to TVA's program and its impending competition with private utilities over price, distribution, and service area.

Lilienthal also had close relationships with other reformers in Roosevelt's circle, including Louis Brandeis, and shared their view that the government operation of some industries was crucial in the protection of public interest.[33] A student of the Progressive fight against private utility "trusts," Lilienthal was a natural choice for the authority's Power Division, and he began his tenure on the board by working with officials in northeastern Mississippi to supply the town of Tupelo with government-generated power. With the ink still drying on the TVA Act, Lilienthal promised Mississippians that power from Wilson Dam would bring industries to the state and supply cheap electricity to farmers and households across the valley.[34]

Lilienthal saw public power as both an opportunity to raise the standard of living in the South and a weapon to stop the abuses of private utilities in the region. Speaking to the Memphis Rotary Club, Lilienthal promised that electric power would improve "the quality and variety of commodities" and "break down the division between the country man and city man." Lilienthal praised the idea of a power "yardstick" to demonstrate reasonable rates and expose the unreasonable prices charged by southern utilities. He also knew that, with lower rates, he would need to raise consumption, and industrial development was a perfect means to do so.[35] Lilienthal argued that successful power policy created "a balanced area of concentrated industrial activity, including some cities of substantial size, good farms and reasonably favorable distribution possibilities."[36] His was a different future than that envisioned by A. E. Morgan. Large cities with concentrated industries were an anathema to Morgan, who saw them as unbalanced and self-serving, just like the cotton-based agriculture of the South. The two found room for agreement in the need to bring electricity to the farmer, but where the chairman consistently placed power second to small cooperative communities, Lilienthal made electricity the center of his plan for recovery and reform. From the outset, he planned to increase the South's electric usage, decrease rates by a "drastic revision," and work with "electric manufacturing and allied industries" to create new jobs.[37]

Thus, Lilienthal stressed industrial development early in his career, echoing Roosevelt's call for increased southern purchasing power and sharing the president's consumerism. In fact, as one biographer has noted, Lilienthal embodied the paradox shared by many in Roosevelt's inner circle, combining support for federal development with an appeal that also captured those conservatives who supported "enhancement of business and individualism."[38] Speaking on the future of the region (and using rhetoric reminiscent of Henry Ford's supporters a decade earlier), Lilienthal promised that "the Tennessee Valley region is to be the scene of an expansion of industry which in the course of the coming decade will change the economic life of the South." He portrayed residents as pioneers on the "frontier" of industrial life, and promised that the government would provide the large blocks of power needed for industrial use without the high rates private utilities charged for their "financial misdeeds." Lilienthal also planned to use TVA's engineers, technicians, and business experts to help advance the industrial program. Only large-scale industry gave the South the "abundance of goods" that might raise the standard of living and address the problems of unemployment, poverty, and general economic insecurity.[39]

In May 1934, Lilienthal began pushing for the creation of an Industrial Development Division to work in conjunction with his Power Division. Noting that future hydroelectric projects would give TVA an expanded amount of available power, he argued that an industrial development program would "find a way to absorb the vast supply of power we are creating, on a favorable business basis and yet consistent with the Authority's social objectives and policies."[40] The Industrial Division worked with municipalities to expand their electrical capacity and recruit industries to use TVA power. It also coordinated incoming businesses with the agency's larger program for the valley and ensured adherence to New Deal industrial policies, with fair labor practices, decentralization of business, and an emphasis on increasing local purchasing power. Thus, only a year after the agency formed, the mechanism was in place by which valley leaders and government officials might cooperate to bring industry to the region. Building on the spirit that emerged in the debates over Muscle Shoals, locals had an increasingly willing partner in a program of economic development that looked forward to the coming Sunbelt boom.

Within months of the signing of the TVA Act, the newly manned board authorized construction on the hydroelectric dams that formed the foundation for the agency's work in the Tennessee Valley. The speed of the decision brought praise from many residents eager to see improvement on the river, but TVA had little time to formulate policies for land acquisition and population removal. Even as the agency began working with farmers and businessmen to improve the economy, social workers struggled to address the overwhelming poverty left by years of agricultural mismanagement. Thousands of residents came into contact with TVA not through agricultural demonstrations, power contracts, or jobs in new industries, but through land negotiations, property clearing, and eviction proceedings. By 1940, TVA's relocation program became more institutionalized, but the intervening years saw three reservoirs created in North Alabama, each with its own circumstances and specific problems. The agency's interaction with the population of the Wheeler, Pickwick, and Guntersville reservoirs highlights a building conversation on development in the valley. Forced to sacrifice their land, livelihood, and way of life, many residents demanded direct commercial assistance from TVA; in doing so, they challenged the government agency to take a more active role in the industrialization of the regional economy and helped shift its mission from balanced growth to industrial development.

In October 1933, Roosevelt diverted $7,000,000 from the funds allocated to TVA by Congress for the construction of Norris Dam to begin work on Wheeler Dam, sixteen miles upriver from Wilson at the site of "Dam 3." The president's primary concern was unemployment, but the dam also generated hydroelectricity, extended a navigable channel to the city of Guntersville, Alabama, and controlled seasonal flooding around the city of Decatur.[41] TVA eventually purchased 100,000 acres of land above the dam in preparation for the flooding that created the Wheeler Reservoir, effectively uprooting 835 families, nearly equally divided by race. Of those displaced by the reservoir, only 100 made their living in areas other than farming, including fishing, small industries (sawmills, for example), and, in a few cases, bootlegging.[42] The land along the river, washed by occasional flooding, was the most productive, and thus most valuable, in the region. It was held on larger farms, worked by tenants and laborers for shares and wages. A total of 700 families lived on farms in the affected area, though only 52 owned their land; the rest worked as tenants, sharecroppers, or wage laborers making, on average, less than one dollar per day.[43] The prospects for successful relocation were grim. Only 2 percent of inhabitants had finished high school, and only two people interviewed had attended college; 80 percent of the children were below their average grade level, and 25 percent did not attend school regularly. Only 33 people in the area had any kind of industrial work experience.[44]

Initial plans called for the TVA to resettle families on new farms but, from the outset, the agency understood that relocation would be a problem. The people had no livestock, no machinery, and no assets to help in securing a new home or farm. They were "localized," as researchers noted, since most had lived in the same community for years. Unsurprisingly, the majority of those relocated chose to remain in the area, taxing an already overcrowded tenant population in a state that boasted the smallest average farm holding in the country. Even worse, as the New Deal farm program, the Agricultural Adjustment Administration (AAA), brought benefits to farm owners, tenants across the region were pushed off land to fill the strictures of crop reduction.[45] Even as TVA sought to put residents to work and to begin its resource management policy, its program demanded the dislocation of the very people it hoped to help.[46] Within the first year of its creation, the agency struggled to accommodate families without jobs, without homes, and without the means of starting new lives. TVA kept a detailed record of its interaction with the people of the valley, and the stories uncovered by case workers provide keen insight into the problems faced in bringing relief to the region.

For the area's more prominent residents, removal posed little financial problem. John Fuqua, a white bachelor and corn and cotton farmer, rented nearly 700 acres on Gilchrist Island, bringing in an estimated $3,000 per year and living in the "most prominent house on the island" while maintaining a "high" standard of living. A case worker noted that Fuqua "represents the old South: big, fat, hospitable, comfortable, thriving in the responsibility of his farm and his man serfs who work for $.50 a day and board, and who evidently worship him"; his notoriety led to a common phrase among local tenants: "Mr. So-and-So is almost as good as Mr. Fuqua." TVA first contacted Fuqua in 1935, when he treated the case workers to fish, peas, tomatoes, cornbread, molasses, buttermilk, and a string of oaths and outbursts demanding the reason for the visit. Agency officials informed him they would be purchasing most of his land and his home and inquired into any removal plans. Fuqua gave a common response—he hoped to rent acreage and continue farming, and he expected TVA to help him find a new place to live. He planned to finish harvesting his crops before taking possession of new rental property, but in January 1936, the weather forced action. The Tennessee River threatened "serious flood danger" due to heavy rains, and case workers told everyone below flood level, including Fuqua, to move as quickly as possible. Within the week, Fuqua removed to a new farm, though the new land could not compare to his former holdings and his house was in "poor repair."[47]

Other owners were not as concerned for their tenants and workers. J. G. Finley lived in the town of Decatur but owned farmland on an island in the Tennessee River. The case worker assigned to the island characterized the land as "flat, fertile, and cultivable . . . the best looking farm I have seen down here" and described irrigation ditches and thousands of dollars of farming equipment. Finley, farming corn and cotton, did not make a similar investment in his workers. He refused to allow TVA representatives onto his island, but his white resident manager, Charlie Webb, spoke to case workers. Webb made $1.50 per day, more than double the "poverty wage" of $0.50–0.70 paid to Finley's laborers. Charly Hodges, a black renter, worked as a farm laborer for Finley and, despite the loss of an arm in a cotton-gin accident, proved "very efficient with a plow." Finley provided a home for Hodges, his mother, and a brother, but the house stood in "bad" condition.[48] Hodges's situation was typical of life on Finley Island. Conditions were "squalid," and wages were too low to provide any hope for successful relocation. When Finley sold the island to TVA, workers were "turned out" and rendered "helpless—even by comparison with sharecroppers."[49] Finley gave vague promises of assistance, but in May 1936, after removal, case workers found Hodges and his brother renting a home in Decatur, working as day laborers when jobs became available.[50] Finley gave more assistance to his manager, agreeing to allow Webb to use his boat to move his family's possessions from the island into a house Finley owned in Decatur, but in October, case workers found Webb employed as a day laborer as well. The case worker considered Webb's relocation "satisfactory" since he found work closer to a school and other community resources, but Webb disagreed, complaining of the loss of livelihood after his removal from the island.[51]

Finley's relationship with his workers and with TVA illustrates one of the major flaws in the agency's relocation policy. The TVA Act specifically gave the board the power of eminent domain to ease land acquisition. While not legally required, TVA also made a determined effort to work with the families that moved from the reservoir area. Case workers met with each family and noted their living conditions, available resources, job history and future prospects, and plans for relocation. The agency appointed social workers familiar with the people of the region and their way of life, hoping to inspire "complete confidence" among affected families.[52] However, the TVA Act did not give the agency the ability to offer direct aid, instead requiring the authority's representatives to refer those in need to national and state relief agencies. As a later removal manual noted, the agency could only "interpret the needs of reservoir families to interested agencies and . . . interpret outside agencies to the reservoir group.[53] More specifically, TVA might list farms for sale, but families were forced to look elsewhere for loans or financial advice on purchasing them. Workers referred cases to state boards, farmers' organizations, and other New Deal programs, creating a bureaucratic network of aid groups that limited the ability of TVA to assist fully the farmers and workers displaced by its projects. The authority could force Finley to sell his property to the government, but it had little or no recourse when he refused to care for the workers and tenants the sale displaced.

Unsurprisingly, many families found removal a stressful process, especially those without the means or ability to find a farm or home comparable to the one taken by the government. Some families were homeless even before relocation, and TVA's workers found themselves in the unwanted position of evicting squatters and "transients" from land near the river.[54] Buddy Cole's situation is an extreme example of the difficulties that could arise in such a removal. Cole, his wife, and two children squatted in a two-room house on the estate of a local farmer. Raising poultry and fishing, Cole earned less than a hundred dollars per year. The family presented a real challenge for relocation. Cole was a skilled carpenter, but an accident and the resulting infection led to the amputation of both legs, and he survived by selling fish caught in the Tennessee. Cole constructed a metal slide from his home to a boat on the shore, using his hands to pull himself down the slide and into the vessel. His son rode a bicycle into Huntsville to sell the catch, but epileptic fits prevented him from working in local industry. Cole's wife, Ruth, had previously worked in textile mills around Huntsville with brothers and sisters, but as the Depression closed mills in the city, Ruth and her family found themselves unemployed.[55] As the family looked toward the future, their options were extremely limited. Cole needed a plot of land adjacent to the river to continue fishing, but his wife would almost certainly have to find work in local industry for the family to make ends meet.

In early 1936, TVA purchased the estate on which the Coles squatted. The heirs could not agree on providing for the Coles, who had only verbal permission to live on the land from the deceased owner. By March, the family's case worker had little hope for an adequate settlement for the family. Workers genuinely wanted to help Cole and his family, but their fate lay outside the realm of TVA's influence. The estate's heirs controlled the disposition of funds from the purchase, and the Coles had no legal right to the land or even the house they occupied. Her hands tied, the case worker informed Cole: "I realize that this seems very hard and unjust but there is nothing TVA can do about it." The agency took possession of the land and according to guidelines for condemnation proceedings, put Cole's small home up for auction. He pleaded with TVA leaders for assistance. The agency helped Cole buy back his house, contacting local farmers to ensure that no one topped Cole's bid of two dollars for the structure, but the family had no means of moving the house, even after taking outright possession.[56]

That summer, Cole began dismantling his home board by board and ordered additional materials to build a houseboat, which he hoped to moor off public land somewhere along the river. TVA asked local hardware stores to donate materials for his boat, but his physical handicap made construction difficult. By November 1936, over a year since the Coles were first contacted by the agency, the family had almost finished their "substantial and durable" new home (that is, the houseboat), and had begun moving from the tent that had provided shelter since the demolition of their original house. Cole floated his boat to Huntsville, where he moored off Alabama Bridge Corporation property near the Whitesburg Bridge. Cole kept fishing, but his wife was unable to find employment in the town's cotton mills, slowed by the Depression or closed due to ongoing textile strikes. The process left Cole bitter. Once completely cooperative with TVA, Cole had become "defiant and resentful," and he threatened to remove timber illegally from TVA land as retribution for his losses.[57]

Cole's case is atypical, but it does suggest important limitations the government agency faced in providing aid and assistance. Like the Coles, many Tennessee Valley farmers lived on and worked small farms under oral contracts with their landlords. When TVA took land, its negotiations with landowners usually included resident tenants, but payment for tenants' homes or land was largely left to the owners' discretion. Some owners worked to help their laborers and tenants find new homes and jobs, but many chose to leave them to their own devices. TVA searched for state assistance for displaced tenants, and as in the Coles' case, the agency worked to aid families without the resources to help themselves. In the end, however, the government faced strict limitations. The authority could work to get Cole possession of his home, but could not give him financial assistance to obtain the materials to build again or to purchase land. Instead, the agency had to ask local citizens, businesses, and state agencies to provide for his family's needs. Faced with such difficulties, many in TVA and throughout the valley hoped that, by improving the regional economy, the authority might provide a kind of financial assistance to the displaced.

TVA's approach to the dispossessed proved fairly similar to that of other New Deal programs, particularly the Farm Security Administration and the Agricultural Adjustment Administration. When the AAA paid landowners to reduce planting and allow fields to lay fallow, many owners used the opportunity to displace sharecroppers and tenants and replace them with farm machinery and wage labor. New Deal programs, including the TVA, tried to provide recourse for the "surplus" of population in farming regions, working through the Resettlement Administration and its successor, the Farm Security Administration, but such aid went largely to those farmers with the means to farm independently. Neither the AAA, the RA, nor the FSA had the funds to help all sharecroppers and tenants find both land and the resources necessary to farm successfully. As Secretary of Agriculture Henry Wallace noted to First Lady Eleanor Roosevelt, the "millions" of surplus people on farms could not return to farming in any profitable way. The solution to the agricultural depression was not "making more farms or more farmers"—it was "making more city employment." In what one historian called a "cruel but effective winnowing process," the realities of a changing market and the programs of the New Deal allowed only the most profitable and efficient farmers to continue cultivating while the remaining agricultural population transitioned to life in towns and cities and to jobs in businesses and factories.[58] When the Tennessee River surged onto farms and fields in late 1936, it covered more than land. The river brought a symbolic close to the predominance of agriculture in the region, pointing to a new commercial and industrial future that TVA and other groups would struggle to embrace in the coming years.

In February, TVA made its final report on removal activities at Wheeler. The agency began by acknowledging that, in its attempts to readjust widespread tenancy, it actually worsened the problem by "taking thousands of acres of fertile land out of production . . . causing 835 families to relocate in an already over-populated area." The report also noted that local relief agencies were "not equipped to handle this problem immediately," and an attempt to work with the Resettlement Administration led to a year of "watchful waiting" with no real result.[59] The Alabama Extension Service did help some, finding farms for owners who received money from TVA, but owners made up only one-sixteenth of the total population. By the time the service published its report, 823 of the 835 families had moved from their land "without recourse to legal eviction"; however, conditions in areas around the new Wheeler Reservoir suggested a less successful result. Only 39 percent of families moved to locations with better access to community resources, and only 37 percent moved to better housing conditions. The majority found themselves in conditions similar to before, though a third now lived in "unsatisfactory housing."[60] Only 8 percent of families moved to land that had better soil, while nearly 70 percent were on land "generally poor and less satisfactory than land on which [the family] formerly lived."[61] Months after the authority closed the Wheeler field office and began operating the newly finished dam, the report concluded that further work toward readjusting the population to its new physical and economic environment was sorely needed.[62]

TVA faced similar challenges at the future sites of the Pickwick and Guntersville reservoirs, though in both cases the characteristics of the flooded land differed from those of Wheeler. Neither Pickwick nor Guntersville had as large a tenant population as Wheeler. Of the 600 farm families affected by flooding at Pickwick, 70 percent did not own the land they farmed, compared to over 90 percent of the families at Wheeler. At Pickwick, the major concern was the flooding of two towns, Waterloo and Riverton, both of which lay on land that would be partially covered by the reservoir.[63] Despite the different situations at Pickwick and Wheeler, the agency came to a similar conclusion: TVA could not simply move families and hope that their new circumstances would allow for a better economic foundation for their community. Readjustment meant a longer, more involved process of working with individuals and groups to provide instruction in new farming methods, encouraging business relocation to affected areas, and job training to assist residents to adapt to industrial employment, whether on TVA projects or in private companies. As at Wheeler, TVA took the best farmland at Pickwick, leaving opportunities scarcer than before. Available land and homes were nearly impossible to find, and those that had land or buildings to sell demanded high premiums or even cash considerations. Several families at Pickwick, as at Wheeler, simply moved onto the narrow portions of land adjoining the reservoir, waiting for TVA to force them off of what had become government property.

Pickwick provides a telling example of other "dislocations" associated with TVA's activities in the valley. Mancil Milligan left a job as a schoolteacher to help build the dam at Pickwick. In 1935, he began working as a public safety officer at the "Negro Camp," the segregated housing facilities built for black construction and clearance workers. Milligan noticed a change in his lifestyle almost immediately. The authority tore down old shotgun houses and built new sturdy homes for workers and their families. TVA also paid good wages, and Milligan used his newfound income to buy an electric iron, a refrigerator, a fan, and a radio.[64] His life illustrated the benefits of a government agency providing both employment and cheap electricity. Yet as the *de facto* police force and fire department, Milligan's fellow public safety officers also witnessed the seamy side ventures that accompanied rising income. Pickwick Village, built to house construction workers at the dam, was full of single men with money to burn, and as Milligan noted, a community of "beer joints and gambling joints and wild women" soon sprang up nearby. Called "Slab Town," the collection of shacks attracted construction and clearance crews leaving their shifts. Milligan remembered that the agency "resented Slab Town being there . . . and did everything they could to suppress it to have a decent place for their employees and the community as a whole."[65]

TVA tried to limit the town's effects on its employees, dismissing workers whose "performance suffered because of Slab Town's influence," but the town persisted. Unable to buy property in the town, which was tied up in leases and overpriced, the agency asked Milligan and his fellow officers to reign in disturbances.[66] The Public Safety Force was overmatched. Despite attempts to close down bootleggers and gambling halls, beer joint owners plied their craft out in the open—one female owner confidently strolled around her room naked with the lights on and shades open. A fellow officer recommended Milligan buy a "big club" or a gun since the job "was just about as rough as could be."[67] In the end, Slab Town did little to affect TVA's overall legacy of economic progress, but its existence does illustrate one of the negative consequences of growth. The authority hoped that, by building dams and employing locals, it would create a different culture, the foundation for a new type of community in the valley. But even as it created villages of workers, it could not dictate their every action. If TVA was to bring progress, it needed to plan for every eventuality.

Unlike Wheeler or Pickwick, the Guntersville relocation program included a comparatively large town. With a population of nearly 3,000, Guntersville nestled in a bend in the Tennessee River and, like Waterloo, relied on the river for daily life. When TVA began planning a dam for the city, it realized that the changes would have a major impact on the community. Flooding would submerge the city's railroad connection and the associated industries lining the tracks, including a cotton mill and warehouse, a lumber mill, a basket factory, oil and gasoline storage facilities, and electric and water substations.[68] As with Pickwick and Wheeler, the dam took the area's best farmland out of circulation; however, at Guntersville, the city's economy also stood to lose much of the woodland fueling the timber industries and, by covering the town's major highway connections, the dam would disrupt commercial activities. Planners were optimistic that Guntersville could eventually recover, even prosper, with cheap electricity and protection from flooding, but they admitted that the transition would be onerous: "it should be recognized that the loss of trading territory and the probable loss of its wood-working industries will necessitate a period of readjustment for Guntersville which will be doubly difficult since it will follow the boom period of dam construction."[69]

Removal activities at Guntersville ended in 1939 on the eve of TVA's mobilization for the national defense build-up that preceded World War II, and the results spoke volumes for the agency's work in North Alabama. In its final report, the Population Readjustment Division called its work a "long-time program" that required the participation of state and federal relief agencies to help the affected communities meet their social and economic problems. As the report succinctly concluded, "An awakened and enlightened community becomes cognizant of all its social and economic ills."[70] Of the 1,200 families removed from the Guntersville Reservoir area, 67 percent left farmland, and many looked to Alabama's Agricultural Extension Service for help learning to cultivate new land, finding new houses and farms, and making other adjustments. Extension workers met individually with families and assisted in the moving process. Of 667 tenant families, only 45 became owners after moving. The vast majority either became tenants on new farms or left agriculture altogether.[71]

The immediate results of TVA's program were not what officials had hoped to accomplish. Instead of helping revitalize agriculture, removal activities exacerbated the tenancy problem. The best land lay under newly created reservoirs while farmers struggled to adapt to less productive farmland. Combined with the AAA's acreage reduction programs, TVA's work made land even scarcer while forcing thousands of families into the land market. Agency planners hoped that fertilizer production from the Muscle Shoals plants and education programs would make the remaining land more productive (thus supporting more farmers per acre), but they also realized that, for many, readjustment meant trading the mule and plow for a job in local factories. The improvements to the Tennessee River at Guntersville may have adversely affected some of the local industries in the short run but, as officials argued, improved transportation, cheap electricity, increased agricultural productivity, and recreation opportunities would bring permanent and "far-reaching" progress for industrial development at Guntersville, as well as TVA's other reservoir projects.[72]

Publicly, the Tennessee Valley Authority bragged about the success of its removal policies. At Wheeler, Pickwick, and Guntersville, the agency condemned only 13 percent of the land needed for its reservoir because of a refusal to sell.[73] Yet statistics fail to illustrate the ways in which some residents attempted to resist relocation. Some felt TVA had undervalued their land. At Guntersville, a group of 66 citizens formed the Tennessee Valley Land Owners Protective Association and contacted Representative John Sparkman to protest "low prices paid by the TVA." Not only did the policy "destroy" the community by removing churches, roads, and other basic services, the unfair payments prevented the relocated from finding a new home and farm that compared to the one purchased by the agency. The landowners decided that a court fight would be too expensive, and looked to Sparkman to plead their case with the authority.[74] After similar letters from other Guntersville residents, Sparkman agreed that some of the prices paid to landowners seemed "unfair," but he admitted that the agency's outlined policy for compensation was legally binding and that there was little Congress could do to help.[75]

Others accused TVA of dishonest practices. W. B. Rudder of Section, Alabama, complained to Sparkman that the authority condemned the land of his orphaned brother's children, forcing them to accept a low price and pay the cost of the transaction. He noted the importance of land, especially to children without another source of income: "Their property is a life time's worth of a little family, is their just and right."[76] J. W. Knight created the Tennessee Valley Landowners Mutual Aid Agency to assist families in the Wheeler area who felt mistreated. Running ads in local papers, the agency explained the proper steps for legal acquisition and suggested that TVA's average price paid undercut official estimates by more than half. Knight wrote to Senator Lister Hill, asking him to lead the Military Affairs Committee in an investigation of land purchase practices, and he included three personal statements by black residents forced to sell land to the agency. Anna Kirby was told that she would not receive more than $834 for sixty acres of land in Lawrence County, and to try to get a better price would be "useless." Spot Foster gave a similar account, detailing an ultimatum from his caseworker that forced him to sell for much less than his land was worth. Fannie Smith sold twenty acres for TVA's price after being told that, if she refused the initial offer, "they would cover the land up with water and it would not be of any value to [her]."[77] The results of the cases are unrecorded, though most complainants found it difficult to challenge TVA's actions, given the legal foundation for land seizure and the popularity of economic relief in a severely depressed region.

The experiences of Kirby, Foster, and Smith were repeated across the Tennessee Valley. Only those with the financial resources and willpower dared to enter into a lengthy legal battle with the federal government. Some turned to representatives like Sparkman and Hill, who balanced a few angry dispossessed families against a population desperate for assistance. Many begrudgingly accepted TVA's offer for their homes and farms with the belief that no real alternative existed. Historians have criticized removal polices for failing to follow the dispossessed landowners more fully after relocating. Instead of working with locals to adapt to a modern economy, TVA simply helped farmers find new real estate, and even then, only when aid agencies were able to assist in the process. Left to seize their own opportunities, the dislocated placed their hope in the economic revitalization that would hopefully accompany the agency's program. Forced off of productive farmland, in some cases held by families for generations, Valley residents trusted that their sacrifice would be repaid with prosperity.[78]

As valley residents left homes and farms surrounding the Tennessee River, the TVA began working to implement the improvements that would bring a new economy to the region. Much of TVA's early work took an indirect approach to economic development. Following A. E. Morgan's calls for balanced growth of agriculture and industry, the agency relied on a program of instruction and training in both farm and factory work. TVA employed hundreds of workers at the old nitrate plants (which adapted to produce phosphate fertilizer) and thousands more in dam construction and reservoir clearance.[79] The jobs provided emergency relief for residents, and though temporary, gave a boost to the local economy and on-the-job training for future work in the private sector. In its employment practices, TVA demonstrated a willingness to challenge, but not overturn, the prevailing social and cultural practices in the South, giving its economic program a larger ideological goal that fit with the chairman's vision. Throughout the 1930s, TVA implemented that vision across the region, yet even as the agency worked to recast the valley's socioeconomic future, locals made their own plans. Some happily followed along with TVA's agenda, participating in training programs, planting new crops, and testing TVA's fertilizer in their fields. Others pushed TVA to take a more active role in building the regional economy, calling for more jobs and assistance in civic growth and development.

After families moved from TVA property, the agency brought in crews of clearance workers and construction laborers drawn from the local population. At Wheeler, 3,600 men worked to clear timber off of soon-to-be-flooded land. As on other projects, TVA segregated workers by race, with several black clearance crews employing between 700 and 800 residents. Clearance work required few skills, allowing the agency to hire many men who could not find jobs on construction crews or in the operation of the dams and powerhouses. For other residents, work on dam projects provided a steady job with wages almost as high as in those found in private manufacturing. The agency reported receiving a thousand applications per day for work in its construction program, even after TVA specifically limited nonprofessional jobs to locals. To help with the overload, the U.S. Civil Service Commission held examinations in valley centers, requiring potential workers to take reading and mechanical aptitude assessments. The commission even provided a "nonlanguage" test for applicants with little or no formal education. The examinations weeded out those unwilling or unable to train for construction work (more than half of initial applicants never took the examination, a fear of failure that admittedly helped TVA screen job seekers).[80]

Wheeler proved instructive in a number of ways. The civil service examinations resulted in a "superior corps of workers" that allowed TVA to promote foremen and other construction supervisors "from the ranks," and many transferred to other dam projects across the valley. The benefits were not relegated to government projects. As Mancil Milligan noted, "If you were a carpenter, you had a job. If he [*sic*] was a farmer, he could sell everything that he grew to the [workers]. If he was a merchant, his business was good. If he was an automobile mechanic, he had a good job. So everybody got a piece of the pie, and we built the dam."[81] As time progressed, TVA created training courses for dam work and recreational programs that acted to "increase the efficiency of men on the job, to allow employees to prepare for other jobs inside and outside the Authority, [and] to provide for the general educational, recreational, and social needs of employees and their families."[82] At construction sites, TVA built dorms, separated by race and sex, and offered courses in math, blueprint reading, electricity, concrete, pipe-fitting, tooling, and welding, all skills needed in dam construction and maintenance, and all applicable for jobs beyond the agency's immediate work in the area.[83]

TVA's attitude toward dam workers exemplifies its early position on economic training and development. Faced with thousands of tenants and other farmers forced off of their land, the agency implemented a program to employ residents and train them to oversee the very construction program that had displaced them. TVA drew technicians and engineers largely from government service, particularly the Army Corps of Engineers. Some came from the private sector, including a surprising number from Aluminum Company of America, or ALCOA, already developing a close relationship with the government in the 1930s.[84] However, these educated technicians were supplemented by Alabamians, Georgians, and Tennesseans no longer able to make a living growing cotton and corn. By employing some of the region's surplus farm labor, TVA eased demands on dwindling acreage while providing immediate work relief and training for future skilled and semi-skilled labor.

Such training lay at the center of A. E. Morgan's vision for the region's economic future. The chairman praised the "initiative and self-directive" nature of valley residents—the very traits necessary for successful employment on TVA jobs and work in the private sector.[85] He began implementing his larger training program at Muscle Shoals in early 1935. With construction underway at Wheeler, the program was partially attributed to self-interest—trained workers built better dams. Yet Morgan envisioned a much larger goal for educated men and women, hoping to "train employees to become artisans in the possible industrial development of this area, and to take a definite place in an improved agricultural-industrial society."[86] TVA worked with the city of Sheffield to develop an elementary and high-school education program at Wilson Dam and cooperated with the State Teacher's College at Florence (later the University of North Alabama) to create an adult education program open to TVA employees and the surrounding community.[87] F. W. Reeves, an independent consultant hired to examine the agency's overall training program, gave the data for February 1936, showing the overwhelming popularity of TVA's educational programs. Over 1,600 people enrolled in sixty-three occupational training activities, including mathematics, blueprint drafting, and personnel administration. Almost 10,000 participated in planned recreation, 7,000 attended informal discussion groups, 600 officially enrolled in adult education classes, and over 7,000 attended eighty informational film screenings. TVA created farm shops to rent agricultural and mechanical tools to local residents, and dispatched mobile libraries that traveled to clearance sites, loaning nearly 19,000 books to 5,000 borrowers.[88] Such numbers led TVA to declare its training program a success, allowing staffers to "satisfy their needs for increased capacities."[89]

In addition to his efforts to train workers, Chairman Morgan encouraged worker organization on TVA projects, hoping that by doing so he would encourage southern industries to be more conscientious in their treatment of labor. When creating hiring and employment policies, he insisted on consulting with labor organizations and ensured that the authority would support collective bargaining and union independence. Though the efforts would not mature until he left the agency, Morgan remained proud of his efforts to include unions in the creation of TVA policy: "So far as I know, this was the first occasion in this country where the rights and responsibilities of labor and management for all crafts on large public projects were arrived at by negotiation and expressed in an inclusive labor policy."[90] For Morgan, unionization was more than just a means to provide an organized, self-policed labor force. Cooperation with unions was a "yardstick" as much as TVA's power rates—a means of "proving" to southern companies that labor organization could be a beneficial, even profitable aspect of the new southern economy.

A. E. Morgan specifically promised to raise the standard of living in black communities in the region, but his vision aligned closely with the racial mores of the South. TVA offered training in trades and homemaking skills to black men and women, enlarging, in Morgan's words, their "social outlook" and providing a base for a "new approach to the race question" and "a new economic era for the South."[91] Morgan's attitude toward black workers exhibits both the promises and limitations the agency brought to white and black residents. He assumed African Americans lived in "degenerate" conditions that needed to be rectified, despite the overwhelming evidence that poverty did not follow a color line. Morgan did attempt to bring relief to residents of all races but, in adopting the prejudices of southern society, he failed to include African Americans fully in TVA's program and set an unfortunate precedent for the agency's policies on race and development.

One of the more telling criticisms of TVA's position came from A. W. Davis, the chair of the Colbert County Negro Citizens League. Davis wrote to local Probate Judge C. E. Carmichael to protest TVA's lack of "practical understanding of the people in the Valley," particularly the African American community.

Davis hoped that the agency would create a position, "Director of Negro Planning," staffed by a black citizen who would better understand the needs of African American communities. He suggested Norman T. Thomas, a janitor in TVA's Fertilizer Department at Muscle Shoals who received an education from Talladega College and had seven years of teaching experience in local schools. He ended optimistically: "We are of the opinion that the Authority should know that we, as a race, still believe in it; and that if we can get started right we shall be able to regain some of the lost time of earlier years." TVA remained circumspect. Carmichael and John Sparkman forwarded the correspondence to Director of Personnel (and future Chairman of the Board) Gordon R. Clapp after approving of Davis's suggestion and praising Thomas's character. Clapp promised to keep Thomas in mind "when the question is brought up," but the discussion ended there.[92]

But perhaps its greatest failure to include African Americans in plans for economic revitalization came with TVA's inability to provide employment for the black sharecroppers and tenant farmers forced off the region's farmland. This became painfully clear as Clapp, who was named General Manager in 1939, tried to address a list of grievances given by Charles E. Houston in a brief on TVA's race relations. Houston charged that TVA failed to develop an integrated policy and instead considered blacks as "a labor commodity rather than as citizens." He specifically pointed to the agency's failure to combat the racism that depressed black participation, including social pressure and malicious rumors at the Norris Dam site and abuse and mistreatment at Chickamauga Dam which kept blacks from joining unions. Instead of helping the black community, Houston argued, TVA introduced more severe patterns of segregation and closed opportunities for blacks in employment, recreation, and job training.[93]

In response, Clapp emphasized the agency's general policy of nondiscrimination and proportional employment, in which the authority promised to hire African Americans in proportion to their share of a given community's population. He admitted that TVA had no official policy specifically designed to address race relations, no "yardstick" equivalent to policies on labor and electric rates, and he stated that the board "has not felt that it was given a special assignment to reconstruct the racial relationship of the population of the South." Clapp clearly believed that, while the agency had a responsibility to include the black population in the economic improvement program, it should not attempt to change the social order. TVA was simply preparing for the "more obvious needs" of the community.[94] Clapp and the board based policy on their own interpretation of the needs of local blacks without considering the expectations and desires of the African American community.[95]

A. E. Morgan consistently approached his work from the position of an administrator, judging the region's needs and determining a set of programs that would best meet that perception. He rarely sought guidance from the people of the valley, choosing instead to rely on case workers, course instructors, and civil service professionals to interact with those affected by removal, local employment, and community training. This led to conflicts with groups who felt left out of TVA's program, such as black communities underemployed on government projects. Such an approach also prevented Morgan from hearing or comprehending the plans of residents who carried their own specific expectations about the benefits of TVA's presence. While Morgan pressed for a communal economy, many valley leaders re-aired demands for directed development, suggesting that new jobs and paychecks might replace the livelihoods lost to the reservoir program.

Across the area, residents responded to the advent of TVA with their own plans for regional improvement. This was especially true of the business community. In Florence, the chamber of commerce celebrated the coming of the TVA after more than a decade of false starts. Leaders immediately began advertising cheap power, mineral deposits, local services, ample labor, and available land, introducing their community as "One of the South's Most Beautiful Cities." Within weeks, Florence began negotiations with industries looking to locate in the region and planned for a municipal power plant to distribute TVA power.[96] Despite warnings to be patient, potential workers flooded the valley, and realty companies again bought and sold lots based on the promise of future prosperity. Governor Benjamin M. Miller received telegrams begging for jobs, despite his lack of official connections to the federal project. George F. Davis, who eventually found work as a machinist at the Muscle Shoals plants, best enunciated the optimism: "TVA was young and everybody had high hopes of having a job."[97]

Even as TVA formulated policy, Florence prepared for its future and businessmen moved to take advantage of the attention. G. E. Orley began planning a new, "modern" hotel, only to be told by TVA officials that the agency was not yet prepared to begin development in the Muscle Shoals region and that private improvements were being "discouraged."[98] Nevertheless, the *Times* encouraged the city to "come out of swaddling clothes and put on pants" to prepare for "commercial and industrial importance." With a more active campaign for growth, city leaders could provide the "inducements" needed to bring in industry.[99] Here was the chance Florence had awaited since the excitement of the initial announcement for the nitrate plants. In the words of the incoming Alabama governor, Frank Dixon, Florence and the rest of the valley were preparing themselves for "the final realization of the dreams of the people" for "the reorganization of society itself."[100]

Of all the cities and towns in the region, Decatur seemed to have the greatest promise for growth under TVA's larger resource management plans. The largest city in North Alabama, with nearly 15,600 residents in 1930, the city lay within the reach of power from Wilson Dam and, with the completion of Wheeler Dam, the area enjoyed a surplus of power that would easily accommodate a number of factories.[101] The Depression hit Decatur particularly hard, affecting both the surrounding agricultural counties of Limestone and Lawrence and the city itself in Morgan County. As Decatur attorney John Caddell remembered, the valley was "broke, sick, [and] discouraged." After counting thirty-three "industries" in the 1930, by 1932 the town leaned heavily on the only major industry left, the Louisville & Nashville Railroad shop.[102] Nearly every resident relied on the company's paychecks, whether as direct income or in the form of customers and patrons. The shop closed just before TVA entered the valley, creating a real economic crisis. From June to December 1933, Caddell earned only seventy-six dollars from his practice and almost left the area.[103] Yet the small city had potential. Located on the southern bank of the Tennessee in the center of the valley, Decatur was an ideal transportation hub for regional products. The surrounding agricultural community provided a large potential market for consumer goods and a source for foodstuff and raw materials. Plus the city boasted an active leadership, willing to grasp any opportunity to revitalize the economy. TVA brought such an opportunity.

As one resident noted, TVA "put the spark back in the growth of Decatur."[104] The city immediately began using low power rates to sell itself to industrial prospects. In 1935, local leaders worked with TVA officials and the state government to attract a Chicago aluminum plant. Governor Bibb Graves formed the Alabama Industrial Authority, a state bureau authorized to assist private companies expanding on government loans, to help the plant relocate in the area.[105] That same year, thanks in part to Decatur's civic leadership, the Ingalls Iron Works purchased eight acres of riverfront property to build boats and barges in expectation of increased navigation on the river. The plant praised the city's efforts to create a "successfully planned community of activity and progress."[106]

The driving force behind Decatur's growth was Barrett Shelton, the editor of the city's newspaper, the *Decatur Daily*. Born in Tennessee in 1902, Shelton moved with his father to Decatur in 1911 to found the *Daily*. In 1924, upon the death of his father, he became the editor and publisher. As his city pushed for industrial prospects, Shelton cultivated relationships with Sparkman, Hill, and Lilienthal, the TVA official most receptive to plans for industrial growth and economic development. In March 1937, he asked Sparkman and Lilienthal to help bring in 500–1,000 jobs to the city to help boost consumer sales. In Shelton's view, the city was "ready to go and with no place to go."[107]

Lilienthal responded, sending economic advisors to Decatur to work with the editor and other business leaders. In 1937, the city was in the midst of negotiations over its municipal power plant, but TVA representatives promised that, as soon as Decatur received power from the agency, industries would follow. They also suggested technical studies to evaluate the city's available resources, particularly those on local farms. For Shelton, Decatur's economic success was a reflection of TVA's progress: "So long as Decatur remains in her present position, one of unsoundness and one of comparative poverty, she will be no advertisement for the effectiveness of TVA. A down-at-the-heel town cannot prove good advertising." The losses caused by the depression did more than take jobs out of the area—economic trouble led to a decline in "civic consciousness" that the limited programs of private utilities, particularly Alabama Power, proved unable to address. The city was "groping" for new leadership, and TVA's assistance was needed to put Decatur back on track.[108]

Shelton and his fellow boosters' aggressive development program could not land every available industry, but working in concert with city officials, congressmen, and TVA, they began to change Decatur's economy. In addition to the Ingalls Shipbuilding plant, the city received investments from the Gulf Refining Company and Standard Oil, both of which built terminals on the river to supply fuel to the growing valley.[109] After a visit by Harcourt Morgan, Shelton and his fellow leaders scraped together three thousand dollars, formed a chamber of commerce, and hired a manager. As Shelton later recalled, "This was how we began. We began right at the source, right at the roots of the community."[110] At the end of the 1930s, Decatur began to realize the kind of industrial development that became widespread in the following decade, even as it put in place the local leadership that could continue such growth. The city set an important precedent for Lilienthal and TVA's program, and as the nation geared for war, the agency played a more active role in bringing manufacturers to Decatur and the rest of the region.

As Florence, Decatur, and communities across the region moved toward industrial development, a corresponding ideological change occurred in TVA's boardroom. Residents largely embraced the entrance of the authority, but support for TVA did not translate into a wholehearted acceptance of A. E. Morgan's communal utopia. In fact, as the people of the valley moved from flooded farmland, they looked to the agency for an economic opportunity to replace (or improve upon) jobs lost in the fields. At Waterloo, Florence, Decatur, and Guntersville, and in smaller communities across the region, city leaders hoped that the authority's larger program would include industrialization to accompany resource utilization and electrification. They found an ally in David Lilienthal.

Barely a month after Roosevelt signed the TVA Act, Chairman Morgan and Lilienthal could not agree on the actual mission of the agency. As Lilienthal later remembered, the men realized that their relationship would "require a good deal of working out."[111] In July 1933, overwhelmed by A. E. Morgan's idealistic list of objectives, Lilienthal and Harcourt Morgan pressured the chairman to divide responsibilities. A. E. Morgan retained administrative leadership and oversight of the engineering and construction of hydroelectric dams, Harcourt Morgan took over agricultural programs, and Lilienthal focused on power and legal questions. The chairman resisted the division, fearing that the action hurt the ability of the federal agency to work for the overall development of the region, but Lilienthal found support from Roosevelt, and the division allowed the power director to focus more fully on his area of expertise.[112]

The separation of powers also engendered a lingering resentment. A. E. Morgan believed that, as chairman, he had a responsibility to oversee all aspects of the agency's program. His fellow directors felt differently, and neither Harcourt Morgan nor Lilienthal wanted to include the chairman in decisions concerning their areas of supervision. Lilienthal promoted his own views on power and development involving an increasing reliance on industrialization, and he saw A. E. Morgan's communalism as impractical and impossible to implement.[113] A. E. Morgan thought his vision should remain the centralizing force behind the agency's program, and as Harcourt Morgan, and particularly Lilienthal, began raising objectives, he became obstinate. As TVA historian Marguerite Owen noted, "It is not surprising to discover that men of great ability do not always like each other, nor work together in comfort. . . . What is difficult to comprehend is the Chairman's apparent conviction that when his colleagues' opinions differed from his own it was proof of moral infirmity."[114]

In 1936, David Lilienthal's seat on the board came up for reappointment. With valley towns eagerly scrambling for TVA electricity, most observers assumed he would return with little trouble. Chairman Morgan, however, saw an opportunity to remove a growing threat. He told Secretary of the Interior Harold Ickes that "Lilienthal has hampered him at all stages. . . . He betrays confidences to the newspapers, carries on negotiations for power contracts without contacting [Morgan]."[115] Lilienthal's public persona became a particular worry for the chairman, who would later charge that, while he concerned himself with the technicalities of everyday work, Lilienthal made friends in Washington and in the press to ensure his later ascendancy.[116] Morgan informed Roosevelt that he would resign if Lilienthal returned to the board, but the president did not share his views. Roosevelt appreciated Lilienthal's understanding of the electric business, particularly his aggressive stance toward private utilities, and the two shared a common faith in increased consumption as the answer to the problems of the southern economy. He reappointed Lilienthal and promised that, if Morgan remained hostile, the chairman would be held responsible for "delaying and perhaps disrupting not only TVA but the whole future."[117] When Lilienthal returned for a second term, Morgan sulked. For a month, he failed to appear at board meetings, a "virtual retirement" that left Lilienthal and Harcourt Morgan to attend to the day-to-day chores of running TVA.[118] When he finally returned, the damage to his credibility was readily apparent.

As Morgan suffered from his public criticism of Lilienthal, he grew closer to the private utilities, the avowed enemy of TVA in the eyes of Roosevelt and Lilienthal. Where Lilienthal built his career in opposition to private power companies, Morgan had fewer qualms about cooperation with utilities like Alabama Power if, in return, TVA could bring relief to the area's farmers and townspeople. He was also less hostile toward Wendell Willkie, whose Commonwealth & Southern owned Alabama Power. Morgan later praised Willkie's work to expand the nation's electric grid, even calling him "progressive."[119]

Where Lilienthal's power program forced communities into economic growth and development, Morgan argued, private power worked at a slower, more conscientious pace. If cooperation with the government lowered rates, Morgan believed that private power companies could fit nicely in his larger vision for the Tennessee Valley.[120]

By 1936, Roosevelt's New Deal agencies were on the defensive against attacks from the private sector, even as the president proved more willing to cooperate in order to further the nation's economic recovery. TVA temporarily defeated its major valley rivals with the Supreme Court's *Ashwander* ruling in 1936 (see chapter 4), but the fight demonstrated the power of utilities to disrupt the agency's operations and, in September, Roosevelt began studying the possibility of a power pool that would connect the transmission systems of TVA and Alabama Power. Lilienthal agreed that a pool would be an asset for the valley, even if it meant trading with the enemy, and he drew up safeguards to protect TVA: the government stipulated that power must come from the cheapest sources in the region, transmission lines must be used jointly, and rates must stay at TVA's lower level. In return, the government would be able to call on a larger supply of power for towns and industries.[121] TVA had much to gain from the prospect of a power pool, since it forced private power to give up resistance and accept the agency's gains along the Tennessee River. As Roosevelt later stated, a pool would "smooth out the peaks and valleys of separate system operations" and "postpone the need for investment in new generating facilities."[122] For private power companies, the pool meant a drastic lowering of rates and a tacit acceptance of competition with government-subsidized electricity throughout the South. Roosevelt approached Wendell Willkie with his idea, but Willkie wanted concessions from TVA. In particular, he expected the government to avoid cities already accepting power from Commonwealth & Southern.[123]

A. E. Morgan made his case publicly in late September, releasing a memorandum giving his "personal views" on the pool. The statement was not issued at the request of the president and did not propose to represent the opinion of TVA. Instead, the chairman outlined his own views of the pool, which differed from those of Roosevelt and Lilienthal. He defended the government's responsibility to generate and distribute electric power, but he stressed that private utilities should be allowed to continue their own power program and receive "fair compensation" for any investment surrendered as part of the pool.[124] He then went further, defending private power investors for asking for protection for their investments (implicitly legitimizing their lawsuits against TVA). He even called for TVA to define its program in hopes of creating "mutual confidence."[125] A. E. Morgan released a copy of his statement to the public and to Willkie before handing it to Lilienthal and Roosevelt. That same day, Willkie came to a conference on the pool, armed with Morgan's memo, ready to utilize the internal conflict to his advantage.[126] Morgan denied that he had supplied his memo to Willkie and the press before the conference, calling it "very inappropriate," but both the president and Lilienthal remained uneasy about Morgan's attempt at independent negotiations.[127] Discussions with Willkie continued through the end of 1936 but failed when Commonwealth & Southern refused to end legal attacks on the government agency. Roosevelt believed the utilities were more concerned with "judicial sabotage" instead of "frank discussions" about the mutual benefits of the pool, and TVA officials began to look for a final resolution of the private utilities problem.[128] However, the greatest casualty of the pool discussions was undoubtedly Chairman Morgan.

In late 1937, A. E. Morgan again found himself at odds with his fellow directors and the president when he publicly backed a legal claim against the agency by Tennessee Senator George L. Berry. The legislator argued that his TVA-flooded property could have produced real profits if mined, and he sued for compensation for the now-inaccessible mineral rights, but TVA's lawyers worked to have the land and its theoretical mineral value declared "worthless."[129] Once again supporting the claims of a litigant against his own agency, the chairman seemed to place opposition to his colleagues over his loyalty to TVA. He refused to concede that his stubbornness injured the authority's reputation, suggesting that his presence as chairman was helping contribute to "decency and effectiveness in government." Morgan supported calls for a congressional investigation into the brewing fight, believing the attention would justify his own position instead of Lilienthal's, but he was increasingly isolated from the agency, and when he attempted to get "evidence" of his claims against Lilienthal, TVA staff refused to give him any information.[130] On March 22, 1938, Roosevelt removed A. E. Morgan from the TVA Board. He charged the former chairman with "making grave and libelous charges," "obstructing the work of the Tennessee Valley Authority," and refusing to give factual evidence of his claims.[131] Harcourt Morgan became the nominal chairman, but Lilienthal drove policy behind the scenes, a result of Harcourt Morgan's reserved personality and Lilienthal's public fame as a proponent of industrial growth and as a defender of public power.

Roosevelt's action ensured a congressional investigation, giving Morgan a chance to express his anger. He recalled that Roosevelt had barely mentioned power when he received the appointment. Instead, the president had stressed economic and social development as a way to improve everyday life in the region: "The picture which he gave me of the possible functions of the TVA was of an undertaking to encourage the decentralization of industry in that region, to help locate people on small farms, and to develop the social and economic resources of the region."[132] In his estimation, the conflict with Roosevelt and the board did not stem from disloyalty, but instead from a fundamental difference between his plan for economic development and that of Lilienthal.

In many ways, Morgan's claims against the agency were justified. TVA had changed under his tenure, moving in a direction that he did not anticipate. As the agency began formulating economic policies for the people of the Tennessee Valley, and as Lilienthal fought to defend public power against its detractors, Roosevelt and many in TVA realized that the idyllic industrial-agricultural utopia Morgan desired would not meet the real and immediate needs of the people of the region. Determined to raise incomes and create a community of consumers, Lilienthal and Roosevelt agreed on the need to bring in industry to provide jobs for those unable to continue in agriculture. And, as valley leaders cooperated with TVA to recruit and attract development, Lilienthal could point to quantifiable examples of success. In 1939, a congressional inquiry dismissed Morgan's charges as "without foundation" and praised the agency's regional development programs, specifically noting Lilienthal's success in proving the feasibility of public ownership of electric facilities.[133] The torch had been passed.

The TVA Board fight and the resulting ascension of David E. Lilienthal positioned the agency on the eve of World War II for a focus on industrial development. Lilienthal's belief in the importance of consumption as the solution to the depressed southern economy, a belief he shared with President Roosevelt and with leading citizens in Decatur, Florence, and across the region, led him to focus on steady employment. His work in TVA's Power Division convinced him that industries using the electricity generated at the authority's dams would provide those much-needed jobs. Morgan's vision, marked by balanced development, educated farmers and trained workers, and communities built on mutual support and interdependence became one of many alternatives to the Sunbelt South. Instead of small, self-sufficient communities in which inhabitants worked in local craft-based industries, grew their own food, and supplied their own needs, the South moved in the direction of a modern economy, geared toward industrial production, commercial agriculture, and business growth. In this shift, Lilienthal found ample room for cooperation with the civic leaders and businessmen of the region, already envisioning such economic development as the surest path to prosperity.

FOUR

PULLING TOGETHER IN THE SAME DIRECTION, 1938–1945

As the Tennessee Valley Authority implemented its program, a group of southerners living and working in Washington, D.C., began holding informal meetings to discuss ways to improve southern society. Loosely affiliated with the Southern Policy Committee (SPC), the group, which included Alabama's relatively liberal congressmen Lister Hill and John Sparkman, covered a number of topics, including "the Southern agrarian crisis, Negroes, rural education, the sharecropper system, natural resources, Huey Long, and TVA."[1] Like President Franklin Roosevelt, many of the participants believed that a solution to the Great Depression would necessarily include economic and social reform in the South. In fact, by the late 1930s, Roosevelt worried that the New Deal, and programs like TVA, had not done enough to address continuing poverty and underdevelopment in the region, and that growing opposition to the New Deal from southern Democrats might make continued reforms difficult. In 1938, Roosevelt asked one of the southerners concerned about conditions in his region, Clark Foreman, for advice. Drawing from conversations with members of the Washington SPC, Foreman suggested that Roosevelt prepare a pamphlet detailing the improvements brought by the New Deal to the South. The president embraced the idea, telling Foreman that "if the people understand the facts . . . they will find their own remedies."[2]

On August 6, 1938, the National Emergency Council, an agency that coordinated and released information on New Deal recovery efforts, printed 100,000 copies of *The Report on Economic Conditions of the South.*[3] In an introductory letter, Roosevelt set the tone for the report's critique of the southern economy: "It is my conviction that the South presents right now the Nation's

No. 1 economic problem—the Nation's problem, not merely the South's. For we have an economic unbalance in the Nation as a whole, due to this very condition of the South."[4] What followed was a litany of economic and social failings. The South had a wealth of physical and human resources, but decades of mismanagement and exploitation rendered those advantages moot—a region "blessed by Nature" boasted the "poorest [people] in the country."[5] The final section of the report suggested a solution: "purchasing power."[6] As the authors noted, the South's "growing population, with vast needs and desires, now largely unfilled, could keep a large part of the rest of the country busy supplying them." With government assistance, "the Nation's greatest untapped market and the market in which American business can expand most easily" would bring the region, as well as the rest of the country, out of the Great Depression.[7]

As the authors addressed the myriad problems associated with the southern economy, they also highlighted some of the work being done by New Deal agencies in the region, including the TVA. While the report mentioned the authority's efforts to make the Tennessee River navigable, the authors failed to account for the larger program that marked the TVA's early years. And, while the report described underconsumption in the South, it overlooked the ways in which community leaders had begun encouraging industrial growth and economic development. Unsurprisingly, many in the region rejected the tenor of the report, even as it enunciated the very problems they sought to address with plans for economic growth. Across the valley, business-minded editors refuted the claims, stressing their communities' efforts to improve the southern economy, and in Knoxville, Tennessee, the TVA Board replied to the report with its own account of progress.

TVA's response highlighted the agency's work to address each economic problem described by the presidential committee. Farmers replenished their soil with TVA fertilizer. Reforestation, protection of wildlife, and careful planning kept southern resources from being wasted. Dams on the Tennessee prevented destructive flooding and provided the power that electrified homes, farms, and businesses at affordable rates. TVA created thousands of jobs on its construction projects and clearance crews and, according to the agency, its self-described policy of non-discrimination set a standard for treatment of southern blacks for other regional businesses. Workers fought the spread of malaria and educated communities on proper nutrition. Finally, the reply noted, the agency developed new industries in the region, which employed those out of work and provided new sources of income that would give southerners a larger share of the national economy.[8]

Valley leaders also refuted the charge that the South was an economic problem for the nation. The *Decatur Daily* boasted that *Fortune* magazine had named the South the "nation's number 1 opportunity," with data offsetting the National Emergency Council's report. Editor Barrett Shelton promised that the region was on the verge of unprecedented development. In fact, he argued, the coming prosperity would cause "painful readjustments in certain Northern industries" as factories decided to relocate where cheap power, transportation, and available labor provided a better business climate. The paper promised that the tendency of some southern leaders to "grovel in ashes strewn by the Emergency Council" did not represent the majority of southerners.[9] Shelton conceded that the South was the poorest section of the country, but he suggested that, in pointing out the problem, Roosevelt's council provided an opportunity to bring in better schools, more industry, and diversified farming. The area needed the "substantial payrolls that come from industry," and that industry would only come with improvements to valley resources.[10] Like TVA officials, valley leaders acknowledged their economic inequality with the rest of the nation but resented the implication that the region had become an economic "problem." Instead, as an economic "opportunity," the region was ready to welcome development, and by the time the *Report on Economic Conditions of the South* was published, leaders in TVA's boardroom and in communities across the valley were prepared to cooperate in pursuit of an improved economy.

In listing the "problems" that marked the southern economy, the report highlighted the changing nature of agriculture in the region. As farms mechanized, a process accelerated by New Deal programs, owners used fewer tenants and sharecroppers. Farmers, more marginalized than ever, moved between cash cropping and part-time labor, never making enough to farm independently and successfully or to diversify crops and plant intelligently, but still unwilling to abandon farming altogether.[11] On top of this, southern farming practices squandered resources, damaged the environment, and ensured that farmers would not and could not grow the foodstuffs that might otherwise address chronic malnutrition.[12] Prescribing efforts to increase the South's "purchasing power," the authors did not necessarily suggest abandoning small-scale agriculture, since changes in methods and types of farming, combined with a higher standard of living, might allow some southerners to stay on the farm. However, given the reality of agriculture in the South, in which declining profitability and government programs drove marginal farmers from the land, many took the report's call for a new focus on consumption to mean a regional shift toward industrial wage labor. This view was echoed in the efforts of civic and business leaders, who sought an industrial alternative during the debate over Muscle Shoals, and in the TVA, where both A. E. Morgan and David Lilienthal proposed alternatives to the dominance of corn and cotton cultivation.

In fact, the ongoing effects of the Depression, the impact of TVA's land acquisition program, and the efforts of developers were already changing the nature of farming throughout the region. In the western Tennessee Valley between 1930 and 1940, the number of farmers dropped from 22,800 to 15,000, while the number of tenants nearly halved (from 17,100 to 8,900); where 75 percent of farmers were either cash or "other" tenants in 1930, only 60 percent were in 1940. The average farm size grew from 55 to 82 acres as marginal farmers sold out to larger landholders, and the acreage planted in cotton and corn dropped from 640,000 to 500,000.[13] Clearly, the nature of farming was shifting as more farmers owned their land (and more of it) and fewer individuals became tenants.

As the report noted, and as numbers demonstrate, marginal and dependent farmers had fewer options by the late 1930s. As demand slackened during the Depression, corn and cotton brought less on the open market. New Deal programs moved the least profitable growers from field to factory, either directly through TVA's flooding program and various efforts at resettlement or indirectly through public works jobs and AAA allotments. Those in the South able to diversify crops, invest in new technology, and operate on a tighter profit margin might remain in farming, but the rest of the South's agricultural population would need an alternative form of income—the industries that valley leaders hoped to recruit. And, by 1938, they found support for such a program in the report's call for "purchasing power," and in the consumer-oriented, development-minded outlook of TVA's David Lilienthal.

In the wake of A. E. Morgan's dismissal in 1938, Harcourt Morgan took over as chairman; however, Lilienthal became the ideological force behind the authority's program. His vision of TVA centered on the production of hydroelectric power—communities would realize real prosperity only when they fully utilized cheap electricity. Partly, this vision was an outgrowth of Lilienthal's focus on the public regulation of power production, and in his years in charge of TVA's Power Division, Lilienthal connected the spread of power to residential and industrial users with economic growth. But his faith in power as a remedy for southern ills was also ideological. Like Roosevelt, and like the National Emergency Council, Lilienthal subscribed to the idea that increased consumption would solve southern economic problems. Given an incentive to buy (whether from a new paycheck provided by a recently recruited industry, or from a desire to utilize electricity now available at home), southerners would put money into the regional and national economy. Lilienthal quickly found opportunities to implement his program as he extended TVA's coverage area across the Southeast.

As the authority's influence spread out across the Tennessee Valley, however, private utility companies increased their resistance to the agency. With public power on the defensive, Lilienthal pointed to his own work in the region to demonstrate the possibilities inherent in TVA's plan, even as he worked for a final settlement with the utilities. In particular, Lilienthal's struggle with Alabama Power allowed him to enunciate fully his plan for development. He became the public face of the "Power Fight," blasting the utilities and promising cheap power to residents and businesses alike. Just as the "Board Fight" gave Lilienthal control of TVA's program, his victory over the utilities ensured that, across the valley, TVA electricity and the industries that used it would be associated with economic progress.

A subsequent and perhaps even greater boost to Lilienthal's program for economic development came with the defense mobilization surrounding World War II. The agency witnessed a drastic increase in demand for power, particularly by industries ramping up production on government defense contracts. Soon valley residents, like many other southerners, came to equate war factories with economic prosperity, and TVA faced numerous demands from local leaders for assistance bringing industry to the region and providing cheap electricity to businesses seeking to win war work or expand production. By the end of the war, the authority was fully dedicated to industrial growth, working in cooperation with state and local organizations interested in economic development. This relationship was complicated, especially as TVA tried to balance its position as a disinterested arm of the federal government, tasked with overseeing the resources of an entire region, and its efforts to sell power and invest in economic growth within its service area. Even when the authority's leaders defended the agency against charges of favoritism and preferential treatment, their desire for industrial growth, and their support for local initiative in fostering that growth, remained clear. By the mid-1940s, TVA was no longer the agency created at the birth of the New Deal. Instead, under the influence of David Lilienthal and the people of the region, the authority came to focus on directed economic development as the path to prosperity.

Private utilities chafed at the creation of a government power agency, especially when that agency challenged them for business in their existing service area. Within weeks of the signing of the TVA Act, Alabama Power attempted to reassure its customers in the Tri-Cities that TVA could not compete with its service. In an open letter, District Manager J. T. Jackson reminded citizens of the company's eight years of "faithful, continuous and excellent service." Alabama Power's rates ranked among the best in the country, and its surplus power ensured that incoming industries enjoyed ample electricity. Responding to a growing sentiment in municipalities along the Tennessee River for publicly owned power distribution systems, Jackson claimed that cities would tax TVA power (making it more expensive than existing rates) and cut the tax benefits already coming to the area from Alabama Power. The manager did, however, promise that the utility would "gratefully" accept whatever decision the area leaders reached.[14] Jackson's company could not afford to be so gracious. Throughout the Muscle Shoals debate, Alabama Power was a scapegoat for the purported evils of the "power trust," and given the opportunity, towns across the valley clamored for TVA's lower rates.

In June 1933, the city of Sheffield voted 660 to 36 to finance the construction of a municipal power plant to receive TVA current.[15] Florence made a similar decision in "the most momentous" election in the city's history. The *Florence Times* promised that a municipal plant would save the city from "incapable" and "selfish" leadership and allow the citizens to control their own destiny.[16] A popular vote for public power did not always translate into an easy purchase from the private utilities. In early February 1934, the city of Decatur began holding meetings with Alabama Power representatives to negotiate the transfer of the utility's power plant to municipal ownership. The groups sparred over costs as Alabama Power valued properties much higher than city leaders, who largely viewed the plants as a municipal resource.[17] That same month, Tupelo, Mississippi, became the first city to buy electricity directly from the government. Praising TVA, Tupelo's congressman, John Rankin, used the opportunity to blast the private utilities whose rates were, according to his calculations, 4,800 percent higher than the cost of producing the power.[18] Tupelo's contract seemed to prove that power from the government could drastically decrease electricity costs, and for utilities such low rates threatened to put them out of business.

The agency aided municipalities in their negotiations, a fact that irked utilities like Alabama Power. When six valley cities, including Decatur and Florence, negotiated with the utility over property, TVA backed the municipalities' valuation, nearly $300,000 less than Alabama Power's price. On March 15, Decatur signed a twenty-year contract with TVA despite continued uncertainty over the legality of building new transmission lines or buying those owned by the utility company.[19] When city leaders worried that Alabama Power's facilities were in poor condition, TVA agreed to operate the facilities at no cost until the city could take charge of the system.[20] TVA's assistance pushed the legal boundaries of the organization. The TVA Act allowed the agency to produce power and sell it wholesale to consumers, but it could not duplicate private utility facilities where they were already available. Instead of permitting the utilities to operate within their established service area, Lilienthal worked with municipalities to acquire loans and negotiate more forcefully for distribution rights. Alabama Power and its fellow southern utilities were incredulous. Years of service to the community, including rural electrification and industrial development, were repaid with disloyalty. Not surprisingly, as TVA became more active in fighting private utilities, the companies and their investors resisted.

The authority faced a number of legal challenges over its work, but the most prominent case came in September 1934 when a group of Alabama Power stockholders represented by Birmingham attorney Forney Johnson filed suit in Athens, Alabama, enjoining the utility from contracting with TVA in North Alabama.[21] The case, named for plaintiff George Ashwander, charged TVA with the unlawful use of federal funds to expand service in an area already represented by a private company. The stockholders also claimed that Lilienthal's rate system was "illusory, deceptive, and merely a device for promoting public ownership of utilities in the area," a charge that would be repeated throughout TVA's early years.[22]

As the *Ashwander* case traversed the courts, Lilienthal began talks with Commonwealth & Southern's president, Wendell Willkie. At first, Commonwealth & Southern hoped to buy power from TVA and distribute it, treating the agency as a wholesaler. Willkie promised Lilienthal that the Tennessee Valley would never accept public power, using Muscle Shoals as an example of the tenuous nature of government investment. Lilienthal told Willkie that, if he refused to relent, the government would simply take the power market. When municipalities clamored to sign contracts for power, TVA appeared to have the upper hand.[23] Commonwealth & Southern even began tentative discussions of a property transfer, but events in court changed the tone of the conversation. In March 1935, a judge annulled the sale of Alabama Power properties. The ruling also prevented municipalities from receiving government loans to build or purchase distribution systems in Alabama Power's service area. TVA appealed but, in the meantime, the agency faced an immediate halt to its expansion in the region.[24] Cities struggled to continue the takeover of the municipal power plants and, across the valley, negotiations with the utility ended abruptly.

TVA won its appeal, and the *Ashwander* case landed in the Supreme Court, which was in the midst of ruling on the constitutionality of other New Deal programs. Johnson made the case for Alabama Power as a public servant of the people of the state. Several counties joined in Johnson's brief (though none were from the valley), praising the utility for its work bringing textile mills to rural areas with cheap and widespread power. In defense, TVA's legal team argued that the government had a right to use the water flowing over the turbines at its navigation dams for "commercial manufacture and sale of electricity."[25] In February, the court handed down an eight-to-one decision upholding the right of TVA to sell surplus power created at its dams.[26] The decision validated both the construction of hydroelectric dams and the municipal purchases of Alabama Power facilities. George Norris applauded, calling the case a desperate move by the power companies to "pull [their] 'chestnuts' out of the fire."[27] In April 1937, the North Alabama District Court issued an injunction against further litigation initiated by Alabama Power. In May, an appeals court refused to hear cases on the constitutionality of government financing of municipal power projects and lifted all injunctions against the authority.[28] The decisions solidified TVA's position in North Alabama and paved the way for the agency to provide power directly to customers throughout the region.[29]

After losing in court, Commonwealth & Southern began final discussions with TVA to create a permanent boundary for utility service in Alabama. Despite calling a valley-wide sell-off a "last resort in a desperate situation," Willkie suggested setting up a three-man commission to determine the values of properties TVA wanted to obtain.[30] In Alabama, TVA reached a tentative agreement with Alabama Power, purchasing property in Colbert, Limestone, Lawrence, Morgan, Madison, Cullman, Marshall, Jackson, and Cherokee counties, except where municipalities had duplicated existing systems (as in Decatur). TVA paid almost $2.0 million for the property, and the municipalities and cooperatives in North Alabama covered the final $2.6 million.[31] Alabama Power lost 14,000 customers and $400,000 in annual revenue. Local municipalities received control of their distribution systems, and in areas that built duplicate systems, the utility sold or salvaged the old equipment and facilities.[32]

The decision ended seven years of constant fighting between TVA and private utilities, allowing the agency to concentrate on long-term plans for electric development. The struggle also focused an inordinate amount of attention on David Lilienthal and the work of his Power Division. Lilienthal realized that power was stealing the public spotlight away from projects like water control and soil conservation, but he was relatively unconcerned.[33] Instead, he took the victory over the private utilities as a sign that the public had come to accept his vision of economic development.

Soon, Lilienthal enunciated a new program for the government agency—a focus on TVA-sponsored industrial growth as a means of economic revitalization for the region. The contrast with former Chairman A. E. Morgan was abundantly clear. Instead of building self-sufficient communities marked by diversified agriculture and craft-based industry, TVA would use power to bring in jobs and paychecks. At a symposium in Mobile, Alabama, in early 1941, Lilienthal listed the goals of his agency's industrial development program. Industry payrolls would increase personal income, which would then flow into communities, paying for needed goods and services. With more money, southerners would be able to buy the goods produced in new factories, ensuring even further growth as more companies located near an expanding market. Lilienthal promised to work with southern businessmen, officials, engineers, and technicians to create a leadership cadre that would help solve particularly southern problems—training the "men and institutions that can grow and develop to meet the very great, almost overwhelming, opportunities and problems of sound industrial development."[34] Succinctly put, this was Lilienthal's development philosophy, and under his leadership, it became TVA's driving ideology.[35]

As Lilienthal prepared to work with community leaders for economic development, he faced many of the challenges highlighted in the *Report on Economic Conditions of the South*. For instance, Lilienthal understood that industrial employment would only benefit southerners if workers were protected from mistreatment. As the report noted, the failure of unionization in southern industries left workers with no collective bargaining power and no "organized influence on social legislation."[36] Lilienthal understood that workers needed training to prepare the South for a new kind of economy, as well as organization to protect them from the vagaries of the industrial economy. In the spirit of New Deal protections for labor, he worked to set an example for employment practices and worker-management relations that could be replicated in new industries locating in the area.[37]

Under Lilienthal's guidance, TVA continued to emphasize training and education to create a more skilled, more adaptable workforce to staff both government agencies and private corporations relocating to the valley. The lack of a skilled labor force troubled Lilienthal, who understood that higher-paying jobs required a basic level of education unavailable to many southern workers. He noted that this problem had seriously hampered efforts to boost regional incomes. For instance, Vultee Aircraft in Nashville informed the War Plant Site Board that it was unable to expand its operations, even with increased defense demand, because "Southern labor was not readily teachable for the requirements of aircraft production." For Lilienthal, such statements made the hope of future defense investment in the South "dismal."[38] He understood that TVA was well on the way to solving the problem with proven training programs. The agency simply needed to find trainers specialized in the technical knowledge required in new industries, particularly those involved in the growing defense effort.[39]

In supporting worker training and unionization, Lilienthal's TVA continued practices put in place by former chairman A. E. Morgan. By the time TVA officially released its labor policy, Morgan had left in disgrace; however, the agreement incorporated the former chairman's opinions on the value of a unionized workplace. TVA and the Tennessee Valley Trades and Labor Council released their "General Agreement" in August 1940, just as the agency escalated its wartime operations. The "Council," an amalgamation of several American Federation of Labor–affiliated unions, became the sole representative for workers on TVA projects, an exclusivity that provided for a concrete set of negotiating bodies and policies, even as it limited workers' options.[40] Stressing the agency's public persona and its growing importance to the defense effort, TVA's leaders convinced the council to waive its right to strike during disputes (a pledge common in public agencies and private companies during the war). In return, the federal agency agreed to maintain operating conditions in times of unrest and specifically guaranteed the workers' right to organize and choose their own leadership. Under the agreement, unions determined their jurisdictions and job requirements without interference from management, and workers created their own work schedules, though the authority reserved the right to delegate jobs to those workers most capable of completing tasks. The agreement also specified the mechanism for settling workplace disputes. Council representatives met directly with TVA's personnel director, and claims not settled in a face-to-face meeting were recommended to an "impartial referee" appointed by a joint board of adjustments consisting of two representatives each from TVA and the council.[41]

The agreement was, at heart, a compromise between unionized workers and government management. It encouraged worker organization in a region actively hostile to unionization in textile mills and tenant fields, and both sides hoped it would serve as an example to companies across the South, proving that union agreements could facilitate worker and management cooperation without affecting production. Lilienthal praised the wartime operation of the general agreement. In late 1943 he referred to wage negotiations with the council as the "briefest conference in our history." An unnamed "old, white-haired boilermaker" agreed: "I never sat through a wage negotiation like this in my whole life, where you talk facts all the time, just facts and no cussing and storming around."[42]

TVA supplemented the labor agreement with corporate propaganda, which proved particularly useful in maintaining loyalty among non-unionized workers. TVA stressed the importance of each employee in "regional and national development and the war effort."[43] Programs highlighted the agency's history and its attempts to correct the social and economic conditions of the Tennessee Valley. TVA's leadership envisioned "maximum employee morale," creating a work environment that stressed willful participation and discouraged dissension in the ranks.[44] The patriotic appeal fit nicely with TVA's larger training and education program—workers learning particular skills or trades would also receive instruction in their "purpose," as well as the role of their division and the larger goals and ideology of the authority. TVA's leaders believed that the agency's wartime labor experience proved the wisdom of its program. The agency contributed greatly to defense production in the region, with no major work stoppages or production slow-downs. By the mid-1940s, management-labor cooperation seemed to be a success, at least from TVA officials' perspective.

Like A. E. Morgan, Lilienthal also struggled to address racial inequality while implementing TVA's program. Lilienthal shared the prejudices of many "liberal" whites in his generation. He believed that black southerners would obtain equal rights through economic opportunity, not legislation targeting unequal and unfair legal and social practices or forcing racial integration. Lilienthal was truly concerned about the inability of African Americans to participate in the agency's development program, and he admitted to Frank McSherry, the deputy director for labor supply and training on the War Production Board, that the "disturbing" employment problems faced by black southerners were one of the main sources of resistance to the full utilization of southern manpower in war industry.[45] However, Lilienthal's personal ideology limited possible solutions. The chairman recorded a 1942 conversation with his daughter, Nancy, who grew upset over a "White Only" sign at the TVA picnic ground on Norris Lake, near Knoxville. Afraid his daughter was developing a "radical" streak, he cautioned her to see racial attitudes as a "fact," even if those views were based on meaningless "social distinctions." His fatherly advice underlined his attitude: "The thing to do was to try, patiently and with considerable difficulty, to remove some of the causes of race feeling, but to stand like a rock on the right of each Negro to an opportunity to work and to learn as much as he was capable of learning, on his merits."[46] Only those African Americans willing to take advantage of the opportunities presented to them could prove their inherent worth. This was the philosophy behind his agency's minority policy.

TVA examined minority employment in the agency on the eve of World War II at the request of the Personnel Department. Director G. F. Gant discovered that, during April 1941, black employment amounted to 10 percent of the total workforce. However, of that percentage, only 6 percent of annual trades positions (permanent skilled jobs) and less than 4 percent of salaried positions were staffed by African Americans. Of the "relatively permanent" trades jobs, 14 percent of workers were black, and 15 percent of the temporary hourly workers were black. Clearly, African American workers were not receiving their share of skilled, stable positions. The Personnel Department noted that, while the construction program continued, maintaining the "proportional" employment rule would be easy since many low-skilled jobs would be available. However, with construction winding down across the valley, the agency would soon face the challenge of increasing the number of black workers in annual salaried and permanent trade positions.[47] TVA's failure to maintain an adequate level of black employment, even by the agency's own standards, pointed to a much larger problem: an inability to include the black community in TVA's work and the economic development that it hoped to encourage.

The agency was not alone in facing pressure to address discrimination and inequality as it expanded activities during the national defense crisis. Across the South, the wartime demand for workers led companies to hire African Americans in larger numbers. Despite the persistence of segregation after World War I, African Americans determined to use the opportunities presented by mobilization to make serious inroads into racial inequality, an effort nicknamed the "Double-V" campaign. In the summer of 1941, in response to labor leader A. Philip Randolph's threatened March on Washington, President Roosevelt created the Fair Employment Practices Committee to investigate instances of discrimination and to enforce equal hiring and promotion practices in companies operating under wartime defense contracts.[48] As with TVA, the dual pressure of the "Double-V" campaign and the government's willingness to address racial discrimination led to tension. In Alabama, tempers flared on a number of defense projects, most notably in Mobile as the city boomed with the production of ships.

The violence at Alabama Dry Dock and Shipping Company (ADDSCO) stemmed from the convergence of discriminatory hiring practices, labor organization, and the federal government's early attempts to address prejudice on defense projects. The demand for ships, and particularly the quick production of merchant ships, resurrected the languishing shipworks in Mobile. Workers flooded into the city, taking jobs at companies like ADDSCO and stressing the city's housing market and public services. ADDSCO alone counted 30,000 workers, 7,000 of whom were African American. Black workers were an essential part of the Port City's waterfront, though as in the rest of the region they were only hired for low-paying, low-skilled laborer and helper positions. While African Americans staffed "inferior" positions, locals and labor unions alike accepted an "integrated" workforce. The war challenged that stasis; new arrivals from rural Alabama and surrounding states unfamiliar and unaccepting of the status quo "were more likely to see the very presence of black workers as a threat to their social status and economic leverage."[49] ADDSCO proved more willing than other shipyards to hire black workers, with 20 percent of its workforce African American compared to 10 percent of the rest of Mobile's waterfront industries. But, as elsewhere, African

Americans at ADDSCO were not appointed to skilled positions. Taken as a whole, the persistence of workplace segregation and economic inequality made conditions particularly unbearable for the African American community in Mobile because the influx of workers and the rise in income, combined with wartime rationing, led to spikes in rents, prices, and the general cost of living.[50]

In August 1942, tensions flared when a white bus driver shot and killed a black soldier stationed at nearby Brookley Field, an Army Air Corps base. A compromise between the local branch of the National Association for the Advancement of Colored People (NAACP) and the bus company forestalled a major protest, but the city was on edge. Three months later, in response to complaints from black workers, the FEPC ordered Mobile's shipyards, including ADDSCO, to integrate skilled labor positions. The company stalled until May 24, 1943, when twelve black men were appointed welders. They worked their shift, largely without incident, but the next morning, 4,000 white laborers and onlookers retaliated, attacking black unskilled laborers with rough clubs, pipes, and other makeshift weapons. Soldiers from Brookley were dispatched to restore order, but not before at least 50 African Americans were injured. Almost 1,000 black workers requested transfers (all were denied due to the high demand for unskilled labor in the city), and many whites walked off the job once African Americans returned to work. ADDSCO responded to the violence by creating segregated shipyards, employing skilled black workers only on separate, black worksites.[51]

The Tennessee Valley did not experience the level of racial strife that struck Mobile, though African Americans in the valley were no less willing to push for greater participation in the wartime economy, and particularly in TVA's work in the region. And as in Mobile, whites resisted changes to the status quo. The agency's proportional hiring practices did seek to include black workers in significant numbers yet, as at ADDSCO, TVA clearly struggled to place black workers in skilled, higher-paying permanent and salaried positions, a fact made clear in the company's own reporting. And given TVA's mission of regional growth and development, the agency also failed to include black communities as active participants in planning and operations in the region. When black leaders challenged TVA to integrate, they meant more than hiring workers—they meant full inclusion in the authority's vision for the valley.

In late 1945, NAACP President Walter White inquired about housing conditions on valley projects. General Manager Gordon Clapp responded for Lilienthal, describing TVA's policy of supplying housing, education, recreation, and medical care for all workers. He noted that black workers and their families lived in separate-but-equal housing, either in existing communities or in the "limited housing" (dorms or cottages) TVA supplied at job sites. Clapp acknowledged that his agency's policy conformed to "established laws and customs in the area which . . . cannot be ignored without detrimentally affecting TVA's ability to carry on its construction and operating responsibilities." As the construction program came to a close, the agency relied on existing communities to house workers, ensuring that black workers were relegated to segregated neighborhoods, schools, and medical centers.[52] Here, stated plainly, was TVA's real dilemma. The agency needed to ensure cooperation among white community leaders in order to continue with construction projects, resource management, and other development programs. The authority insisted on the hiring of black workers, but only as far as allowed by the community, and TVA would only address instances of racial inequality when actual conflict arose.

TVA's black workers experienced discrimination first-hand. The Labor Council provided little protection for black workers, who found too few allies among the white mid-level managers and project supervisors overseeing daily work life. Separate construction and clearance crews solved this problem in the earliest days, but as the agency faced demands to integrate its workplace, conflict became more widespread. In 1943, three African American men were appointed as guards at Wilson Dam. White guards threatened to "riot" if their black co-workers staffed the positions, even promising to "throw the negroes in the river" if they wore their uniforms or carried weapons. Harold Pounders, an Office of Price Administration official in Florence, defended the white workers, blaming FEPC legislation for allowing the African American community to "progress too rapidly and to [*sic*] far." He asked Congressman John Sparkman to "do something for the benefit of these white guards and the other white employees at TVA." The congressman responded with surprise, promising Pounders that he would discuss the problem with Lilienthal who, he thought, would not hire black workers "without regard to the place or type of work" or "where friction might result." He asked Lilienthal to reconsider employing black workers in precarious positions. Lilienthal promised that the hiring had been made with careful consideration as to the proportion of African Americans in the Wilson Dam community and the character of those employed. In his estimation, the guards proved their competence in previous occupations, had the respect of the community, and "were known personally to a large number of the Authority's employees at Wilson Dam." TVA held a joint discussion with "over 200 members" of the Safety Service, calming fears, and the issue faded from record.[53] The incident reveals the difficulties faced by black workers under TVA's racial policy. True, the agency included the African American community in its hiring practices, yet by working within existing southern racial boundaries, the authority struggled to allow black workers access to the supervisory and management positions that would help guard against discrimination and prejudicial violence. Black workers continued to occupy the lowest rungs of the TVA ladder, forced to rely on the willingness of officials to defend their right to work.

The continuing influence of A. E. Morgan's labor and racial policies did not stem from Lilienthal's fond memories of the former chairman, or from some unwillingness to change the direction of TVA's program. Instead, the earlier policies fit Lilienthal's own objectives for development. TVA's labor agreement exemplified how cooperation between workers and management could result in a more efficient, fully functional workforce. The policy had real limits—TVA decided which unions would represent workers and used its status as a government agency, operating under a state of national emergency, to curtail certain avenues of protest. The general agreement provided workers with a promise of self-government and the agency with a guarantee of uninterrupted production. Workers kept jobs, income flowed into communities, and thousands of "happy" employees provided great publicity for Lilienthal's industrial recruitment plans.

In the same vein, TVA's policy on race relations sought to address the economic needs of African Americans without challenging social barriers. Insisting on "proportional employment," Lilienthal and Authority officials hoped to extend the benefits of TVA, particularly employment, while working within the bounds of what most white southerners considered "acceptable"—they would defend the right to employment, but little else. Granted, this policy did much to include African Americans (proportionately) in the benefits of the TVA's work. And the problems TVA's black workers faced, relegated to lower-paid and lower-skilled positions, were typical for the African Americans in the wartime United States. Given the realities of operating in the segregated South, the authority's position is somewhat understandable. However, the agency might have done more—operating under the mantle of the federal government and with a stated mission of including communities in their own development, TVA had a unique opportunity to allow African American leaders and workers a greater say in the future of the region. In the end, TVA's leaders sought to preserve a positive working relationship with the valley's existing civic leadership and hoped that the increased income and economic opportunities presented by the agency would benefit all residents, regardless of race.

World War II brought profound changes to the South, and the Tennessee Valley Authority was prepared to martial those changes for the good of the valley's citizens. From the outset, TVA hoped to use defense mobilization to remake the regional economy. In October 1939, David Lilienthal submitted a report to President Roosevelt, listing the ways in which TVA might be useful to the nation during the wartime emergency. Some of his suggestions recalled the agency's original mission. Lilienthal noted that, in the past six years, the authority had built a vast regional network of technicians and instructors who could help implement large-scale programs quickly and efficiently. Lilienthal also boasted a proven record of success in working with local leaders to remove families from reservoir areas, organize aid, and facilitate resource conservation. However, he went on to suggest measures more in line with his own conception of TVA's mission. Lilienthal argued that the national defense emergency could provide "the occasion for a permanent improvement of [TVA's] regional house-keeping." TVA might have to shelve efforts in soil fertility, forestry, and other "exhaustible" resources, he admitted, but in doing so, the agency would undoubtedly realize the "best feasible adjustment of resources to production quotas to the end that with the passing of the emergency, instead of a depleted region super-imposing its woes upon the inevitable shock of 'normalcy,' a virile, well-balanced economy shall assist the nation in its orderly return to peace-time pursuits."[54] A. E. Morgan would never have considered such radical changes. Lilienthal proposed the scuttling of several TVA activities, including resource conservation programs that had been integral to the original purpose as laid out in the TVA Act of 1933.

As TVA prepared to go to war in the 1940s, Lilienthal grasped the opportunity presented by the defense effort and, under his influence, TVA completely abandoned Morgan's communal idealism and adapted to a new political and economic environment. The agency produced power for defense industries, public and private, bringing jobs for the unemployed and wages for the destitute. Lilienthal, who was named chairman of the board of directors in 1941, matured his relationship with leaders across the valley, who found TVA ready to cooperate fully in programs of industrial recruitment and community development. By 1945, residents saw the agency as a regional arbiter of economic development, peddling electricity as a means of bringing industry to towns and communities along the Tennessee River. In conjunction with community leaders throughout the valley, Lilienthal's TVA ushered the region into the Sunbelt South, an economy centered on industrial and commercial growth, encouraged by the federal government, and embraced by regional boosters seeking economic prosperity above everything else.

Much has been written about the impact of World War II and the domestic defense effort on the southern economy. The location of armories, camps, arsenals, and a number of war-related manufacturers provided a much-needed boost for the "Nation's No. 1 economic problem." Tenant farmers and agricultural laborers who left the land during the 1930s found jobs in southern defense centers as "bulldozers [ploughed] military bases out of the 'Old Plantation.'"[55] In Alabama, for instance, non-agricultural employment rose by 26.3 percent, outpacing the rest of the South and the nation as a whole.[56] As the region's young men and women shipped to Europe, Africa, Asia, the Pacific, and camps and defense facilities across the country, those who remained at home experienced dramatic changes. The dislocations that accompanied the war challenged the racial status quo, providing further impetus for the fight for civil rights, guaranteed the right to organize for southern workers, and helped undermine the strength of conservative southern politicians.[57]

In May 1940, Lilienthal met with Roosevelt's secretary of commerce, Harry Hopkins, and promised that TVA could implement national defense plans across the Southeast. Hopkins suggested that the agency focus on activities within its authority, including research assistance in attracting private factories for planes, guns, and munitions; training workers for industry; and planning for the expansion of the power supply (all suggestions in line with Lilienthal's vision for TVA's participation in the defense effort).[58] However, with an extensive infrastructure in place, TVA hoped to contribute more than just planning and recruiting. Howard Menhinick, the director of the Department of Regional Studies, provided an extensive list of the services the agency offered. In particular, Menhinick noted, TVA might avoid the "overloading of federal offices" that accompanied the defense effort by coordinating interaction between federal programs and local and state administration. Menhinick also offered to take control of regional training, transportation, housing, planning, and even stockpiling programs.[59]

Lilienthal understood that the agency's greatest contribution would be recruiting and supplying defense plants in the area. He told residents that, despite "growing pains," new industries would soon relocate to the Tennessee Valley: "Growth of industry in the South . . . has been inevitable. The change has been coming gradually, and it was right that it should, but national defense needs have accelerated the pace. Now the South is ready."[60] TVA gave the nation the "stamina for emergency efforts" through its numerous programs for the valley, particularly power generation, and only an organization like the agency, providing navigation, fertilizer, electricity, and administrative cooperation could provide the workmen, machinery, and sheer industrial capacity to run the "vast industrial machine" that supported the armed forces. TVA's electricity drove the war effort, and in powering the plants, "vindicated" congressional decisions to provide funds.[61]

In 1935, when Lilienthal asked for House Military Affairs Committee for money to expand power generation, he was rejected since "so little industry of military significance" was located in the valley.[62] In 1940, the situation was markedly different. War industries demanded a rapid increase in TVA's electrical output. Congressmen rushed through appropriations measures that would allow TVA to expand facilities at dams and steam plants across the region, including an initial $65 million to expand generating capacity to meet the growing needs of defense plants. In North Alabama, for instance, the facilities at Muscle Shoals shifted to munitions and explosives production, placing increased demand on power from TVA's hydroelectric dams.[63] Some feared that demand would outstrip supply, leaving the armed forces and local consumers without power. Hearing rumors that the nation as a whole would soon face a power shortage, Sparkman wrote to then-Chairman Harcourt Morgan, suggesting an expansion of the facilities at Wilson Dam. General Manager Gordon Clapp tried to allay the representative's fears, promising that TVA engineers were studying the possibility of increased capacity, but focusing on areas where the need was greatest. Sparkman persisted, highlighting the fear among area officials that the booming defense economy would pass over the valley for lack of electricity. At the risk of sounding "over-insistent," he pressed Clapp for a decision, stating that, in efforts to recruit the Reynolds

Metals Company, power considerations could be the deciding factor. Concerned about the continued development of North Alabama, Sparkman wanted to be sure that the power was available.[64]

The best example of TVA's commitment to industrial production during the defense effort was its relationship with the Aluminum Company of America's manufacturing plant near Knoxville. In the 1930s, TVA cooperated with ALCOA to connect some of the manufacturer's hydroelectric facilities to the government network, including the site of Fontana Dam in western North Carolina. The agreement allowed TVA to control electric facilities within its boundaries, and in return, ALCOA called on the authority to provide more power as needed. The war made this contract extremely valuable to the aluminum company. In his journal, Lilienthal noted that his agency was "carrying" ALCOA above its contractual obligations, knowing that aluminum was so valuable to the war effort that TVA could not force ALCOA to renegotiate. The situation became "uncomfortable" because some industries and communities were forced to go without power so that the company could continue increasing production.[65]

The relationship created concern elsewhere in the valley, where leaders wanted assurance that TVA would reserve enough power for their own development plans. Worried about industries in North Alabama, Sparkman wrote to Lilienthal expressing concern that TVA and ALCOA had entered into an "alliance" and that, in the authority's case, "the whole Defense Program has served to make the big, bigger." Both Clapp and Lilienthal responded, sending the congressman a copy of TVA's contract with ALCOA and allaying fears that the agency had become a power-manufacturing trust. Lilienthal agreed with the "unhappy" fact that some big companies and agencies were increasing in size and profit margin during the crisis, but TVA could do little about ALCOA's size and suggested the government work to support small business.[66]

In fact, groups sometimes fought to ensure that their particular area received enough power to participate in the defense movement. Sparkman's concerns about a TVA-ALCOA "alliance" largely stemmed from his fears that the Chemical Warfare Arsenal scheduled to be built in Huntsville would be unable to contract for enough power, defeating development in the area. In September 1941, officials from TVA and Huntsville's municipal power system met in Knoxville to outline an agreement. Lilienthal hoped to provide electricity directly to the government facility, but Sparkman insisted on the city's right to buy and sell TVA power. Accompanied by the City of Huntsville

Electric System's manager, Karl Woltersdorf, a former Alabama Power district manager, he argued that the city purchased the municipal plant from Alabama Power in order to facilitate Huntsville's growth. If TVA cut Huntsville out of the negotiations, the action would reverse the outcome of the "Power Fight" of the 1930s. Worse, the city plant required "heavy capital expenditures" to meet increased demand, and only contracts with large buyers (like the arsenal) would help recapture the financial losses.[67] Defense mobilization fulfilled the hopes of municipal plants across the valley, seeing the increased industrial demand that Lilienthal and TVA had promised. But now, presented with the possibility of vastly increased profits, the government agency attempted to interpose itself between supplier and customer.

Events elsewhere increased Huntsville's fears. In late October 1941, the Office of Production Management called for power rationing in the Southeast to ensure sufficient electricity for defense industries. Federal officials implored domestic customers to reduce power usage in order to "ease the burden on industry, to prevent factory shutdowns, and to maintain payrolls," both in war industries and in other companies forced to scale back production.[68] At the same time, TVA was embroiled in a fight to supply Chattanooga's Volunteer Ordnance Works. Chattanooga's municipal system also wanted to power its local defense project, and as in North Alabama, TVA hoped to circumvent the city to provide power directly to a fellow government agency. As negotiations grew heated, Sparkman again wrote to Lilienthal, carefully outlining his understanding of TVA's role in power production and distribution. He warned that the agency could not sell power directly to a consumer—the TVA Act only provided for wholesale distribution to municipal groups and rural cooperatives.[69] In early November, Lilienthal announced TVA would withdraw its proposal to supply power to the Chattanooga plant, though he reasserted his belief that the agency had the right to do so. The "spirit of competition" was against TVA's policy of cooperation with distributors, but Lilienthal insisted that direct power supply was a preferable option when dealing with government plants.[70] A victory for Chattanooga seemed a victory for Huntsville, and Sparkman received a promise from Lilienthal that he would not participate in a competitive bidding process unless specifically directed by the War Department to do so.[71]

The relief was short-lived. Less than three weeks later, the War Department informed Sparkman and the municipal electric system that it would contract directly with TVA for the lowest possible electric rate, a "Federal

Department dealing directly with a Federal agency." Woltersdorf complained that the government had "taken advantage of our friendly attitude."[72] In the end, Woltersdorf realized he was fighting a losing battle. The War Department requisitioned TVA power for national defense requirements and paid a "government rate" comparable to the contracts the agency held with cities and municipalities in the valley.[73] In hindsight, the fight to supply the arsenals proved overblown. With the culmination of the national crisis, municipal electric systems took over power contracts and witnessed an explosion in customers associated with the rapidly expanding facilities. Yet the disagreement provides an interesting insight into TVA's wartime industrial growth. Arsenals, ordnance works, and associated companies demanded enormous blocks of prioritized power, returning a sure profit to any provider. Hoping to encourage further investment, the agency sought to give defense projects the best price possible, even if the resulting contracts failed to take into account community leaders' plans for growth.

As this conflict demonstrates, TVA did not always receive full cooperation from the people of the valley. While locals largely supported the agency's efforts to recruit industry to the region, they expected Lilienthal to extend the benefits to each community. When the chairman made decisions that seemed preferential, as with ALCOA, Chattanooga, or Huntsville, civic leaders and their representatives in Washington, D.C., cried foul. Lilienthal's TVA attempted to remain a "regional agency" as its efforts turned to directed economic development. Yet, as wartime conflicts suggested, that "regional" outlook sometimes challenged local expectations for growth.

No defense industry in North Alabama received as much wartime attention from TVA as the Reynolds Metals Company. When the Virginia business announced its decision to locate in the valley in 1940, locals praised TVA officials and congressional leaders for their work in negotiating with the company's president, Richard R. Reynolds. In particular, Senator Lister Hill formed a personal relationship with the aluminum manufacturer, making daily calls and petitioning the Reconstruction Finance Corporation for loans and TVA for a favorable power contract.[74] Florence's T. M. Rogers, a long-time proponent of valley development, and Allen J. Roulhac of Sheffield worked diligently to convince Hill and Sparkman to help bring the facility to Sheffield. As Roulhac noted, the Tennessee Valley, and Sheffield in particular, were "located in the territory served by public power, in an area which certainly needs industrial development of high order badly [and] should be a most desirable location for any kind of national defense or peace time industry." Cheap, available electricity was a crucial determinant in the decision, making negotiations with TVA especially important. Sparkman set up meetings with Reynolds and TVA representatives, who promised to make an "equitable" contract with the company. Rogers agreed to pay all of the expenses of local leaders who helped show Reynolds officials the site at Sheffield. He saw the initial financial outlay as an investment in the district's future: "The best thing I see about the Reynolds Metal Company is the fact that it will make available aluminum for other industries, both large and small, who would be interested in locating here due not only to cheap power but local materials."[75] Local and federal leaders cooperated in their attempt to influence the decision. Sparkman worked with TVA to formalize power contracts, and when he realized that Reynolds was concerned with transportation and material availability, he contacted Rogers and Roulac, asking the businessmen to find "anyone competent" to advertise the area.[76]

Alabama's representatives remained outwardly impartial, assuring inquiring groups that they would work equally for every community able to accommodate the plant, but by late summer, Sheffield had become the clear front-runner. In fact, the only major obstacle to immediate construction was TVA's electric rate. Reynolds wanted the same rate as the other regional aluminum manufacturer, ALCOA. J. A. Krug, the authority's chief power engineer, promised to match ALCOA's rate for secondary power (electricity produced during times of low water), but he offered only the standard industrial rate for primary power (drawn from normal or high water running through the dam) with a 10 percent discount if the plant connected directly to a TVA dam. Krug promised to supply power as soon as possible, but Hill was frustrated with the agency's efforts: "I cannot but feel that if Dr. [Harcourt] Morgan and Mr. Lilienthal had evidenced proper interest in the matter, the aluminum plant would now be under construction in the Tennessee Valley area."[77]

The negotiations proved a rocky beginning to the relationship between Reynolds and TVA. Nevertheless, in mid-September, Sparkman's secretary informed Rogers and Roulhac that a tentative contract had been signed to locate the plant at Sheffield, and on October 7, 1940, the news became public. Reynolds Metal Company began construction on a facility just two miles from Wilson Dam. Within six months, Reynolds promised to employ 1,250 men working to produce aluminum for the American Army Air Corps. The factory replaced "fields of lespedeza, turnips, potatoes and cotton," consumed a million dollars in TVA power, and, except for "key men," employed all-local labor.[78] An economic victory for the Tri-Cities, the Reynolds Metal Company was also a symbolic change for the region, since the plant was literally built on the fields of cotton that once dominated the region.

Bringing Reynolds to the Tennessee Valley was undoubtedly a success story for North Alabama and a perfect example of the style of industrial recruitment that marked the Sunbelt economy. Seeking businesses interested in war work, developers cooperated with the region's representatives in Washington, D.C., to target Reynolds. The company was then "sold" on the climate (broadly defined) of the region, particularly cheap TVA power, ample natural resources, available plant sites, and transportation. Both government and business leaders wooed Reynolds officials, demonstrating their willingness to work closely with the company and ensure its success. TVA was very much a part of the proposal, working as much as possible to ensure more business for itself and for the valley. The campaign borrowed from earlier efforts to "boost" the economy, including the work of civic groups in Florence in the 1920s and Decatur in the 1930s, and by the 1940s, such work was becoming standard practice.

However, as successful as the valley was in attracting Reynolds, locals found that working with the federal government could prove complicated. In the case of TVA, the agency was tasked with region-wide development. The authority could work to bring industry to the valley at large, but Lilienthal was hesitant to give one particular community an advantage over its neighbors. The agency might help attract Reynolds to the region, publishing resources and rates, but TVA would not locate Reynolds in Sheffield at the expense of another valley town. Instead, civic leaders in a particular community would need to take the initiative. When development worked, as it did in the initial efforts to snare Reynolds, residents praised TVA. Yet when the agency's regional imperative hampered efforts (as in the conflict over providing power to arsenals), locals chafed at the restrictions. Again, TVA's negotiations with Reynolds are illustrative.

Almost as soon as the Reynolds plant was completed in the summer of 1941, the company began planning to expand. After initial inquiries into sites around the region, the company decided to add to its existing property near Sheffield in the aptly named town of Listerhill. With an increased loan from the RFC, the company's officials expected to increase output in Sheffield drastically on the strength of the wartime demand for domestically produced aluminum.[79] Despite the importance attached to their work in the valley, Reynolds officials felt TVA favored the ALCOA plant in Tennessee with lower rates, government assistance, and an unfounded priority for their product. In early 1942, TVA demanded a revenue guarantee from the Alabama plant as a "minimum protection to the Government's interests for the benefit of Reynolds Metals Company." Reynolds officials called the request a violation of regular business practices, particularly while the company operated under the provisions placed on it by the RFC while it paid back its loan—in the minds of its operators, Reynolds was a "government plant." When TVA suggested the RFC make that title official by taking full responsibility for the facilities, the company's representatives became "exercised" and demanded to be included in all discussions between TVA and RFC concerning Reynolds. In fact, the aluminum company had already begun buying equipment and gearing for increased production. Without a sure contract for power, its work to expand might be a wasted investment and a costly mistake.[80] For new TVA Board member James Pope, negotiations with Reynolds were "unsavory" and left him with a "feeling of nausea." He asserted that the board had to be sure that "the interests of TVA, i.e. the Government, are protected."[81] A few weeks later, tempers cooled to the point that Lilienthal and Reynolds found an "acceptable" solution by which TVA would power the plants, though neither side felt particularly happy about the agreement. Lilienthal told the board that, having protested the actions of the company's executives, he would let the matter stand, considering the nature of the wartime emergency. The agency could not be seen as preventing the production of aluminum, especially when the RFC had funded the plant's expansion.[82]

With Reynolds moving into full production, Senator Hill praised the company's efforts. He recalled meeting with Richard Reynolds in 1940 while the Virginian prepared to choose a site for his southern plant. Reynolds told Hill that light metals would play an important role in determining victory or defeat (especially when used for manufacturing aircraft), and Hill praised the businessman's foresight, citing a May 1941 letter in which Reynolds had asked the Office of Production Management to increase aluminum production through subsidies to manufacturers (Hill failed to specify how much Reynolds and Alabama benefited from such a decision). While American factories were "lulled to sleep," Hill claimed, Reynolds had acted without orders, payment, or even government protection to mortgage his existing factories to supply aluminum for the war effort.[83] The company received similar praise from the

Alabama State Chamber of Commerce, which claimed Reynolds began a "new era" with its Listerhill plant, building the equivalent of six thousand bombers a year. The chamber echoed Hill in its estimation of the company's self-sacrifice in taking on the "hazardous business."[84] The high praise of both Hill and the Alabama chamber differed markedly from the reputation that Reynolds held among TVA's officials. While Hill applauded the company's self-sacrifice, Lilienthal and the board noted Reynolds Metals's potential for profiteering and double-dealing. For the authority, Reynolds Metals Company was a boon to the local economy, but in the big picture it was one defense company asking for special treatment in a section of the country populated with several wartime industries eager to draw TVA power. For the leaders of North Alabama, and particularly the communities surrounding the plant, though, Reynolds was the cornerstone of a revitalized economy and an example of successful development strategy.[85]

The aluminum company remained an integral part of the region's economy for several decades. However, the wartime rate dispute demonstrated the potential for conflict inherent in Lilienthal's plans for industrial development. In TVA's guise as a regional arbiter, the chairman believed that, as long as power rates encouraged industrial development across the valley, those rates were "fair," even if internal discrepancies existed. In North Alabama, officials saw "favorable" rates at ALCOA as a troubling sign for local development. If TVA chose to lower power rates only in Knoxville, industrial recruitment in Florence, Decatur, and Huntsville would suffer. As much as TVA fostered cooperation and mutual support for growth and development among communities, the agency's work could also cause conflict and competition.

In North Alabama, civic and business leaders embraced Lilienthal's program of economic development, even as they quibbled over the agency's actions. Yet not all of TVA's original proponents shared the new chairman's perspective, and even as the authority solidified its new direction during the defense effort, it found increased opposition in Congress from those who believed it was no longer the agency it was created to be. In particular, Tennessee Senator Kenneth McKellar became an outspoken opponent of Lilienthal's leadership. Representing a number of valley counties, McKellar worked closely with Senator George Norris in the 1920s after the future "Father of TVA" agreed to include fertilizer production in his government operation plans for Muscle Shoals. McKellar introduced amendments ensuring that TVA power could be sold to municipalities and cooperatives, and after Roosevelt's election, he claimed to be "perfectly delighted" with the prospect of the government's development of the Tennessee River watershed.[86] McKellar believed that only the federal government could adequately oversee such a massive undertaking and ensure that the benefits went to residents in need of assistance.

As economic development became the driving ideology behind the agency's actions in the valley, however, McKellar argued that the authority had exceeded its original intent, citing numerous examples of its misuse of funds, lack of oversight, and policies injurious to farmers. In particular, he questioned the continued flooding of farmland in East Tennessee which, he argued, was antithetical to TVA's mission to assist in the rehabilitation of southern agriculture. When he attempted to block the continued construction of Douglas Dam above Knoxville, needed to power the valley's growing economy, he found that his sentiments were not shared by his fellow congressmen. As TVA's Marguerite Owen noted, McKellar's "choler appeared to be inexhaustible, and his diligence in obstruction was unremitting. He was, however, confronting a president determined that war production should not be threatened by a power shortage."[87] With war industries placing an enormous drain on regional power reserves, dam construction was necessary to keep soldiers armed and planes in the air. The *Huntsville Times* warned that McKellar's "inopportune" actions "would strike vitally at [TVA's] program, and upset a major portion of the nation's war effort."[88]

At its heart, McKellar's disgust with TVA centered on a larger opposition to the decline of agriculture, and underneath the "choler," his critiques noted the ongoing shift away from a predominantly farm-based economy. The war added to the flight from farm to factory as marginal farmers who had survived the Depression and remained on the land during the New Deal took jobs in defense factories for high wages. David Lilienthal's TVA was, perhaps, a handy target for those, like McKellar, who believed that the federal government was aiding in this transition. This was consistent with his early support for the agency. A. E. Morgan's TVA hoped that communities would become self-sufficient by farming more efficiently and supplementing farm income with home and craft-based production. TVA's initial hydroelectric program provided the power needed for electrified farms and small businesses. By 1940, though, new leadership, the wartime emergency, and the shifting southern economy meant an expansion of TVA, producing power for large-scale industry. Now that the people of the valley were becoming wage-paid consumers, McKellar saw himself as one of the last defenders of a dying agricultural alternative.

McKellar also balked at the authority's spending practices and, in 1942, he introduced a bill that allowed Congress to oversee more closely the funds appropriated to TVA. He called Lilienthal and Chief Power Engineer J. A. Krug the "gold-dust twins" of the agency, citing thousands of automobiles, travel pay for Lilienthal to publicize TVA's actions (and oppose McKellar's criticisms), and several unnecessary projects, amounting to a "carte blanche" that had to be checked.[89] McKellar's former allies denounced his "interference" with the war effort. Norris listed the benefits "endangered" by the criticism: 470,000 customers, five thousand miles of transmission lines, nineteen generating plants, and essential defense businesses across the valley. The Nebraskan promised that such oversight would make TVA unable to fulfill its role in producing power, forcing the agency to "turn in its receipts" and killing its flexibility.[90] According to his journal, Lilienthal welcomed the attacks, even the personal affronts, as "a perfect demonstration of the difference between predatory politics and baseness in public life, and the thing that TVA stood for." McKellar's critique proved what the chairman felt all along—working solely within the government would only hamper TVA's larger vision. Locals supported the authority's relative independence from government oversight. Lilienthal specifically cited Decatur's leadership, including Barrett Shelton, whose success in using TVA to bring in business showed that the agency influenced residents to call for development on their own.[91]

The House of Representatives defeated the McKellar Amendment in June, but the senator continued his "unremitting and unrelenting . . . attacks on the TVA." In early 1943, he introduced legislation making federal employees who earned over $4,500 per year subject to congressional approval. Valley leaders worried that the amendment would "give him a throttle hold upon TVA personnel and technicians."[92] Barrett Shelton asked Alabama Governor Chauncey Sparks to contact Senator John H. Bankhead Jr. in an attempt to fight on behalf of TVA's program for "the farming people of the state." Lister Hill told a concerned group of city commissioners from Muscle Shoals that he was doing everything in his power to defeat McKellar. The Huntsville Chamber of Commerce began a letter-writing campaign to induce congressmen across the country to kill the legislation.[93] For the valley, the opposition was more than a power play by McKellar. By endangering the authority's independence, the senator was striking at an economic lifeline connecting the people to the prosperity of the defense boom. Not only did Lilienthal and his agency provide dams, plants, factories, fertilizer, and electricity, but as both Hill and Lilienthal noted, TVA buttressed the people's confidence, convincing them that their own actions could make a difference in the local economy.[94] Hill specifically defended the importance of the agency's flexibility: "We were setting up something new and different. . . . It was necessary to give TVA a flexibility and an initiative such as that enjoyed largely by private corporations."[95] Without the freedom to hire consultants and other workers to communicate with community leaders and local groups, and without the discretion to direct funds to needed projects, TVA would be relegated to a very limited governmental role supplying power to whichever entity Congress deemed worthy.

As TVA's supporters mobilized behind the agency, McKellar was increasingly isolated. His colleagues in the Tennessee delegation expressed their support for the authority, and Lilienthal and other representatives of TVA made speeches across Tennessee.[96] McKellar called the chairman "oily, eely, designing, [and] corrupt" and criticized his increased power in the agency: "He is just as much in control of that Board, and everything that pertains to the TVA, the dams, and the funds, as Hitler is in control of Germany."[97] This criticism, in particular, points to a more insidious opposition, based not on Lilienthal's actions as chairman, but on his Jewish background. Calling him "oily" and "designing," McKellar invoked an offensive, stereotypical caricature that few of Lilienthal's other critics echoed, even those supportive of McKellar's other points of contention. Though the senator did voice legitimate concerns about the direction of TVA's policies, he enveloped them with racism and prejudice, and thus helped to discredit himself and his cause.

In June 1944, McKellar's amendments were removed from the TVA appropriation bill in committee. In March 1945, he again tried to tighten federal oversight of the agency, but his wartime campaign proved that he could not overcome the massive public support for the authority in valley communities and in the halls of Congress.[98] McKellar's fight, however distasteful his personal attacks on the chairman were, highlighted just how far Lilienthal had moved away from the idealism of TVA's origins during the Great Depression and early New Deal. A. E. Morgan envisioned an agency with the ability to draw on the authority and sheer resources of the government to remake the physical and social landscape of the region. The government took charge in relocating farmers, building dams, controlling malaria, conducting employment training, running demonstration farms, and overseeing experimental fertilizer programs—the generation of power for industrial uses was not a priority. Lilienthal rejected that valuation, and the defense mobilization of the American economy allowed him to flex the agency's industrial muscle in cooperation with the residents he sought to aid. Communities across the South used TVA's assistance to market low electric rates, available labor, and ample resources to defense industries. As Hill noted, the agency was created "for the people." How those people chose to utilize their gift would be an important force in the redirection of the authority's program.

From its inception, TVA was envisioned as a "grass-roots" organization, a government agency that sought the input of the people it was directed to help. David Lilienthal certainly agreed, and he empowered residents as developers, boosting income through industries recruited to the area to take advantage of TVA's cheap, available power. Under A. E. Morgan, TVA centered on locals recruited into temporary relief work and trained in better farming practices. Lilienthal's agency still targeted unsuccessful farmers, but he transferred attention from TVA's agronomists and social workers to its economists and planners. He organized meetings with local and state leaders, instructing them in methods of industrial recruitment, interorganizational cooperation, and infrastructure development. The authority's new focus convinced many communities to create civic improvement associations, and valley cities with existing chambers of commerce and development groups found in TVA a willing partner in progress. Even as Lilienthal used the opportunity of the defense effort to move the agency in a new direction, local development groups continued to push him to go further with pleas for assistance and examples of startling success.

Lilienthal's development initiative came just as southern states, including Alabama, began their own state-organized industrial development programs. In 1936, Mississippi's leaders created the Balance Agriculture with Industry program, empowering the state government to seek out industrial investment.[99] In Alabama, the legislature enacted the Alabama State Planning Commission in 1935, but limited its actions until 1939, when the commission gained the ability to advertise state resources to nonresident companies.[100] In 1937, Alabama Power's Tom Martin founded the Alabama State Chamber of Commerce, hoping to organize statewide efforts to attract and retain business.[101] Frank Dixon, elected governor in 1938, proved more receptive to development than his predecessors. In 1940, he traveled to New York, speaking to an investment club on the need for industrialization to supplement the southern agricultural economy.[102] Dixon and the State Planning Commission tentatively began organizing to sell the state to interested industries across the country. The commission studied the drainage basin around Mobile, conducted detailed investigations into the state's park, recreation, and forestry resources, and released a report on the housing and population problems created in war industry communities.[103] In 1943, the commission became the Alabama State Planning Board (ASPB), but its mission remained the same; the ASPB worked with communities to prepare for development, conducted large regional improvement projects, oversaw statewide public works, and ensured that wartime industry transferred seamlessly into peacetime pursuits.[104]

The businessmen of the state did not awaken overnight. The Florence Chamber of Commerce had been active since World War I, seeking industries to offset the stalemate over the proposed government facility at Muscle Shoals. Decatur and communities across the region initiated their own programs in response to the opportunities presented by the entrance of TVA in the 1930s. North Alabama was truly ahead of the state in its embrace of economic development activities. Yet the 1940s saw an expansion of local activities just as a new statewide enterprise sought to streamline the state's progress. The defense boom helped, but TVA's work with these local and state agencies provided an impetus to grow and coordinate that transformed a motley collection of local groups into a region-wide network of developers.

Early in its existence, the Alabama State Planning Board fostered a relationship with TVA to help meet the demands of the Alabama counties located within the authority's service area. Beginning in 1940, TVA set up a cooperative exchange with the state organization, providing its vast regional research mechanism in the hopes that the ASPB could more closely oversee and manage the local community development groups that put its plans into action.[105] In 1943, the cooperation became even more formalized when the two signed a seven-year contract. TVA provided a full-time planning technician to the state agency and reimbursed all expenses.[106]

The relationship matured during the defense boom as TVA and the ASPB cooperated to facilitate industrial development while working to assist communities upended by rapid economic growth. Lilienthal praised the "excellent" work of the ASPB, particularly in Guntersville, where the transition from agriculture to industry and recreation "presented a host of new problems and new opportunities requiring energetic and farsighted local action." The ASPB worked with the city to create a zoning ordinance, a municipal park, a boat harbor, and studies for future growth. In Muscle Shoals, the state board designed a public housing program to meet demand on defense projects. The ASPB and TVA worked together to provide solutions for the "serious community development problems associated with the current intensive national-defense expansions."[107]

Lilienthal hoped to foster community leadership in industrial recruitment and economic planning and, in its relationship with the ASPB, TVA insisted on an approach that encouraged local initiative. The two groups cooperated with Florence's planning commission to create a detailed map of the city, including new subdivisions built during the defense boom. In Sheffield, the groups helped the city formalize its building code and conduct studies for a sewer system.[108] In 1944, at the request of Governor Sparks, TVA's Director of Regional Studies Menhinick drafted a formal program of operation for the ASPB, hoping to guide the state board into the postwar years. At the heart of the authority's instructions was a provision to stimulate local planning, encouraging the ASPB to guide local agencies just as TVA guided the ASPB by creating multi-county cooperation and cataloging regional resources.[109] Menhinick stressed the larger picture: "When many people are thinking and working on the same problems and all are pulling together in the same direction, there is created a wealth of manpower, ingenuity, and ideas which could never be supplied by a limited number of federal or state personnel."[110] TVA hoped to create a system of oversight and instruction that would streamline industrial recruitment. Under the agency's guidance, communities would cooperate with each other instead of undercutting bids or stealing prospects. Lilienthal stressed that economic revitalization would only come when communities used their inherent resources to bring in industries, increasing the purchasing power of residents and pumping money into the area that could be used for needed improvements. Working with state agencies like the Alabama State Planning Board, the chairman was able to implement that plan in a carefully organized manner.[111]

The authority took time to foster relationships with state agencies, but it also worked directly on the local level with civic organizations and with individual businesses looking to relocate or expand operations. TVA's relationship with companies such as Reynolds could be characterized by tense negotiations and competing motivations, but cooperation with civic organizations occurred with relatively little disagreement. Across the valley, civic agencies fully embraced Lilienthal's program of industrial development. Decatur, in particular, continued its cooperation with the agency, finding its new leadership more acquiescent in plans for industrial recruitment. Led by the editor of the *Decatur Daily*, Barrett Shelton, and the Decatur Chamber of Commerce, the city's enthusiasm for development and its wartime economic growth spurred Lilienthal's transformation of TVA's program, even as that program encouraged the valley to rely on industry to create economic opportunity.

In September 1939, weeks after Germany's invasion of Poland, Shelton began pressing Decatur's case for defense investment. He first turned to Lister Hill, claiming that Decatur "[had] these things coming to us," and he called for defense plants that would "[belong] to the Tennessee Valley section of Alabama." Hill reassured the editor that he was focused on that very goal.[112] In May 1940, Shelton contacted Harcourt Morgan in an attempt to convince TVA to bring wartime industry to his city. He asked the new Chairman Morgan to meet with him and Alabama State Chamber of Commerce President Benjamin Russell in the hope that TVA would give North Alabama, which was "in a most uncomfortable industrial position," information on industrial relocation requests received by the state agency.[113] General Manager Clapp attempted to remain impartial, agreeing that many communities like Decatur would want to take advantage of TVA's program, but that the authority had to remain "regional." Clapp cited many of his agency's accomplishments, such as navigation, flood control, and electricity, but he instructed the editor that these would only benefit Decatur and the rest of the valley if he and his colleagues chose to "work toward their full utilization." Clapp promised to send a representative to help the city attract new industries, and recommended that Shelton pursue development based on "the application of local initiative and ingenuity toward the creation of new wealth and new income through entirely new enterprises."[114]

City leaders continued to press TVA for assistance, but they refused to wait on the agency to take a more active interest in Decatur's growth and instead continued their work to build the city's economy. In October 1940, the Nebraska Consolidated Mills announced the construction of an eight-hundred-barrel-per-day flour processing plant, employing 75 workers.[115] In 1941, in cooperation with TVA, the city won the Southern Aviation Training School on land just north of the city across the Tennessee River. Decatur Chamber of Commerce President John M. Nelson hoped that the school would be the foundation for even further defense investment.[116] Such active leadership made Decatur the ideal example of Lilienthal's plans. After a trip through North Alabama, Lilienthal called the city a "grand experiment." Just four years earlier, Decatur was "in admittedly bad shape," looking for industry to revitalize the area's economy.[117] By 1940, the city had a population of over 16,000 with nearly 5,500 wage earners, more than double the number in 1930, though Decatur added only 1,000 new residents.[118] As Lilienthal noted, "Instead of crying about the ruin which was coming because much of the farming land was flooded by Wheeler Dam, [Decatur's civic leaders] used their heads." Shelton, in particular, had the "brains and spirit" to realize that the newly navigable river would bring in industry.[119]

Industrial attraction, however important, was not enough, as events soon proved. New facilities and the expansion of existing industries forced leaders to consider the quality of economic growth. Shelton regularly editorialized on the subject. He quoted a McComb County, Mississippi, newspaper on the growth of "boom towns" marked by economic speculation, immorality, and crowded conditions; for valley leaders, this concern for the consequences of unregulated growth stretched back to the conditions in Muscle Shoals during the days of the Ford offer, as well as life in TVA's construction villages, particularly "Slab Town" at Pickwick Dam. Shelton warned that only Decatur's "slow and methodical" growth would save it from a similar fate. He praised the confidence of local workers, who not only wanted employment and steady income, but also a better city, and worked toward that goal.[120] Decatur launched an $820,000 public improvement program to build four new school buildings, pave twelve city blocks, and locate a new marine park on an island in the Tennessee River.[121] In 1941, the city organized an official planning commission, designed to cooperate with both TVA and the various federal war agencies directing defense funds across the country. The commission prepared zoning ordinances and looked into the use of the Tennessee River waterfront, including land purchased by TVA but unused for Wheeler Reservoir, and Ingalls Shipbuilding expanded onto adjacent TVA property.[122] Rising employment and waterfront industries put a strain on the city's outdated sewer system, and in conjunction with federal agencies such as the Public Housing Authority, the commission worked to update the municipal water supply and extend utilities to industrial and residential developments.[123]

In 1943, Shelton proudly boasted of his city's growth. On the occasion of TVA's tenth anniversary, he quoted an unnamed Decatur businessman who told Lilienthal, "We are building a city here, not necessarily a bigger city, but a better city, a city that will live, that will not blow down in the face of ill economic winds."[124] The story may have been apocryphal, but its sentiments undoubtedly pleased the chairman. Shelton understood the necessities of economic growth. He looked to TVA for assistance, but also guided local leaders, whose initiative brought new industries to the city while preparing its infrastructure for further expansion. Following its rapid wartime growth, the city's postwar future would largely prove anti-climactic, especially as nearby Huntsville eclipsed it in size and economic strength. Yet the relationship between the federal agency and Decatur's local leadership exhibited the remarkable transformation in TVA's vision.

Close cooperation with community leaders was an essential part of TVA's larger plans for postwar development as well. In August 1943, the University of Alabama's Dr. Raymond Paty, who would eventually be named to the TVA Board, foresaw a "violent, perhaps swift transition" to peacetime economics when the war ended, a process that could only be alleviated by immediate planning in cooperation with local businesses and communities.[125] One of the main concerns for the authority was the disposition of the numerous war plants that began scaling back production and employment as the conflict overseas drew to a close. TVA's cheap electricity brought numerous arsenals, camps, and storage facilities to the Tennessee Valley, and in 1944, Commerce Department chief John Ferris worked with government officials to bring local groups into the discussion on the utilization of surplus plants and the role communities would need to play in the "disposition" of their defense facilities.[126] Leaders like Barrett Shelton had become an integral part of the region's economic future, helping to prepare their communities for the future.

As the nation readied for life after the war, the authority incorporated its development program and its relationship with local and state groups into its everyday activities. In February 1945, Ferris produced a report on TVA's work with community development groups in an attempt to "clarify" the relationship, a sure sign that the agency planned to continue the cooperation into the foreseeable future. While the report referred to the work with the groups as "developmental in nature," it also noted that local leaders played an increasingly important role in the "orderly transition from a predominately raw materials economy to more diversified forms and higher levels of economic activity."[127] Again, TVA stressed the need for local initiative, encouraging businessmen to make the crucial decisions to start and expand businesses. Ferris's department recommended a special staff committee to foster cooperation between area groups, determine "realistic" investments and returns, and serve as an impartial jury to solve "technical bottlenecks" to development.[128]

TVA leaders hoped that the valley's growth would build on the advantages brought by the research capabilities and resource improvement programs of the agency.

That December, TVA held a conference with representatives of the state planning commissions within its borders. In the first session, Ferris clearly stated the importance of the commissions' work, recalling the earliest language of A. E. Morgan's TVA: "The objective is a rising standard of living for the people of the region resulting from their direct participation in conserving and making use of the resources of national wealth of the region as a whole."[129] Yet Ferris's plans for community development groups fit squarely in Lilienthal's vision. Ferris noted that modern industrial development required technical knowledge in an area's available resources and potential. TVA's trained staff, with connections to universities across the valley, and its position as an impartial government agency allowed it to serve as an information center, working with state and community-development groups looking to attract different companies. TVA was a "technical partner" to the people responsible for development.[130] Alabama State Planning Board Director W. O. Dobbins actively participated, freely discussing his state's successes and failures. He praised Alabamians for having "the initiative, imagination and resources to promote this development." TVA's representatives lauded Dobbins, whose actions were exactly what they expected from state commissions and just what they hoped to encourage in communities across the region.[131] The conference attendees worked to establish a clear set of objectives for TVA and state and local committees and a concrete methodology for regional development, premised on the fact that the region's "primary objective" should be to generate industry with TVA and the state commissions serving as "a catalyser and advisor."[132] Thus, by the end of World War II, the authority committed itself to encouraging local development committees to bring industry to the South.

Ferris's report and the first State Planning Commission Conference embodied TVA's new program, which took shape with Lilienthal's emergence from the "Board Fight" and came into its own during the "Power Fight" and the agency's participation in the World War II defense effort. In order to revitalize the southern economy, Lilienthal demanded a reconsideration of the basic relationship between the agency and its customers. It would no longer seek to create an industrial-agricultural utopia marked by small, homegrown factories interspersed with self-sustaining family farms—Morgan's communalism gave way to Lilienthal's consumerism. Under his care, TVA actively encouraged the industrial development of the Tennessee Valley as a means of boosting southern (and national) "purchasing power." Factories reserved blocks of TVA power, ensured the agency's continued operation and expansion, and brought jobs for the unemployed and payrolls for struggling communities. Valley leaders welcomed the change in policy. In Florence, Decatur, Guntersville, and communities all along the river, public and private organizations fostered an intimate relationship with TVA's planners that continued well into the postwar years. Leaders like Barrett Shelton embraced the assistance, working with Lilienthal in aggressive recruitment campaigns. World War II provided a tremendous boost. Defense orders flooded into the Southeast as government and private plants took advantage of cheap labor, cheap power, and a favorable business environment. By 1945, the Tennessee Valley had come to rely on industry for continued prosperity built on a growing cooperation between local communities and the federal government.

In 1944, David Lilienthal published *TVA: Democracy on the March*, a laudatory account of the agency's work. In particular, he noted that government investment and private initiative combined to "create new jobs, relieve human drudgery, give new life and fruitfulness to worn-out lands, put yokes upon the streams, and transmute the minerals of the earth and the plants of the field into machines of wizardry to spin out the stuff of a way of life new to this world."[133] A. E. Morgan did not rejoice in Lilienthal's "machines of wizardry." As he would later recall in his own account: "Individual self-interest is not an adequate basis for an enduring democracy or a healthy society. . . . Democracy can survive only in a society whose members have a sense and an understanding of their lives as parts of the ongoing totality of life and a loyalty to the totality that is greater than that to their own group and self-interest."[134] Morgan never forgave Lilienthal for his role in the "Board Fight" of 1938, and his recollections belied a continued dislike for the new chairman's policies. However, in his critique of his former agency's redirection, Morgan uncovered an important shortcoming. In embracing industrial development, Lilienthal began to defer many decisions to community leaders and business owners—he allowed them to embrace their own goals and short-term gain in exchange for a broad-based program of long-lasting socio-economic change. No longer concentrating on dam construction or comprehensive resource management, Lilienthal's agency transferred the responsibility for development to the state planning boards and civic organizations that directly interacted with the companies they were trying to entice into their community.

David Lilienthal's TVA cooperated with local leadership in the growth of the southern economy, and he truly believed that, as newly employed southerners made money and reinvested that money in the region's economy, the South would no longer be the nation's economic problem. Yet even as southerners found jobs and made money, an important alternative vision for the South was abandoned. By the war years, TVA no longer served as an active guide for the valley, as a "yardstick" for an economy and society that might operate more fairly and responsibly. Acquiescing to local mores in the interest of growth and cooperation, Lilienthal's TVA failed to ensure that African Americans received an equal voice in the future of the region, that all residents and workers had a say in the direction of their community, or even that incoming industries cared for the people and environment that drew them to the valley in the first place. Thus, by the 1950s, even as TVA came to embrace fully its role in facilitating development alongside local leaders, the agency found itself recasting and reconsidering its mission to revitalize the Tennessee Valley.

On February 21, 1919, the Mechanical Department at Nitrate Plant No. 2 in Muscle Shoals, Alabama, held a "Farewell Dinner" signaling the end of wartime operations. In hindsight, the dinner also symbolized the termination of work at the plant as Congress began debating the future of the project. *Courtesy of Florence-Lauderdale Public Library.*

Construction on Wilson Dam was completed in 1924 amidst local and national discussions over its utility and purpose. *Courtesy of Florence-Lauderdale Public Library.*

Just weeks before his inauguration, in January 1933, Franklin D. Roosevelt visited the Shoals to assure residents of his determination to develop the regional economy. *Courtesy of Stephen Rickard and Florence-Lauderdale Public Library.*

TVA case workers interviewed families affected by reservoir construction across the Tennessee Valley. In this photo, a TVA employee interviews the Murphy family of North Carolina. *Kodak Negative File, 1933–76, Records of the TVA, National Archives, Southeast Region, Morrow, Georgia.*

Guntersville, Alabama, was one of the larger cities affected by TVA's program of planned flooding. As in towns across the Tennessee Valley, the TVA sought to ameliorate the effects of such drastic changes by encouraging local leaders to engage in civic planning and economic development. *Library of Congress.*

Barrett Shelton, the editor of the *Decatur Daily*, worked closely with David Lilienthal on behalf of growth and development in the Tennessee Valley. Here, Shelton, *left*, meets with Lilienthal, *right*, in Decatur. *Courtesy of Barrett C. Shelton Jr.*

Congressman Robert E. Jones became one of the strongest defenders of TVA and its efforts in the valley. Here, Jones, *left*, consults with Dr. Wernher von Braun on the layout of research facilities at the University of Alabama at Huntsville. *Courtesy of Marshall Space Flight Center, NASA.*

FIVE

AN AGENCY OF ITS OWN CREATION 1945–1960

The decline of the New Dealers began almost as soon as they assumed power. Many of President Franklin Roosevelt's most vaunted programs fell to legal challenges and faulty oversight. His "court-packing" scheme alienated those who feared he had assumed too much power and, in 1937, the U.S. economy entered a sharp recession, proving to many of Roosevelt's detractors that his experimentation had not solved the economic crisis. By the late 1930s and early 1940s, the New Deal took a secondary role as the country shifted to wartime footing—as Roosevelt himself noted in a December 1943 press conference, "Dr. New Deal" became "Dr. Win-the-War."[1] The government quickly became a willing partner of business in the name of economic growth and defense production. At the same time, an increasing awareness of racial inequality, spurred by wartime activism from African Americans and Gunnar Myrdal's eye-opening *An American Dilemma,* convinced some New Dealers of the need for a new focus on civil rights.[2] New Deal liberals did not completely abandon their Depression-era efforts at reform. They still called for the federal government to maintain a "safety net" for those Americans in need of assistance, but they focused much of their attention on maintaining the economic gains made during the war, hoping that prosperity would spread as widely as possible. Inspired by the belief that the Great Depression was a result of underconsumption, liberals turned to government spending to help industry expand. Encouraged by Washington, D.C., successful businesses hired workers and fed consumers, whose daily activities then powered the American economy.[3]

The TVA of the 1940s, 1950s, and 1960s fit within this larger transition. Many of the agency's leaders were convinced that the South suffered from a lack of "purchasing power," David Lilienthal especially, and during World War II the agency worked to locate industry in communities across the valley. When the country began to demobilize, TVA's leadership continued the economic development programs begun under Lilienthal, encouraging state and local organizations to approach and entice manufacturers to relocate in the region, advertising vacated plants and government-owned parcels of land along the Tennessee River, and providing detailed surveys on available resources. As TVA officials continued to facilitate economic expansion, they also focused new attention on recreation and tourism as an additional source of income for community growth. Decatur exemplified the agency's maturing development strategy. The city lay at the center of the region's postwar resurgence, with active local boosters and a close working relationship with the authority. "The Decatur Story" became synonymous with TVA's success, even as the city was eclipsed by Huntsville's remarkable growth. Despite losing Lilienthal to the Atomic Energy Commission in 1946, the TVA Board continued his program for the valley. Its successes and failures helped southerners embrace a new industrial and commercial base and a culture of professional economic development.

In 1947, TVA's Commerce Department held a meeting of the directors of state planning and development agencies at the site of TVA's Fontana Dam in North Carolina. The conference reasserted the authority's stand on cooperation with civic and business leaders as a central aspect of its postwar program. In his opening remarks, Director John Ferris listed the assumptions underlying TVA's relationship with the attendees. Building on TVA's experience fielding complaints of preferential treatment during the defense effort, he stressed that the initiative for development lay primarily with individual communities. As an agency for regional resource management, TVA supervised the growth of all valley businesses. For more localized attention, he noted, development groups representing individual communities, or several nearby communities, should use TVA's guidance to create an environment favorable to growth.[4] After delineating the authority's role, Ferris gave specific instructions, describing how a "coalition" of valley agencies could work independently, as well as in conjunction with each other and with TVA, to serve as a "technical partner" to communities interested in attracting industry. Ferris quoted an early TVA report on local development to instruct the conference's attendees: "The planning of the Valley's future must be the democratic labor of many agencies and many individuals, and final success is as much a matter of general initiative as of general consent."[5] In the years after the war, TVA fully committed itself to the industrial growth of the region and encouraged state and community groups to do the same.

Alabama's W. O. Dobbins was an active participant in TVA's development conferences, and his State Planning Board continued to cooperate with the authority to further the fortunes of North Alabama. In the years following World War II, the state agency, operating as the de facto postwar planning organization for Alabama, worked feverishly to preserve the advantages that defense investment introduced in the state.[6] In 1947, Dobbins's group produced a massive ten-volume study of state industrial resources entitled *Alabama's Industrial Opportunities*. Each volume catalogued manufacturers in a given industrial sector, from agricultural products to electrical machinery. The publication presented the wide variety of resources the state offered industrialists while embracing an optimistic vision of the state's future. In an introduction reprinted in each volume, Dobbins wrote, "The people of Alabama look forward to an improved economic and social order. The foundations of the future rest upon the development of industries which will utilize the resources, labor, and capital of the state."[7] In an accompanying summary, Dobbins boasted that his state had "many attractions for industrial leaders," particularly mineral resources; cheap labor, fuel, and electricity; and a strong regional market.[8]

TVA's influence on the state agency is readily apparent. Like fellow leaders of state industrial groups across the South, Dobbins created a rudimentary database of industrial information, available for any community interested in recruiting industry. Granted, the State Planning Board assumed a larger responsibility for interaction with prospective industries than the federal agency but, like TVA, Dobbins's group relied largely on local and regional development organizations to take the first step. Discussing the usage of TVA lands in North Alabama, Dobbins pledged to assist in the valley's growth by creating a general development plan, encouraging local and county planning boards to act, and providing them with technical assistance.[9]

After World War II, state-based development programs proliferated in the South. Many began in the 1930s, as the New Deal–era penchant for resource planning led to state-specific industrial directories like those issued by Dobbins's Board. By the 1940s, around one-third of southern states produced such directories, and many state agencies moved toward a more active industrial recruitment policy, particularly as competition increased.[10] In Tennessee, the state industrial board promoted economic opportunity by maintaining a list of facilities available in each community. In Mississippi, the BAWI program supported legislation allowing municipalities to issue bonds that could then be used to purchase land and buildings for incoming factories.[11] In South Carolina, the government advertised through chambers of commerce, provided tax exemptions to interested clients, and financed the expansion of community services.[12] Like many other state leaders, South Carolina's governor, Fritz Hollings, encouraged "safaris" to New York City in which political and business leaders "sold" the state to companies interested in relocating.[13] As in Alabama, southern governors became "salespersons for their state."[14] Across the region, development efforts matured into active, organized efforts to bring business to the Southeast.

Alabama followed many of its fellow southern states in building on prewar and wartime growth to create a more favorable environment for the recruitment of industries. In 1949, Alabama's state legislature passed the Cater Act, authorizing the formation of municipal industrial development boards and empowering them to acquire and furnish land, sell and lease property, and issue bonds. The 1951 Wallace Act (sponsored by future governor George C. Wallace) followed, allowing municipal governments to finance the construction and outfitting of facilities for incoming businesses, as well as any other improvements needed on manufacturing and commercial projects. As the two acts suggested, the state government took a more active role in industrial development across Alabama.[15] The state board changed its name to reflect the increased emphasis, becoming the State Planning *and Industrial* Board (though its actions changed little). After World War II, it focused on industrial recruitment as the most promising possibility for economic advancement. Through the 1950s, the group continued to collect information and coordinate work with local developers. The Cater and Wallace acts mobilized community groups and civic clubs to sponsor industrial parks and to prepare factory sites for potential industrial clients. In fact, the laws specifically encouraged facility and site planning in industrial recruitment. TVA's developers wholeheartedly embraced the practice, which allowed the agency to use its substantial regional land holdings as an incentive for economic growth.

By the 1950s, TVA's construction program was a distant memory, especially in North Alabama, where over a decade had passed since the authority finished work on the dam at Guntersville. From time to time, the agency renovated its facilities, even adding new coal-fired steam plants to dam sites in order to meet postwar residential and industrial demand, but for the most part, TVA no longer needed acres of waterfront property as insurance against an untamed flood or as potential dam sites. Instead, the land had become valuable as the setting for future industrial growth. Located alongside a main navigation artery, in a zone of cheap power and labor, TVA's waterfront sites proved the perfect asset for regional development. In 1955, the agency began assisting state and local groups in utilizing its available land. The Government Relations and Economics Staff released a report on industries situated alongside authority reservoirs. The bureau surveyed 107 waterfront establishments, including 56 manufacturing plants accounting for three-quarters of the $2.3 billion invested on the waterfront.[16] The report noted an additional 63 sites, consisting of 74,500 acres suitable for industrial use. Despite the number of locations, the "choice" spots were limited, so careful planning was needed to match industrial requirements with the specifics of each site. Leaders promised that "[many] waterfront communities will find it in their self-interest to reserve, plan, and develop much of their remaining waterfront land exclusively for industries."[17] In particular, TVA recommended pulp and paper mills, inorganic chemical plants, synthetic fiber manufacturers, and electro-metallurgical producers, all of which made use of the water supply for cooling and transportation.[18]

Such recommendations fit squarely within TVA leaders' conception of how land and water resources might best be utilized or "conserved." In considering the waters of the Tennessee, the open land on its shores, and the woodlands of the region, the agency's planners viewed resources to be sold, consumed, and transformed into products and income. This vision was well within the concept of utilitarian conservation that informed TVA's dam and reservoir plans: natural resources should be used intelligently for the improvement of the area in which they are located. Suggesting that the pines and hardwoods, located in such close conjunction with an ample source of water, might be perfect for new pulp and paper mills, was not so different, at least in TVA's eyes, than suggesting that a "tamed" and managed Tennessee River might power homes and businesses across the valley. The authority did recognize potential problems with such an approach—industries that utilized the river might introduce chemicals and other pollutants into the environment. Ferris warned that the industrial uses of the river had to be balanced with residential, recreational, and even agricultural needs; in his words, the key to planning for waterfront industrial sites was "a well-integrated program using the resources of all responsible agencies to achieve sound development."[19] Yet even this caveat assumed economic development as the central consideration for the use of resources. The adulteration of the river, a serious concern when selling industry on its benefits, was only dangerous if it precluded other uses of its waters.[20]

Planning for the use of land and water resources along the Tennessee necessitated the inclusion of state and local agencies already working with the authority for development. TVA's Aelred J. Gray met with the Alabama state board to discuss land along the shores of TVA reservoirs, valuable as both industrial sites and recreational areas. Gray admitted that the studies of waterfront industrial areas were still in need of "broad planning" and coordination, and that utilization depended largely on the activities of local groups. Dobbins was optimistic that, since "industrialization and urbanization of the South in general and north Alabama in particular was almost certain to occur . . . lands along the reservoir represented a major resource in this development."[21] Gray also held discussions with civic groups in Florence interested in attracting industries to locate along Wilson Reservoir, despite the "high land values" of lakefront lots. TVA convinced Lawrence and Colbert counties to create planning commissions to advertise their sites, and in Decatur, where city planners were already creating a land-use survey, agency officials helped zone industrial land on the river.[22]

By the early 1960s, the agency's land-use policies had matured. In 1961, Government Relations and Economics staffer Charles M. Stephenson called the availability of industrial sites one of the most "pressing problems of local economic development." Site preparation involved a number of "modern" development techniques, including community planning, zoning, subdivision control, highway access, taxation, local transportation, and parking regulation. TVA expected community groups to clear and grade land, provide access to highways and railroads, prepare utilities, and even push local legislation needed by potential businesses.[23] Stephenson recounted successful campaigns by groups that had used site preparation to attract companies. Huntsville Industrial Sites raised its funds from stockholders and built an industrial park with marked success. Guntersville's local development organization purchased a TVA tract alongside the reservoir, dividing the purchase into residential and industrial sites.[24]

Perhaps the greatest success of TVA's land-use policies came in Decatur. Much of the city's industrial growth during the war occurred along the Tennessee River, including Ingalls Shipbuilding, Alabama Flour Mill, and several oil companies. With the end of the war, however, Decatur faced the challenge of expanding its industrial sector, and city leaders looked to the agency for assistance. Ferris's Commerce Department recommended a careful preparation of new sites, extending road, water, and city utilities to waterfront land outside municipal boundaries. TVA even provided preliminary data on eight specific sites, with descriptions, needed improvements, and the estimated cost of getting each ready for industrial use.[25] Studies were informative, but officials wanted to go further to "insure the future availability of waterfront sites for the industrial growth of the Valley." Director J. Ed Campbell of TVA's Reservoir Properties Division suggested creating a checklist of available land, clearing titles, rescinding surplus declarations that made land harder to transfer to private control, and actively matching industries to particular sites.[26]

As a "regional" entity, TVA could only make recommendations. However, encouraged by the authority, state and local groups collected industry-specific data and interacted with interested businesses. Working in conjunction with the State Planning Board, Decatur's City Planning Commission delved even further into the possibilities of waterfront land. Their report recommended contacting manufacturers in need of riverside resources (such as lumber), as well as factories dependent on waterborne transportation (such as agricultural processers, lumber mills, and watercraft manufacturers). The group planned to expand road and rail connections, build conveyors down to the river, and dredge shallow areas, all in an attempt to expand the city's water frontage.[27] Soon, outsiders referred to Decatur's waterfront as Alabama's "Gold Coast," with investments totaling $65 million and companies employing over 5,000 local men and women.[28]

One 66-acre waterfront site was sold in conjunction with adjoining private land to the Worthington Air Conditioning Plant. The company was so sure of its purchase that it began improving the site two months before the public auction, a sign that city leaders worked carefully with potential clients to ensure an easy transition. Worthington officials praised the city: "[Our] selection of Decatur as a manufacturing site was an excellent choice. In fact, we do not know how we could have done better."[29] The chamber of commerce purchased several land tracts, financed by a combination of public subscription and mortgage loans. The city sold two "sizable" sites to industries, including a 357-acre tract to a manufacturing plant. On another plot, Decatur officials removed buildings, graded land, and held a public subscription drive, all in an effort to bring in an industrial client.[30] In addition to Worthington, postwar investment in the city included Monsanto's Chemstrand, Minnesota Mining and Manufacturing (better known as 3M), Wolverine Tube, Expanded Foam Products, Valley Steel Construction, and a number of smaller concerns.[31] Wolverine's leadership specifically cited the waterfront location as a prime consideration in its decision to move operations to Decatur, which overcame competition from 274 communities in eleven different states to win the plant.[32]

As these successes suggest, North Alabama had a number of draws for businesses interested in relocating: pleasant weather, ample resources, cheap non-unionized labor, and cooperative civic and state governments, promising lax regulations and financial incentives. Yet these benefits were prevalent in the emerging Sunbelt, and communities across the South highlighted such "attractions" in a scramble to bring in business. For the Tennessee Valley to best its competition, TVA knew that enthusiastic and organized local and regional developers would be essential. In offering its waterfront properties, TVA hoped to facilitate the work of development agencies, and the agency took advantage of local interest in cooperation whenever possible. In late 1948, Decatur's chief proponent of economic development, Barrett Shelton, pitched the idea of a regional development group to TVA Chairman Gordon Clapp, causing "a great deal of staff discussion." The authority encouraged Shelton, proposing financial cooperation with municipal and county power boards. Clapp suggested that Shelton contact "qualified professionals" versed in the needs of industries, yet objective enough to spread prosperity across North Alabama.[33] Clapp then provided an outline of a "North Alabama Development Council" designed for industrial recruitment. The council, later named North Alabama Associates (NAA), served as an intermediary between TVA, the State Planning Board, and civic and community development groups. Its members gathered and disseminated information on resources in Alabama's Tennessee Valley, encouraged further local organization, and contacted prospective companies.[34] TVA encouraged local power distributors to make a minimum investment in the organization, based on their industrial and commercial receipts; the more business a distributor had, the greater responsibility it had to help its neighbors grow. Founded with funds from the Huntsville and

Decatur electric systems, the NAA eventually expanded to include Florence, Sheffield, and several other valley cities.[35] Giving their approval to Shelton's organization, TVA officials recommended he put a "good man on the job."[36]

Shelton found that man in T. D. "Tom" Johnson, the former director of Alabama Power's Industrial Development Division and twenty-year veteran of industrial recruiting. After leaving the utility in 1943, Johnson took a job at the Vanity Fair Mills in Monroeville, Alabama, eventually traveling to Reading, Pennsylvania, before returning to Alabama in 1948 to get back into his "old line of work and first love."[37] At NAA, Johnson divided his time between research and promotion, carefully documenting the advantages of the valley, making personal contacts, and releasing publicity pieces. TVA enthusiastically supported his efforts; as Johnson noted after a visit with officials at headquarters: "I came away with the deep feeling that [the] Tennessee Valley Authority had a wealth of information that would be most useful in our work [and] that we would receive their wholehearted cooperation in our efforts to develop new industry in the Valley."[38] Johnson quickly found himself fighting to keep defense money flowing to North Alabama. He helped reactivate Huntsville's Redstone Arsenal and offered his services to congressmen John Sparkman, Lister Hill, and Robert E. "Bob" Jones, who hoped to locate a hydrogen bomb plant in the region. Sparkman related his confidence in Johnson to the Atomic Energy Commission's General Manager Carroll L. Wilson, calling the developer a "good man" who "will do a good job if called upon."[39]

One of Johnson's first projects in North Alabama proved to be his most difficult and, ultimately, his most disappointing. In 1949, TVA lobbied for the Air Force's proposed Air Engineering Development Center, listing four valley cities as possible locations: Huntsville and Florence in Alabama and Tullahoma and Smyrna in Tennessee. Huntsville was an early favorite. The city's then-defunct arsenal provided ample land already owned by the government, with ready-made facilities awaiting occupation. The Army had proven Huntsville's worth as a secure, well-powered city able to absorb the planned boom that accompanied defense investment. As one TVA report claimed, "Huntsville is an attractive and progressive community which demonstrated in World War II its ability to provide for a substantial increase in population." The government even had another facility nearby, Camp Forrest in Tullahoma (fifty miles from Huntsville and itself a candidate for the facility), which provided a test-flight space without removing "good agricultural land" from the regional farming economy.[40]

TVA prepared to expand the arsenal site to meet the center's needs, and planners assured the Air Force that, even though the surrounding land was in "one of the most productive areas in the Tennessee Valley," the two hundred families occupying tracts adjoining the arsenal reservation were not organized in "well-established communities."[41] Johnson and the NAA led the regional effort to convince the Air Force to locate in Alabama, cooperating with local civic groups, particularly the Huntsville Industrial Expansion Committee (HIEC), but with no success. Tullahoma proved a better fit, though the proximity to Huntsville allowed the city and surrounding communities to gain some jobs. In the end, the expansion of Redstone Arsenal, announced the same year, proved a much greater victory, bringing thousands of jobs and millions of dollars to the community and quickly outpacing Tullahoma; however, the loss left Johnson dejected.[42] He later recalled, "There was quite a let-down in Huntsville. Naturally, it was difficult for me to keep my chin up."[43] The failed bid for the Air Engineering Development Center provided quick on-the-job training for Johnson, as well as a clear example of the necessity of organizational cooperation in the pursuit of potential industries—government and private alike.

Even as Johnson and NAA lobbied for the AEDC, the group juggled a number of other projects that ultimately proved more profitable—a "silver lining in the clouds" that lingered from that first failure.[44] Johnson continued his work to lease the surplus Huntsville Arsenal properties, helping bring the Wernher von Braun team to Alabama. He traveled to New York City in May 1950 to talk with officials at Monsanto Chemicals, experiencing "disgust, heartaches, and joy without limit" when he located a subsidiary, Chemstrand, in Decatur.[45] Such trips became Johnson's main tool in attracting industry. As he told the Hartselle Chamber of Commerce, he visited a number of northern cities, well versed on the corporations looking to relocate and the names of important officials at each business. Johnson's efficiency allowed him to call on more businesses per trip, yielding "the maximum of results."[46] NAA worked to interest businesses in the old Dallas Manufacturing Company properties in Huntsville, one of a number of defunct textile mills in the valley. In 1951, Nashville's General Shoe Company leased the property.[47]

As Johnson noted, however, economic development work entailed more failure than success. NAA spent thousands of dollars attempting to bring the Air Reduction Company to Huntsville, hosting engineers and preparing detailed mineral studies. The company decided instead to locate near Paducah, Kentucky (another city booming on TVA power), alongside Goodrich Tires,

Pennsylvania Salt, and DuPont Chemicals. Johnson met with Owens-Corning to place a fiberglass plant in the valley, only to learn that the region's gas infrastructure could not accommodate the company's needs. Another great disappointment was Courtaulds, a textile manufacturer whose Lustre Fibres division wanted to locate in the South. Johnson worked with representatives of the corporation for two years, making numerous trips to New York to discuss the region's business opportunities. After weeks of heated negotiations, officials took an option on a tract on the Tennessee River just south of Huntsville. The company began planning for construction, paying engineers to study the site, but at "the 11th hour," Mobile produced a better counter-offer and the company located farther south.[48] Despite losses, Johnson remained optimistic about the valley's future: "Patience and persistence are essential elements if we are to be successful in industrial development. . . . When a prospect is lost we must be out after someone else, again making studies of a special nature to develop a new interest to the point of their location."[49]

Johnson's persistence certainly paid dividends. The revitalization of the arsenal alone cemented his legacy as an architect of the postwar boom. Monsanto, which opened with two hundred jobs in 1952, expanded dramatically throughout the 1950s and 1960s. Worthington Air Conditioners, growing rapidly in the postwar economy, planned to reach $5 billion in sales by 1958, promising to be "good neighbors" to the community. In 1959, 3M announced plans to construct a $4.5 million plant west of Decatur to produce the water- and stain-repellant chemical Scotchguard.[50] Many of the companies NAA attracted bought sites along the Tennessee River, utilizing the water for industrial processes, the river for navigation, and contracting with municipalities for large amounts of cheap TVA electricity. Johnson relied on the authority to conduct and distribute research on the valley's offerings and, in return, the developer brought in business to help the agency grow. TVA's relationship with NAA proved remarkably beneficial to both parties, and the agency looked to such regional organizations to carry out its vision of economic success.

Decatur's leadership, and particularly Barrett Shelton, grasped the potential inherent in TVA's program. He kept in constant contact with the authority, asked for information, petitioned for funds for city improvement, used the agency's influence to spur the Decatur Chamber of Commerce to action, and aided in the creation of a regional development organization. TVA's leaders encouraged Shelton's work; it provided a great advertisement for the agency's ability to use resource development and cheap power to revitalize the economy. In 1950, the city had a population of 19,974, with 7,500 residents gainfully employed. According to census records, male workers were predominantly operatives or craftsmen and foreman, positions associated with industrial employment.[51] By 1960, the numbers were even more promising for TVA's program. As the population approached 30,000, the city boasted 10,700 workers, still dominated by craftsmen, operatives, managers, and professionals.[52] Whereas in 1950 surrounding Morgan County still boasted a plurality of farmers and farm laborers, in 1960 manufacturing outpaced agriculture in the county by 6,000 to 1,800 workers, respectively.[53]

In late 1949, Shelton was invited to speak before the United Nations Scientific Conference on the Conservation and Utilization of Resources on behalf of TVA's ongoing work. In a speech entitled "The Decatur Story," he praised the authority for its assistance in transforming Decatur "from nothin' to somethin'" in their fifteen-year partnership. He told his audience how the Depression doomed the city's one major industry, a railroad shop, and how reliance on cotton relegated the city to poverty. Soon, however, TVA encouraged the city to rid itself of the "old order" and "build toward a diversified agriculture and a diversified industry." At the end of the 1940s, the valley boasted eighty-seven manufacturers (up twenty-six in the past eight years) with a combined payroll of $12.6 million. For Shelton, the greatest change was the new mindset of the people of his city, who had become more confident and who now possessed a better "spirit" that would "go far" in attracting more industries.[54] As he later wrote in a guest editorial for the *Huntsville Times,* "We are no longer afraid. We are confident. We know what we can do." Shelton praised TVA for "a vigorous and intelligent effort," but the editor equally credited the region's population: "TVA is not a magic wand. TVA would be helpless to activate community progress without the brains and energies of a free people."[55] He ended on a note of confidence in the region's economic future: "[Our] people are constantly at work on new plans to perfect a soundly begun economic system so that our people might have opportunities to earn better things of life."[56]

Like many southern communities eager to participate in the Sunbelt boom, those in the valley boasted a number of attractive prospects for potential business. TVA's work on the Tennessee made the river navigable and accessible, ensuring that businesses could ship goods easily and take water for industrial purposes, and cheap, dependable hydroelectricity powered homes and businesses alike. The population, so recently marginal farmers, was willing to take low-skilled wage work—as Morgan County's numbers showed, more and more were leaving the land for jobs in industry. The state's anti-union environment meant a relatively captive workforce. Alabama, like its neighbors, proved extremely accommodating to incoming businesses, ready to extend tax breaks, help with financing, and even prepare sites for construction. Across the South, such draws had become commonplace, so much so that active recruitment on behalf of a town or community could make the difference between economic growth and stagnation. Here, the work of people like Shelton and Johnson, especially when done in conjunction with a like-minded TVA, proved essential. Civic leaders across the region ensured that business considered the valley for relocating and starting companies. Their efforts resulted in a surge of development that reshaped the region's economy and brought the Tennessee Valley into the Sunbelt South.

Focusing so much of their attention on industrial development, civic leaders left little time or energy to consider the consequences of such rapid growth. When municipalities worked with TVA or state agencies to extend public utilities or city services, they did so primarily to attract industry. Yet in the years after the war effort, a few scholars and professionals began to consider the effects of industrial growth in the South. Some who studied economic modernization criticized the tax exemptions and promotional campaigns that induced companies to relocate to the South. Development experts Calvin Hoover and B. U. Ratchford suggested that agencies and organizations act "intelligently" to bring in business while insuring healthy growth by fostering "a sound labor code," resource management, "a sound, fair tax system, and "more technical training and research."[57] In retrospect, Hoover and Ratchford were right to question the nature of southern development strategies. States and communities competed to offer the most attractive environment for industrial growth, cutting corporate taxes, ignoring destructive environmental practices, and privileging the needs of business management over the welfare of low-paid, non-unionized workers.[58] For southern civic leaders and their colleagues in the federal government, however, the benefits of growth outweighed the costs. In a presentation at the Southern Economic Association in 1953, TVA's Stefan Robock best enunciated the agency's point of view: "Further economic progress for the Southeast depends largely upon the continuation of rapid industrialization trends of the past."[59]

For the most part, the wartime emergency gave TVA and its regional groups little time for introspection. But, even as Robock and TVA continued the agency's program of "rapid industrialization," the authority began preliminary investigations into the stresses of growth. In 1953, TVA released the *Childersburg Pilot Study*, an "exploratory" examination of Childersburg, Alabama, thirty miles southeast of Birmingham. Childersburg sat well outside TVA's boundaries, but agency officials saw a perfect opportunity to investigate the long-term consequences of industrialization for a small, southern community. Conducted in conjunction with an eleven-person interdisciplinary committee from Auburn University, the study sought to understand the city's defense boom and its consequent struggle to cope with demobilization.

Prewar Childersburg was a small farming and textile town without paved streets, streetlights, or sufficient water or power. In January 1941, the government built a smokeless powder plant in the city which, after a number of additions, employed 25,000 men and women, 6,500 of whom moved to the city for work. The city struggled to house the workers and their families, establishing boarding houses, government barracks, and trailer parks on every available lot. Traffic was horrendous (pedestrians had to wait up to an hour just to cross downtown streets), and the city's muddy roads became treacherous, leading to snarls. City leaders were overwhelmed to the point of inactivity. Instead of working to adapt their community to the bustle of industrial life, the leadership decided "it is only temporary and can't last, so let's pitch in and make money while we can; there's always time for other things later."[60]

When conditions began to affect the workforce, government officials tried to alleviate the problems, expanding city services and building roads, homes, hospitals, and schools, but Childersburg's leadership provided little assistance. In fact, when stress forced the mayor to resign, the office remained unoccupied for two years with no one willing to take the job.[61] The end of the war exacerbated the situation. Only 300 of the original 25,000 workers were retained at the plant, and the population of the city dropped from 9,000 to less than 6,000 almost overnight. The sudden removal of income spurred leaders into cautious action, and in cooperation with Alabama Power President Tom Martin, Childersburg began planning for the future of the vacant plant. North American Rayon Company and a northern newsprint company decided to locate in the city in the early 1950s, thanks to local financing and site preparation, but the damage had been done. When the newsprint company advertised 856 openings, 40,000 job seekers sent applications. Worse, only 83 of the openings were for skilled positions, and just 14 Childersburg residents were given jobs in the company's administration. Most of the skilled workforce in the city came from outside Alabama.[62]

The influx of new business did little to meet immediate needs. In order to attract the two companies, Childersburg authorized a ten-year tax concession, ensuring that none of the financial benefits of economic growth trickled down to the ailing school system or any other municipal service. Housing built during the war was "semi-permanent" and deteriorating, creating both a surplus of houses and a lack of suitable living quarters, especially for families. Schools continued to face overcrowding, with classes held in auditoriums, halls, and even in school buses. Demand for hospitals, leisure activities, and churches outpaced the city's offerings.[63] Sociologists determined that conditions in the boom town adversely affected the children of workers attracted by the plant.[64] The Childersburg study provided a warning for any leader hoping to encourage industrial growth. The defense boom and bust greatly affected the city and surrounding country, in ways that were not always readily apparent, and in ways that provided no easy solution.

TVA's immediate response to the Childersburg report was to call for more regional planning, paying particular attention to the "environment" (broadly defined) of industrial communities. In late 1953, TVA officials and their Auburn University colleagues held the first of a series of meetings with Alabama Chamber of Commerce and Alabama Power leaders to discuss the problems of rapid industrialization. At first, state and utility officials failed to understand the real purpose of the meeting: "There was . . . a tendency on the part of the representatives from the Chamber of Commerce and Alabama Power and Light to push the project in the direction of industrial promotion."[65] TVA's representatives, including Stefan Robock, stressed larger considerations: "It is not enough for a community to attract industry, it must hold it and keep others coming. It must prepare for expansion, be ready to absorb the people and solve the associated problems." Here was the central purpose of the Childersburg study; however, some leaders refused to learn the lesson. Alabama Power Vice-President Cooper Green continued to call for industrial recruitment, telling the assembly, "We must try to sell industry on Alabama." Others began to get the message; one attendee replied, "The goal is what will we do [*sic*] if industry comes to our community."[66] In the end, TVA failed to convince the businessmen of the need for integrative studies to solve community problems, but Robock did note that the pilot study and the cooperation between TVA and Auburn began to break down barriers.[67] It also highlighted the differences between state business leaders, pushing for development, and TVA, which had begun to consider some of the consequences of such growth.

The Childersburg study and the Auburn conferences evidenced a growing realization among some in TVA that true economic development required more than simply encouraging local communities to attract industries. Cities and counties only benefited from the jobs and paychecks of a company if the surrounding community adequately prepared for the consequences of economic growth. Thus, the agency was forced to address an issue its founders had debated in the years before World War II. Both A. E. Morgan and, to an extent, Franklin Roosevelt argued for a social revolution to accompany the economic revival of the Tennessee Valley. They called for an end to the "rugged individualism" that had hampered communal cooperation and had perpetuated the failing cotton monoculture. By the 1950s, southerners had seemingly swapped one economic problem for another. In an attempt to create employment and incomes, TVA's leaders again fostered single-minded economic growth, albeit a kinder, gentler program that brought accompanying benefits of navigation, flood control, agricultural education, electrification, and resource planning. Yet in encouraging industrialization, they failed to bring real community development that would extend the benefits of prosperity to all inhabitants, and the hurried nature of the defense crisis exacerbated the situation.

In the 1950s and 1960s, TVA struggled to encourage economic growth while managing the region's resources as intelligently as possible. The complicated approach that emerged from this mindset was best exemplified by the agency's attempt to promote recreation. In his address asking Congress to pass the TVA Act of 1933, Roosevelt stressed the importance of local cooperation in the development of recreation areas.[68] In fact, recreation played a key role in the New Deal. Civilian Conservation Corps workers built lodges, pavilions, and other amenities at national and state parks across the country. Both the Public Works Administration and the Civil Works Administration included maintenance programs for park facilities. Roosevelt saw recreation as a potentially valuable means of relieving stress and buttressing American confidence, not to mention a source of employment for millions out of work. Within the Tennessee Valley Authority, recreation largely took a back seat in the 1930s to dam construction, relief employment, and power expansion. In 1940, the president noticed as much when he addressed the growing opinion that TVA had been created solely to produce electricity. In a message to Congress, he warned, "It is coming to be realized more and more that in the improvement of our American civilization we cannot stop at hospitals and schools any more than we can confine ourselves to strictly economic subjects. Recreation in its broad sense is a definite factor in the improvement of the bodies and minds of our future citizens."[69]

Dam construction provided a ready-made resource for recreational development in North Alabama. By 1940, the Tennessee River had been tamed, creating Pickwick, Wilson, Wheeler, and Guntersville reservoirs in North Alabama. As Regional Planning Studies Director E. S. Draper noted, the "viciously swirling" Tennessee was replaced by placid, scenic lakes surrounded by government-owned land. The reservoirs boasted 600,000 acres of water, waterside parks and boat docks, and nearly all included plans for further development, including cabins, stables for horseback riding, hiking trails, and educational facilities.[70] With the end of World War II, the country's newfound wealth and leisure time boosted opportunities for recreation. By 1950, over $7 million in personal watercraft plied the waters of TVA lakes, and summer cottages dotted reservoir shorelines. The authority encouraged such growth, cleaning up access areas on the banks of the river, selling camp and lodge sites, encouraging boat purchases, and regulating construction on its waterfront tracts in an attempt to balance financial gain and natural beauty.[71]

In addition to boating, hiking, picnicking, and horseback riding, TVA encouraged hunting and fishing on the acres of public land surrounding the reservoirs. For many in North Alabama, such activities were an important part of rural life, but the authority supported recreational wildlife management as a source of tourism revenue.[72] Encouraged by the agency, in 1938 Roosevelt set aside 41,000 acres of TVA land in Limestone, Madison, and Morgan counties alongside Wheeler Reservoir for the Wheeler Wildlife Refuge, protecting the waterfowl that migrated annually between the Gulf of Mexico and the Great Lakes.[73] As the steward of waterfront land, TVA jealously protected the right of the public to hunt and fish along the shore. When a group of locals purchased land on Wheeler Reservoir at auction and attempted to section the tract into private lots with cabins, TVA forced the businessmen to remove the buildings. They complained, but TVA General Manager George F. Gant held the line, citing the agency's "minimum rights" to ensure public use. The tract was one of the few access points to the reservoir and a popular spot for hunting and fishing, and the public agency determined to protect its recreational advantages.[74]

As municipalities and counties realized the value of recreational planning, many looked to TVA for help. In 1952, for instance, Huntsville's City Planning Commission asked the authority to help create a more orderly plan for the city's recreational facilities. Compared to Decatur, Florence, or Guntersville, Huntsville's access to the river was fairly limited, but TVA owned land away from the river as well, and the agency's holdings provided a base for the growing city's leisure needs. Municipal leaders noted TVA's willingness to set aside land and facilities for public use, including Little Mountain State Park at Guntersville and Joe Wheeler State Park west of Athens. Huntsville's parks were woefully inadequate, particularly city playgrounds, and planners hoped that the government agency would help create a recreational space that might allow the city to continue its expansion. The group gave specific acreage needs (323.97 for whites, 102.93 for blacks) and even noted the areas where each park could be placed.[75] As with industrial recruitment, cities found TVA a valuable ally in the desire for further recreational development.

More than any other city, Guntersville, Alabama, took advantage of its new lakeside location to boost the local economy. The city exploited the "new resource base," hosting an annual motorboat race with an attendance that regularly exceeded 50,000 per year. E. S. Draper suggested that "Waters of the lake, spouting outboard motors, cruisers, and yachts, where bottom lands formerly were devoted to corn, may be the harbinger of a new day."[76] *Huntsville Times* reporter Eleanor Hutchens predicted that Guntersville's main source of income would switch from agriculture to "play."[77]

As with industrial development, a desire for further recreational investment created difficult choices. As Guntersville grew, the city needed updated sewage disposal plants, partly to decrease the amount of pollution released into the river (and thus into the increasingly popular reservoir). When the city asked TVA to sell land along the reservoir for one dollar as a means of assistance, the agency refused. Chairman Herbert Vogel sympathized with the city's plight, but noted the extent to which property values along the river had risen—from $57 per acre when TVA purchased the land for the reservoir to over $1,100 per acre for lakeside plots. In 1956, Vogel told Mayor T. E. Martin that because his city had become "a highly desirable recreational and industrial community . . . such desirable and expensive properties" could not be sold for such paltry rates, even for the expansion of city services.[78] While tourism made Guntersville relatively wealthy, the rise in property values complicated community development.

In some cases, the authority found itself forced to choose between recreation and the use of waterfront property for industrial purposes. In such cases, the agency turned to industry, with its greater potential for income creation and economic diversification. In 1967, for instance, Huntsville's civic development group wanted to add acreage in the Wheeler Wildlife Refuge to a specially zoned industrial park. TVA accommodated the businessmen, drawing the ire of regional conservationists like L. C. Bartmess, a member of the North Alabama Conservation League. Bartmess complained to Congressman Bob Jones that the encroachments for "industrial purposes" compromised the integrity of the refuge, threatening its existence and the benefits it brought to the region. He made the choice clear: "We cannot emphasize too strongly our interest and desire for business and industrial development along the river, but believe this can well be done without destroying one of our greatest natural assets." TVA Chairman Aubrey Wagner remained unconvinced. He responded to Jones that the "relatively narrow" strip of the refuge sold to Huntsville had almost no effect on the integrity of the preserve. Instead, he praised the work of the city's leadership, who were "working on a plan to diversify and strengthen the economy" and who would use the land by "promoting additional industrial development."[79] The agency valued recreation, but the promise of industrial growth outweighed the needs of outdoor enthusiasts.

By the 1960s, TVA could count recreation among its more successful programs for the economic growth of the valley. Reservoirs covered nearly half a million acres and created 10,000 miles of new shoreline. In 1960 alone, over forty-two million visitors came to TVA lakes to boat, fish, hike, hunt, and camp. The reservoirs created waterborne activities that had been rare in the region; before TVA, the Tennessee River was much too narrow, fast-moving, and shallow to accommodate the millions of people who now toured the region. The authority preserved public use of the river, working closely with state, local, and even private groups operating the numerous parks, boat ramps, cabins, lodges, and marinas along the Tennessee. The statistics spoke to the program's success. Fishing increased fifty-fold on valley reservoirs by 1960. Recreational use also increased steadily after World War II, topping ten million visits in 1960.[80] For TVA planners, recreation was more than just resource planning. As Guntersville's success showed, recreational development created real economic benefits for towns located along or near reservoirs. The agency encouraged locals to promote tourism in their areas, setting aside land and cooperating with state and local agencies to found refuges, regulate access, and protect the public's right to "play" on the river. In a nation with free time and even freer finances, the valley's natural resources provided the perfect opportunity for economic growth, as long as communities worked to realize it.

By the mid-1960s, TVA's program for economic revitalization had matured and expanded well beyond the bounds of its original New Deal manifestation. In the wake of the defense effort, the authority focused the bulk of its time and energy on economic development, particularly the facilitation of local and regional organizations tasked to attract industry to the Tennessee Valley. In some regards, this program continued a tradition older than TVA, begun in the years following World War I as businessmen and municipal leaders in the Tri-Cities sought to encourage growth as federal investment at Muscle Shoals stalled. Still, the agency brought a new enthusiasm to the effort. Officials worked closely with area-wide groups such as the North Alabama Associates and local chambers of commerce, particularly Decatur's, using diverse methods from data collection to planning assistance and site procurement in order to ensure the region's place as a center for public and private investment. As an agent of industrialization, the authority finally abandoned resource conservation and regional planning for economic development.

As this transformation occurred, TVA faced a series of challenges from those in and out of power, concerned with the agency's new direction and methodology. During the war, TVA weathered criticism from the likes of Senator Kenneth McKellar, thanks to popular support from the valley and the agency's integral role in powering defense industries. With the end of the wartime emergency, though, came a more serious threat. As the postwar TVA powered incoming industries and a booming population of homeowners, it experienced newfound hostility in Congress from a resurgent Republican Party, and the election of Dwight D. Eisenhower in 1952 further concerned the agency's leadership. Unsure of the president's attitude toward the aging New Deal program, TVA fought to maintain its boundaries, particularly during the Dixon-Yates controversy of 1954. Fiscal conservatives were not the agency's only challenge in the postwar years. As African Americans battled the southern status quo, TVA's acquiescence in segregation also faced opposition. Even its much vaunted labor policy failed to contain worker discontent. Finally, the resource-driven authority found itself confronting the environmental effects of its economic policies. The political and social challenges of the 1950s marked TVA's program for economic growth as indelibly as its successes.

In fact, the TVA that emerged from the political and social challenges of the 1950s and 1960s embodied the transformation of the valley itself. The authority defended its race and labor policies, afraid to alienate southern boosters and industrialists interested in regional investment. Faced with evidence of environmental pollution, a direct challenge to the agency's stated purpose of conserving natural resources, TVA's leaders defended the businesses that populated the valley, superficially correcting the most grievous problems while protecting further investment. Yet just as social challenges helped delineate the authority's role in southern life, political antagonism gave ultimate expression to its economic transformation. Hounded by opponents loathe to add funds or responsibility to a powerful federal agency, authority leaders turned to privatization, hoping to remove their programs from the threat of political action or budget cuts. Supported by valley leaders, TVA officials demanded and won the right to finance their agency, ensuring that each industry and customer attracted to the region contributed to the authority's continued growth. By the mid-1960s, the transition away from New Deal idealism was complete. TVA became an agent of regional development, encouraging residents to organize, to prepare their communities for growth, and to attract the businesses that made that growth possible.

Over the course of the 1950s and 1960s, Robert E. Jones became the most strident of the authority's defenders in Congress. Born in Jackson County in the northeast corner of Alabama, Jones served as a county judge in Scottsboro before joining the Navy during World War II. In 1946, Jones ran in a special primary for the congressional seat of John Sparkman, who succeeded John H. Bankhead Jr. in the Senate. Throughout the campaign, the judge stressed two issues that would characterize his political career: agricultural assistance and "full support" for TVA.[81] Jones defeated eleven challengers to claim the seat and, in his first major vote, Jones helped appoint Gordon Clapp chair of the TVA Board of Directors. When Tennessee's Kenneth McKellar criticized the agency, Jones rose to its defense, inviting Republican congressmen to North Alabama to see "the real story of the Valley Authority . . . which demonstrated that a heretofore economically depressed area, when given the means, could successfully lift itself by its own bootstraps."[82] He also protected TVA from cuts in the agency's appropriations, claiming that Republican cost-cutting measures "[go] against common sense and [respond] to the wishes of one of the most greedy [*sic*] and ambitious lobbies this Congress has ever seen."[83] For his defense of the authority, he earned a telling nickname, "Mr. TVA."[84]

In retrospect, Jones's defense of the agency came at a crucial point in the authority's transformation—as fellow Congressman Carl Elliott claimed,

Jones's efforts were "like an arm in the dike against the angry waters threatening TVA."[85] For Jones, TVA became a point of pride, a government program benefiting his state and community. Even as the agency abandoned its New Deal roots, Jones continued to see the authority and farm relief as essential to continued prosperity. In addition to his work for TVA, he secured Federal Housing Authority funds for farm buildings, fought to raise cotton quotas, and supported waterways development that improved navigation in the state—Jones was instrumental in providing legislation for the creation of the Tennessee-Tombigbee Waterway, connecting the Tennessee River to the Tombigbee and the Gulf of Mexico. In every action he took, Jones hoped to maintain economic growth in the region, whether that growth came from industry, agriculture, or other federal investments.

As the authority turned to economic development, it faced charges of favoritism, misappropriation, and disregard for farmers. Its congressional defenders, particularly Jones, Sparkman, and Hill, ceaselessly defended the changing program. TVA's congressional supporters expected a Republican attack on the New Deal agency, but more disturbing than Republican opposition was the acquiescence of fellow Democrats in attempts to limit TVA's funds. Massachusetts's John F. Kennedy Jr. gave his support to reduced appropriations, arguing that the continued financing of the authority would drive industries from Massachusetts to the Tennessee Valley in search of cheap power. Jones defended private interests locating in the valley: "I assume that the gentleman will agree that an important freedom in our economy is the freedom of management to locate where it will—to consider the availability of raw materials, of labor, of markets, in selecting the place it will live." Instead of criticizing the textile and shoe manufacturers, Jones suggested, Kennedy needed to curtail the private power companies whose high rates had driven away his region's industry.[86] Kennedy's argument was not new. In fact, as early as the 1880s, when southerners began building cotton mills to process the region's crops, New Englanders feared that southern economic growth came at their expense. Given the agency's need for congressional support, however, Kennedy's re-airing of the criticisms did not inspire confidence among those hoping to see the valley continue its progress.[87]

Yet the greatest threat to TVA's financial health seemed to be the fiscal conservatism and small-government ideology of President Dwight D. Eisenhower. In December 1952, the *Huntsville Times* suggested that the incoming Republican administration showed a "lack of enthusiasm" for the agency and quoted four unnamed Democratic congressmen who feared that Eisenhower would "choke [TVA] to death."[88] For his part, Eisenhower remained circumspect on the future of the agency. He praised it for its work in the valley, including the creation of new industries, the conservation of natural resources, the promotion of national defense, and flood control. He tried to ease concerns: "Certainly there would be no disposition on my part to impair the effective working out of TVA." Yet Eisenhower had no desire to see the agency grow even larger. He warned that TVA was not a "rigid pattern" for development elsewhere, and he used the authority as an example of "creeping socialism," implying, among other things, a stealthy attempt on the part of TVA leaders to expand their power at the expense of private enterprise.[89] He also echoed the fears of New England congressmen, who provided "reliable information" that the authority was "growing huge on federal taxes and producing cheap, government-subsidized power drawing industry away from these other states and creating unemployment in their industrial towns."[90] Eisenhower refused to acquiesce in the expansion of a government monopoly on power, and he recommended support of local power sources, including the creation of independent public power plants, built by county cooperatives, cities, and even states.[91]

In October 1953, Tennessee Governor Frank Clement approached President Eisenhower, asking for his support for appropriations to TVA for construction of a new steam plant at Fulton, Tennessee. Much of the increased demand in the area came from defense projects, particularly the Atomic Energy Commission (AEC) plant at Paducah, but Eisenhower saw the situation in Western Tennessee as the perfect chance to cap TVA's growth. He told Clement that Memphis, a growing urban area with booming power demands, should build its own plant, even though the action would break an existing contract for TVA power. Chairman Gordon Clapp warned Eisenhower that no private utility wanted to assume the risks of financing a plant to provide power for the uncertain needs of defense work, but the president ordered the Bureau of the Budget and the AEC to work together to find an alternative to increasing the "burden" on the federal government (i.e., funding TVA's expansion).[92] Encouraged by the president's stance, two private power companies offered their services: Middle South Utilities, chaired by Edgar H. Dixon, and Southern Company, headed by Eugene Yates. Dixon and Yates formed the Mississippi Valley Generating Company and began negotiations on a contract for construction and operation of a generation plant across the Mississippi River from Memphis in Arkansas. The new company, usually referred to as "Dixon-Yates," agreed to construct a power line with TVA, which would purchase the power and distribute it to the defense plant at Paducah. The final agreement gave Dixon-Yates insurance against the vagaries of federal funding by forcing TVA to buy a set amount of power regardless of need. The Dixon-Yates contract placed the "political football" of power squarely in the hands of the Republican administration.[93]

Alabama's congressional delegation rose to TVA's defense. Bob Jones asked Attorney General Herbert Brownell Jr. to investigate the legality of the contract.[94] Lister Hill reassured his constituents that he was doing all he could to stop the Eisenhower administration in its attempt to "destroy TVA and our public power policy."[95] Hill, in particular, played a major role in combating the proposed contract. The Alabama senator began a close scrutiny of the administration's role in promoting the Dixon-Yates contract and found that a temporary consultant to the Bureau of the Budget named Adolphe Wenzell was, at the time, also employed by the First Boston Corporation, the project's financier. Eisenhower charged that the Wenzell connection was a "regrettable error" and a "diversion from the main issue," but the evidence seemed to support claims that Republicans were conducting an underhanded battle to halt TVA's progress.[96] The Dixon-Yates contract also spurred local action. A group of concerned residents formed the "Citizens for TVA, Incorporated," a nonprofit organization designed to "maintain a strong and effective TVA" and to create a central organizing body for the defense of the agency. John Sparkman praised President George Dempster and the "Citizens" for their "outstanding and productive" work, and encouraged a publicity campaign to boost morale.[97]

Such local support for the agency was crucial to its campaign against Dixon-Yates. The TVA Board did little to contest Eisenhower's claims, afraid that any outburst would result in retaliation by the administration. These fears were realized later that year, when Chairman Gordon Clapp's seat on the board expired. Clapp had been with the authority from 1933, ascending from director of personnel to general manager and finally to the chairmanship when David Lilienthal resigned to join the AEC. Eisenhower refused to renominate Clapp and instead replaced him with Brigadier General Herbert D. Vogel, recently retired from the Army Corps of Engineers. Eisenhower hoped that Vogel would ease the passage of Dixon-Yates by forcing TVA's cooperation. The president's plan worked; TVA agreed to accept the energy produced at the

Dixon-Yates plant, and the private utility held a celebration with an elaborate groundbreaking ceremony and a victory parade.[98]

The party proved hasty. Hill's revelation of the intrigue between the Bureau of the Budget and Dixon-Yates caused many to take a second look at the government contract, including Memphis's municipal leadership. When TVA's contract with Memphis expired in 1955, city officials decided not to renew the agreement, opting instead to build an independent municipal electric plant. Without the growing urban area on its network, TVA was able to meet AEC demand. The yet-to-be-built Dixon-Yates plant was no longer needed, and the White House cancelled the contract.[99] Neither party could claim a real victory, though both tried. Eisenhower noted that, in building an independent plant, Memphis followed his prescription for allowing natural resource development to occur at the local level, and with local initiative. Edgar Dixon and Eugene Yates sued the federal government for the cancelled contract and eventually won $1.9 million in damages, a decision Eisenhower felt "right." He concluded that the "government has the power to help human beings in need. It has also the responsibility to stimulate people to exercise initiative on their own behalf."[100] In his eyes, at least, Dixon-Yates inspired Memphis to do just that.

Ironically, TVA had the same goal; however, the president's actions had roused the valley to action and earned the ire of Alabama's delegation and their colleagues, who were determined to protect the agency's role in regional development. "Mr. TVA" perhaps best enunciated the anger at Eisenhower's actions. Jones called the controversy "a story of cunning speculators with a bold plan to obtain a 'fast buck' while acting in total disregard for the public interest."[101] The scandal, coming as it did on the heels of congressional attempts to limit the agency's appropriations, demonstrated the changing climate for federal funding. The authority could no longer assume that the government would provide for increasing demand. As the valley used more and more electricity, domestically and industrially, TVA had to find a new way to meet its needs. By the mid-1950s, its legislative supporters were planning for a future in which TVA would have the ability to fund itself.

A hostile administration was not the authority's only concern in the postwar years. As the agency's leadership defended its financial existence, the board also faced challenges to established policies that seemed increasingly out-of-date in the changing national climate. Long concerned about the intelligent use of resources, growing environmental concerns forced the authority to reconsider its stance on pollution, particularly in the recreational waters that had become an important part of its economic development program. TVA also faced challenges to its labor policies. A. E. Morgan had praised the forward-looking nature of TVA's agreement with labor unions, encouraging cooperation, collective bargaining, and negotiated arbitration, and well into the 1940s, the lack of overt labor strife seemed to prove him right. In the 1950s, however, workers began to push for greater autonomy, forcing TVA to reconsider its union policy. Finally, the agency's approach to racial inclusion proved inadequate when judged beside the rising tide of civil rights protest across the country. Up to the 1940s, TVA had encouraged proportional employment in its offices and facilities, but had largely held to the color line. As African Americans began challenging Jim Crow in earnest, TVA's policies failed to stand up to scrutiny, and the agency's leaders defended their programs even as they sought to maintain racial stability across the region.

TVA's response to the social challenges of the 1950s and 1960s is important in situating the agency in the drive for economic development that marked the Sunbelt boom. As civic leaders, state governments, and federal agents looked to recruit industry to the South, they catered to incoming businesses. This not only meant preparing sites and providing tax increases, it also meant highlighting the South's anti-union policies and general lack of environmental regulation. For TVA, such practices seemingly ran averse to its mission. The agency was tasked with ensuring the intelligent conservation of the region's resources, but allowing a business unregulated access to the ecosystem might undermine TVA's work. Likewise, promising an open shop to incoming industries directly opposed the authority's efforts to ensure organization on its own projects, the labor "yardstick" it hoped to encourage in the region. Yet, by the 1950s, TVA found itself forced to balance its social prerogative with its efforts to attract business. And, just as the agency worked to facilitate civic participation in development and insulate itself from opposition at the federal level, TVA, like other booster organizations in the Sunbelt, privileged economic growth.

For an agency that demanded such a drastic physical change of the southern landscape, TVA evoked surprisingly little environmental concern among residents through World War II. This was partly due to the nature of the agency's initial approach to development, which introduced forestry, erosion protection, and resource protection to the region, addressing the most egregious environmental problems of the Depression-era South. Residents were also wary to challenge the program bringing jobs and income to their communities.

The Depression and the wartime emergency provided little opportunity for criticism from those benefiting from TVA's actions. By 1945, however, the end of the defense effort combined with a growing concern for the consequences of industrial development to draw attention to pollution in the area. That year, TVA's Health and Safety Department released a detailed study of pollution in the Tennessee River system, thanks in part to pressure from state health departments. In addition to untreated sewage from municipalities, the valley's streams and rivers also carried waste from pulp and paper mills, textile mills, cellulose plants, and wartime metals and chemicals industries; studies showed pollution numbers nearly double prewar levels.[102] When industries began to recover during the postwar years, the agency's engineers posited that "an increase [in pollution] will result with the unfolding of anticipated expansion."[103] In a nod to the increasing importance of recreation in the authority's program for economic development, researchers concluded that pollution would have its largest impact on tourism on the region's lakes. Boating might continue to prosper "if the aesthetic requirements can be overlooked," but swimming and fishing would be seriously hampered by contaminated water, limiting broad-range recreation facilities.[104] Pollution had become both a consequence of economic progress and a serious impediment to continued growth.

By the early 1950s, little had been done to solve the growing problem. In 1953, the *Huntsville Times* reported that pollution in the state's section of the Tennessee River increased 35 percent from 1941 with little action from Alabama's state or city governments. No Alabama cities topped the list of the valley's biggest problem areas (all were in Tennessee, Virginia, and North Carolina), but the region faced a worsening problem. One resident wrote Bob Jones, complaining that the TVA facility at Muscle Shoals "turned a lot of phosphorous loose into the Tenn. River killing thousands of pounds of fish." Soon afterwards, the agency's fertilizer plant "loosed another chemical into the river that has come through our water system into our homes which has a bad odor and is making people sick." Jones contacted the agency, which made a careful investigation into the incidents. General Manager John Oliver admitted that the first release occurred when "elemental phosphorous originating from an undetected source in the TVA chemical plant" created a "large" fish kill in the upper end of Pickwick Lake. The second incident came from a release of diphenyl oxide, or "Dowtherm," from the Phosphate Development Works at Muscle Shoals, operated by the Army since World War II. Oliver promised that TVA would work closely with the Army to prevent further spillage, but refused to accept responsibility for the pollution or issue a rebuke to the Army, which had become an important partner in the region's growth.[105]

As late as 1967, pollution remained a concern for residents. In a talk with the Decatur Kiwanis Club, Bob Jones admitted as much, linking concern for the region's natural resources with its economic future. He asked assembled community leaders to join him in "safeguarding the water quality of our fine lakes and streams as we successfully court industrial expansion, develop our towns and cities, and make greater and greater demands on our existing water supply."[106] He praised action by the government, the public, and even some industries to call attention to the importance of environmental awareness, but noted that the Tennessee Valley faced an impending crisis. With industry "knock[ing] on our door" and Americans coming to the region to "boat and fish and to build homes on the lakeshores," the valley needed a "well-ordered and closely supervised" partnership between the public and industry to maintain the region's natural health.[107] He concluded with an appeal to TVA to become a "watchdog," cleaning the region's waters and devising a plan to help both the public and industry prepare for conservation.[108] Jones's concerns signified just how little TVA had done to combat pollution. Without a more comprehensive plan for environmental protection, the agency would soon face a serious problem that might limit or even negate economic development.

Unlike comprehensive pollution control, labor held an important place in TVA's vision. By the end of World War II, the labor "yardstick" set up by A. E. Morgan and David Lilienthal seemed successful; TVA experienced no major work stoppages, and a 1948 report by the University of Chicago's Committee on Human Relations in Industry praised the agency's policies as proof that "patient and clear-sighted men can construct the sort of human relations structure they believe in."[109] Researchers discovered that the agency's workers felt like an essential part of TVA's mission of change. As one employee told a committee investigator, "I've walked out here in the south when there were laws on the books against it, but striking against TVA would be like striking against ourselves." The report concluded that "TVA approximates the ideal concept of union-management cooperation."[110]

By 1950, however, labor unrest began to expose shortcomings in the vaunted "Agreement." In designating the Tennessee Valley Trades and Labor Council as the "official" union for laborers, TVA strictly limited workers' organizational choices. The agreement made communication and negotiation easy since TVA's leaders always knew whom to contact when conflict arose, but workers who felt misrepresented had little recourse. In 1951, a group of workers from the International Association of Machinists (IAM) complained when TVA asked them to join a council affiliate. According to representatives, workers who refused were told that they would be fired. As the complaint noted, the central problem was job loss. The authority terminated some machinist jobs and assigned emergency repairs to engineers, even though some of the tasks required machinist-specific skills. The IAM members were not only forced to switch affiliations, but they also watched as the council supported the transfer of skilled positions from machinists to those less capable. The workers threatened to take steps to "rectify the injustice," a thinly veiled reference to striking.[111] Authority officials denied the charges, standing by their agreement with the council. A month later, Director of Personnel Harry L. Case issued a general notice to all employees stressing TVA's belief in "democratic labor relations" and reminding workers of the well-established channels for complaints. The agreement left "no jurisdiction" for work stoppages, and because TVA was a government agency, strikes were illegal on its projects.[112] Case made clear TVA's willingness to prosecute any workers who refused to follow the channels agreed upon by the council and authority.

In September 1951, the machinists struck, setting up picket lines at Boone Dam in Tennessee. The council ordered its members to cross the line, undermining the machinists' actions. The disgruntled workers extended their protest to Hales Bar, Chickamauga, Chattanooga, and, in Alabama, Widows Creek, but again, council laborers broke the picket lines. In the end, TVA claimed victory, insisting that the strikes were an illegal act and that the authority had always enjoyed good relations with its workers.[113] Chairman Clapp defended TVA's policies: "What we have emphasized is giving employees responsibility." He pointed to the decentralized supervision that allowed employees to oversee many of their own projects. He praised the fluid promotion lines that created a large pool of increasingly skilled workers, and thus, a standing cohort of potential employees.[114] Yet as the machinists' strike indicated, TVA's support for the workforce was limited to its own prescription for labor. Workers had the right to organize, but only to create a more efficient workforce. When disputes threatened to close projects needed to improve the region and power homes and businesses, TVA's needs came first. In that respect, the agency was not so different from other southern industries.

Just as TVA's leaders praised the agency's labor relations as a much-needed example for southern employee management, they also pointed to its stance toward African American employees as beneficial and instructive. Even as the valley's African American population resisted inequality more aggressively in the postwar era, the agency insisted that its approach to minority employment was fair. When Harry Truman's Executive Order 9980 challenged race-based hiring practices in the South, TVA informed its workers of the order through posters, pamphlets, and group meetings, and instructed supervisors and managers on how to handle complaints.[115] Publicity was enough for the board, but black leaders saw things differently. In 1953, Humphrey May, a representative of the Cement Mason's Local 826 called for an investigation into TVA's unfair employment practices. Despite a legacy of skilled labor stretching back to Reconstruction, May noted, black laborers had become the victims of discriminatory employment, thanks largely to the recognition of unions that refused to allow black members. When TVA looked to the council for workers to employ on projects, the lack of black union members meant that only whites received skilled jobs. Soon, May argued, skilled work would become completely synonymous with "white" work.[116] TVA responded as it always had, emphasizing hiring provisions based on "merit and efficiency." Clapp pointed to African American journeymen carpenters and linemen, labor foremen, and "helpers" in skilled crafts. Despite noting the problem of finding blacks with the experience or skills needed for trades labor, he assured the federal officials that TVA was doing all it could to train and employ skilled black workers for the agency's jobs.[117]

A greater challenge to TVA came in 1957 when a federal court struck down the segregated operation of public parks. The authority, which worked closely with state and local governments in preparing recreational facilities before leaving area leaders in control, had invested time and money in a dual system of parks, but the ruling gave TVA cause for introspection. General Manager (and future TVA Board member) Aubrey J. "Red" Wagner asked J. Ed Campbell, the director of reservoir properties, for recommendations on an official response. Campbell noted TVA's dedication to equal access to reservoirs (through segregated facilities); however, he feared that the legislation would result in a number of park closings, leading to severe restrictions on TVA's recreational program. With public attitudes "still in the process of change," Campbell foresaw the "likelihood of closure" for parks along Alabama's reservoirs.[118] Yet he remained optimistic. As long as TVA maintained a minimum number of open parks, the agency might "exert leadership toward resolving the basic issues involved." Campbell argued that, as a leaseholder, TVA should demand that, upon signing a lease or renewal, the prospective operator agree to a policy of integration.[119] Wagner and the board approved the recommendations.

The board failed to take serious action to resolve inequality in hiring practices on its own but, by 1960, the board tentatively moved to provide equal access to recreational facilities. The agency's role as a "leader" in race relations was questionable at best. Its policies were very similar to other business groups interested in attracting businesses to the South, demanding integration as required by law but doing little else to address continued prejudice. Operating in cooperation with state and local governments and organizations predicated on segregation, the agency again compromised its idealistic views. No longer able to act as a "yardstick" in racial equality or labor-management relations, TVA's leadership resigned itself to economic advancement and moderate social change. Any more would endanger the thousands of jobs and millions of dollars pouring into the region.

By 1960, two accomplishments proved TVA's ability to weather the decade's storms: the Self-Financing Bill and the Tributary Area Development Program. The programs did more than culminate years of struggle—they cemented the transition from an agency based on planning and resource conservation to one dedicated to economic development. TVA spurred economic growth by encouraging local groups to act in their own interest by creating industrial jobs. The benefits accrued back to TVA in the form of power profits, which allowed for further growth and expansion. In the process, the authority came to embody the drive for and culture of development that characterized the Sunbelt South.

As a concept, self-financing tantalized TVA's leaders. During the original debate over the authority in the 1930s, some proponents demanded that the agency be allowed to use revenue from its power sales to fund the expansion of generating capability. For fiscal conservatives, this provided a means for the agency to fund its own growth without placing a burden on the government. For New Deal liberals, a self-financed TVA would be encouraged to extend its benefits to as many as possible, since more customers translated to larger profit margins. In these early debates, however, arguments against such legislation proved stronger. For two decades, TVA submitted its proposed budgetary needs to Congress, which debated the merits of the request before doling out funds to the agency. During the 1930s and 1940s, the authority's congressional opponents, particularly Senator Kenneth McKellar, used appropriations debates to challenge aspects of its program they found distasteful, but New Deal majorities ensured that, for the most part, funds were available when needed. By the 1950s, however, consensus became particularly difficult to achieve, and the agency's problems culminated in the Dixon-Yates controversy. The Eisenhower administration and a divided Congress proved much more hostile to TVA's plans for expansion, and in response, the authority's supporters revisited the idea of self-financing.

In 1955, the Citizens for TVA, fresh from its campaign against the Dixon-Yates contract, presented "Sources of Capital for the TVA Power System" with the assistance of the TVA Board, detailing the authority's need to fund itself. By 1957, the group argued, half of TVA's annual output would go to federal defense agencies. Any failure to provide electricity would be a detriment to national security, not to mention a blow to the agency's many domestic and business customers. TVA needed the ability to build when necessitated by demand for electricity, regardless of the political tilt of Congress. The report concluded with a proposed amendment to the TVA Act that authorized the agency to issue bonds secured by its own revenues.[120] Such a plan would push the authority much closer to operating as a private industry, but would also provide the kind of financial security that would insulate the agency from the vagaries of congressional majority.

In March 1956, as Congress debated cuts in TVA's appropriations, Bob Jones raised the issue of self-financing. In a telling comparison, he asked his fellow legislators to recognize that "industrial development and economic growth in the Tennessee Valley should not be treated any differently than industrial development and economic growth in the other regions of the United States."[121] While valley companies brought a new way of life to residents, the accompanying prosperity placed demands on TVA's power resources. Cuts in TVA's appropriations meant capping growth and telling industry to locate elsewhere. As he noted, "Surely the Congress will act responsibly, and accept this opportunity to support an agency of its own creation and without a cent of appropriation being necessary."[122] Jones's bill gave TVA the power to issue revenue bonds to "provide the additions to power capacity required to keep up with the growing load of the area it serves."[123] He pointed to the agency's legacy of success from its early construction program to its participation in the defense effort—a veritable investment pitch—and found support across the valley. Louis Eckl, the editor of the *Florence Times* and a representative of the Associated Tennessee Valley Chambers of Commerce, backed the "sound and workable legislation" that allowed the authority to continue providing the power needed by expanding industry in the valley.[124]

Private utilities led the opposition to self-financing, afraid that passage of the legislation removed the one roadblock to TVA's complete dominance of the Southeast. Jones noted as much in a 1958 speech, citing the "hostility" of private utilities seeking to "erect an insulating wall around the TVA." He instructed his constituents to "be up in arms," since a private power victory would allow for higher rates, poorer service, and fewer industrial clients.[125] Once again, Alabama Power was a scapegoat, and valley leaders denounced the company as "a principal in a vicious and concentrated attack against TVA" in hearings on the bill. The utility's parent, Southern Company, called the authority a "socialistic monster" seeking to expand public power at the expense of private utilities. Jones responded that bond issues were an important financial tool in a free-enterprise system.[126] The debate highlighted TVA's amorphous position as both a public and private agency. When Southern Company called TVA "socialistic" and the U.S. Chamber of Commerce denigrated the agency's favored position, both recalled the public nature of TVA, a federal agency using its position to expand operations. Yet Jones and the valley chambers increasingly preferred to see the authority as a private entity, a belief that helped them make the case for a financing system based on that of private enterprise.

The House Public Works Committee approved the bill but, in the Rules Committee, Virginia's Howard Smith refused to allow the plan to reach the floor.[127] Jones, the "spark plug" behind the bill, reintroduced his legislation during the next session with guarantees that TVA would not encroach on new territory (particularly that of Alabama Power). John Sparkman pushed the plan through the Senate, noting its benefit for Alabama's "great industrial development."[128] In July 1959, the Senate passed the Self-Financing Bill, sending it to a joint committee to draft the final version. Despite private power's "measure of success" limiting TVA's territorial expansion with a final geographic boundary for the agency, the legislation was a victory for the forces of TVA.[129] The board no longer had to rely on Congress to obtain funds for new plants or more lines. For the valley's representatives and business leaders, the legislation meant freedom from the annual lobbying and debating that accompanied appropriations fights. For the residents of TVA's service area, the success heralded continued economic expansion. Even Eisenhower noted the victory. In his memoirs, he recalled signing the self-financing bill into law, making the agency more "businesslike," something TVA wanted as well.[130]

Even as the Self-Financing Bill made TVA "businesslike," the agency held to its larger mandate to extend its efforts to residents throughout the Tennessee River watershed. This included plans for industrialization in underdeveloped communities where the authority could afford to fund comprehensive electrification and economic development, even though returns on an investment might be decades in the making. TVA's program in smaller communities came under the organizational oversight of the Tributary Area Development Program (TAD). On the surface, TAD seemed a return to the original idealism of the early TVA—a comprehensive program for the revitalization of underdeveloped areas within the Tennessee Valley. In reality, the program sought to encourage isolated communities to embrace the same type of growth that had occurred along the Tennessee River in places like Decatur and Florence. TAD embodied many of the successes and failures of TVA's program and marked another fulfillment of Lilienthal's program, as well as the vision of development that civic and business leaders promoted throughout the agency's existence.

In her history of TVA, Marguerite Owen situated the beginning of TAD in 1950 in the Beech River watershed of west central Tennessee, sixty-five miles northwest of Florence. Community leaders contacted the TVA Board, asking for assistance dredging the river and clearing the channel connecting their community to the Tennessee River. TVA's leaders sensed an opportunity to turn their attention to this often-ignored area and encouraged civic groups to think more broadly about the "total resource development" of the Beech River region.[131] The Eisenhower administration's demands for governmental economy challenged the existence of the fledgling program but, by the late 1950s, citizens had sponsored a new courthouse in Lexington, controlled erosion with new pastures and tree plantings, and attracted several small industrial plants employing 2,300 residents. The success at Beech River suggested that smaller communities across the valley could "promote economic well-being" and become "pleasanter places to live in" by creating their own Tributary Area Development associations.[132] Beech River was soon joined by a number of other "depressed" communities looking to improve their economy in conjunction with TVA.

In 1959, the authority's Walter L. Criley met with mayors and other county and city officials from various communities in northern Alabama and southern Tennessee. The group had recently formed the Elk River Development

Association (ERDA) and adopted a program of navigation, flood control, dam construction, and industrial and recreational development on the tributary—in essence, a miniature TVA.[133] Authority officials were encouraged by the meeting, and board member Brook Hays praised the group's "voluntary, non-government collaboration."[134] In his opinion, ERDA proved that, given the opportunity, local leaders would work to better their community. Just as TVA encouraged valley chambers of commerce and groups like NAA, ERDA became the face of TVA's efforts in smaller communities along the Elk River. The leaders of the ERDA looked to the authority for assistance, but the relationship did not always tend toward cooperation. Instead, by 1961, the group began enunciating a very different vision of growth than that promoted by TVA.

In early 1961, ERDA President Joe Sir complained about Chairman Vogel to his senator, Lister Hill. Sir wanted to build a dam and reservoir on the Elk River, improving navigation and flood control. Vogel had other ideas. The chairman told Hill that Sir "failed to understand fully TVA's position and objectives," and he used Beech River as an example—the region had nine new industries, including 1,500 new jobs in forestry and timber industries alone. With TVA's help, the same progress could be made in the Elk River watershed.[135] As he related to Sir, no "sound economic justification" existed for dams (in itself, a telling statement). Vogel suggested that the "abilities and enthusiasm" of ERDA could be better directed toward a comprehensive plan that included recreational facilities and industrial development. In his response, Sir clarified this "difference in approach." ERDA shared the authority's desire for "an integrated effort for economic growth," and river control was simply the group's first concern in the long-term development of the area.[136] Where Vogel envisioned a program to inject direct benefits through employment and income creation, Sir wanted a much broader development that would create the foundation for future growth—much like the earliest land-use programs of A. E. Morgan's TVA. By 1960, the authority could no longer countenance full-scale river development unless the returns could justify the investment.

In the end, Sir acquiesced. The next year, ERDA and TVA's Water Control Planning Division studied the water supply in the Elk River Basin, proposing a "single, large 'wet' industry" such as a paper mill to increase the industrial presence in the area. The next month, ERDA produced a report on regional employment and income status, detailing underemployment on local farms and calling for "increased personal income" and the use of local raw materials. The group planned to meet with TVA to decide the "major direction" of its development activities.[137] ERDA and TVA began work on a tributary area training program to help local families with little income or schooling prepare for jobs in the "large employers of labor" that TVA and the local organizations would attract.[138] Dependent on the agency for assistance in obtaining federal funds, accessing studies and surveys of the region, and planning for future growth, ERDA resigned itself to industrialization without broader river development. When given the opportunity to encourage a return to the kind of revitalization first envisioned in the New Deal, TVA decided instead to call for jobs and income, a decision three decades in the making.

After World War II, the Tennessee Valley Authority solidified the direction of economic growth in the Tennessee Valley. Working in conjunction with local, state, and regional development groups, the authority encouraged industrialization as its central approach to economic modernization. TVA paid more attention to the social costs of industrial growth in the years after the war, but the agency failed to call for changes when those changes would jeopardize development. Instead, the authority committed itself to the idea of progress envisioned by David Lilienthal and celebrated when communities organized to recruit industry. By 1960, aided by congressional allies and valley supporters, TVA became a self-funded agency, able to direct its activities largely as it saw fit, and the Tributary Area Development program demonstrated the authority's continued commitment to industrial recruitment, relegating comprehensive resource development to a subsidiary role.

TVA was certainly not alone in its decision to privilege industrial growth; the agency found ample support and encouragement among local and state groups, and the movement toward investment in the private sector echoed in the actions of other federal government agencies. In Huntsville, the defense boom created a major federal presence in the city, an Army facility that would later be joined by a NASA civilian space center. Both the Army and NASA cooperated closely with private industry, even as locals continued to press their leaders to bring additional jobs and paychecks to the region. More than any other city in the region, Huntsville's remarkable expansion in the 1940s, 1950s, and 1960s illustrated the full extent of federal, state, and local cooperation in the economic development of the Tennessee Valley.

SIX

HUNTSVILLE HAS WHAT IT TAKES 1940–1949

By 1940, Decatur, Alabama, blossomed with new industry and an active program of economic development, spearheaded by civic and business leaders in cooperation with the Tennessee Valley Authority. Just north of the Tennessee River, however, the city of Huntsville languished. In one of the first popular accounts of TVA's work in the region, written in 1939, Willson Whitman noted Huntsville's failure to take advantage of the agency's bounty. With cheap government power, the city "could have been a sort of capital again," but instead, leaders watched as the textile mills that underwrote municipal finances faltered in the face of labor conflict, increasing costs, and decreasing profits.[1] The city's economic decline was dramatic. At the turn of the twentieth century, Huntsville was the second-largest cotton-mill city in the South, a processing center for the fields of North Alabama and central Tennessee. A 1919 chamber of commerce pamphlet placed the city "in the forefront among Southern commercial centers." The chamber boasted that, if a wall were erected around Huntsville and Madison County, the area would prove completely self-sufficient, thanks largely to the economic strength of the city's textile mills.[2]

Dallas Mills typified the industrial economy of the city. In 1891, a combination of local businessmen, a group of investors from Nashville, and a large contingent of New York financiers founded the mill. The workers came from the farms of the valley, leaving tenant agreements and share contracts for an industrial wage. By 1915, Dallas's mill village boasted 120 houses and 64 tenement buildings.[3] In 1924, Huntsville as a whole had 4,750 textile workers in a city with a reported population in 1920 of 8,000, 7,000 of whom were over the age of seven.[4] The Depression forced mills across the county to "collapse like a deck of cards"; Dallas lost $270,039 in 1930 alone.[5] The 1934 national textile strike was costly as well, with increased unemployment, lost wages, and worsening conditions. Combined with a national slump in cotton production, the textile industry was "a shell of its former self."[6] In 1939, Huntsville counted only 17 manufacturers employing a total of 133 workers.[7] The failed industries left numerous vacant buildings and thousands of unemployed workers to fend for themselves. On the eve of the war, the decline of the cotton industry in Huntsville created an economic crisis for the city.

Like civic leaders across the valley, Huntsville's business community saw the World War II–era defense mobilization as a great opportunity. John M. Nelson, the manager of the chamber of commerce, noted as much in a letter to Representative John Sparkman. Citing the industrial recruitment "victories" of Alabama cities like Decatur, he argued that "there should certainly be some place in the picture into which Huntsville would fit." Nelson pointed to repaved streets and expanded public services and promised to "step in and make a fight for anything that may be planned." Sparkman warned against the "exaggerated idea" that developments were so widespread as to be easily obtained, but he promised to relay information on the mill properties standing vacant.[8] Nelson and his cohorts attempted to convince Reynolds Aluminum to choose Huntsville. Appeals went to Sparkman, Tom Johnson (still with Alabama Power at the time), and Richard Reynolds, advertising Huntsville's viability as a center for the defense industry.[9] Reynolds decided to locate at the Sheffield site, but Huntsville's leaders took the loss in stride and immediately asked for federal assistance with other prospects.

After continued appeals to Sparkman, the congressman responded with a list of his attempts on behalf of the city. He had encouraged improvements to Huntsville's airport, telling the chamber to contact aviation manufacturers personally, though his efforts would not bear fruit until late 1944, when Capital Airlines provided the first airline service to Huntsville–Madison County Airport.[10] He listed the city's resources with the Associated Industries of Alabama, advertising the growing number of available textile-mill properties. Yet he refrained from making promises that would unjustly raise hopes. Asked about Huntsville's possibilities for a government facility, Sparkman told city commissioner J. B. Van Valkenburgh, "Congressmen have absolutely nothing to do with the location of these plants," and noted that industries chose sites based on natural resources and the labor market. He was even more pessimistic in a response to the chamber's secretary, Claude H. Pipes: "I am firmly convinced from my knowledge of the plans and studies of the War Department that we cannot hope to get any so-called 'War Baby' in Madison County. We simply are not properly located for it."[11]

Sparkman's suggestion that politicians could not influence the location of war plants was only partially true, and its sentiment belies the role that southern Democrats played in the region's industrial development. In fact, Alabama's congressional delegation was essential to the state's efforts to attract business. Dating back to the Muscle Shoals crisis, powerful Democratic lawmakers ensured that Alabama (and other southern states) received ample federal aid and provided a friendly climate for business investment. Alabamians understood this, contacting senators like John H. Bankhead Sr., John H. Bankhead Jr., Lister Hill, and John Sparkman and congressmen like Edward Almon, William Bankhead, and Bob Jones for assistance. Such long-serving representatives, re-elected thanks to the staid politics of the one-party, segregated South, were well connected and politically valuable to the national Democratic party; as such, they were a critical resource in the quest for industry. However, political connections alone did not create development, and across the region, veteran Democratic congressmen sought the same benefits as Alabama's delegates. The region's prosperity may have been aided by senators and representatives, but it was driven by the work of locals who pushed their politicians to use their influence for growth and who shaped their communities for development. The resulting federal-local cooperation ultimately helped to lift the valley over its regional competition.

By early 1941, as other southern communities experienced economic revitalization at the hands of government plants and camps, Huntsville fell behind. Sparkman's doubts about the city's chances echoed the palpable pessimism among the local leadership. An editorial in *The* (Huntsville) *Mercury* attempted to spur the populace to action, asking "are we willing to take crumbs that fall from the rich man's table? Or do we want to go after some new blood and money?"[12] Recalling the failed attempt to land Reynolds Aluminum, some complained that their congressmen had neglected the city in favor of development at Sheffield and Decatur.[13] Sparkman's falling popularity illustrated just how important government connections were to local communities interested in joining the nation's defense boom. In neighboring Decatur, Shelton's relationship with TVA helped the city grow, while Nelson and the Huntsville Chamber of Commerce received bleak reports. For Sparkman and his fellow congressmen, the appeals were incessant. As Sparkman counseled caution and realism, Senator Lister Hill gave similar advice to valley residents, informing constituents that he simply could not get a plant for every interested community.[14] Considering the success of their neighbors, Huntsville's leaders worried that Sparkman and Hill would fail to include their city in the revitalization of the region's economy.

In reality, the duo had actively pursued opportunities for Huntsville since the beginning of the wartime economic boom, but the nature of defense work forced the politicians to maintain a level of discretion. As early as 1937, the congressmen knew that the Army hoped to build a new chemical warfare arsenal in the South and, in October, two unnamed War Department officials visited the most likely valley candidate for a new facility, the Muscle Shoals fertilizer plants. In particular, Shoals area leaders hoped to utilize Plant 1, which had remained idle when TVA began production at Plant 2. In March 1938, Sparkman informed Florence businessman T. M. Rogers that the community should be prepared since "one of the officers who made the inspection tour is a good friend of mine, and I see him every few days." He made similar promises to the Sheffield Board of Commerce, informing the group that he took every opportunity to ensure that the Tennessee Valley would be "definitely tied in" with the defense program.[15] The Muscle Shoals facilities did play an important role in the nation's armament. Dedicated to munitions manufacturing in times of war, they changed production from fertilizer to chemical weapons. By the early 1940s, however, spurred by the pleas of valley leaders, Sparkman and Hill turned their attention to another community in need of industrial development.

In early June 1941, Huntsville retailer George Mahoney received a telegram from an official with the Nashville, Chattanooga, and St. Louis Railroad, informing him that two men would soon arrive from Baltimore with an interest in land in southwestern Madison County on the Tennessee River. Lieutenant Colonel Charles Ernest Loucks, a War Department official, and R. F. Graef of the Washington, D.C., engineering firm Whitman, Requardt, and Smith, were greeted at the station by Mahoney and fellow businessman Lawrence Goldsmith. As Goldsmith later informed Sparkman, "They were not inclined to talk very much, but knew exactly what they wanted, and where they wanted to go." The officials told their guides that they needed 1,500 acres for a building site, surrounded by 30,000 acres as part of the larger project reservation. Sparkman immediately went to work, querying his colleagues in the War

Department and conferring with Lister Hill. They learned that Loucks and Graef were scouting locations for a proposed chemical warfare arsenal, and Huntsville was one of five sites under consideration. Goldsmith waxed dramatic: "Huntsville is counting on you," he wrote to Sparkman, "This is our only chance."[16]

The War Department's Chemical Warfare Service ranked Huntsville second, but after talking with the Alabama congressmen, officials promised to visit the Madison County site personally before coming to a final decision.[17] Huntsville faced stiff competition. The city of Memphis, within the reach of cheap TVA power, was a clear frontrunner for the chemical plant, and Tennessee Senator Kenneth McKellar used his considerable influence to lobby for the site. However, Sparkman and Hill consistently promoted Huntsville and North Alabama—as Hill wryly noted, "We are in a 'cat and dog' fight with [the rival locations,] but I think John Sparkman and I can handle the situation."[18] Hill's bureaucratic clout and Sparkman's ties to War Department officials gave the lawmakers enough influence to ensure that Huntsville would receive a fair evaluation, even if the city was not the Army's first choice.

As important as Sparkman and Hill were to the decision, without local action, Huntsville would have likely remained a dying mill town. Community leaders, particularly Mayor A. W. McAllister and Goldsmith and Mahoney, gladly took the lead role in pressing the city's case to the visiting officials. Huntsvillians remained in constant contact with Sparkman and Hill, as well as the War Department. Goldsmith and Mahoney hosted surveyors and engineers, showed available sites, and organized meals, transportation, and accommodation. When Chief of the Chemical Warfare Service William Porter and Army Colonel William English came to Huntsville in late June, the city jumped to the top position on the War Department's short list, a move partially due to congressional influence, but heavily impacted by their tour of the region. When Porter left Huntsville, he told Goldsmith that the city would receive his vote. Goldsmith noted to Sparkman, "I think George and myself did a good job for two country lads. We entertained them royally." Sparkman replied, "[Porter] reports that you fellows really took care of him and Colonel English and that they were delighted with Huntsville and with the proposed site."[19]

Such enthusiasm was part of the city's larger zeal for new development. Business leaders, concerned that the failing mills would bring the community down with them, jumped at the opportunity to locate a defense plant in the county. They provided a solid local front for Sparkman and Hill's legislative wrangling. However, in their excitement, they also demonstrated the *ad hoc* nature of Huntsville's economic development program. Mahoney and Goldsmith sprang to action only after the decision to investigate the city had been made and the possibility of an arsenal was brought to their attention, and they relied heavily on Sparkman and Hill throughout the entire process. In fact, Huntsville's leadership did little to contact industries that hoped to expand during the war effort—instead, they appealed to Washington and Montgomery. For Huntsville to prosper, local leaders needed the funds, the direction, and the confidence to act on their own initiative to bring industries to the region. In short, Huntsville's boosters needed to learn the ways and means of Sunbelt economic development.

The location of a chemical warfare arsenal in Huntsville signaled the beginning of a great transformation in the city. Huntsville benefited from a number of distinct advantages. Thanks to TVA, the region enjoyed cheap power, plentiful water, and improved transportation networks, and the ongoing cooperation between valley leaders and authority officials provided a wealth of experience in local, state, and federal cooperation. The region's congressional leadership worked diligently for local development. As in Florence and Decatur, Huntsville's community leaders believed government investment to be the first step in the economic revitalization of their city. And, once growth began, Huntsville's leaders sought to maintain both the relationship and the industrial growth that resulted from it. The city's boosters worked frantically to accommodate government projects and add to the city's financial base. The interaction between local and federal developers, and the maturation of their efforts in the face of success and failure, characterized the city's new economy and signaled the region's complete acceptance of a Sunbelt-style ethos of growth and development.

On July 2, 1941, John Sparkman sent a confidential note to Barrett Shelton, informing the *Decatur Daily* editor that the Army had chosen Huntsville for its chemical warfare arsenal, awaiting only President Roosevelt's signature before the decision could be made public. The next day, Sparkman's office issued telegrams and a press release formally announcing the $41.3 million project and a $6.0 million adjoining ordnance plant. The arsenal would manufacture "smoke materials and other chemical warfare agents" on 30,000 acres alongside two railroad lines and the Tennessee River, and the ordnance plant would store and prepare shell casings. More importantly for Huntsville's struggling economy, the project would employ thousands of workers for construction and operation with "a high percentage of the operating labor . . . drawn from the community within a radius of 25 to 30 miles of the Arsenal site."[20]

Sparkman's release stuck to the official details of the project, but local leaders expounded on the decision. The *Huntsville Times* praised Sparkman and Hill for carrying the needs of the Tennessee Valley to Washington and promoting the region's beneficial location and resources to those making the important decision. The paper also recognized the community leaders who hosted the visiting engineers and army officers on inspections of the area. Mahoney and Goldsmith "contributed a great deal in making their stay pleasant and presenting the social, manufacturing and other manifold advantages of the city and county." The plant was not a "war baby," the paper promised, but a permanent part of the regional economy, housing a staff of officers, enlisted personnel, and civilian workers that called Huntsville home and whose "salaries and wages will flow into the channels of trade of this city and this section."[21]

Most residents were as ecstatic as the *Times*. News of the decision leaked the night before, thanks in part to off-the-cuff comments by Alabama congressman Frank Boykin and subsequent radio broadcasts—as one leader noted, "even all the cooks and the houseboys have heard about the proposed plant." On July 3, when the news officially broke, the public erupted in celebration. Rents rose rapidly, owners called in leases, and the city witnessed a boom that recalled the days of Henry Ford's offer for Muscle Shoals. The editor of the *Huntsville Times*, Reese Amis, wisely predicted, "It's going to be hard to get people to keep their heads."[22] Sparkman became a local hero, solidifying his reputation and ensuring his eventual promotion to the Senate. As Amis noted to the congressman, "It will do you a world of good and stop some croakers who have been saying that you have been trying to turn everything to the Tri-Cities." Sparkman tried to share the praise with Hill, but he continued to receive most of the credit. In a 1990 interview, George F. Davis attested to the Alabamian's legacy: "[Sparkman] was the one that got all the arsenal coming to Huntsville."[23]

The city soon received a taste of the dislocation that accompanied economic development. As with TVA's reservoir construction program, the first consideration in the actual location of Huntsville Arsenal was the acquisition of land. Nearly 550 families lived on the planned reservation, 70 percent of whom were African American tenant farmers. The arsenal also displaced thirty-one known cemeteries (white and black), three black schools, eleven black churches and one white church.[24] In fact, the 30,000 acres set aside for the arsenal proved a study in contrasts. The site boasted one of Madison County's oldest homes, the Lanier place, and Cedar Grove Methodist Church, one of the region's oldest churches, and the surrounding fields were worked by black farm laborers—the situation recalled the antebellum South's plantation economy as much as the twentieth-century New South economy.[25] In a matter of months, the Old South gave way to a Sunbelt defense industry, manufacturing shells for the American war effort.

Relocation began immediately. In late July, three black families vacated a 160-acre plot needed as headquarters for the construction operation. The Army paid the farmers for their crops, but unable to find new farms in time, officials moved the families to temporary housing near Alabama Agricultural and Mechanical University on the opposite side of the city.[26] In total, the government paid $600,000 for eighty-one tracts of land, and 112 families required a sum of $2,000 in additional moving expenses. Nearly half of the families relocated to farms in Madison County, and 180 families moved into town and sought employment at the arsenal.[27] As with TVA's massive relocation efforts, the War Department faced many of the same challenges and, once again, government officials struggled to meet the needs of the displaced.

In late July, the Farm Security Administration set up a relocation office to act as a "clearing house," listing land for sale or rent in the valley. As one official noted, "Our intention is to get new homes for these people as near their old communities as we can."[28] This was overly optimistic. Thanks to TVA, much of the region's best farmland lay under acres of water, and removal policies made scarce farmland that much rarer. This lack of land combined with increasing demand to drive up prices on remaining fields. The government needed a temporary expedient to let land values calm before permanently settling families, so the FSA began building prefabricated homes, providing temporary residence for the thousands of farmers across the Southeast who lost their homesteads in the name of national defense.[29] Given the circumstances of removal, the FSA provided a chance for removed families to continue their accustomed way of life. Yet prefabricated homes scattered throughout the county could not replace an attachment to the land developed over decades of family farming or the kind of localized knowledge that meant success or failure for marginal farmers. The FSA provided some additional assistance, including grants for moving expenses and rehabilitation loans.[30] For many, however, the help was not enough to keep them on the farm, and just as in the aftermath of TVA's land acquisition campaign and the subsequent reservoir program, the agency could not provide the land and equipment that farmers needed to compete in a changed agricultural economy. Instead, the move provided an added encouragement to seek a living off the farm and made industrial development that much more important for the city and region.

Physical displacement was only one aspect of the larger transition facing agricultural interests in the arsenal area. The "attractive jobs" at the arsenal offered benefits and job security lacking in the agricultural sector and paid up to five times the average daily wage of farm laborers in Madison County.[31] Within days of the announcement, John H. Wall wrote Sparkman for work, fearing the arsenal would "terminate my farming activity." Kathleen Jones came to a similar conclusion, noting that the plant would disrupt local farm labor.[32] For those residents that relied on a cheap, available workforce, the arsenal provided a direct challenge. By March 1942, farm owners were reporting labor shortages, leaving fields uncultivated and crops unharvested.[33] And, given the larger labor shortage affecting the United States as industries geared for the defense program and millions of men and women left to serve in the armed forces, such strains were magnified. As George F. Davis remembered, the arsenal upset the "old settlers": "All their hired help left, and they couldn't hire anyone. They had people who did all their chores for them. So they all left, because they got good jobs." One friend of Davis's went to the "little settlement" where "the poor people lived" to recruit someone to do her laundry. The "poor people," however, were no longer looking for work. One told Davis's friend that, with jobs at the arsenal, "[we're] trying to hire somebody to work for us."[34]

For many more Huntsvillians, jobs on the government reservation meant a welcome economic boost at the end of a long depression. News of the defense project brought a flood of requests to Sparkman for employment. Claude Hudson of Elkmont, a rural town in northern Limestone County, asked the congressman for employment information less than a week after the plant became public knowledge. With Sparkman's assistance, Hudson applied for a guard position and was hired in early November.[35] Sparkman also recommended Marland M. Fowler, a "poor man with a wife and three children," for a position at the arsenal.[36] By late August, construction crews and initial employment at the plant reached 1,300; in early November, numbers surpassed 5,000 and payroll topped $175,000.[37] Pearl Harbor added to the boom conditions. The arsenal began twenty-four-hour operations, and contractors sped construction at the still-unfinished Redstone Ordnance Plant, bringing total employment to over 10,000 civilians. The arsenal's personnel office stayed open for sixteen-hour days, sometimes processing as many as 70 job applicants per hour.[38]

With the demands of war boosting ordnance production, nearly every applicant expected to receive a job. Cecil Brooks of Trinity complained to Sparkman that "several" area men were "not being fairly dealt with" by arsenal personnel, who refused to offer them jobs. Brooks resigned his position as a teacher to obtain defense work, and his failure to find a job left him unemployed. He also heard that many of those with positions in upper-level management were from out of state. Upon investigation, Sparkman learned that Huntsville Arsenal was "98% staffed" by mid-December and that some of the hires had come from outside the valley, despite promises by officials that the arsenal would observe local-preference employment. As one engineering-firm official told the congressman, "We can assure you that there has never been any idea of calling men from distant points if we can find the qualified men here who have the experience and knowledge necessary to do the work called for." However, when trained men could not be drawn from Huntsville and Madison County, "it has become quite necessary that we do get the men with the required experience."[39] Brooks voiced concerns already shared by many in the valley and in Washington. As arsenal officials staffed managerial and professional positions, they found local labor unprepared to meet the plant's needs. In order to maintain the benefits of the facility's payroll, Huntsville's community leaders needed to find ways to train local workers for a new economy.

In September, 300 men and women attended open registration for classes at a defense training center connected with the University of Alabama and temporarily housed at Huntsville High School. According to Supervisor Warren C. Moore, the free courses were designed "to fill definite needs in the national defense program." Six hours each week, students learned basic accounting, structural design, mechanical and electrical maintenance, supervision, industrial engineering, chemistry, and other technical skills useful at the construction site and on production lines at the arsenal and other defense facilities.[40] George Davis enrolled in a "refresher course" simply by expressing interest in the class and received textbooks from the university. His instructor was a technician from the Edgewood (Massachusetts) Chemical Warfare Arsenal.[41] The government-sponsored coursework was crucial to staffing at the arsenal, and those who participated undoubtedly found the transition to the production line easier than those without basic training in manufacturing. Yet the extension center did little to prepare the community for modern industry. The trainees became line workers and foremen, prepared for their specific jobs. They did not become engineers or chemists, whose skills easily translated into higher-paying jobs in the public and private sector. Without a more highly skilled workforce, Huntsville struggled to staff postwar defense industries and to maintain its economic advantages.[42]

Government employment meant better paychecks and rudimentary on-the-job training for workers leaving the tenant fields or the mill village, but perhaps the greatest change in the lives of those hired on at the arsenal came with the government's encouragement of union labor. Huntsvillians were no stranger to unions; labor activity at the town's cotton mills was a common occurrence in the Depression years when falling wages and New Deal legislation encouraged workers to create a common front. In fact, in July 1934, the United Textile Workers began the Great Strike Wave in the city, as 5,000 millhands walked off their jobs and "flying squads" of organizers threatened anyone trying to return to work. Though southern and central Alabama mills continued running, between 16,000 and 23,000 of the state's entire textile workforce of 40,000 participated. The UTW strike threatened an already weak textile industry and soured the city's business leadership on the unionization of local workers.[43]

Mill owners constantly battled their organized workforce with the assistance of local and state authorities, but the war effort provided a completely different environment. Embodied in the National War Labor Board's efforts to maintain, protect, and even increase organization among southern workers, the federal government encouraged union membership on its projects.[44] In September, E. S. Coffey, personnel director for the construction company working on the arsenal, announced that only union labor would be employed at the Huntsville site, creating a closed shop for the International Hod Carriers. The statement brought immediate criticism. City Commission Chairman Joe Van Valkenburgh received complaints that the company forced applicants to "pay tribute" to get jobs, referring to the initiation fee and weekly dues required of union members. The *Huntsville Times* demanded a congressional investigation into the "labor racket" in which the "forgotten man" was forced to pay to work for "his own government."[45] As craftsmen came into Huntsville, one reporter noted, they "seem to know exactly who to see, and what to do to obtain prompt employment," while local laborers paid their dues and waited in the Hod Carriers' headquarters waiting to be called to work.[46] The attention brought results. The construction quartermaster, Major Neil McKay, transferred to Arkansas, and Coffey resigned. Worker selection became the responsibility of the Alabama State Employment Service.[47]

The newly appointed construction quartermaster, Carl Breitweiser, immediately stirred further discontent. In an attempt to cut costs and increase efficiency, he began using semi-skilled and unskilled laborers to lay pipes, replacing unionized plumbers. In response to the jurisdictional challenge, the plumbers walked off the job to "attend a funeral." The *Huntsville Times* backed Breitwieser, who was "making an honest, vigorous effort to build the arsenal as cheaply as possible . . . and as rapidly as possible." The striking workers were "trying to throw monkey wrenches" into the project, and the paper called for law enforcement to investigate union activity.[48]

The Japanese attack on Pearl Harbor and the U.S. entrance into World War II worsened public perception of unionization at the arsenal. The Hod Carriers lost all responsibility for employment; laborers were not required to join a union, and all hiring was taken over by the newly staffed construction-personnel office. The plumbers immediately returned to work, offering to work one day each week without pay (the government declined the offer). The war brought a new immediacy to the project, and the construction and operational crews were placed on two ten-hour shifts with an intervening four-hour maintenance shift, seven days per week. The Chemical Warfare Service posted bulletins around the facility, noting that production at Huntsville Arsenal would "play an important part in the nation's war effort."[49] The unwritten implication for any labor activity that hampered shell manufacturing was evident.

When electricians struck in early January 1942, asking for a wage increase, the public responded with hostility. Breitwieser immediately held a conference with union leaders and assured them that pay would rise; the electricians were back at work by the beginning of the night shift. Yet the ten-hour strike had greater reverberations. The *Huntsville Times* asked, "Is there no PATRIOTISM, no LOYALTY from these people who are among the highest paid labor men in the country?" The workers struck despite "the known fact that American soldiers and civilians are being killed by the Japs." Days later, the paper remained incensed, calling for workers to stay on the job. Worker organization was a privilege to be enjoyed only after wartime production met the country's needs.[50]

Labor received the message. Activity sharply dropped at the arsenal as the war continued, and the electricians' short strike in January 1942 was the last major wartime work disturbance at the plant. In July 1943, Sparkman praised workers at the facility: "We not only have labor that wants to work and avoid trouble, but is the finest in the United States."[51] The war buttressed anti-labor sentiment in the city, discouraging union activity as traitorous when increased production could help end the war in Europe, Africa, and the Pacific. Even as TVA boasted a "progressive" labor policy, Huntsvillians continued to view organization and activity at their government facility with suspicion, and workers learned that unionization remained extremely difficult in the modernizing South.

The transition from field to factory at the arsenal facility brought another challenge for many new employees: interaction with African American and women workers taking advantage of the influx of jobs. Of course, southern women were no strangers to industrial labor. As Jacquelyn Dowd Hall and others have noted, white women were "welcomed with open arms" into cotton mills, providing cheap, unskilled labor (and sometimes, an assurance of their children's even cheaper labor).[52] Huntsville, dotted with cotton mills, boasted a workforce which included many white women, and the Depression made women's labor a necessity for many families. While some industries preferred to hire only male "breadwinners," the dire economic straits meant that every family member able to earn a wage needed to look for work.

With thousands of farm families heading for the city, and with the increase in job opportunities at the arsenal facility, women joined men in asking for employment. After being laid off from her job at a local mill, Christabel Burleson of Hartselle asked Sparkman for help in transferring from "an industry which has little or no future at the present" to the arsenal, and the congressman encouraged her to apply through the Civil Service for a position.[53] Gladys McCurry, Sparkman's widowed sister, initially wrote her brother attempting to get her son (his nephew) a job, mentioning casually that "I wish I could get on at the plant too. Seems there would be something, filing papers, [answering] telephones and such that I could do."[54] Sparkman contacted arsenal commander R. C. Ditto on McCurry's behalf; Ditto sent her an application promising "first consideration" for any available job, and Sparkman promised to go with her to the interview. In April 1942, McCurry interviewed with a "mighty nice lady" for a position paying $105.00 per month, and Sparkman promised Ditto would "take care" of her.[55] Granted, Sparkman put forward extra effort to secure McCurry a position, but his sister's request was typical of many women that sought work at Huntsville Arsenal. As Nancy Dickson, a stenographer who moved to the facility with her husband, recalled, "When I learned the amount of salary earned by a temporary Civil Service clerk-stenographer—$135 per month, sixty-five percent more than the salary I had earned in Memphis, the mud and the rain and our dreadful room seemed more bearable."[56] With hundreds of clerical, housekeeping, and service positions available, the government plant offered women an admittedly gender-specific economic alternative.

At first, Huntsville Arsenal's female employees were relegated to clerical positions and lighter production-line work, leaving the "heavy labor" for men. Yet as the draft called the city's male labor force to war, the arsenal began a more expansive hiring of women. In January 1942, officials announced an increase in the age limits for employment for women and a raise in pay to five dollars per day. Female employees produced, inspected, and tested materials and mechanical parts, jobs normally given to the arsenal's male workforce.[57] Huntsville Arsenal staffed an "all-girl" line, part promotional gimmick and part necessity as male workers took other positions or shipped out to fight.[58] The *Huntsville Times* praised the "she-women" who were "rapidly moving into the he-men jobs." These "industrial amazons" trained to take on "difficult man-sized jobs" as their husbands, fiancés, sons, fathers, and brothers fought overseas. The *Times* assured readers that "[most] of the women do their own housework before or after their shifts," but traditional gender roles were definitely strained by wartime circumstances.[59] The *Birmingham News* suggested as much (though in gendered language) when it described one female worker in Huntsville as a "slim girl, weighing merely 105 pounds" who could "do anything on the line that any man can do."[60] As women took new positions in the plants, they benefited from the same specialized training that had been offered to male workers. The University of Alabama extension center offered classes for female defense workers, and by December 1942, nearly 40 percent of production workers at the plant were women.[61]

As women began to take prominent roles in production at plants across the valley, they shared in the dangers that accompanied chemical weapons manufacturing. Accounts from the region's other major chemical facility, the

Muscle Shoals plant, illustrate the changing nature of female employment. In 1943, Geraldine Byrd learned that TVA planned to hire women at the old fertilizer plant. She took an entrance exam and began as a cooler operator, making sure that water flowed into chambers that cooled nitric acid. As Byrd recalled, conditions were "terrible"—buildings opened to the elements, exposing the workers to unpredictable Alabama weather. She recalled, "When the sun in the afternoon hit those towers and those nitric acid fumes come off, it would just take every bit of the skin off of you. We went to New Orleans one time and we told everybody we had been sunbathing. The skin on our faces was peeling off so badly."[62] Byrd remained at Muscle Shoals until 1954, though she expected to be terminated at the end of the war effort. She told her interviewer that she had been advised by officials that "we were just really hired [for] the war years."[63] Women workers may have occupied the jobs temporarily, but while manning the production lines, they shared the labor and danger of their male counterparts.

Women were not the only beneficiaries of the expanded economic opportunities. Shelby Johnson wrote to Sparkman in late November 1941 asking about opportunities for black men at the arsenal. When Johnson contacted the Huntsville Chamber of Commerce about training opportunities for the black community, his request was brushed aside. He looked to his congressman for assistance: "[All] these years in my loyalty to Huntsville and America and my struggling to send two children to college to prepare them so that they can sustain themselves [and] the best that they can offer them at the arsenal is a job making beds in the bunk houses at twelve dollars per week. It makes me feel that all of my efforts have gone for naught!" Johnson's daughter, a social worker trained at Howard University, applied for work in the rapidly expanding city, but was told that "there were not enough Negroes in one locality and that a white person would fill the job better." Black farmers forced off their land to make room for the arsenal were denied access to the benefits that came from the government investment. Johnson enunciated feelings that had begun to spread throughout the black community: "We know that there is some distinction between the races but for the jobs that Negroes are qualified to do and never appointed makes us wonder." Sparkman professed sympathy, but told Johnson that racial restrictions in the labor unions and a lack of black men looking for training limited opportunities at the facility. He complimented Johnson's "fine outlook and civic mindedness," but cautioned him that "progress comes slowly."[64]

The war sped that "progress," though black workers never enjoyed the same opportunities as their white counterparts. By early 1943, enough black workers found jobs at the arsenal that the city council worked to develop a new segregated housing unit at the "circus grounds" east of the city.[65] Upon returning to Huntsville for a thirty-six-day leave in 1945, Private First Class Freddie L. Rice noted the small changes overcoming the southern town. Places that had once refused to hire blacks now integrated their staff. Rice was pleasantly surprised to find that African Americans were "being upgraded and integrated in war industries" in Huntsville.[66] Black workers never enjoyed the same opportunities as their white counterparts, but they did make real gains during the defense emergency that would create a more solid economic foundation for the social and political advances of the coming decades.

African American women found work at the arsenal harder to obtain. While some black men worked on the production line alongside their white neighbors, the lack of adequate segregated facilities kept the demand for black women low. As base historian Kaylene Hughes noted, black women also suffered from fears by the officials at the arsenal that the performance of all women, but particularly African Americans, was "an unknown quantity."[67] Racial and gendered stereotypes proved formidable boundaries, but the demands of the war helped push officials to overcome their hesitancy. In 1943, arsenal officials concluded negotiations with Atlanta University to hire one hundred black female graduates.[68] When PFC Rice returned to Huntsville, the sight of African American women staffing clerical positions surprised him more than any other change. The sight "almost paralyzed him. . . . He couldn't move." Rice had hoped to join the Great Migration and settle in Toledo, Ohio, upon discharge, where segregation and prejudice seemed less overt. However, upon witnessing the changes which had come over Huntsville, the private felt that returning home might not be as bad as he had once thought. He would still face discrimination, but "those girls working in the arsenal office make me think things might change."[69]

Change was certainly a fact of life in Huntsville in the early 1940s. The rapid expansion of the arsenal and the national defense effort placed demands on Huntsville and Madison County's agricultural economy. As the farms and mills faced increasingly hard times, the government project provided higher pay and better job security. Huntsvillians accepted positions as civilian guards, machine operators, and line foremen; they entered a new workforce in which labor organization was a constant fact of life, job training was a necessary part of the workday, and female and black co-workers shared the morning commute. Southern customs did not disappear. Segregated facilities ensured that little interracial interaction occurred off of the production line and outside the office, and female employees, white and black, continued to be placed largely in clerical and service positions traditionally considered "women's work." Yet Private Rice's comments are indicative of the ways in which the city began to deal with the new facts of economic life. If Huntsville's citizens wanted prosperity, they would have to accept social change, however limited.

Challenges to the southern racial and gender status quo were not the only changes to the former mill town. Commissioner Loula Dunn of the Alabama Department of Public Welfare noted as much in a speech prepared for Governor Frank W. Dixon in June 1941, a month before the arsenal decision became public. Dunn wrote, "The impact of national defense on local government may well be illustrated by the rapidly changing scope of public welfare services. . . . In areas where a sleepy village has become a boom town over night, a community or a local government cannot be expected to cope with its problems unaided, but requires the combined effort of all three governmental levels."[70] Huntsville's leaders realized that municipal growth required quick thinking to accommodate an expanding population. Hundreds of unemployed men flocked to the city, hoping to find a job at the arsenal or at any of the businesses riding the wave of prosperity. Traffic increased substantially, as did demands for municipal water, electricity, and sewage, taxing an infrastructure unprepared for the influx of people. Yet perhaps the greatest concern came with the demand for housing for the thousands of new employees, forcing civic leaders to look to state and federal authorities for assistance in creating a stable community out of boom conditions. They marshaled the city's resources to prepare for rapid growth and, in the process, learned invaluable lessons that would serve developers and residents in the years ahead.

Coming on the heels of economic depression, the defense boom brought welcome relief across the South. At first, however, the jobs and paychecks were localized in the towns near government facilities, causing a migration of men, women, and children hoping to find work. The effects of such rapid growth could be substantial, as Childersburg's experience proved, and Huntsville was no exception. Job seekers became a "serious" problem for the city. Homeless men and women slept in their cars, on the steps of the courthouse, and on benches in the city's central park. One employee recalled, "The park in the night flickered with cigarettes as well as the usual lightning bugs. A hum of snores mixed with laughter, and singing blended with nature's choir of frogs and crickets."[71] Sanitation lagged and crime spiked. Many, unable to find work, were reduced to begging on the street.[72]

Those able to find work further troubled city services. In 1940, Huntsville was a city of 13,000, with a workforce of just over 5,500.[73] In November 1941, the arsenal alone employed nearly that many, and at its height in 1943, the facility approached 17,000 employees. Madison Pike, the main road into the arsenal, was clogged with workers in the mornings and evenings. Rain made conditions worse, as did the rationing of rubber and metals that might be used to repair automobiles, and by March 1942, Huntsville's leaders looked for state funding to pave all existing roads into the facility and to build several new arteries to ease the gridlock.[74] Arsenal officials encouraged workers to use buses and, when public transportation became overcrowded, told employees to carpool.[75]

Other city systems faced similar strains. Demands for city water forced leaders to add new pumps to the municipal water system. The City of Huntsville Electric System frantically negotiated with the Tennessee Valley Authority for more power, hoping to maintain a lucrative electric contract even as wartime demand brought rate hikes.[76] The Huntsville Hospital Board of Trustees begged the federal government for funds, explaining that "hospital facilities were not sufficient to accommodate the increase of business that would be incident to the increase of population." The arsenal's leadership seconded the hospital's request, noting that the hazardous nature of chemical weapon production and the possibility of a major accident at the arsenal "is sufficient reason to consider the hospital addition an absolute necessity for the war effort." Federal funds allowed the hospital to build three additions with fifty-four new beds.[77] Even Huntsville's public library adapted to meet the arsenal's demands, adding more technical books to be used in training classes. As one librarian noted, "It is no uncommon sight now to see a carpenter, or a plumber, perhaps in overalls, perusing the news periodicals, or struggling with notes on chemistry at one of the reading tables."[78]

The nature of production at the ordnance facility also caused some concern over the environmental impact of the plant, though unlike demands on the hospital, library, roads, or schools, city leaders did little to address such worries. In fact, the lack of action on the ecological disruption that accompanied Huntsville Arsenal's growth says much about the region's economic priorities and coincides neatly with the larger approach of TVA and local leaders to the question of the environmental impact of industrial growth. Within two days of the formal announcement, Donald Isom, the president of the Tennessee Valley Wildlife Federation, asked Hill to consider the ecological footprint of the proposed facility: "Owing to the nature of the refuse from such a plant as this we sincerely hope that a filter or settling pool will not be overlooked in the original plan." Hill assured Isom that Chemical Warfare Service officials had promised that operations would not harm the local fish and wildlife.[79] Subsequent events proved the senator wrong.

The chemicals produced at the plant were certainly dangerous. As George Davis recalled, accidents occasionally led to injuries. In one particularly gruesome case, phosphorus pipes burst, spewing 2,300-degree liquid and burning several people, including some of Davis's neighbors. Davis transferred to Muscle Shoals after the accident, hoping to avoid being "blown up."[80] John McDaniel, hired in 1942 to manufacture mustard gas, remembered the precautions workers had to take: "To do this work, it would be necessary for me to wear clothes impregnated with a substance to prevent the mustard gas fumes from coming in contact with the skin. The long johns underwear were thick with the substance, as were the socks, coveralls, shoes and hat. I have scars today on my wrists where I was careless in joining the underwear sleeves and the gloves."[81]

Assured that the arsenal's production lines were safe, the city did little to contain the chemicals on the reservation. In fact, the importance given to the arsenal's output meant that any environmental concerns came second to defense needs; as arsenal commander R. C. Ditto told Sparkman, conservation officials in Madison County understood that the "production of the Arsenal had to come first." Not all Huntsvillians were acquiescent. Louis Collier complained to Sparkman that indiscriminate dumping had "robbed us of a considerable area for hunting and fishing" and promised to ruin any chance of using the surrounding land after the war. In fact, despite claims of safety, Collier found dead fish floating down Indian Creek, obviously originating from the arsenal reservation. Sparkman contacted officials, who promised the congressman that water was analyzed "almost hourly" to ensure low concentrations, though some instances of contamination "while regretted, are unavoidable and incident to war."[82]

In 1947, a year after production ceased, Colonel Sterling E. Whiteside Jr. finally commented on the periodic fish kills that occurred on both Indian Creek and Big Spring Creek. Despite "continuous and tedious" precautions, he admitted, some chemicals escaped safety mechanisms. Huntsville's industrial sewer system simply did not have the catch basins needed to keep pollutants out of the surrounding environment.[83] Though the arsenal used water to produce and clean materials, staff did not begin treating wastewater until the 1970s. In 1981, water on the reservation tested positive for cancer-causing agents, but the army continued to downplay the pollution and did little to stop toxic releases.[84] The shift to missile production did little to lessen the impact of the government facility on the environment, though increased public attention did bring to light the challenge Huntsville faced in attempting to balance prosperity and ecological safety.

Huntsville faced a greater adjustment to its booming economy in its struggle to provide affordable rental housing to new employees and their families. Housing prices and rents skyrocketed within days of the announcement of the arsenal's location in the city, and the Alabama congressional delegation moved quickly to secure funding for a federal housing development that might take pressure off of the city. The Madison County Defense Council called for more homes, and city and county officials requested $2.5 million to expand "all public facilities," a sure sign that the city was unprepared for the population increase.[85] Sparkman appealed to his constituents, asking renters and sellers to "be sane and sensible" and avoid rent and price gouging. He warned, "There will be a day of reckoning for those who engage in excessive speculation."[86] Claude Pipes, the manager of the Huntsville Chamber of Commerce, asked Sparkman to help get the city declared a "defense area," allowing homebuilders to access federal funds as well as rationed building materials in order to meet the demand. The chamber fielded hundreds of requests for homes each day, and Pipes worried that the real "rush" had not yet occurred. The congressman promised that the federal government could carefully survey the city's housing needs, but Huntsville could not wait on surveys.[87]

A week after making the request, the city advised residents to "fix up" any old or abandoned property to prepare living quarters for renters. The Farm Security Administration, which had provided prefabricated housing for farmers dislocated from the arsenal reservation, gave the city twenty government trailers, the first of over three hundred that went to defense workers. In a speech to the Conference of American Governors, Alabama's Frank Dixon enunciated Huntsville's concerns: "[These] governments are faced with the overnight creation of boom towns. . . . The spiral of high rents and high prices already beginning to prevail is one which brings sleepless nights to our public officials." With increased demand, Huntsville's rents climbed 23 percent higher than prewar levels.[88]

Relief came in February 1942, when the Federal Works Agency sent an assistant administrator to the city to oversee the construction of affordable, permanent housing. The county board of commissioners approved a new subdivision west of the city, specifically to house arsenal employees. In April, the Office of Price Administration officially designated Madison County a "defense area," allowing officials to fix rent at April 1941 levels and provide assistance for tenants facing inflated rates.[89] The next month, a House committee began formal investigation into defense migration across the South, determined to discover "exactly what has happened to change dozens of sleepy, happy-go-lucky Southern towns into hectic, overcrowded modern versions of a gold rush." Arsenal officials R. C. Ditto and Carroll Hudson spoke to the inquiry, giving projected employment figures. Ditto defended his staff, which he felt was "cooperating splendidly" with community leaders trying to update and expand city services and facilities. On a visit, John H. Tolan, the Democratic California representative who chaired the committee, praised the city for adapting "more efficiently and quietly [to] the impact of its war projects than has any other defense center I have visited."[90]

Tolan's comments failed to capture city leaders' struggles to adjust to defense conditions throughout the 1940s and 1950s. Arsenal workers collected paychecks, but rising prices ensured that the increased prosperity would not reach all Huntsvillians equally. City leaders welcomed the arsenal as economic relief, but higher wages also meant localized inflation. As the *Huntsville Times* noted, both white and black workers in the lower pay scales "have not enjoyed wage or salary increases at all comparable to the income enjoyed by those employed at these concerns. Rents have gone up, food has increased, clothing has advanced. They have been caught between the upper and nether millstones. The last few months have ground them."[91] Government action came too late to help many still struggling to turn their earnings into a better life; rent control was simply the government "rushing in to lock the stable after the horse has escaped." The housing situation pointed to the mixed benefits already apparent a year after the celebrations that marked the arsenal's coming.[92]

Housing problems plagued Huntsville's leadership throughout the war. When the arsenal added several hundred jobs in September 1942, the influx of new workers combined with rubber shortages (resulting in a lack of tires that prevented many from commuting) to boost demand near the plant.

Housing project managers told city officials that residences were occupied as soon as constructed, and that many projects had waiting lists for homes. Those Huntsvillians not employed at the arsenal faced even stiffer competition since they were ineligible for defense housing.[93] In June 1943, officials ordered 150 occupants of the government trailer park to vacate the camp in the hope that the renters would move to vacant Federal Housing Authority homes scattered across the city. Even though many took advantage of the defense housing, most of the inhabitants could not afford the mandatory move. War production salaries "will not allow them to pay the prices demanded for rent of available houses."[94]

As late as 1945, Sparkman pressed the NHA for money for additional housing near the facility, though federal officials warned that housing needs might be "temporary." As Madison Town Clerk J. C. Gormley noted, however, the wartime demand had not slackened: "Since work started at the arsenals there has been a great demand for houses at Madison and every available room here has been occupied and a large number of garages have been remodeled into living quarters and each one has a waiting list."[95] Despite cooperation from the federal government, Huntsville's leadership never balanced the supply of low-rent accommodations with the demand from the city's workforce. During the initial boom, the chamber of commerce struggled to find adequate housing, yet even when subdivisions sprang up around the city, housing remained scarce for low-wage labor. Considering the speed with which the arsenal located, the community did all it could to meet demands. As the city continued to grow in the postwar years, however, the leadership had ample time to build on its wartime experiences. By the 1950s, the Huntsville Chamber of Commerce was better prepared to adjust to the city's continued economic development.

By 1943, Huntsville Arsenal was in full production. The facility's mortar shells and smoke pots helped disguise U.S. ground operations in North Africa and Italy. The "goop" bombs carrying highly flammable chemicals set Japanese cities alight; as Secretary of War Robert Patterson noted after the war, "The blackened shambles of Tokyo, Yokohama, Osaka, and other Japanese war centers presented graphic testimony to the made-in-America fires that rained from the skies." The plant produced nearly twenty railroad-car loads of finished ammo each day, totaling millions of rounds over the course of the conflict.[96]

Yet even as the arsenal helped win the war, Huntsville's community leadership turned its attention to peacetime concerns. Government representatives and arsenal officials consistently promised that the facility would continue operating well into the postwar years, but across the city and throughout the Tennessee Valley, businessmen worried that the booming prosperity inspired by the government defense industry would disappear just as fighting men and women returned home looking for work. As the fortunes of Huntsville Arsenal flagged and the war effort slowed, the concerns convinced the city's leaders to work for the industrial development of the region. Amidst calls for diversification, Huntsville's leadership embraced a new economic direction for the old mill town.

Afraid that demobilization would bring economic ruin, in 1943 the *Huntsville Times* began running three "postwar objectives" on its editorial page for the remainder of the war. The city needed to complete its regional airport, build a new highway to attract both commercial and tourist traffic, and, most importantly, prepare the "unneeded portions" of the arsenal reservation for use by private industry. The paper stated in no uncertain terms: "[The arsenals] have wrought a vast change in this whole area. . . . But the war will be over some day, perhaps sooner than a great many believe. These arsenals then will largely close down. Most of the local labor that has been employed in them will be without jobs." Such pessimism had largely been absent as the ordnance facilities on the Huntsville reservation steadily increased production, but the time had come for a practical assessment.[97]

Across the nation, government agencies worried about the transition from a wartime to a peacetime economy. Huntsville provided a perfect opportunity for speculation, and in 1943 the Department of Labor released a report on the city's wartime growth and recommendations for its future. Researchers called the city "an outstanding example of how drastically war has changed the peacetime way of life in a large number of areas."[98] With the end of the war in sight, government officials worried that decreasing employment at Huntsville Arsenal threatened severe dislocation. Soon, officials worried, former ordnance workers would need jobs, but cotton mills would not return to pre-Depression levels, and the location of the arsenal reservation ensured that many former farmers would not be able to return to the fields. The report painted a grim picture for the newly unemployed: "The end of the war will find them no longer spread abroad, but lodged in numbers in such centers as Huntsville, and many will have no work to which to turn."[99] For the city to survive, the government needed to help Huntsville address its problems. The report noted, "Whether it will require action to reestablish small farmers on the land, to employ the unemployed until private industry can make room for them, or to do whatever else Congress may decide to do, that responsibility is an obligation owed to Huntsville by the national Government."[100]

At the state and local level, leaders began to discuss their own role in reconversion. The state's postwar planning commission, the Alabama State Planning Board, was generally optimistic, though its members fretted over the potential for dislocation. Huntsville, Anniston, Childersburg, Gadsden, Birmingham, and Mobile anticipated "localized problems" as defense plants attempted to convert to peacetime uses.[101] In a letter to Congressman Sparkman, J. A. Senter, a General Development Agent for the Nashville, Chattanooga, and St. Louis Railroad (which had rail lines connected to the arsenals) best captured the anxiety that already worried city leaders: "When the war is over, I am very much afraid that the Huntsville operation will close down, throw a great many people out of work, and necessitate the securing of an industry to take up this labor loss, or we will find deplorable conditions existing in that section."[102] As Huntsville soon discovered, reconversion was a long, tortuous process.

The city received its first scare in August 1943, when Concan Ordnance Company negotiated to assume control of the arsenals. Weeks before, Raymond Paty told Sparkman of the overwhelming need for postwar planning, particularly "prompt conversion of war plants to peace-time production," but the Concan negotiations caught the congressman by surprise.[103] Sparkman immediately contacted then–Under Secretary of War Patterson, expressing fears that privatization would decrease employment, impair morale (since workers would no longer be directly employed by the national war effort), and cost the government money. Patterson's office agreed that some changes would occur, perhaps even some downsizing, but officials promised that as many workers as possible would be transferred to similar jobs in defense or other private industries. Major General L. H. Campbell tried to assure Sparkman and his constituents, noting that Concan "has an efficient and successful record as an operator of a similar plant."[104] In fact, by 1943, many government facilities were beginning to privatize, hoping to free military personnel for active duty. Anniston's defense facility announced a deal with Chrysler, and while the discussions in Huntsville remained "mystifying," the city warmed to the idea that the arsenals would continue employing local workers, even if at reduced levels.[105] In November, the agreement fell apart. The War Department announced that "conditions had changed" because, as Sparkman confided to Reese Amis, the private company was afraid that the workforce "wouldn't stick." Both men were relieved. Amis called the failed deal "good," and the congressmen agreed that the deal was "a mistake."[106] The arsenals remained government facilities, but the scare convinced many in the city to be proactive in preparing for the postwar economy.

In late September 1944, members of the Huntsville Chamber of Commerce, encouraged by representatives of the Nashville, Chattanooga, and St. Louis Railroad, formed the Huntsville Industrial Expansion Committee (HIEC). The organization immediately began planning for a peacetime economy that might, or might not, include Huntsville Arsenal and Redstone Ordnance Plant. The committee's first act was a subscription drive, asking local businesses to donate money to be used in its campaign to bring new industries to Huntsville. In June 1945, John Blue, the owner of an eponymous North Carolina farm implement factory, decided to move his business to Huntsville. A month later, the General Shoe Corporation of Nashville, Tennessee, occupied one of Huntsville's old mill properties. The chamber of commerce and its industrial expansion group worked out the deals that brought both companies to the city. In early 1946, the HIEC began taking interested industrialists on tours of available properties and boasted a membership of over two hundred and a bankroll of twenty-five thousand dollars.[107]

Early on, the HIEC's campaign found support in Washington, especially from Congressman Sparkman. In May 1946, George Mahoney, who was elected president of the HIEC, and Sparkman helped Barrett Shelton locate Wolverine Tube Company in nearby Decatur. The company praised Sparkman's efforts. He also worked to provide the resources by which Huntsville could sell itself to larger companies. In April, he obtained a contract with a natural gas company to provide Huntsville with access to gas, which would assist the city in negotiations with large industries.[108] In 1949, Congressman Bob Jones worked with locals to show properties to industries looking for plant sites.[109] Huntsville's federal representatives leant the HIEC and other civic leaders their influence in the drive to diversify the city's economy.

The group's first substantial push for industry came in November 1946 with the publication of "Huntsville Has What It Takes." The brochure, designed by the HIEC in consultation with TVA officials, set out the benefits of locating industry in Huntsville and served as the city's main promotional tool in contacts with interested companies. Detailed descriptions of Huntsville's resources were prefaced by testimonials from the city's leading industrialists, including the arsenal's Carroll Hudson, General Shoe's James A. Jackson, and John Blue. Jackson and Hudson praised North Alabama labor that "readily adapts itself to the manufacturing industry," and Blue specifically thanked the HIEC for helping his company locate in Huntsville.[110] The pamphlet's authors stressed the physical and cultural resources available throughout the Tennessee Valley, including the area's labor supply. The HIEC described local manpower as fully trained, thanks to the arsenals; in doing so, the committee revealed its fears of a future without the government projects: "An estimated 90 percent of this tried and tested personnel is still on the scene—most of it going back to its farm and city homes in the area. It is available for Huntsville's new industries."[111] Seeking a diversified economy to relieve the city's dependence on the government arsenals, "Huntsville Has What It Takes" provided both a sales brochure and a window to the concerns of city leaders for their area economy.

The HIEC was not North Alabama's first civic development organization. In addition to the chambers of commerce that worked to attract business to communities across the valley, a number of organizations emerged to address the need for economic growth. In Florence and the Tri-Cities, for instance, civic and business leaders joined together to sell their region during the Muscle Shoals crisis, raising funds and extending assistance to locate industries in the area. Decatur's business community pressed TVA to help recruit industry and cooperated wholeheartedly when the agency moved in that direction, eventually forming the region-wide NAA in 1948. However, the nature of Huntsville's economic crisis led the city's leaders and the HIEC to expand and mature their development program beyond the scope of most of its regional colleagues and predecessors. In doing so, the HIEC and Huntsville's business and civic leaders facilitated a Sunbelt-style booster ethos in the heart of the Tennessee Valley.

Even as the HIEC worked to bring new industries to the city, the arsenals began to scale back activity. In August 1945, the arsenals cut contracts, eventually dropping $97 million worth of work in the weeks following the war. Huntsville Arsenal furloughed one-third of its workers (mostly women), and Redstone implemented a (reduced) forty-hour week.[112] Soon, city leaders faced the problem of employing the workers that once filled the arsenals, as well as returning veterans and those displaced from the farm economy. In November 1946, when the HIEC pamphlet arrived in Huntsville, the number of unemployed around the city reached 4,000.[113] Some industries took advantage of the arsenal properties, including the American Rubber Company and the Keller Motor Corporation, but the nature of the arsenals' chemical work made the transition to private industry difficult. Many buildings were contaminated, and some property on the reservation had to be fenced off due to excess chemical corruption. The *Huntsville Times* tried to remain optimistic, promising that the arsenal properties would allow "large private industries" to locate in the area (even though leasing had failed to find industries willing to move into the properties), yet the optimism belied the lengths to which those most concerned with Huntsville's economy went to try to keep the arsenals active.[114]

In February 1947, only a skeleton crew remained at the government reservation. A gas-mask plant which had temporarily occupied Huntsville Arsenal closed, laying off 280 workers. Only 241 workers and three officers staffed the "reserve ordnance arsenal" and administrative force at Redstone.[115] In December, the arsenal properties were declared surplus and listed for sale.[116] Placed on standby, the facility eventually employed 1,500 civilian and military workers for "maintenance and upkeep," but compared to a wartime peak of over 10,000, the immediate postwar employment was a severe disappointment for those hoping the arsenals would become a permanent fixture of Huntsville's business community.[117] As the HIEC worked to bring in new industries to take the place of defense jobs, Sparkman, Jones, and Hill held a series of meetings with Secretary of the Army Kenneth Royall in an attempt to convince him to retain the facilities. Sparkman pointed to a series of personal investigations that proved the cost to keep Huntsville Arsenal active was comparable to the cost of any other chemical warfare arsenal. He argued that "conditions" in the Tennessee Valley, particularly "power and water," outweighed those of any other potential site. City leaders made hurried appeals to Army officials, voters flooded Hill's office with petitions, and the HIEC begged arsenal leaders to keep the facilities active.[118]

Despite the heavy push for a diverse economy, civic boosters realized the importance of the defense project, no matter how anemic it seemed in comparison to its booming wartime business. Negotiations with Royall failed, and the disappointment of Huntsville's business leadership was palpable, but the *Huntsville Times* tried to find a silver lining. The "passing" of the government facility "brought regrets from most, some fear and trepidation to many, and a feeling of relief to others, that the issue finally is settled." The gradual nature of the closing helped "cushion the shock." In fact, the vacant facilities constituted a valuable infrastructure with water, power, and transportation connections that would make industrial occupation that much easier. As groups like the HIEC continued to contact private industries, eliciting interest in the old arsenal grounds, the government's departure might even "prove to be a blessing in disguise," the newspaper hoped.[119]

In January 1948, the city moved to catalog the resources on the arsenal reservation, hoping to list the water systems, sewer lines, dock facilities, fire-fighting equipment, highway construction equipment, school buildings, hospital, electric transmission equipment, rail lines, and airport facilities available for interested parties.[120] A number of organizations expressed a desire to use at least part of the facility. Some, like Keller Motors or Solvay Chemical, brought jobs to the city, though they employed a miniscule percentage of the wartime total. In general, demobilization after World War II proved an economic "hiccup" in the sustained postwar boom of the late 1940s and 1950s. Industries found peacetime uses for wartime products, like aluminum, and revived consumer demand after the Depression and wartime rationing fed a growing domestic economy.[121] Yet for communities like Huntsville, a scaled-down federal presence threatened the city's economic livelihood and forced civic leaders to action. Any industrial client was a victory for the city, though as Huntsville's leaders soon realized, the arsenal would be nearly impossible to replace.

Keller Motor Company perfectly exemplified the changed nature of activity on the Huntsville Arsenal reservation. Hubert Mitchell, a Hartselle, Alabama, businessman, inventor, and entrepreneur, founded the company in 1947 with George Keller, who had worked in sales for Studebaker for nearly thirty years. Keller and Mitchell incorporated their company and leased one of the largest buildings in the former Huntsville Arsenal facility to fabricate the Keller Chief and Keller Super Chief, both "lightweight economy cars."[122] The company seemed destined to succeed. By 1947, returning veterans were participating fully in the consumer economy and cheap family cars were a necessity for the booming suburban American middle class. Yet Keller Motors failed to reach its potential. The Huntsville facility never staffed more than a skeleton crew of a hundred workers, and when Keller died of a heart attack in 1949, the company collapsed. Major American automakers like Ford, Chrysler, and General Motors increased production to take advantage of rising postwar demand, leaving Keller little more than an anachronism—a local company unable to compete in a national market.

Others groups hoped to use the expansive reservation for more constructive purposes. The U.S. Public Health Service visited the city to assess the feasibility of turning the administration area of Redstone Arsenal into a regional tuberculosis sanitarium.[123] J. H. Crow Jr. asked Bob Jones for permission to purchase barrack buildings for Sunday school rooms for his church. Superintendent W. G. Hamm of the Huntsville Public School System tried to purchase parts of the old arsenal to buttress the city's crowded educational facilities, and L. H. Pinkston of the Huntsville Chamber of Commerce worked with the Alabama State Department of Education to use the old arsenal headquarters as a trade school, training the newly unemployed for work in incoming industries.[124]

Huntsville Arsenal had been the flagship of the defense effort in the city, and its deactivation threatened the end of the remarkable growth that had characterized the city's early years. Across the Tennessee Valley, communities prepared to recreate the defense boom by attracting industries that could bring renewed prosperity. In Huntsville, however, such economic development largely remained dependent on the fortunes of government contracts and the ability of the community's business leadership to utilize federal investment. Though they were disappointed by the seeming loss of the arsenal, Huntsville's civic leaders learned a valuable lesson in economic development. Government investment had revitalized the ailing textile center, but without an active program of community improvement, the benefits of the defense facilities spread unevenly. Faced with unemployment and strained services, Huntsville's leaders scrambled to adapt. Peacetime demobilization led to a more serious dislocation, and in response to declining jobs and paychecks, the city began a determined effort to bring new business to the region. As city leaders in neighboring Decatur turned to TVA for development assistance, the HIEC worked to supplement and replace government investment with private investment. In conjunction with congressional leaders, the city fought to maintain the federal presence in the region, even as they sought a more diversified economic base.

SEVEN

HOLD ONTO WHAT YOU HAVE WORKED SO HARD TO GET IN, 1949–1960

By late 1948, efforts to revive or replace the demobilized facilities on the Huntsville Arsenal and Redstone Ordnance Plant reservation fully occupied development agencies and officials across the Tennessee Valley. In addition to the Huntsville Industrial Expansion Committee (HIEC), civic leaders looked to the newly formed North Alabama Associates (NAA), to the TVA, to the Army, and to the state's congressional delegation in hopes of finding relief from the looming economic trouble. Yet just when Huntsvillians had resigned themselves to a long campaign to reutilize the facilities, Colonel Carroll Hudson, the former commander of Huntsville Arsenal, announced that he would return to the reservation to command a new Ordnance Department research team studying the use of rockets. The city had "suitable land and facilities for rocket research and development," and the Army hoped to employ a small cadre of technicians engaged in research and development in this relatively new field in military science. Hudson was careful to give a realistic picture of the incoming program. Again and again, the commander cautioned citizens that the new Redstone Arsenal would be very different from its World War II–era precedent, particularly in terms of employment. As Hudson noted, "There is no reason to expect any large expansion at Redstone, comparable to that during the war era." Most of the employees would be trained engineers and technicians, highly educated men and women that, as Hudson's words implied, would likely be drawn from other areas.[1]

But what the new facility lacked in immediate economic impact it made up in national attention and relative stability. Hudson met with the Huntsville Kiwanis Club in April 1949, showing a film on the V-2 rocket as an explosive example of the city's future. Within months of the announcement, Hudson and his crew reequipped laboratories, modified existing facilities to meet new demands, and conducted basic engineering work in preparation for full-scale use of the Redstone properties.[2] The government suspended attempts to lease the rest of the old Huntsville Arsenal reservation and began transferring tracts of land to Hudson's unit. The site was gradually absorbed by Hudson and his technicians, and soon the entire reservation became "Redstone Arsenal." In what Reese Amis, editor of the *Huntsville Times*, called "the most heartening piece of information that has come to this area in some time," Redstone officials announced that they expected to hire 235 workers in 1950 and relocate another 665 from other facilities across the country.[3] Though gradual, the prospect of any increase in employment provided Huntsvillians with a glimmer of hope. Despite pronouncements otherwise, city leaders tentatively looked to the government to again provide a spark for economic growth in the valley.

In early September, a group of scientists from the Army's Ordnance Research and Development Division Sub-Office at Fort Bliss, near El Paso, Texas, visited Huntsville to discuss "problems connected with the rocket research and development program now underway at the arsenal." Among the visitors were thirteen German scientists, recruited at the end of World War II during "Operation Paperclip" to help the United States develop rocket-based weapons. The group included Dr. Eberhard Rees, who later recalled his first visit to the city. Rees had "mixed feelings" upon seeing the town. Despite the wartime boom, Huntsville had retained much of its rural character, a fact that boded ill for a facility demanding high-tech equipment and sophisticated minds to develop, test, and manufacture rockets, and Rees wondered if the city would be able to provide the staff for a complex defense facility. Rees also had personal concerns about the reception he might receive in the South. As he recalled, "I was uncertain whether Huntsville and its population had the progressive spirit and forward-looking attitude for the build-up of a community with a social structure so entirely different from the past."[4]

Rees soon had a chance to test his fears against reality. The September visit was more than just a conference. In October, the valley's congressional delegation, Senators Lister Hill and John Sparkman and Congressman Bob Jones, announced that the entire staff of the Texas facility would relocate to Huntsville. Hudson portrayed the move as one of economy. The laboratories and associated facilities at Fort Bliss were "inadequate," and the Ordnance Department felt that relocation to the unused buildings at Redstone would cost less than a complete refitting elsewhere (Hudson speculated that the Army saved nearly $4.5 million in utilizing the old Huntsville Arsenal grounds). Chief of the Army Rocket Division Holger N. Toftoy also fought for the move. Building off wartime advances in rocketry, the Army made quick strides in the development of anti-aircraft guided missiles. To test the rockets, however, Toftoy needed larger runways than those at Fort Bliss, and the Army searched for an available site with enough space for experimentation. Toftoy found ample room in Huntsville, and asked to use the old arsenal properties.[5] The city celebrated as 500 military personnel and their families, 65 civilian employees, and 100 German scientists, including Rees and Dr. Wernher von Braun, relocated to the valley.

Von Braun became an instant celebrity in the city. Born in Wiritz, Germany, in 1912, he developed an early love of astronomy and, as a young student, joined the lab of rocketry expert Hermann Oberth as an assistant helping with the development of liquid propellants. In 1932, just as the German government evinced a growing interest in the use of rockets, von Braun graduated with a degree in aeronautical engineering and joined the German Ordnance Department, eventually becoming the technical director at the rocket proving ground at Peenemünde on the Baltic Sea. Von Braun played a key role in developing the rockets used against the Allies during the war, most notably the V-2. Von Braun's work in creating the weapon made him a controversial figure after the war. The scientist valued the space-flight possibilities of the V-2 over its military uses, but in accepting Nazi funds, he implicitly cooperated in the Axis war effort. Furthermore, his production facilities made use of Nazi slave labor in camps at Dora and Nordhausen. As he would later tell an interviewer, "We felt no moral scruples about the possible future use of our brainchild. . . . It was simply a question with us of how the golden cow could be milked most successfully."[6] Throughout the rest of his career, von Braun constantly negotiated the fine line between civilian science and military necessity as rockets became paramount to both fields, and he never fully shrugged off the darker implications of his cooperation with Hitler's government.

In January 1945, with the war in Europe drawing to a close, the Russian army neared the rocket facility at Peenemünde. Von Braun and his staff faced an important choice: stay and surrender to the Red Army or move farther south to meet the United States. The scientists voted overwhelmingly to evacuate. Over 5,000 rocket scientists, associates, and family members collected the program's documents and papers and boarded cars emblazoned "Vorhaben zur Besonderen Verwendung" (a mythical "Project for Special Disposition") to evade the numerous Gestapo checkpoints. Von Braun sent his brother, Magnus, to negotiate with the U.S. Forty-fourth Infantry at Bleicherode, and the Allies gladly accepted the collection of German scientific minds and made plans to transport von Braun and his associates to the United States. Chief Toftoy took charge of Operation Paperclip, traveling to the captured missile factory at Mittlewerk and shipping out whole and partial V-2s unused in the war effort. Von Braun and 127 of his Peenemünde colleagues then entered Ordnance Department custody.[7] The scientists traveled to the Aberdeen Proving Ground in Massachusetts, where they began the laborious process of translating and organizing thousands of captured German documents. The team then transferred to Fort Bliss, where they created apartments and laboratories out of an old Army hospital complex. In late 1946, the German scientists began bringing their families to Texas and learning English, preparing to spend the rest of their lives working in the United States.[8]

On April 10, 1950, von Braun, his wife Maria, and their sixteen-month-old daughter, Iris, left El Paso for Huntsville. At first, the city's residents were skeptical of their new neighbors. One young Huntsvillian remembered his first sight of the scientist. Returning from school, he saw a family moving into the house across the street: "The young husband, very blond and handsome in his trenchcoat, and his pretty wife were conversing in a foreign language, possibly German." When he told his father, the older man announced with a shake of his head, "Looks like this neighborhood is going to the dogs."[9] The husband and wife were the von Brauns. In the end, as one popular historian has noted, Huntsville, "with the natural aplomb and courtesy of the Deep South, has taken the foreigners into its hearts and, more importantly, into its homes."[10] The transition was certainly not as easy or smooth as city leaders would have liked, but the economic benefits outweighed the social challenges of rapid economic growth.

Upon arrival, the rocket team set to work. Von Braun hoped to recreate conditions at Peenemünde, housing research and engineering alongside actual production. This "everything-under-one-roof" approach allowed seamless transition between design, experimentation and testing, and manufacturing. The Army, however, had other plans. The Ordnance Department preferred to keep the Army Ballistic Missile Agency (ABMA) as a "research and development organization," contracting parts supply and production to the private sector.[11] This decision helped cement Huntsville's economic future. Had production been allowed to remain "in-house" at Redstone, the city would undoubtedly have continued in the vein of Huntsville Arsenal with a small cadre of skilled researchers and engineers designing and testing rockets, while an army of semi- and unskilled workers operated the production lines, churning out weapons for the battlefield.

Instead, Redstone Arsenal presented the city with a completely new economic environment. The only unskilled civilian jobs on the facility were in construction, housekeeping, catering, and groundskeeping. Redstone occupied the center of a growing contract network, in which von Braun's team and a core workforce of highly educated scientists and engineers directed center activities, farming out the semi-skilled and unskilled production work to industries across the country; it was the very definition of the postwar military-industrial complex: "an interwoven system of production comprising the Pentagon, the armed services, private firms, and political players."[12] Huntsville saw remarkable economic growth in the 1950s and 1960s, but jobs and paychecks for most residents were completely reliant on the ability of city leaders to diversify the local industrial economy.

In this, Huntsville resembled other southern defense centers, struggling to adapt to redevelopment in the wake of postwar demobilization. In Marietta, Georgia, civic leaders actively pursued bomber manufacturer Bell Aircraft by preparing the city for industrial growth and by pressuring their representatives in Washington, D.C., to assist in the project. When the war ended and demand fell, Bell left the community. Hoping to replace the lost money and jobs, the city advertised an available workforce and a proven ability to support defense manufacturing. Soon, the Air Force helped locate a Lockheed facility in the community, providing what one scholar called a "permanent manufacturing presence sustained by ongoing federal contracts." Bell and Lockheed exhibited many of the problems Huntsville faced as Redstone grew throughout the postwar decades, including an imported workforce, tenuous government funds, and the constant demand to balance economic growth and social change.[13]

In spite of the pressures that accompanied growth, Huntsville welcomed the bustle of activity at Redstone Arsenal in the 1950s as a respite from the doldrums of the late 1940s, when most of Huntsville feared a permanent economic decline. Industries relocated in the city, local businesses sprang to life, and civic leaders worked furiously to accommodate a future built on government appropriations. But even as Redstone brought hope, many worried that rocket science would not provide the economic foundation the region needed. While von Braun and his fellow Germans worked to accommodate the needs of the American military, Huntsville's civic and business leaders looked for permanent prosperity. Should the arsenal fail, or even fail to live up to the expectations of its proponents, they hoped to provide an industrial foundation for economic security. In training skilled workers, reorganizing the city to house the booming population, and diversifying local industries, Huntsville's leaders avoided some of the dislocation that seemed an inevitable byproduct of rapid economic growth.

Huntsville's success in the 1950s and 1960s marked the region's full entrance into the modern South, particularly the economy of the emerging Sunbelt. As the city's civic and business leaders sought industry to support and balance the growth of the arsenal, their efforts recalled the work of Florence's community leaders, organizing in response to the debate over Muscle Shoals, and Decatur's citizens, working in close conjunction with TVA to industrialize before, during, and after World War II. The practices certainly shifted and changed as boosterism matured; Huntsville's Space Age civic organizations sought a level of professionalism and efficiency far beyond that of Florence's chamber of commerce in the 1920s. However, the larger similarities are telling—across the decades, the valley's civic and business leaders mobilized for development and cooperated fully with the federal government in the pursuit of economic growth. The city's emergence as a major center of the Sunbelt South is more than a local success story. Huntsville's boom, along with the leaders who worked to encourage and maintain it, highlights the culmination of the valley's long and complex campaign for economic development.

The first private companies to participate in the city's rocket boom accompanied the relocation of the Fort Bliss team. Alongside the German scientists came 102 employees of General Electric, which had contracted with von Braun's team in El Paso.[14] GE soon found itself amid a number of additional concerns. Upon learning of Redstone's new mission, Thiokol moved a division to Huntsville to develop fuel for Army rockets, and within a month, Philadelphia chemicals and plastics manufacturer Rohm and Haas visited Colonel Toftoy to plan for a North Alabama branch.[15] Local companies also benefited from the arsenal and expanded their own production on government investment. Reynolds Aluminum, for instance, received orders for aluminum to be used in missile housings.[16] In return, money that flowed into the outfitting of Redstone benefited the contractors. In June 1951, the government spent $4 million in constructing new laboratories for Rohm and Haas and Thiokol technicians, and public money funded myriad expansions in utilities, roads, and facilities serving employees on the reservation.

Large-scale missile production was not the only source of contracts on the arsenal, and in reality, Huntsvillians and other valley residents benefited as much from small-business agreements as they did from companies like Thiokol. Redstone Arsenal set up a small-business department designed to "assist businessmen here and all over the Valley to get contracts for materials needed in the work at the arsenal." Within a year of the rocket team's move, the office supported a number of industries, including a hundred-employee cartridge-box factory using wood cut and processed in nearby Scottsboro. In the first half of 1951, Redstone let nearly $700,000 in contracts to North Alabama concerns. Colonel Hudson optimistically suggested that the city and region would see a marked increase in contracts to local firms, and by the end of the year, 81 percent of the arsenal's contracts went to fifteen hundred small southeastern companies manufacturing everything from rocket parts to floor coverings to lenses used in research equipment.[17]

Valley companies recognized the value in bidding for government work. Huntsville businessman Walter Eigenbrod wrote Bob Jones asking for his support for a loan for Eigenbrod's Southern Permanent Awning Company, hoping to enlarge facilities to participate in the defense program. Eigenbrod complained of the difficulty of navigating the Washington bureaucracy, but Jones offered little beyond contact information. Eigenbrod then turned to the business community for help. He wrote Reynolds Metals Vice-President Marion Caskie in hopes that his aluminum supplier could provide advice on obtaining a government contract. Caskie was much more accommodating than Jones, sending the awning manufacturer a "Government Sales Kit" that introduced its owners to the contract network. Caskie encouraged Eigenbrod to discuss his company's needs with the Huntsville Chamber of Commerce, and even offered to mention the company to government officials.[18] Decatur Iron and Steel had similar concerns. The company, which produced steel for bridges and buildings, called on Lister Hill for assistance in avoiding the "natural human predilections" that arose in any contract negotiation. Hill promised to use his influence on the Army, stating that he was "most sympathetic" with the company's predicament.[19] Both Southern Awning and Decatur Iron and Steel found themselves in the midst of an economic transition. With the expansion at Redstone Arsenal and the implementation of the contract system, small businesses across the valley adapted to the new and potentially lucrative source of funds.

When combined with expansion at Redstone, rising employment at associated firms appeased city leaders worried about the region's economic future. Even with growth, planners realized that they could not rely solely on the arsenal. For one thing, employment on the reservation was highly uneven. With some production occurring on-site and companies like Thiokol and Rohm and Haas in the city, demand for unskilled and semi-skilled workers did increase, and by 1955, 1,500 military personnel and nearly 6,000 civilian employees worked at Redstone Arsenal, with an annual payroll of $40 million.[20] However, most of the appointments to the facility followed Rees's predictions as a "highly trained" cadre of technicians staffed the arsenal, and the nature of the new jobs did not help those Alabamians lacking the requisite credentials.

In May 1956, when the Alabama Hosiery Mill permanently closed without advance notice, 300 men and women lost their jobs. Many looked to the expanding arsenal as an option. Charles Black contacted Bob Jones on behalf of a number of out-of-work employees, begging for help finding jobs at Redstone. Jones, Hill, and Sparkman jointly contacted Toftoy, asking him to speak to Black. Later in the month, Black and George D. Hartselle Jr., calling themselves the "Employment Committee," visited the arsenal but learned that their congressmen's influence could not create work. Black, Hartselle, and others received applications but were unqualified for every job listed as available.[21] The situation was no better in 1958. Redstone announced an increase of 1,150 jobs in both government and contractor offices, but as the *Huntsville Times* warned, all of the openings were "professional type" and unskilled labor would "not be touched at all."[22] By 1960, one-fifth of Huntsville's male metropolitan workforce was classified professional or technical, and half of those positions were engineers.[23] If the city were truly to enjoy the prosperity promised by Redstone, Huntsville's leadership would need to act decisively to train local workers for skilled positions.

City leaders and arsenal officials hoped that a research university in Huntsville, with programs in math, science, and engineering, would better prepare citizens for full participation in the aerospace economy. The University of

Alabama authorized an official extension campus in the city in late 1949 (in contrast to the temporary defense training program during World War II), offering night classes geared toward work at the government facility. Redstone Arsenal realized the benefits of local training and, in 1951, the extension center reached an agreement to award graduate credits to arsenal personnel "to contribute to the effectiveness of the rocket and guided missile research and development program at Redstone."[24] The center quickly outgrew its temporary residence, with over seventy courses and a student population of 1,000, second in size only to the extension center at Birmingham. In 1957, university trustees began planning for permanent facilities to be located near the arsenal reservation and the numerous aerospace companies populating its fringes. Soon, arsenal leadership called for expanding the extension center, now being referred to as the University of Alabama at Huntsville (UAH), to a four-year program with opportunities for postgraduate work and associated research programs. General Bruce Medaris of Redstone's ABMA defended a fully developed university as essential to the city's growth: "The best prevention for technological unemployment is . . . adequate education and training for our future labor force." Arsenal and municipal leaders hoped that UAH would create the scientists and engineers needed to sustain Huntsville's boom. Medaris's remarks encapsulated the problem: "There is not enough fully prepared manpower available in Alabama to support new industry [and Alabama must] provide the foundation through its public schools, universities, and trade schools."[25]

Two local leaders led the fight for UAH: von Braun and the president of Brown Engineering, Milton K. Cummings. Cummings mobilized the business community, particularly those companies like Brown, directly funded by government contracts based on the technical specifications of rocket and missile production. He offered the city tracts of land for the university campus and held a number of meetings with his colleagues in the HIEC and chamber of commerce, seeking to create an intellectual climate in the city that would "move all mankind to a higher ledge." In 1961, von Braun personally appeared before the Alabama state legislature in support of a $3 million bond issue to build new labs and facilities at UAH. He promised legislators that the funds would create an "educational climate to attract the right people" and ensure that the government programs and associated private industries stayed in the area. Never one to mince words, von Braun made sure that the state's political leaders realized the essential nature of graduate training in the sciences.

According to the scientist, the government located the program in the city because "the Army had a big chunk of spare real estate that served the immediate purpose of providing a home. . . . We've lived in that home for more than 10 years now, and it's about time we got a schoolhouse and everything that goes with it."[26] That December, state voters ratified the bond issue by a four-to-one margin.

A year later, von Braun continued to call for improvements to the university, telling an audience at the University of Alabama in Tuscaloosa, "One of our greatest needs . . . is more trained engineers who can interpret new scientific information and apply it to useful designs, bridging the gap between scientific discoveries and engineering achievements." He called on the government to continue funding local colleges and universities.[27] Von Braun went on to develop a particularly close relationship with UAH, allocating nearly $600,000 to finish construction and reserving some of his research and development for the test stands, labs, and technical equipment located on campus.[28] Von Braun understood a central requirement for lasting economic development: permanent, sustainable growth required a workforce with the skills and training for new and emerging technology.

Inadequate educational facilities were a small part of a larger problem. The revitalization of the arsenal was accompanied by a population explosion in the city. Huntsville began the 1950s as a large town, smaller in population (with 16,500) than both Florence and Decatur in North Alabama. By the end of the decade, the city had become a metropolitan area with over 117,000 inhabitants, 72,000 within city limits that had expanded from four to almost forty square miles.[29] The growing population put a strain on city services, particularly the region's housing supply. The influx of workers at the arsenal, at associated industries, and in the numerous service industries that catered to the growing community overwhelmed the city's scant housing options. In November 1949, only a month after the relocation of the German scientists was announced, HIEC head Fritz Thomas formed the Civic Housing Committee from members of the chamber of commerce. The group immediately began discussions with the Federal Housing Authority to provide homes for incoming scientists and other workers. In a matter of months, the committee members helped form a real estate company, planned for three hundred new houses scattered on sites throughout the city, and authored a subscription campaign for the $50,000 needed to begin construction. The *Huntsville Times* noted the excellent opportunity for investment in rental properties: "These people, who are high salaried, and with fine families, will be a great addition to Huntsville. . . . The speed with which this money is raised and put on the line, will be a test of how much Huntsville wants to expand."[30] In 1951, Huntsville was (again) designated a "defense housing area," with lenient credit terms for new home construction.[31] One arsenal official told the chamber of commerce that the "thing of greatest concern to [General Medaris] is housing for civilians to be imported into the city." If Huntsville could not provide homes for technicians on the reservation, then the nation's defense program could very well be "stymied."[32]

Huntsville's entire infrastructure struggled to accommodate the rapidly growing population. As the arsenal and its associated industries brought in workers, streets congested with cars, classrooms overflowed, and hospital and recreational facilities proved woefully inadequate.[33] In early 1952, Elizabeth Parks Beamguard pleaded with Sparkman for funds to help the public library. The six-person staff could no longer maintain the "pressure of increased population." In particular, the voracious reading habits of the German scientists required "considerable time and work in service." The stress on the library mirrored the pressure placed on hospital administrators, teachers, and numerous city officials who lamented the "inadequate financial medium" to expand necessary programs and services.[34] Some elementary schools threatened to begin operating in shifts, the city's health department warned that the old sewer system was not designed to handle the increased strain, and water works officials promised that a dry summer would lead to a water shortage.[35]

The city council sprang into action. Members voted to survey city services and allocate $8.5 million in local bonds and federal aid to meet the most pressing needs. Hugh Morrow Jr., a Birmingham surveyor hired for the job, suggested a program of planned annexation as a way to increase tax revenues and streamline community development.[36] By 1956, the Madison County delegation in Montgomery had drawn up legislation to annex "practically all of the populated areas surrounding Huntsville" without a vote. The homes, businesses, and facilities in West Huntsville, Huntsville Park, and Lincoln all became part of Greater Huntsville. The legislation, crafted in cooperation with the HIEC, allowed the city to provide sewage disposal and utility coverage to areas around the city, opening up new homes for incoming workers and raising revenue to help pay for citywide improvements.[37]

Not everyone proved as willing to go along with annexation as the city's leaders had hoped. B. C. Brockway carried his protests to the secretary of defense, arguing that he was being "dragged" into the city thanks to the expansion of the arsenal. In return for his cooperation, Brockway demanded that people in the annexed areas be given first shot at jobs opened at the facility. Brockway's bargain was naive, but his sentiments highlighted a growing problem for city leaders.[38] In order to maintain control over the city's expansion, those in charge of Huntsville's infrastructure needed to meet the demands of middle- and upper-class technicians and scientists who worked on the reservation but chose to live in the suburbs. Scrambling to adjust to this new suburban landscape, city leaders largely ignored the needs of those passed over by the defense boom. Leaders assumed that men like Brockway would be swept along in the currents of economic revitalization, little concerned about the life that he would leave behind in the process.[39]

In the late 1950s and early 1960s, annexation proceeded apace. In 1957, the city government purchased a building next to the old courthouse to house "overflowing" city offices and made plans for a new municipal government complex. The city council voted to add a corridor of Madison County stretching from Huntsville to the Tennessee River to the city limits, providing police protection and municipal services and clearing the way for Redstone to expand a 300-house subdivision. Communities north and west of Huntsville joined the city, though one area voted seven to three to remain separate, a sign of continued (if ineffectual) resistance.[40] By 1960, the city had built 10,000 new homes, spent nearly $25 million in electricity, water, sewer, and gas expansions, built new city and county schools, and tripled its police force. The construction of a new major roadway, Memorial Parkway, promised to ease traffic and provide a new strip of retail spaces to serve incoming workers. Huntsville Hospital won a $790,000 Hill-Burton grant to expand its 172-bed facility to 300 beds.[41] Huntsville had become "an American conglomerate—cosmopolitan and busy," gobbling up suburbs and expanding its web of services to reach communities across the central Tennessee Valley.[42] As city leaders pushed to accommodate and encourage growth, however, they left parts of the city behind.

As Huntsville suburbanized, the city's old center fell into neglect. Hannes Luehrsen, an architect who had long worked with von Braun and his team, hoped to address urban stagnation. In 1957, he released a plan to update the downtown, unchanged since "horse and buggy days." A new "City Center" would provide a modern meeting place for the city's political, economic, and social leadership. Luehrsen noted a transformation occurring across the country as the middle and upper classes fled stagnant inner cities for suburbs:

"Adding one subdivision to another does not make a city, nor will outskirt shopping centers or development along highways." The German architect proposed a new civic center, accompanied by a convention hall, new restaurants, theaters, and parks. He noted, "If we plan it right, it has to be more than simply a place for business and traffic, more than just an accumulation of important buildings. . . . It should be the heart of the City, physically and spiritually."[43]

Luehrsen's vision evolved into a city-wide revitalization scheme entitled the "Heart of Huntsville" plan, involving economic diversification, internal improvements, even slum clearance. Echoing a constant fear of Huntsville's business community, the "Heart of Huntsville" program resulted in a city more attractive to new industry. As Mayor R. B. Searcy claimed, the city's new "bold architecture" and "spaciousness" would undoubtedly make it the "world's center of space exploration."[44] Luehrsen argued for more comprehensive development, urging city leaders to make careful study of the "Greater Downtown" area in order to create a core of entertainment, shopping, and meeting places, though Searcy and others focused increasingly on slum clearance as a way of "beautifying" the city and ensuring its appeal to outside investment. Worried that businesses would avoid the city's decaying interior, the mayor valued appearance (and thus, economic recruitment) over practical usage, and Luehrsen soon claimed that city leaders ignored his original conceptions for a design of their own making.[45] Worried about future development, city leaders overlooked the needs of many Huntsvillians for a narrower program to attract business.

More than any other group, the Huntsville Housing Authority took the lead in initializing the Heart of Huntsville plan. Drawing on federal funds as the "striking edge" of its program, the HHA's revitalization encompassed nearly the entire city limits as they lay in 1950 and resulted in the aptly named Von Braun Civic Center, a new parking system, a city hall, a library, a historically recreated nineteenth-century village, a Hilton hotel, and a municipal greenspace, all surrounded by new housing developments. John Sparkman was effervescent concerning the changes made to the city. He ranked slum clearance as one of the two greatest contributions he made to the city's growth (alongside attracting the Chemical Warfare Arsenal in 1941). As he recalled, "We had some of the worst slums to be found anywhere. . . . This area was so infested with vermin that the Health Department recommended that it not be torn down by hand but be burned down." Sparkman then boasted that he was "given the privilege of setting the first house on fire. . . . It was a tremendous fire that cleared the whole area, and it made possible the development of one of the finest and most productive industrial and housing areas in Huntsville."[46]

The revitalization of downtown Huntsville certainly proved beneficial to the city's economic development. The civic center and park provided recreational outlets for affluent engineers, scientists, and technicians while presenting a brochure-ready vista to attract interested companies. Yet the residents of those "vermin-infested" slums were the same low-income, low-skilled workers ignored in the rocket boom. As Huntsville tied its fortunes to defense work, the city's leadership hoped that rising wages would spread to everyone. Slum clearance served as a telling example of the outlook of the city's business leaders, who were concerned about larger economic growth and were willing to encourage community development when it allowed them to attract new industries and preserve government investment.[47]

Throughout the 1950s, Redstone experienced growth that eventually surpassed the levels reached during World War II, and the Army's Redstone, Jupiter, and Saturn rocket programs brought valuable government contracts to the area and made Redstone and Huntsville household names. But even as the arsenal grew, city leaders were never sure of economic security. Beginning in 1956, Secretary of Defense Charles Wilson campaigned to remove the Jupiter program from Army supervision and transfer control to the Air Force. The Eisenhower administration, constantly trying to economize, threatened the Army installation's ample appropriations. In the late 1950s, excitement over economic growth at the arsenal was tempered by fears that budget cuts or inter-service rivalries would wreak havoc with its payroll and contract network. Huntsville resident Walter Wiesman asked the crucial question: "How much does the present prosperity depend on how much money the government is willing to provide to keep many industries going on defense orders?" Bob Jones's response enunciated their fears, foreseeing "serious readjustments" should a change in federal policy or the international environment decrease funding.[48]

The uncertainty spurred civic boosters to intensify their efforts to balance the Redstone payroll with private industry, but a mature industrial recruitment program did not materialize in the city overnight. In fact, the 1950s proved to be a decade of on-the-job training for the chamber of commerce and the HIEC. During the demobilization of the mid-1940s, the groups created a detailed pamphlet, advertising the district for potential investors, but other than general publicity, the organization did little to approach prospective clients. Concerned about the rampant growth of the arsenal and fears of its impermanence, city leaders adopted new strategies soon to be synonymous with Sunbelt boosterism. In doing so, their economic development campaign found a maturity that would make their efforts easier and more successful.

Civic improvement groups had plenty of company in industrial recruitment by the 1950s. In fact, Huntsville's developers actively sought out other communities as successful models. In Mississippi, leaders noted, the Balance Agriculture with Industry Program encouraged legislation giving local governments the authority to issue bonds and build facilities which could then be rented to interested industries. Illustrating that plants could be "bought," the program promised real returns for municipalities like Huntsville, willing to make a similar effort.[49] Closer to home, civic and business leaders looked to Lawrenceburg, Tennessee, a smaller southern city with a similarly active development group. In 1952, Lawrenceburg's leaders attracted a large textile firm, Wamsutta Mills, with a publicly financed bond issue, repaid by rent from the incoming company.[50] Four years later, Murray Ohio Manufacturing Company located in the surrounding county and, by the early 1960s, employed 2,000. Lawrenceburg's growth helped the region transition from agriculture to an industrial economy as locals "set [their] own pattern" for economic growth.[51] Yet, while residents benefitted from paychecks, and as the city and county enjoyed increased tax receipts, the growing population and workforce strained an infrastructure designed for a smaller, rural town. Huntsville's leaders saw in Lawrenceburg an example: the city's success proved the feasibility of a civic development program, but its struggles to prepare for growth encouraged the Alabama city to pay more attention to the social and economic costs of development.

The HIEC also cooperated with nearby municipal groups and regional organizations, particularly Tom Johnson's NAA. Realizing that reliance on the arsenal for growth affected the entire region, Johnson joined Huntsville's diversification efforts and employed his region-wide network of chambers and interested businessmen to bring new jobs to the entire region. Johnson attracted few industries to Huntsville, but his efforts in Decatur, Hartselle, and other towns directed much-needed jobs and funds to the region. He worked to occupy the old Dallas Mills facilities, cooperating with the chamber and the HIEC to lease the property to General Shoe and, eventually, to aerospace companies working in conjunction with the arsenal. Yet Johnson's importance to Huntsville's growth went beyond the immediate work of companies brought to the valley. Johnson's NAA, along with the Wallace and Cater acts and the successes of civic organizations in other southern states, encouraged Huntsville's leaders to continue expanding local efforts and initiative in a more active, and ultimately more professional industrial recruitment campaign.

As Johnson noted in a speech from early 1952, economic development agencies needed to do more than simply advertise their communities. Proudly pointing to NAA, and drawing from decades of experience, Johnson enumerated the "foundation stones" of a successful organization and encouraged groups like the HIEC to broaden their approach. The first step in any campaign, he argued, was to develop a basic collection of raw data on natural resources, manpower, taxes, education, living conditions, and the myriad other aspects of economic and social life in a given region. Armed with an array of statistics, a successful group worked to cultivate close relations with engineering firms, construction companies, and private consulting groups. Next, it created ties with the local business leadership, recruiting bankers, insurers, large business owners—all of whom had the kind of investment capital needed to purchase sites and build facilities in expectation of enormous returns. Finally, Johnson argued that a group should work closely with educational institutions, particularly the University of Alabama and Alabama Polytechnic Institute (and in Huntsville, UAH), which could marshal research capacities in favor of new methods of production and management while providing a skilled workforce—attractive propositions for any interested business.[52] Johnson's "rules" for development closely mirrored the ongoing work by TVA and its civic partners. By the 1950s, the agency had compiled an enormous amount of data and had developed close working relationships with both community leaders and educational institutions. Local boosters then approached businesses, marshaling the support of the authority, to sell the valley as a place for business.

By 1953, Redstone accounted for nearly 7,000 jobs, but growth on the arsenal was not a real source of financial security. As civic leaders knew, Huntsville needed a "good-sized, substantial industry that will give employment to several hundred families."[53] Between 1954 and early 1956, the HIEC scored two major industrial clients: Mallory-Schwarzkopf, a rare metals company, and American Machine and Foundry (AMF). Mallory-Schwarzkopf's decision was partially based on Huntsville's material and labor attractions, but the company also benefited from land that had been specially set aside for them.

The month before the move was announced, Huntsville Industrial Sites, Inc., a nonprofit organization created by the HIEC and funded through the sale of two hundred shares of public stock, purchased 248 acres of surplus Redstone Arsenal land, marketing part of the parcel directly to Mallory-Schwarzkopf.[54] In June 1956, AMF announced its plans to locate an underground manufacturing plant near the Tennessee River. The HIEC acquired land along the river through the direct purchase of property, organized seismological studies of the surrounding area in preparation for construction, and met with officials when they visited Huntsville.[55] Governor Jim Folsom helped by authorizing a highway directly to the facility—as he told *Huntsville Times* editor Reese Amis, "I appreciate the fact that Madison is one county that likes to push forward as well as I do."[56]

Less than a month later, HIEC officials obtained state funding for a dock system to be built on TVA land near the incoming AMF plant, providing a shipping terminal that could be used by any Huntsville operation; the *Huntsville Times* hoped that the terminal would "renew the spirit of industrial expansion."[57] The paper was proved correct in 1959 when, thanks to the HIEC's persistence, Union Carbide's Linde Division leased land near the docks for a liquid nitrogen and oxygen plant to fuel rockets on the Redstone reservation.[58] Even as valley agencies moved to offer surplus TVA property along reservoirs and prepare sites for industrial growth, the HIEC branched into site preparation and more advanced techniques to attract business.

In fact, with the success of Huntsville Industrial Sites, land investment proved to be one of the HIEC's strongest tools in the quest for new industry and, in the late 1950s, its strategy shifted decidedly in that direction. In a report on Huntsville's advantages, the NAA noted the willingness of civic groups to prepare sites for prospective clients, pointing to the spirit of cooperation between the HIEC and the chamber of commerce as an indication that "civic business and governmental leaders are ever mindful of their responsibility to present industry, doing everything possible to bring about their successful and happy operation."[59] Soon, Huntsville's civic and business leadership turned to a strategy becoming popular among other southern development groups—the creation of industrial parks.

In February 1957, the group purchased the old Lincoln Mills properties, renamed it the "Huntsville Industrial Center," and almost immediately saw results when Brown Engineering Company, a Huntsville firm expanding on government contracts, leased the facilities. The civic organization even financed a renovation to prepare Brown's offices. In July 1958, Chrysler, which won the contract to construct the Jupiter rocket, decided to locate at the Industrial Center as well.[60] The site was soon joined by the "Industrial Research Park," and the two sites became key selling points for the HIEC, providing office space and industrial facilities in close proximity to Redstone labs. Alongside UAH and other improvements, the industrial parks had "the dual result of supporting government contract work while it was strong and creating vital pieces of the infrastructure on which the new high technology could prosper."[61] The expansion of the arsenal led the community to prepare for diversified industry, and it convinced civic leaders and the HIEC to move beyond simple publicity to active city planning, and specifically land investments, in order to bring new industries to the area.

Huntsville's "Research Park" filled quickly as the HIEC brought engineering firms, research labs, and high-tech companies to the city, just as other Sunbelt industrial parks began to emerge. The best example of this increasingly popular method of economic development was undoubtedly Research Triangle Park near Raleigh, North Carolina. Begun in 1956 by an organization tasked with locating industrial research labs and facilities, Research Triangle drew support from business leaders, hoping to buttress the state and regional economy, and scholars and researchers from nearby institutions like Duke and the University of North Carolina at Chapel Hill, hoping to take advantage of developing technology.[62] While Huntsville's park realized almost immediate success, Research Triangle grew slowly, at least at first. Despite an active promotional campaign consisting of pamphlets and brochures, as well as private investments in facility construction and preparation, the park did not attract a major industrial client until 1959, and only experienced steady growth after recruiting a federal environmental health sciences center and IBM in 1965.[63] Research Triangle eventually outpaced Huntsville, becoming the epitome of a successful industrial park, but considered jointly, the facilities in Raleigh-Durham and Huntsville illustrate the increasingly modern and professional nature of economic development across the South. The HIEC had come a long way since the publication of a simple brochure.

Despite their city's growth, Huntsville's leaders remained unsatisfied. In 1958, the *Huntsville Times* cautioned against inactivity: "Huntsville badly needs new industry if it is to enjoy the soundest economic health. This area has enjoyed unprecedented prosperity in recent years. . . . However, during the 1930s the community learned first hand the peril of over-dependence on a single industry."[64] Without constant effort, the collapse of the defense industry would leave Huntsville in a position analogous to the Depression-era collapse of the textile industry. At the end of the impassioned plea for further industrial development, the reporter noted another difficulty. Since the late 1940s, two groups had largely spearheaded the efforts for Huntsville: the valley-wide NAA, which had performed some of the initial contacts of industrial clients, and the HIEC, which worked at the community level to address local needs and prepare sites for occupation. While the two organizations had cooperated in the past, "petty jealousy, selfishness, favoritism and apathy" had begun to threaten their combined efforts.[65] While unspecified, the growing rift between the HIEC and the NAA almost certainly revolved around jurisdiction. The NAA was a regional organization, funded by a number of municipal electric systems and businessmen. Johnson's organization sought to place companies in the communities that proved the best fit and boasted the best chance for continued development. Huntsville had long been the single largest contributor to the NAA, thanks to its large and profitable electric distribution system, but to the NAA, it was one community among many hoping for new industry. The HIEC, maturing into a determined economic recruiter, focused exclusively on Huntsville and, to a lesser degree, surrounding Madison County. NAA-recruited industries in Decatur or Scottsboro might employ a few Huntsvillians or bring a minor boost to the county's treasury, but only Huntsville-based companies could secure the city's economic future, and only the HIEC worked exclusively for the city.

Nearly a year after the newspaper first mentioned the growing disagreement, the groups made a relatively clean break. Huntsville and Madison County leaders agreed to limit their work to their own city and county, financed by local businesses and the Huntsville Electric Board, which stopped its contributions to the NAA. Huntsville's developers promised to continue to "balance our wheels" and "add weight on the other side of the rim," but this new, more concentrated effort provided an important opportunity for professionalization. The HIEC, no longer concerned about sharing funds or clients with the NAA, decided to hire a "trained and experienced director" as a full-time, paid position to bring in new industry.[66] No longer led by local businessmen forced to balance the needs of the committee with the daily concerns of running a business, the new HIEC focused solely on industrial recruitment with a trained staff and a well-defined area of operations.

With a growing industrial base and a professionalized development organization, leaders were prepared to confront a major challenge to the continued influx of defense investment at Redstone Arsenal. On October 4, 1957, the Soviet Union launched Sputnik, the first human-made object to orbit the Earth. The von Braun team reacted with "frustration and disappointment," promising that, with the proper funding, the Army would have produced an American satellite and won the "race" to space. General Medaris told the Senate Preparedness Subcommittee that he and the von Braun team wished that "government committees would let them alone so they could do their work."[67] The satellite did not pose a direct threat to the United States, but the symbolic victory in the Cold War space race caused concern among many in the government, afraid that the Soviet success implied a larger advantage in military technology. President Eisenhower hoped to manage the fallout from Sputnik, stressing the need to develop "peaceful" satellites, but the nature of U.S. space research and development proved a real challenge.

Since World War II, rocketry had been predominantly a military science—von Braun and the Army had worked in competition with the Navy and Air Force to obtain funding for missile projects. This inter-service rivalry meant that early rocket production in the United States was inseparable from the Cold War demand for superior military technology. President Eisenhower, however, believed that missile research needed a civilian branch, and the Soviet "victory" in 1957 convinced the president that without a primarily "scientific" mission, American rocket science would fall further behind. In 1958, he called for legislation that would encourage peaceful space technology. In response, Congress passed the National Aeronautics and Space Act, giving civilian control to the development of space technology, except where weapons were concerned. In effect, the legislation created two parallel rocketry programs, one open to the public and one closed to all but the military.[68]

Recognizing that the development of space technology had long been the province of the service branches, Eisenhower allowed the new civilian space agency, named the National Aeronautics and Space Administration (NASA), to "recruit" its research and development staff from the scientific talent of the Army, Navy, and Air Force. The force expected to transfer to NASA included five missions and 2,100 scientists centered in Huntsville, a decision that "aroused" von Braun and his team. The German told the government that some of his scientists would undoubtedly use the opportunity to move to the private sector (an easy move, considering the increasing ties between the military and its contractor companies), and he called the transfer from the Army to NASA "less than prudent." Local leaders agreed, and the *Huntsville Times* warned of "serious implications" for the effectiveness of the Army's ballistic missile program and for the economic health of the city if von Braun's team left.[69]

In the end, the government recommended the transfer of von Braun and his team from the Army to NASA, but also allowed the rocket scientists to remain on the Redstone reservation. The decision pleased Huntsvillians, who realized that the location of a major NASA facility in the city would further boost federal investment. Yet in "stripping" the German scientists away, Eisenhower effectively ended Redstone Arsenal's military-based space plans. Instead, the Air Force would largely control weaponized rocketry and satellite development.[70] Medaris was angered by the decision, but he promised that the Army would continue to work on space projects, since their expertise would be used as a "contract service" for NASA. Huntsville's mayor, though happy that von Braun's team would remain, expressed the Army's feelings: "As a reward for [the Army's] magnificent and indisputable record, the Department of Defense not only umpires the Army out of the ball park but steals all the balls as well."[71] Sparkman asked Eisenhower not to "cannibalize" the Army's team, and Bob Jones noted the "psychological effect" of the uncertainty surrounding the team's future. He asked Eisenhower to make a final decision, which would be "a good service to them . . . in turn for their continued efficiency and morale."[72]

In October 1959, two years after Sputnik, Eisenhower officially asked Congress to move the team to NASA, consolidating their projects, including the Saturn rocket, under NASA's civilian oversight. The president called the transfer a "new opportunity for [von Braun's team] to contribute their special capabilities directly to the expanding civilian space program." Keith Glennan, the new head of NASA, praised the decision and the Army's former scientists, noting their "dedicated teamwork and cordial relationships."[73] NASA continued to work with the Army, sharing facilities on the arsenal and cooperating on several existing and new projects. NASA had a separate budget, and a separate "contiguous area" on the reservation, though many of the buildings were split between the two groups while a NASA headquarters was constructed.[74] Work proceeded apace, and researchers on both sides adjusted to the new situation. Huntsville, too, learned to embrace the new government agency making a home on the arsenal, but the implications of the transfer underscored the precarious government funds. In an address to the Huntsville Rotary Club, General Medaris provided the call-to-arms: "Continue your efforts to broaden the industrial base and thus provide new opportunities for employment while providing the community with a built-in safeguard against the inevitable displacement that must be expected in a dynamic technology."[75]

In March 1960, the House of Representatives approved a $915 million budget for NASA, including $27 million for construction on the arsenal and an additional $75 million in new hires, payroll increases, and a heavier project load. As Bob Jones noted, the benefits would undoubtedly spread throughout the community: "These huge expenditures will solidify the position of Huntsville as the rocket capital of the nation and should give all of us a feeling of confidence and security about the future of the area." NASA Director Glennan agreed, promising "steady, sound growth."[76] The space agency built a new home on the arsenal reservation at the George C. Marshall Space Flight Center, though much of their work continued in the same general area where they had labored for a decade. Marshall officials transferred 500 technicians from other government facilities and hired 1,200 for administrative and support work.[77] Despite the new facilities, the rapid staff increase caused immediate problems at Redstone, and both Sparkman and Hill received numerous requests for funds to expand existing offices and build new ones. The congressmen supported the $4.5 million Independent Offices Appropriation Bill, hoping to move government scientists from rented space in the Huntsville Industrial Center and temporary offices in renovated army barracks and huts.[78]

In September, Eisenhower publicly dedicated the Marshall Center with words of encouragement for the assembled public. He called the Army's accomplishments "the product of unrestrained human talents and energy and restless probing for the betterment of humanity," and looked forward to the successful continuation of the scientists' work. In praising the accomplishments of the von Braun team's Army career, the president hoped to salve the wounds caused by the transfer to NASA. Yet Eisenhower also pointed to NASA's future triumphs. Success in the civilian agency came without the "domineering bureaucracy" of an overarching government or military oversight committee. NASA would be free to employ the "courage," "talents," and "imagination" of its own researchers, but also of private industry.[79]

Eisenhower's comments suggested a larger restructuring of the relationship between government research offices and the business community. Though nowhere near as self-contained as during World War II, the Redstone Arsenal of the 1950s still relied, to some extent, on in-house research and development. Von Braun's team conducted scientific investigations, built prototypes, and tested rockets. The team relied on the private sector to manufacture parts and equipment that had largely been tested, as well as items that the team could not produce on its own. Companies with contracts for Redstone work brought business to Huntsville, and civic and business leaders saw a steady stream of profits from the arsenal. The Army's 1,500-mile Jupiter rocket exemplified the cooperation that marked government-industry relations before the advent of NASA. As one reporter for the *Washington Post* noted, the missile had been developed and tested by government scientists and engineers, and the team at Redstone provided almost all of the engineering work, including the construction of prototypes used during the experimental phase. Private industry carried out the plans and specifications developed by Redstone. Proponents of this system praised the Army for its ability to check private costs and profits—some even made the auspicious comparison between Redstone's oversight and TVA's "yardstick."[80]

In fact, the two were remarkably similar in principle. The "yardstick" power rates were designed to provide guidelines for distributors of TVA electricity while undermining the influence of privately owned utilities. Likewise, Redstone officials hoped that they could set guidelines for the contract corporations that drew up plans and specifications. A rocket designed, tested, and prototyped at Redstone would, in theory, prove much cheaper to mass produce than one designed completely in-house at Chrysler or Douglas, where the companies' staff could charge higher rates for each stage of development and production. Still, the private sector benefited from the relationship with the Army's missile program. By 1958, a quarter of the arsenal's budget was dedicated to small businesses, with an additional 20 percent of money going to larger prime contractors being spent on smaller subcontracts. Over 4,000 private employees worked alongside the Army's scientists; the largest contractor on base was Thiokol, followed by Chrysler and Rohm and Haas, all of which had offices in the city.[81] The Army's system served Huntsville well, providing a relatively steady stream of high-paying technicians working in von Braun's labs and a number of workers in smaller factories scattered across the valley, making components used on the German's rockets.

For the fiscally conservative, though, the Army's system centered too much responsibility in von Braun's laboratories, and proved overly expensive to the federal government, which paid for the scientists' myriad research programs, tests, and missile prototypes. Unlike the Army, the Air Force contracted out much of its design, research, development, and production to private companies. One retired Air Force general who presided over a private organization of aircraft manufacturers noted that, by allowing private companies to oversee complete development of each rocket, his former service cut out the cost of middlemen. He told a reporter that "the Government arsenal has about outlived its usefulness."[82] Many in the government backed such claims. In 1959, General Medaris faced a congressional subcommittee investigating the Army's contract system as part of the larger inter-service rivalry for missile work that resulted in the creation of NASA. Congresswoman Martha Wright Griffiths of Michigan asked Medaris why work on the Jupiter had been split between Chrysler, headquartered in her home state, and Hayes, an aircraft company with offices in Birmingham, Alabama. The congresswoman cited Chrysler's diligence in performing up to Redstone's standards, even claiming that the success of the Jupiter program rested largely on Chrysler's involvement. The unspoken implication was that if the Army, like the Air Force, had given the entire contract to the Michigan manufacturer, then Medaris might have avoided a confusing and expensive web of contractors and subcontractors. Medaris fired back, defending the Army's system. He cited his arsenal's numerous successes and told Griffiths that, by keeping part of the process in-house, he could act as needed to ensure production. He informed investigators that Hayes had been chosen to complete some emergency work since it was close enough to Huntsville for a quick turnaround on the project. Hayes officials backed Medaris's claims, explaining that the Redstone team "did [itself] a favor having Hayes Aircraft Corporation handle certain of their emergency work here in Alabama where changes and coordination could be carried out at the least possible expense and delay."[83]

Eisenhower agreed with Griffiths. In creating NASA, the president adopted the Air Force system, tasking scientists, like those on von Braun's team, with initial design and research while leaving most of the development and actual production to the private sector. The contract system fit with the president's larger concern with government economizing, as well as the civilian mission of the space agency. Privatization took some of the decision-making responsibilities away from von Braun, but it greatly enhanced the possibilities for economic growth in the city of Huntsville. With the NASA team more reliant on the private sector, business leaders looked to attract more companies to the valley. Eisenhower's decision also continued the process of localization in the industrial development of the Tennessee Valley. By 1960, the federal government was no longer willing to manage the industrial growth of the region. Instead, through NASA, Washington provided a stream of appropriations that filtered through Marshall to a number of private aerospace concerns, which then managed their own workers and subcontractors. Thus, even as the Tennessee Valley Authority increasingly relied on the work of civic and regional development organizations to carry out its plans for economic growth, the other major source of government development funds, the rocket and space program at Redstone and Marshall, left the development of new industry to its major contractors and the municipal groups concerned with the area's diversification.

In September 1960, von Braun invited 380 representatives of major industries to an orientation conference, hoping to "enable industry to understand the support Marshall Space Flight Center will require in its present and future missions and objectives." Of its $360 million budget, Marshall planned to dedicate a "choice cut" to the "maximum capabilities of private industry."[84] Von Braun and his team unveiled blueprints for the upcoming line of Saturn space vehicles, took industrialists on tours of the new labs and testing grounds, and featured speeches from the directors of each department.[85] NASA Director Glennan was a firm believer in the benefits accrued from a close relationship with private industry, but Marshall's director was a reluctant contract manager.[86] Von Braun chaffed at the government's removal of a large part of his team's development work. Even worse, his earlier fears were proven true when a number of his original German colleagues used the shift from the Army to NASA to leave for more lucrative positions at private companies. The scientists cited "concern over their ability to provide a college education for their children," and the defections hinted at the larger problem: the inability of the government to compete with a private pay scale. Others formed their own companies, including a small group of technicians and engineers who left Marshall to found Space Craft Incorporated (SCI), developing satellite and missile equipment for their former colleagues.[87]

Of the myriad companies that contracted with Marshall for work, many were large national companies with the capacity to manufacture the rocket bodies and intricate engines required for space flight. News releases consistently listed work going to Chrysler and Seattle-based Boeing. In 1962, for instance, California's Lockheed Missile and Space Company was selected by NASA for the development and production of the Reactor in Flight Test vehicle, a contract worth $180 million. In September 1962 alone, Boeing was awarded a $7.3 million contract for a comprehensive rocket design, test, and launch program—that same month, Alabama-based companies won a combined $7.7 million in contracts.[88] Not all money awarded to national companies fled Huntsville; Boeing and Chrysler both maintained offices in the city, solving problems that arose and providing a quick response on new contracts. Lockheed purchased an eighty-acre tract in the city's industrial park to coordinate contracts with Marshall. The recruitment work was largely accomplished by the HIEC, and Lockheed specifically praised the proximity of UAH as a source of future training. The *Huntsville Times* called the decision "one of great importance" and hoped it would prove an "ice-breaker" for other aerospace firms. California-based Lear Siegler chose Huntsville as the site of a plant just days after Lockheed. The electronics company employed two hundred, though nearly half came from California.[89]

These "victories" for the city's economy were mixed blessings. The influx of highly paid, highly skilled technicians and engineers certainly boosted tax revenue and provided a new repository of business for Huntsville's retail and service sectors. However, the specialized knowledge needed in the design and construction of space vehicles often required years of advanced education, something few native Huntsvillians possessed. Von Braun's work for UAH proved an important addition to the city, but the fact that Lear Siegler needed to bring almost half of its staff from the West Coast points to the real challenge city leaders faced. The HIEC continued its work to diversify the city's business population, but the group also looked to bring in more and more aerospace companies to fill Marshall's (and Redstone's) contract demands. Hoping that rising economic fortunes would benefit all Huntsvillians, the city's leadership failed to truly address the needs of all residents.

Leaders in Washington and local industrialists tried to ensure that a number of businesses benefited from defense contracts. In 1961, President John F. Kennedy directed the Defense Department to channel contracts to areas with "chronic heavy labor surpluses." Major General August Schomburg, the ABMA commander, contacted his local contractors, including Lew Jeffers at Hayes Aircraft, and asked for assistance in awarding subcontracts to the smaller businesses in the area. Jeffers happily concurred, welcoming the increased business.[90] He also realized the need to keep contracts flowing to Alabama companies. The local offices of Boeing and Lockheed, completely dependent on a relationship with NASA, contributed to the city's treasury, but they were small outposts of international corporations, and they did little to buttress the overall economic health of the region. Cognizant of the need to support local growth, the space center specifically directed contracts to companies like Hayes Aircraft, hoping to keep the funds completely within the boundaries of the region. In January 1962, for instance, Marshall let $15 million (of a total $82 million) to Alabama companies, including $100,000 in Decatur and $6 million in Huntsville ($4.8 million alone to Brown Engineering). In April 1963, four state firms won a total of nine contracts, garnering $27.6 million in government funds.[91]

Von Braun championed local businesses and encouraged the city's leadership to develop companies that could successfully compete for government contracts and weather changes at the government facility. In a speech to the annual chamber of commerce banquet, Marshall's director encouraged his audience to make "long-range contributions" to the city's growth. He praised the city's work to improve the racial climate and the formation of a local Better Business Bureau but called for more work to improve Huntsville's hospital and recreation facilities, better traffic management, a city beautification program, and a new focus on education. He asked the city's leading citizens, "Are we doing enough for those less fortunate families who are bypassed by the big space and missile boom. . . . Are we doing everything possible to attract more diversified industry to the community?"[92]

He made similar suggestions in a 1965 speech to the Alabama Chamber of Commerce Board, in which he explicitly acknowledged the importance of his center's work in Huntsville. With 21,800 employees in the city, split between 7,000 civil service and 14,800 contract workers, Marshall's presence "has impacted heavily on Alabama's prosperity." Statistics backed the scientist's claims—in 1965, 75 percent of those employed in Huntsville had jobs "tied directly to government missile and space activities."[93] Von Braun estimated that he paid $215 million to his employees, who then spent $130 million in retail purchases and $6.5 million in income tax payments. His conclusion was both an appreciation of Alabama's encouragement of local growth and a warning to those who had come to rely heavily on federal funds: "I think we should admit to the fact that much of our prosperity is due to federal programs being carried out in the state. . . . [O]ne cannot fail to see the tremendous impact these programs are having on the state's economy."[94] The ability of local firms to compete for NASA contracts was crucial to the region's continued prosperity, as were businesses relatively independent of government expenditures.

Perhaps more than any other local business, Brown Engineering exemplified the success that could result from a close relationship with the government facilities. In 1953, Marietta Tool and Engineering Company located in the city to work with Redstone Arsenal. After receiving $40,000 in working capital from local investors, the company won its first contract, a fin-and-rudder design on the Army's Redstone missile. The company began expanding on government contracts, eventually changing its name to Brown Engineering after an Indiana industrialist bought the controlling interest. In the late 1950s, Milton K. Cummings took over as president and personally led the firm into the space age. Cummings began his career as a clerk for a cotton merchant, but he worked his way up to become a financier. By 1959, Cummings and Brown were prepared to help Redstone and Marshall with locally based missile engineering, eventually becoming the center's largest engineering support contractor.[95]

With a talented firm in such close proximity, von Braun depended on Brown's services. In 1965, for instance, Brown won a $12.4 million contract from Marshall for support labs to research and develop propulsion systems and vehicle designs. The company employed 920 technicians under the contract, outnumbering many of the larger companies' local offices in the city. Cummings consistently adapted to meet Marshall's needs, underscoring his company's reliance on the government facility. When von Braun's team planned to activate the Michoud testing facility outside New Orleans, Brown set up offices in Louisiana.[96] Brown also offered to lease testing facilities to Space Craft Inc. (SCI), hoping to be included in valuable subcontracts from its fellow Huntsville firm.[97] Cummings led his company to pursue government funds aggressively, and in return, Brown reaped millions of dollars in engineering contracts.

Brown Engineering combined profit-seeking with a real desire to see Huntsville grow, and Cummings's community-development work illustrates the interconnected nature of private business, federal funds, and local progress. Cummings became an active partner of the HIEC, personally financing the creation of both the Huntsville Industrial Center and Industrial Research Park, later known as Cummings Research Park in his honor. Seeking to provide a space for the incoming aerospace offices, Cummings and Huntsville Industrial Sites purchased 150 acres on land adjoining both the arsenal reservation and the growing campus at UAH. Brown Engineering relocated to one tract, and Cummings sold the remaining plots to other firms at cost. Research Park became a major selling point for the HIEC's continuing diversification and, soon after, an important source of funding for continued scientific training. Huntsville Industrial Sites renamed itself the University of Alabama at Huntsville Foundation and added more acreage, hoping to use funds from the sale of property to improve UAH. As companies such as IBM and Boeing bought space, they contributed to the programs at the university that trained the city's workers to compete for jobs.[98] As chair of the Research Institute Committee, Cummings helped von Braun organize the campaign that brought state support to the remarkable growth of UAH, and he consistently encouraged math and science in secondary schools and undergraduate programs. In 1961, Cummings proposed a "counsel and guidance seminar and tour" in conjunction with Marshall and area universities, introducing local high-school and college students to missile and space work. Brown actively sought cooperation from other local firms, hoping to create a community-wide foundation for the employment of Huntsvillians and Alabamians in highly skilled positions.[99] Granted, not all firms were as interested as Brown in municipal improvement and civic responsibility, and Cummings certainly profited from increased activity on the arsenal. Like the city's leadership, however, he realized that the success of Redstone and NASA determined his own fortunes as well as those of the Rocket City.

Federal funds flowed into Huntsville during the late 1950s and early 1960s, and as Marshall's contracts spread throughout the region and nation, business in the valley boomed. Chrysler, Boeing, Brown, SCI, and others hired new scientists and engineers, who then spent money in the city's restaurants and shopping malls and paid taxes to the cities and counties of the Tennessee Valley. As such, Huntsville was a Sunbelt success story, boasting a modern economy built on federal investment and associated private industry, encouraged by a community of developers interested in selling their city to businesses. Yet growth brought change, and as Huntsville's neighbors had learned, accommodating the dislocations of growth was essential to maintaining prosperity. This was especially true in Huntsville, a southern city whose racial mores lagged behind national and international opinion.

Throughout its wartime boom and postwar bust, Redstone Arsenal provided an opportunity for employment for the valley's African American population, but economic gains did not result in political or social equality, and Huntsville, like its neighbors, carefully maintained a segregated environment. The views of the region's leaders were best enunciated by one of its native sons, Senator John Sparkman. Answering inquiries from around the country on his position on the Supreme Court's *Brown vs. Board of Education* decision, Sparkman characterized the stance of fellow white southern New Deal liberals and "progressive" civic and business elites. He gladly took credit for his role in drafting the "Southern Manifesto," a document signed by a number of southern congressmen and governors protesting the ruling and warning against school desegregation. He stressed, "I believe that any effort to force changes against the will of the people may well set back the progress that has been made over the years."[100] Sparkman, like TVA's A. E. Morgan and David Lilienthal, was content to reinforce southern segregation laws while encouraging black Alabamians to use economic opportunity to make social gains. Yet the very investment that provided that "economic opportunity" also challenged the status quo, and government funds proved to be a potent weapon in the civil rights movement as the revitalization of Redstone Arsenal drew federal attention to Huntsville.

In late 1958, syndicated columnist Drew Pearson warned members of the HIEC that the United States might curtail military spending in the South because of its "race problems."[101] Pearson's comments highlighted a growing concern. As the federal government moved to address the most blatant forms of segregation, southern resistance to change increased. Officials were loath to invest more money in a region that increasingly demanded "states' rights" and used anti-government rhetoric to protest civil rights laws. In 1964, an unnamed NASA official released a statement warning that Huntsville might lose its space activity unless "its people show a greater appreciation of this economic plum and abandon their hate the federal government attitude." The *New York Times* reported a government discussion on a proposed transfer of Marshall's staff to NASA's New Orleans facility due to Alabama's refusal to integrate. The paper attributed the proposed relocation to Alabama's "social conditions" and called it a "direct slap at Gov. George C. Wallace . . . and the racial policies of his state."[102] The threat to the valley's livelihood brought a response. Sparkman received an influx of letters begging him to "hold onto what you have worked so hard to get in," and the senator immediately contacted NASA and President Lyndon Johnson, who promised that the announcement was a rumor and that Marshall would remain untouched.[103]

Even if the government refused to act, Alabama's image did have an effect on Marshall's programs, as civil rights reactionism in Birmingham, Montgomery, and Selma brought negative national attention to the state. The government facilities relied heavily on well-educated scientists and technicians recruited from northern and western universities since, as with many southern Sunbelt communities, Huntsville could not provide sufficiently skilled workers to meet the demands of rocket and missile development. As Alabama became synonymous with violent opposition to racial equality, Redstone and Marshall found recruitment increasingly difficult. A proud proponent of the city of Huntsville, Wernher von Braun begged city and state leaders to improve race relations. In a June 1965 speech to the Alabama Chamber of Commerce, he cited a letter published in the *Congressional Record* in which three University of Rochester (New York) students stated that they would refuse to take a job in Alabama "due to the unfavorable posture of this state in racial matters." As von Braun added, a number of his recruiters had received similar "testimonials-in-reverse." He asked the assembled businessmen and businesswomen to take a "positive and constructive" approach to solving the state's problems, and counseled that "we should work hard to shed the labels of obstructionism and defiance that have been applied to us." Von Braun praised the "admirable" and "courageous" work of the statewide Committee of One Hundred, a group of business leaders working to "accommodate the forces of change" in communities looking to attract industry.[104] Alabama needed to repair its reputation if its businesses, public and private, were to recruit top-level researchers and technicians.

Huntsville and North Alabama largely avoided the overt public conflict that marked civil rights activity in the rest of the state and, in fact, the need to protect federal investment forced the city's leaders to accept moderate change. This is perhaps most apparent in the process by which Huntsville integrated its public schools. In March 1959, Washington, D.C., NAACP Director Clarence Mitchell accused military authorities of cooperating with segregationists on two defense facilities: Little Rock Air Force Base in Arkansas and Redstone Arsenal, where base officials sold twenty-one acres of land to the city for a segregated elementary school. Mitchell argued that, instead of giving the city land, the Army should have built an integrated school on the property, and he argued that, at Redstone, officials were cooperating with a city in active defiance of the *Brown* ruling.[105] In response, the Department of Defense moved to integrate arsenal schools, an act that Alabama Governor John Patterson likened to a declaration of war. Madison Pike School was one of only two segregated schools drawing all of its students from military districts (along with a school in Abilene, Texas), and it had escaped federal attention since it was operated by the local school system. Patterson prepared to fight the government, claiming that federal authorities had no jurisdiction over local schools and promising to enact a state law that allowed local school boards to shut down schools under a "threat of violence."[106] The *Huntsville Times* preached caution, noting the "sound reasoning [of] leaders of both races" and instructing locals to avoid "excitement or rash action" in favor of the city's legal defenses.[107]

Mitchell pressed his case as the Department of Defense investigated. In 1962, still awaiting government action, he charged government leaders with "pussyfooting." The arsenal's African American staff also grew impatient. A sergeant stationed at Redstone petitioned the Huntsville School Board to allow his daughter to attend a white school located closer to the sergeant's home than the nearest black school.[108] In January 1963, the U.S. government asked a federal court in Huntsville to issue a court order forcing the city and county school systems to end discriminatory education practices affecting black military and civilian families working for the Army at Redstone. The government specifically noted $4.4 million in investments in Huntsville schools and threatened the removal of federal funds if the schools continued to obstruct integration. Federal officials argued that, when the school board accepted the money, it had agreed that the facilities "will be available to the children for whose education contributions are provided . . . on the same terms."[109]

Similar problems affected UAH. Even as the government forced the city and county to integrate, the University of Alabama cancelled a course at the Huntsville extension center when Joan Cashin, the African American wife of local dentist and civil rights leader John Cashin, applied for admission. UAH officials claimed that they were unable to procure a speaker for the class, but the underlying motives were clear to Cashin. Asked about the incident, she stated, "My main regret is that Alabama, through the university, has in effect put a brake on better race relations which have been developing here." Ironically, Cashin was able to apply largely due to the center's desire to increase participation in its programs on the arsenal. She attempted to enroll in a class with no educational prerequisites and no official credit upon completion, a course offered by the university to attract white arsenal workers who wanted to train for better positions.[110]

Two months later, UAH again rejected two black students that administrators claimed did not meet admission requirements. Both men were government employees; Marvin Carroll was an electronics engineer at Redstone's Army Missile Command, and Dave McGlathery was a mathematician at Marshall. At first, the university attempted to deal with the crisis quietly. Hoping to prevent the "stand in the schoolhouse door" promised by Governor George Wallace should the state's universities face forced integration, UAH officials contacted McGlathery's boss and asked him to "discourage" his employee's application, but the scientist refused to comply. Dr. Ernest Stuhlinger, a top aide to von Braun, told McGathery that he had a right to enroll in the class. Von Braun cautioned McGathery that he might want to consider dropping his application if it appeared he would become a "martyr," but both McGathery and Carroll received encouragement from their superiors, and both were told that the government would pay their tuition costs.[111] The support from Marshall and Redstone was unsurprising. Federal aerospace programs required highly trained technicians, and the government's support for UAH was founded on the need to train workers for defense needs. In May, the men filed suit for admission to UAH, alleging that "the university has a contract with the Government under which Federal employees are entitled to training at the center." Their suit was accompanied by one from Tuscaloosa, in which three other black students hoped to transfer to the university.[112] A federal judge ruled that the Justice Department could not sue for integration for the sole purpose of abolishing discrimination. Governor Wallace quickly asserted control, ordering the National Guard to Tuscaloosa and laying a "tight security net" of state troopers over the Huntsville branch, citing a need to prevent mob violence.[113]

The events in Tuscaloosa are a well-known part of the civil rights movement narrative. Wallace's "stand in the schoolhouse door" at Foster Auditorium, the national press coverage, federal action, and the enrollment of Vivian Malone and James Hood demonstrated the courage of black students and a handful of white supporters in the face of overwhelming racist opposition, fanned by Wallace's rhetoric and actions. Yet in Huntsville, the quiet resolution to the desegregation crisis demonstrated the growing influence of the government reservation on local politics and perfectly illustrates the way in which federal economic development transformed the social environment of a community as much as its business climate. As the *Washington Post* reported, Huntsville residents largely rejected Wallace in favor of "their main preoccupations—the Redstone Arsenal moon rocket project, rooting out crabgrass and wangling new Space contracts." In fact, the city was in the process of desegregating its lunch counters, thanks to a sit-in by local high-school students; a black doctor was admitted to the local branch of the American Medical Association; and the first black policemen was appointed.[114] Much of the change was the direct result of the federal presence. At the municipal golf course, for instance, blacks were allotted "equal" use two days every week. The segregation of the course ended abruptly when white federal workers "swarmed in" on a day reserved for black golfers. When they returned the favor on a day reserved for whites, segregated play ended.[115]

The desegregation of UAH was equally anti-climactic. Even as Wallace took his "stand" in Tuscaloosa, McGlathery "walked unescorted through a front door of the university's extension center" in Huntsville. The *Chicago Defender* quoted Mayor Searcy, who said, "We do not expect trouble. . . . And we're going to see that law and order is preserved." Federalized troops were placed on standby alert at the local National Guard armory on Wallace's orders, but they remained there, avoiding the campus. McGlathery even commented that his registration "speaks well for the city of Huntsville, the state of Alabama, and the country as a whole." The *Washington Post* described the events in the city with optimism: "If Bull Connor and Governor Wallace speak for the dark and retrograde prejudices in the state, the youth of Alabama—Negro and white—are setting a different and brighter example for their elders."[116]

The city school system prepared for an equally uneventful integration. In September 1963, four black students enrolled in white public schools, and in January 1964, ten more entered for the second semester. Most of the students testing the segregated schools were children of arsenal employees. Wallace issued a public statement against desegregation, but promised not to interfere since "Huntsville officials had not requested his help." Huntsville's Police Chief Floyd Dyar later remembered the integration as being "smooth as silk."[117] The contrast with Tuscaloosa was telling. Granted, Huntsville did not immediately embrace civil rights—city and federal officials only addressed segregation laws and practices after the determined efforts of local African Americans. Yet in Huntsville, racial boundaries fell relatively quietly. The difference was the presence of the federal government and the desire of local leaders to maintain good relations with their most important investors. The arsenal and space-center employees, recruited from across the country, created a constituency that supported integration, and the federal government made it clear that continued investment required basic equality and public desegregation. The city's reliance on the continued economic health of the defense facilities meant that local leaders, from the mayor to the businessmen whose companies depended on government contracts, accepted such changes as a necessary part of growth. In that regard, Huntsville resembled other business-oriented cities in the Sunbelt, where "the maintenance of white supremacy . . . slipped from its traditionally dominant position and the primary objective for the South's business leaders became economic growth."[118] Huntsville's experience was atypical, measured against the rest of Alabama, where "efforts to promote industry . . . were dull and marred by anti–civil rights violence perpetrated by white thugs who were cheered on by state and local government officials."[119] In the valley, at least, social change was part and parcel of the economic development that came with federal attention.

Redstone and Marshall forever altered the social and economic fabric of Huntsville. In little more than a decade, the city went from the depths of despair, faced with the loss of textile mills and a government munitions plant, to the center of the national missile-defense and civilian space-flight efforts. Highly skilled and well-paid scientists spent their earnings in the city, fueling malls, shopping centers, and restaurants. The government's presence was felt in the new university, a new art museum, and a new symphony, but also in the relatively quiet integration of the UAH and the city's schools. However, not all of the changes came from prosperity. In fact, one of the most important transformations experienced by the community came in large part thanks to the fear of economic collapse. The rapid growth of Redstone and Marshall caused concern among business leaders, afraid that decommission lurked around the corner. In the 1960s, the Huntsville–Madison County Chamber of Commerce and the HIEC completed the maturation of their industrialization campaign in the city. In doing so, the groups culminated a decades-long process by which local business leadership used the specter of government withdrawal to solidify the economic future of their city, their state, and their South.

By the early 1960s, business leaders in Huntsville had adopted many practices consistent with fully modernized, fully professionalized municipal development organizations. The chamber of commerce boasted a city beautification campaign, extending from downtown revitalization (the "Heart of Huntsville" program) and slum clearance to park construction. The chamber worked closely with technicians to reorganize traffic flow and update an aging infrastructure, and its members encouraged the municipal government to annex nearby communities in order to support the increasingly suburban nature of the city's workforce. The chamber also worked closely with the HIEC, having decided to focus solely on the economic development of Huntsville and Madison County at the expense of cooperation with regional and state groups. Encouraged by local entrepreneurs, particularly Brown Engineering's Milton K. Cummings, the HIEC and a number of associated nonprofit concerns began investing in commercial real estate, building industrial facilities, staffing research parks, and accommodating the needs of prospective clients in advance of a decision to locate in the area. In 1960, the HIEC began an internal reorganization and repurposing that, when completed, signaled Huntsville's emergence as a major player in the Sunbelt economy.

As the group worked to cut ties with the NAA, the HIEC commissioned Fantus Area Research, Inc., a New York firm specializing in resource surveys for industrial prospects, to study the city. After several months, Fantus returned with an optimistic report, citing ten types of industry suited to Huntsville, from laboratory furniture to prefabricated housing. The city had numerous advantages, including favorable water resources, plentiful raw materials, low labor costs, cheap electricity, an expansive utility system, and a number of potential plant sites. Fantus recommended continued efforts by the HIEC, even providing five possible industrial recruits, and encouraged the civic group to hire a development specialist and continue expanding health, education, and utility facilities to meet growing needs.[120]

In December, the HIEC hired Guy B. Nerren as executive director. Nerren had previously served as an assistant director of industrial and community development for Mississippi's Delta Council and, upon arrival, he prepared to right an "economic wheel" that had become "steadily . . . out of balance with the expansion of the missile-space industry and the continued dormancy of private industrial development."[121] Nerren went to work, accompanied by a paid staff and the continued support of HIEC's members in the business community, led by W. L. Halsey Jr., a wholesale grocer. In May 1961, Halsey announced that Cleveland, Ohio, firm Parker Aircraft had decided to locate a fifty-man plant at the Huntsville Industrial Center, serving Marshall.[122] Parker represented another business tied to the fortunes of the arsenal, but Halsey understood the need for positive action. Informed that Governor John Patterson was considering a statewide decrease of its aviation fuel tax, Halsey petitioned him to sign a bill on the subject. He explained that his organization was desperately working to bring in industry dependent on air transportation, and the state's high taxes had ensured that "jet air travel has by passed [*sic*] Alabama." That same month, the HIEC sponsored an amendment to Alabama's Wallace and Cater industrial development acts that allowed the city to finance the construction of industrial plants, with bonds to be repaid from site leases.[123] As Halsey told the *New York Times*, "We feel that we should continue to strengthen our program of assistance to all groups of manufacturers in the Huntsville area. With all our natural advantages and with continued hard work by the people in the Huntsville area, we are confident that our industrial growth will continue."[124]

In 1963, Halsey, Nerren, and other HIEC officers left for the West Coast in an ambitious recruiting drive. Such trips were increasingly routine by the group's standards, yet it exemplified both the continued push for diversification and the transformation of the HIEC into a professional booster organization. In February, they arrived in California and met with officials from Aerojet-General, an aerospace company planning to purchase sites at Cummings Research Park alongside a number of new tenants, including IBM, Lockheed, Northrup, and General Electric. While in California, the men set up meetings with executives at multiple aerospace companies, including Ford's Aeronautic Division, Rocketdyne, and Lear Siegler. They distributed pamphlets and brochures extolling Huntsville's general industrial climate and, more specifically, the properties available in Research Park. Halsey looked to Washington for assistance, sending his itinerary to Sparkman, who wrote letters to the officials who met with them. Sparkman promised his cooperation, and many companies showed interest in moving their operations to the area.[125]

The campaign helped solidify some of the industries already expanding in the area, including Aerojet, Northrup, Lockheed, and Lear Siegler. Furthermore, the HIEC proved itself adept at the art of industrial recruitment, combining publicity, personal attention, federal support, and community development in a unified drive for industry. By 1968, Research Park boasted fifteen industries, a million square feet in building space, 10,000 employees, and an annual payroll of nearly $100 million. The 200-acre park was part of 1,500 acres owned by the UAH Foundation throughout the city, all geared toward the recruitment of new industry by the HIEC.[126] Having begun in 1946 with a pamphlet, the HIEC matured into a true civic booster organization, led by professional businessmen with tried and tested methods for approaching and attracting international companies to Huntsville.

NASA Administrator James E. Webb summed up Huntsville's economic transformation in an address to University of Alabama alumni at the National

Press Club in 1965. He claimed that NASA had built a "Southern Crescent" with federal money that was "bound to generate a diversification of industry throughout all the Southern States" and which realized its greatest potential with "the vision and the resourcefulness of the civic and business leaders" of the city.[127] Webb pictured a diversified economy, one built by a combination of federal money and an active local business community. That combination was also the goal of Huntsville's civic leaders, and by 1965, they could point to evidence of their success. Industries associated with Redstone and Marshall employed highly skilled workers manufacturing guidance systems, synthetic fibers, and aluminum rocket bodies. Across the valley, factories produced fertilizer, aluminum, polyester, air conditioners, and a number of goods unconnected to the space or missile program.[128] Redstone Arsenal, and later Marshall Space Flight Center, poured money into the city in the form of contracts, payroll, and taxes, but they were never seen, at least by Huntsville's business leaders, as a solid foundation for economic prosperity. Creating publicity pieces, investing in land, actively soliciting business, providing hospitality for visiting officials, and raising money for improvements, the HIEC worked tirelessly to bring new industry to the city and to prepare the community for continued economic growth.

Boosters could not completely wean the city from its dependence on federal money. Redstone and Marshall employed too many and meant too much to the city's treasury. No amount of recruiting could offset the substantial growth on the government reservation. However, the work of the chamber of commerce and the HIEC, civic development organizations, regional groups like NAA, and TVA created a significant number of employment alternatives across the Tennessee Valley. The "Rocket City" still felt the sting of funding cuts, yet the diversification work of the 1950s and 1960s ensured that, when appropriations fell, as they would in the late 1960s and 1970s, the city experienced no serious economic dislocation and, in fact, enjoyed a foundation on which to build future prosperity.

CONCLUSION

A GREAT PLACE TO DO BUSINESS

On July 16, 1969, a Saturn V rocket blasted off from Cape Canaveral, Florida, carrying astronauts Neil Armstrong, "Buzz" Aldrin, and Michael Collins to the moon. The rocket was designed and tested, in part, by Wernher von Braun's staff at Marshall Space Flight Center and manufactured by thousands of contractor companies, many with offices in Huntsville.[1] Putting a man on the moon certainly demonstrated the productive power of Huntsville's aerospace economy; however, the victory also presaged troubling times for the "Rocket City." Without the mobilizing force of the moon mission, and given a declining national economy, NASA faced serious budget cutbacks that challenged the continued strength of the defense industry in the Tennessee Valley. As government agencies shifted priorities, the city's leaders once more sprang into action, seeking to diversify an economy too dependent on federal investment. Such efforts not only underline the ongoing ethos of economic development among Huntsville's civic leaders, but also highlight the close and complex relationship that the people of the region shared with those government agencies active in the local economy.

Even before Apollo XI made history, Huntsville looked to an uncertain future. The *Huntsville Times* foresaw a drop of over 1,000 workers at Marshall in the first half of 1969, reflecting slowed contracts as the Apollo program reached its apex.[2] The next year, 1970, was even worse, a year that that government employees "would rather forget than relive." *Explorer I*, the first U.S. satellite and the first of many successes by von Braun's missile team at Redstone, burned as it reentered Earth's atmosphere, symbolically ending the heady days of the Space Race. Huntsville's best-known resident, rocket engineer Wernher von Braun, left his post at Marshall for a position with NASA in Washington, D.C., and seven of his German team members were let go from the space center, along with one-third of the complex's specialists. In what one writer called Redstone Arsenal's "toughest year" to date, 1,100 employees were let go and 700 more were transferred to more active facilities elsewhere in the country, a number that included Otto Hirschler, the last member of the German rocket team still working at the arsenal.[3]

The *Times* tried to remain optimistic and made diversification one of its overarching goals for the decade of the 1970s. The paper promised that the city had "a viable research and development capacity" that could "attract manufacturers of space exploration hardware." Yet aerospace work alone would not preserve the prosperity. City leaders needed to focus on planning and recruitment, carefully laying out the benefits of working in Huntsville, selling the city, purchasing lots and preparing them for industries, training future employees, and seeking venture capital—the tools that had proven so successful in the past. The paper concluded with a telling statement of the city's economic policy: "Proud as we are of local space industry, eager as we are to see it expanded, assured prosperity in the '70s will require a broader more diverse economic base."[4] Only one year after the emotional high of the moon landing, 1970 truly seemed a year of endings for Huntsville; however, the reporter ended on a note of cautious optimism: "Somehow, in retrospect, the year was neither boom nor gloom."[5]

In spite of a list of budget cuts, layoffs, and losses, Huntsville's economy had merited a judgment that would undoubtedly make many cities across the country envious, and in reality, the "gloom" of the 1970s was not as overwhelming as it seemed. Huntsville still enjoyed an influx of federal funds. Together, Marshall and Redstone brought over $250 million into Huntsville's economy and, while nowhere near their peak, both facilities employed tens of thousands of workers. Across the city, missile and electronics companies thrived on lucrative government contracts, populating large research parks and spending money in Huntsville's shops and malls. The city had weathered economic cutbacks before, and city leaders had every expectation that Huntsville would again survive a period of decreased funding. This hesitant optimism in the face of real economic concerns exhibits the remarkable nature of Huntsville's economic development.

Boosters redoubled their efforts in the face of reductions at Marshall, which reached a nadir of 5,000 workers in the mid-1970s, and continued to pursue industry and improve the business environment. As scholars noted,

"[The] reductions had a relatively moderate impact on the local economy due to considerable local growth tied to a very effective industrial development program." Even though between 1966 and 1973, 2,000 government and 9,000 private employees lost their job, Huntsville's boosters brought 7,500 new positions to the community.[6] The decade saw the completion of Huntsville's downtown revitalization projects, helping the city boost retail sales.[7] In 1972, Owens-Corning announced its decision to locate a fiberglass manufacturing plant at the industrial park.[8] Much of the growth in the 1970s came from electronics and research companies, locating in Huntsville or expanding existing facilities and employing some of the technicians and engineers let go from Redstone and Marshall. In 1978, Universal Data Systems (later bought by Motorola), Englehard Industries, and SCI Systems increased both office space and employment at Research Park.[9] Many older companies adapted to the new economy. Brown Engineering merged with California-based Teledyne Engineering and began shifting its focus to computer software. The 1970s saw Teledyne Brown take on new contracts for missile defense systems with the Army at Redstone, but also with foreign defense agencies.[10] Building on the accomplishments of Huntsville's city leaders, industries took up much of the slack when Redstone and Marshall faced retrenchment. When Ronald Reagan poured funds into defense spending, Huntsville's economy was better prepared to face the shocking (re)growth of its government facilities.

In 1982, Huntsville's developers left on another recruitment drive to California, focused specifically on high-tech companies. The trip complemented the flow of Huntsville's shifting economy, and when unemployment rose across the country in the recession of the early 1980s, Huntsville's remained the lowest in the state. Recruiting went well and, by 1985, Huntsville was second only to San Diego in concentration of high-tech employees to total employment.[11] Granted, much of this growth could be traced to the foundation laid by Marshall and Redstone, and federal investment remained a crucial part of the city's overall health. Government contracts brought engineers and technicians to Huntsville, and even though the agencies had declined in the 1970s, their contracts, as well as the promise of future contracts, kept many businesses working through the slump. However, the growth also depended on the work performed by Huntsville's city leaders. The 1982 trip built on a tradition of working with companies to move them to the "Rocket City." Actively recruiting companies that fit their notion of a balanced economy, groups like the HIEC and the UAH Foundation created an environment that encouraged further growth. Cummings Research Park provided protectively zoned land between the government reservation and UAH, with its graduate programs in engineering, and alongside other defense contractors. By 1990, Research Park was the second largest industrial park in the world, with 16,000 workers, and one-fifth of Huntsville's 133,000 workers were employed in aerospace and related industries.[12]

Integraph, a company formed in Huntsville by five engineers from IBM, symbolizes the city's remarkable growth in the face of national economic troubles. During the 1970s, Integraph worked on missile systems with Redstone, as well as digital mapping programs that could be used by municipalities for city planning purposes. By the 1980s, the company focused largely on interactive graphics, filling contracts with defense agencies and reaping the benefits of Reagan-era defense spending. By 1991, a little over twenty years after its founding, Integraph was a Fortune 500 company with offices in fifty countries and almost $1.2 billion in revenue. UAH economics professor Niles Shoening noted the city's success in weathering the down periods: "When you look back on Huntsville's economy in the 1980s, you can't even find the national recession of 1981 and 1982 in the data in Huntsville. . . . Our economy is just different."[13]

By the early 1990s, as Marshall engineered space shuttles and Redstone worked on Patriot missiles for the first Gulf War, Huntsvillians still worried about the health of their city's economy. Yet city officials had been surprisingly successful in balancing the federal facilities with a diverse economy. True, the city was still largely dependent (and continues to be) on Marshall Space Flight Center and Redstone Arsenal for employment, tax revenue, and contract work; however, as the slump of the 1970s showed, Huntsville's economy was diverse enough to survive the retrenchment that came with budget cuts and recession. The Huntsville Industrial Expansion Committee, the Chamber of Commerce, the UAH Foundation, and other groups developed and implemented a professional civic booster program to bring new industries to the city in the expectation of fluctuating government funds. City leaders proved adept in adapting to the needs of federal agencies and private businesses. They were unusually foresighted in anticipating development, but they benefited from the city's great selling points: its proximity to transportation networks, cheap TVA power, active government installations, and the relationship that they had developed with each other and with the federal government.

Close cooperation and consultation with the federal government continues to be essential to the Tennessee Valley's growth and prosperity. On May 13,

2005, the Defense Department proposed relocating two major Army commands and the "bulk of the nation's missile defense work" to Huntsville's Redstone Arsenal as part of the Base Realignment Closure Commission's [BRAC] recommendations. The move encompassed 4,700 positions on military bases in the Washington, D.C., metropolitan area and, for Huntsvillians, it promised growth in numerous sectors of the city's economy.[14] As in the 1960s, Huntsville became the beneficiary of federal largess, and once again, city leaders rushed to prepare for new jobs, new business, and an expanding local economy. While a sluggish national economy ensured that the relocation did not occur as quickly as Huntsville's leadership might have hoped, the influx of new families and increased growth at the government reservation recalled the arsenal's postwar expansion. City leaders continued to worry about accommodating the growth; Joe Vallely, Huntsville's director of economic development, noted that "we are optimistic . . . [but] we know we have to work on infrastructure. Sometimes, that's housing, but it's [also] traffic, schools and office space."[15]

As the impact of the BRAC decision demonstrates, the process by which the Tennessee Valley industrialized across the twentieth century remains relevant in the twenty-first. The federal government continues to appropriate funds and direct investment to the valley. Civic leaders still encourage federal investment, working to prepare communities for future growth while directing development toward local goals. The negotiation that characterized relations between federal, state, and local organizations continues to mark the region's ongoing prosperity. Even as globalization expands and complicates the Sunbelt economy, valley residents have proven more than capable of recruiting, nurturing, and sustaining growth, as several recent developments demonstrate.

The BRAC announcement gave cause for celebration to Huntsville's leaders, reminiscent of the announcements of the location of Redstone Arsenal and the revitalization that accompanied the arrival of Wernher von Braun and his team. Senator Richard Shelby called the proposal "a big step for Huntsville and North Alabama." His colleague, Jeff Sessions, went further: "I think it reflects a belief that the city has the capacity and the economy and culture to sustain these commands and . . . in the future you would see the Madison County community be a center for top defense issues."[16] The direct beneficiaries of the base realignment were the city's defense contractors. Lockheed-Martin moved to a $30 million building in Cummings Research Park and, as an executive from the Huntsville office noted, "From Lockheed Martin's perspective, we recognize that there is a lot of growth potential here in the community."[17] In

2011, real estate professionals prepared to develop a 468-acre site bordering Redstone for a $1 billion office park to house companies contracting with the expanded facility.[18] The defense boom expected to accompany the BRAC decision has cemented Huntsville's reliance on Redstone Arsenal and Marshall Space Flight Center and their network of contractors spread across North Alabama. In 2008, the city boasted 40,000 aerospace and defense employees—one of every twelve Huntsvillians was a scientist, engineer, or technician. Over 200 contractors were located in the valley, and the defense realignment will skew the imbalance even further. Despite municipal developers' best efforts, Huntsville remains heavily reliant on defense for economic growth, and the community continues to struggle to maintain its relationship with the federal government.

If the realignment served to emphasize Huntsville's overreliance on defense spending, it also highlighted the problems of a one-industry economy. Defense contractors require well-educated and highly skilled employees, a fact not lost on proponents of the BRAC move. Announcing the decision, *Huntsville Times* reporter Shelby G. Spires noted that the expected jobs were mostly "high-paying, white collar jobs," and as part of the larger shuffle, Redstone planned to lose the "lower wage, military trainee jobs" held by soldiers who were "rarely allowed off base."[19] In fact, as the relocation progressed, city leaders found that more than half of the jobs (57 percent) went to newcomers to the city. While some businessmen applauded "new growth" from new arrivals, city leaders clearly continue to struggle to spread incoming prosperity to all Huntsvillians.[20] Granted, the base expansion has created new retail demand for the city's shops and service industries, but many retail jobs entail extra training. Kathy Evans of the Huntsville Career Center noted the increased interest in employment in Huntsville, citing the communications firm Verizon as an example. The company planned to employ 1,200 at a new call center in the city but needed employees with a background in technology. Verizon officials praised Huntsville as an ideal environment for technology-based companies: "Huntsville is a growing city. . . . The business climate is favorable; the work force that is already there is highly skilled. That certainly fits well with our company."[21] Verizon's optimism exemplifies the kind of growth inherent in the BRAC decision, but it also belies the city's continued economic imbalance. Defense contractors and other high-tech companies require educated and trained workers. For the vast majority of North Alabamians, the direct benefits of the BRAC decision will have to trickle down the economic ladder.

Increased employment at Redstone, Marshall, and the valley's contractor companies has also strained the city's infrastructure. As with the postwar defense boom, the rapid influx of new hires caused city leaders to scramble to accommodate the incoming workers and their families. In 2008, Madison County annexed 2,000 acres in neighboring Limestone County for residential development, with nearly 1,400 homes planned or under construction across the county. In the communities surrounding Huntsville, "affordable land" and "good schools" spurred building booms. Since 2004 (the year before the BRAC announcement), real estate closings have more than doubled in the city, and new subdivisions have quickly filled available land.[22] Schools have also faced increased pressure. Officials planned for the possibility of 10,000 new students in Madison County alone by 2012, in addition to the growing region's natural increase, and local school systems face a "unique dilemma" in assisting already overcrowded schools prepare for the remarkable expansion. For instance, Hazel Green, a community seeing increased interest from incoming BRAC families, scrambled to find room for 1,300 students in a school designed for 900.[23]

In order to truly benefit from new workers, new paychecks, and a growing economy, Huntsville and its surrounding communities must expand an already taxed infrastructure. Once again, municipal leaders find themselves facing the promise and the difficulty of relying on federal investment for economic growth. For some, at least, the price of prosperity simply is not worth the cost. As one local noted in an editorial to the *Huntsville Times*, "I remember when Huntsville and Madison County used to be a wonderful place to live. Now it seems as though the politicians, bureaucrats and developers can't get enough growth. I can't be the only native Madison County resident who feels this way, but personally, I don't want another wave of so-called prosperity."[24]

TVA, too, has continued industrial recruitment, following a pattern similar to that begun by David Lilienthal and his successors in the postwar years. In fact, in a highly publicized recent campaign, the agency successfully brought a Volkswagen manufacturing plant to Chattanooga, which narrowly edged out another TVA site in North Alabama. The competition arose between two authority "megasites," tracts organized by the government utility to attract national and international companies, particularly automotive manufacturers, to the Tennessee River watershed. In order to obtain the support of TVA developers, each "megasite" must have at least 700 acres of developable land; must be immediately available; must have completed environmental and geotechnical testing; must be near interstate highways, railways, and suppliers; and must have plenty of available laborers. The requirements necessitated an active development program with civic leaders able to prepare their communities for growth in conjunction with the federal agency. After the agency received twenty-six applications, a private consulting company certified nine sites, five of which have sold since 2005. TVA, in cooperation with local and state organizations, recruited Toyota, Peterbilt and Kenworth Trucks, SeverCorr Steel, and Dow-Corning to relocate to the valley, adding billions to the regional economy. In 2008 alone, thanks largely to a Tupelo, Mississippi, Toyota plant, TVA boasted $5.6 billion in new investment in its area of operations.[25]

The "megasites" expanded the scope of TVA's already vibrant site development program. In the late 1940s, faced with thousands of acres of waterfront land and no real demand for continued dam and reservoir construction, the authority began marketing its land to manufacturers, hoping to bring jobs and paychecks to the valley. Decades later, TVA continues to use site preparation and advertisement to improve the regional economy. Admittedly, the scale of the authority's work has increased: TVA's "megasites" attract global companies, bringing billions of dollars in investments and hiring thousands to staff assembly lines. And, according to development professionals, such "larger-scope economic development efforts" helped the agency pioneer a new form of "site certification and marketing."[26] However, the underlying sentiment remains unchanged. As TVA Senior Vice-President of Economic Development John Bradley told one reporter, "[Volkswagen's decision] is an enormous economic development boost for the Tennessee Valley. . . . It reinforces the region's position as a leading automotive manufacturing corridor and demonstrates once again that the Valley is a great place to do business."[27]

As TVA and Huntsville demonstrate, the federal government continues to play an important role in the valley's economic growth, providing investment and guidance to municipal leaders. Yet perhaps the most telling example of the persistence of the development ethos in North Alabama is the continued work of regional organizations. In 1963, Tom Johnson's North Alabama Associates reorganized as the North Alabama Industrial Development Association, yet the central mission remained unchanged: "[NAIDA] works with the local economic development agencies throughout North Alabama, the Alabama Development Office and many other agencies to recruit industry for North Alabama. NAIDA advertises the region's advantages, particularly its defense infrastructure, the growing presence of automotive suppliers, and the continued strength of chemical production and processing."[28] The organization still draws on a number of state and local benefits, including financial incentives such as twenty-year tax credits, construction and equipment tax abatements, and even site-preparation grants. As the group carefully notes, North Alabama's labor force draws on a "hardworking agrarian lifestyle" with "a strong work ethic" that has translated into "a right to work state with little union activity."[29] NAIDA represents a vibrant tradition of local and regional encouragement for economic growth in the Tennessee Valley, directing federal investment, recruiting and attracting manufacturers, and contributing to the increasingly global nature of Sunbelt growth.

The Tennessee Valley experienced remarkable economic growth in the middle of the twentieth century, driven by active civic and commercial organizations dedicated to economic development and determined to work closely with the federal government to attract industry and to prepare their towns and cities for growth. As early as the Muscle Shoals debate after World War I, civic groups pressed the government for assistance, quickly learning that such assistance was not guaranteed and that, when given, it did not always take the form that the people of the valley expected. In conjunction with TVA and Redstone Arsenal, however, groups in Decatur, Huntsville, and communities across the region organized to sell themselves in the hopes of bringing lasting prosperity. By the 1950s and 1960s, as the government came to focus on disinterested investment, city and business leaders were well versed in the ways and means of development. Professional boosters could look to a long history of working with the federal government to ensure economic growth on former cotton fields and in former textile mills.

Valley residents also learned that economic growth brought serious social changes. Companies hired African Americans, who used their newfound positions to push for greater say in the segregated South, and women, who challenged the stereotypical assumptions about women's roles at work. Businesses also forced southerners to consider the impact of growth on the natural environment. Communities sold industry on the resources available along the Tennessee River, then balked when companies fouled the water, killed wildlife, and threatened continued use of the region's natural wealth. Other changes came as a direct result of government intervention. In Huntsville, city leaders quietly integrated schools and universities, afraid that negative attention would result in a withdrawal of federal funds. Agencies mandated unionization, with mixed results, on TVA projects and in defense industries. Such changes were as much a part of growth as prosperity, and as locals pushed for development, they came to understand that, in campaigning for business, they had to prepare their communities for new and different ways of life.

The changes of the twentieth century reshaped life in the Tennessee Valley, and statistics help to illustrate the ways in which the valley of 1960 would have been unrecognizable to the people of 1910 and 1920. In 1910, less than 63 percent of children aged six to fourteen attended school regularly; by 1960, the number reached 97 percent. Between 1940 and 1960 alone, the percentage of residents having completed four years of high school rose from 6.5 percent to over 20 percent. Wage and income data document improved standards of living. In 1920, the average wage earner brought home $875 per year, just more than the state average. Through the Depression, the valley's wages dropped more precipitously than in the rest of Alabama, falling to $690 on the eve of World War II. By 1960, the combination of a booming regional economy and national prosperity brought the average to over $2,800 per year. Between 1950 and 1960, median family income rose from almost $1,400 to $3,790 (the state kept pace, rising from $1,580 to $3,940 on the strength of the valley, as well as growth in Birmingham and Mobile).[30]

County-by-county data is even more revealing, particularly for those counties directly affected by economic development. Colbert and Lauderdale counties, led by the active civic organizations of Florence and the early work at Muscle Shoals, outpaced the rest of the state in average wages in 1920 and 1930. Though they fell below the state average in 1940, the median income in 1950 and 1960 for the two counties was still nearly $500 more than the rest of the state. The cooperation between TVA and Decatur's business community helped the River City best the state average, boasting higher wage averages in 1940 and a higher median income in 1960. Nowhere is the difference more apparent than in Huntsville. Through World War II, Madison County trailed the rest of the state in average wages, median years of school completed, and in percentage of adults who had completed four years of high school. Income still lagged in 1950, though schooling reached the state average. By 1960, the influence of the arsenal reservation was clear: the county's median income was nearly $5,500 ($1,500 more than Alabama as a whole), students averaged nearly eleven years in school, and nearly a quarter of adults had at least four years of high-school education.[31]

The absence of such active development is equally apparent, particularly in Lawrence County, located between Decatur (to the east) and Muscle Shoals (to the west). Between 1920 and 1960, average wages and median income in the county never reached the state average; in the depths of the Depression, Lawrence County's average wage was just $520 when the rest of the state made over $850. In 1940, the Census Department would not release wage data since only one business operated in the county (and thus, the information would not be confidential). By 1960, when both Colbert and Morgan County reported median incomes well over $4,000, Lawrence's residents averaged under $2,400. In 1910, a quarter of Lawrence County's adults were illiterate and barely half of school-aged children attended school. By 1960, school attendance had improved dramatically, but citizens were still undereducated when compared to the state and regional average. Only 13 percent of adults had four years of high school, and the county average was under eight years of schooling. Lawrence County benefited indirectly from growth in Decatur or Florence; undoubtedly some residents commuted to work in nearby cities that were expanding on private and public investment. But the county never experienced development on a par with its neighbors, and instead remained in the shadow of the valley's Sunbelt communities. As an exception, its slow-moving economy provides a stark and telling contrast for the success stories that surround it.[32]

Nowhere was the overall change more apparent than in the shift from farm to factory. In 1920, the Tennessee Valley was overwhelmingly agricultural. In the counties along the Tennessee River, nearly 40,000 people made a living farming while fewer than 9,000 earned wages. Excepting Madison County and Morgan County, both of which had textile mills, the remaining counties boasted ten farmers for every wage earner. On the whole, there were more owners in the valley than in other parts of the South—43 percent of farms were run by owners—though such small farms, dominated by cash crops like corn and cotton, meant that many of the owners were marginal and no better off than the 57 percent who were tenants and sharecroppers. As civic groups demanded economic development, they pointed to the dire straits facing farmers in the region. Without an alternative, they argued, the overreliance on cotton would send marginal owners into tenancy, marginal tenants into wage labor, and all into poverty. In Florence, Decatur, and in Huntsville, boosters posited industrialization as an alternative to farming, a way to bring prosperity in the form of paychecks and investment that would help those unable to continue on the land find new ways to survive. Assisted by federal farm practices and reforms, developers participated in the economic shift that unseated agriculture as the primary occupation in the valley and across the South, and by 1960, farming was practiced by a distinct minority in the region. Of the 140,000 residents of the counties along the river that reported earning a wage or salary, only 18,000 identified as working in agriculture, on farms averaging 113 acres, double the average in 1920. Tenancy dropped dramatically as well, down to only 29 percent of farm operators. Farming had become the occupation of larger landowners, while residents without the means to own large amounts of land or invest in equipment and labor turned to industrial work for sustenance.

As telling as such statistics might be, they fail to capture the impact that federal development had on the everyday lives of the people of the Tennessee Valley. Holland Greer, whose father was a towboat pilot on Wheeler Reservoir, captured the coming of prosperity. The income and employment was "just a God-send," the "greatest thing that ever happened to . . . those people that came off the farm." Greer described the waning fortunes of cotton agriculture. Where once farmers could expect cotton "four, five, six feet high," on the eve of TVA's entrance, farmers had "farmed the nutrients out of the land" with cotton only a "half knee-high." Then the authority "came in at a good time to rescue a whole bunch of those people." Along with Reynolds Aluminum, TVA "worked thousands of people, they bought farms and built houses, and really lived a good life compared to what it was before." Greer concluded wistfully, telling his interviewer, "Big time, you know, we were on a roll back then."[33]

Huston Cobb's story is similar. Cobb's grandfather, a tenant farmer, embodied the challenges of marginal agriculture. Having mortgaged his crop and his tools, a bad crop left him "broke-up" and forced him off the land. When TVA's construction program began, however, Cobb's relatives found employment; he remembered the ease of getting work when "folks would go up [to the construction site] and lie around on the ground, and a man come out and say, 'You, you, you.'" Cobb's father took a job with TVA, starting in 1934, and his family was "up-town, out of the field back over there."[34]

As a teenager, George Davis took a job at the nitrate plants in Muscle Shoals. As work slowed, he moved to Huntsville, trying farming but eventually taking work in the textile mills in order to make ends meet. In the years before the arsenal, it was a "little sleepy town" where "everybody knew everybody else's business." Davis trained to work at the arsenal, but when an accident at the arsenal injured people on his street, he applied for a job at TVA as a machinist in the repair shop. In 1990, he remembered just how popular the agency had been during the height of its work in the region: "TVA was young and everybody had high hopes of having a job. Not only working for TVA, but it brought in new industries and things like that in the Valley. Even little plants would work 50 people or 25, but they had a job, very industrious."[35]

Yet one story, more than any other, captures the nature of the changes that overtook the valley's economy in the middle of the twentieth century. Told by people in and out of the Tennessee Valley and remembered by officials at TVA and average citizens, it concerns a visit made by David Lilienthal to the city of Decatur. One of the more meaningful reminisces comes from John Caddell, an attorney who, in 1943, served as president of the Decatur Chamber of Commerce. At first, Caddell had been wary of TVA, particularly its treatment of Alabama Power. But as the authority made clear its willingness to work with communities on their own development, Caddell became a convert. He accompanied Barrett Shelton to meet with Lilienthal, "the real heart and soul of the development." As Caddell listened, Shelton asked Lilienthal, "What are you going to do for us?" Lilienthal responded, "Not a goddamn thing. I'm just going to teach you how to do something for yourselves."[36]

For Shelton and Caddell, the notion that TVA would work to serve the larger mission of the city's civic and business leaders fit perfectly with their vision for the future. Like their fellow boosters across the valley, and their predecessors and successors, they viewed federal investment as a means to an end, and they cultivated a close relationship with men like Lilienthal as a way to help attract and direct development to the region. In the 1920s, Florence's chamber of commerce pushed for action on Muscle Shoals, even as they looked to local organization as a way to offset the stalled federal facilities. In the 1930s, 1940s, and 1950s, leaders throughout the region, but particularly in Decatur, worked with David Lilienthal and TVA to attract private investment and to organize active development agencies at the local and regional level. During and after World War II, civic groups in Huntsville led the drive to bring federal facilities, increase defense investment, and diversify the community with private industry. At each step, growth brought dislocation, and the people of the valley struggled to adjust to change as agriculture declined, as civil rights and unionization became crucial considerations for industrial location and expansion, and as the impact of development on the environment threatened to undermine the region's health. Still, one factor remained (and remains) preeminent: thanks to the region's active civic leaders and business community, and the close relationship they forged and maintained with an increasingly development-conscious federal government, the Tennessee Valley came to symbolize the prosperity, however promising and problematic, of the Sunbelt South.

ACKNOWLEDGMENTS

First and foremost, I want to thank my family for their unrelenting support. My parents, Steve and Bonnie, and my sister and her family—Meghan, John David, Jack, and Georgia Chambless—have given me words of encouragement and consolation more times than I can count. The farther south we move, the more essential they have been as my connection to the Tennessee Valley, and the work is stronger for their help. I am also grateful for the enthusiasm and support that my in-laws, Frank and Barbara McCollum, as well as Frank III and Richard and their families, have shown for my studies and this project. Since beginning work on this topic, I lost both sets of grandparents: Lewis and Ora Downs and Reeder and Mary Lee Barnett. Their lives, their love of history, and their insistence that the past matters drew me to the field and set me on a constant quest to know more about the world they inhabited.

My years as a student prepared me to spend countless hours poring over the written word, both in archives and in the innumerable drafts that resulted in this book. As an undergraduate at Birmingham-Southern College, I learned to research and write from Dave Ullrich, Matt Levey, Bill Nicholas, Sam Stayer, Guy Hubbs, and Mark Lester. Dr. Lester, in particular, became an unofficial advisor and my first mentor as a scholar. My professors at the University of Alabama—Margaret Abruzzo, John Beeler, Greg Dorr, Tony Freyer, Paul Gorman, Paul Hagenloh, Andrew Huebner, Hasan Jeffries, Howard Jones, Micki McElya, Josh Rothman, Harold Selesky, and George Williamson—challenged me to care deeply about the past. Lisa Lindquist-Dorr, George Rable, and David Beito read an earlier, much rougher version and pushed me to think more broadly about the causes and consequences of economic development for the South. Another early source of support, Peter Coclanis, began by providing positive feedback after a panel at the Southern Historical Association, brought me to the Global American South Conference at the University of North Carolina, and encouraged me to pursue publication. I am eternally grateful to my professor, advisor, career counselor, and personal mentor, Kari Frederickson. She found me bewildered as a new graduate student and led me to pursue a deep-seated interest in the history of the modern South. She helped direct my thoughts and reined me in when I wandered off course, but she also allowed me the freedom to figure out how to tell the story in a way that was meaningful to me. The university, the College of Arts and Sciences, and the Department of History offered me a number of funding opportunities, including a Graduate Council Fellowship, several assistantships, scholarships, stipends, and a generous departmental fellowship. My fellow grad students created a supportive community. Thank you especially to Charity Carney, Jill Cooley, Daniel Menestres, Joe Danielson, and Kris Teters. Ryan Floyd is a lifelong friend; he took time from a busy work and family schedule to proofread and edit, and he has to be sick of reading various versions of this manuscript.

During several years in the limbo of adjunct and visiting positions, I found sympathy and encouragement from Jim Day, Ruth Truss, Clark Hultquist, and Amanda Fox at the University of Montevallo; Randy Law, Victoria Ott, and Debbie Smith at Birmingham-Southern College; and Chris Maynard and Martha Frances Graham at the University of North Alabama. Thank you also to the faculty in the History Department at the University of Alabama at Birmingham, particularly Carolyn Conley, Colin Davis, Harriet Amos Doss, Brian Steele, John Van Sant, and Walter Ward, for a great year and an invaluable experience. While at UAB, I was lucky enough to "try out" the material from this project with a group of MA students in two seminars. Their input on the South's relationship to the federal government and on the New Deal certainly contributed to my work.

Last year, I had the great fortune to find a position at the University of Mobile. The administration and faculty have encouraged my work and professional growth, and the students' enthusiasm for learning provides a constant reminder of why I love teaching. I am especially grateful to Mark Foley and Audrey Eubanks, to Dwight Steedley, Tom Bevill, and Lonnie Burnett, and my colleagues "on the hall" who have become like a second family: Michael Robinson, Casey Cooper, Joe West, Jeremiah Sullins, Julie Biskner, Luke Brekke, Adele Hermann, Ted Mashburn, and Cindy Godwin.

My research took me throughout the state of Alabama and the Southeast, and a number of people provided valuable advice and assistance. Bill Tharpe at the Alabama Power Corporate Archives helped me explore the debate over Muscle Shoals and the arrival of TVA from the perspective of the state utility, and Leah Rawls Atkins shared her perspective on the utility's role in the development of the region. The Special Collections staff at W. S. Hoole Library at the University of Alabama and the Louis Salmon Library at the University of Alabama in Huntsville helped me to navigate the personal papers of John Sparkman, Lister Hill, and Bob Jones, and the staff at Auburn University's Draughon Library guided me through the Alabama Cooperative Extension papers with ease. On this and other projects, I have spent countless hours in Alabama's State Department of Archives and History; the facilities are impressive, and the staff is warm and friendly. Their assistance made the papers of innumerable state and local politicians readily accessible. I am also indebted to the archivists at the National Archives branch in Morrow, Georgia, who introduced me to the labyrinth of files on TVA and NASA, and who put up with intermittent appearances and innumerable requests and questions. Clint Alley at the Florence-Lauderdale Public Library gave me access to oral histories of the TVA years, and the staff at the Huntsville Public Library directed me to material on Redstone and Marshall. Mike Wright, Brian Odom, and Kim Mason Henry at Marshall Space Flight Center cheerfully fielded questions on the space program. J. Tate Godfrey, Cindy Burns, and Jason Wright gave me access to the files of Tom Johnson at the North Alabama Industrial Development Association, and Barrett Shelton Jr. provided photos and stories of his father's work for the region. Greg Warren helped turn old slides into usable photos. David Goldfield and the outside readers for LSU Press helped me to sharpen my argument and refine my work. Lee Sioles, Catherine Kadair, and Stan Ivester made this readable, and Rand Dotson made the entire process a joy.

Parts of this work have been presented at a number of conferences, including those of the Southern Historical Association, the Alabama Historical Association, the Agricultural History Society, and the Society for American City and Regional Planning History. In their comments, Kenneth Lipartito, Sarah Phillips, Monica Gisolfi, and Mark Rose helped to sharpen my arguments, and along with a number of insightful comments and questions from audiences and fellow panel members, their advice was constructive and encouraging.

This book is dedicated to the two most important people in my life. My wife, Sarah, followed me from Birmingham to Mobile and put up with the uncertainty of life during and after grad school. She is a source of never-ending encouragement and gentle pressure, constant love and friendship, and the reason this is possible. My son, Graham, is the greatest gift I have ever received. I can only hope that one day he'll read this book and understand why his dad already had so many gray hairs.

NOTES

INTRODUCTION: BRISK MEN, ENERGETIC OF MOVEMENT AND SPEECH

1. Kirkpatrick Sale in *Power Shift*, qtd. in Numan V. Bartley, *The New South, 1945–1980* (Baton Rouge: Louisiana State University Press, 1995), 431.

2. Thomas Wolfe, "Boom Town," in *The Complete Short Stories of Thomas Wolfe*, ed. Francis E. Skipp (New York: Charles Scribner's Sons, 1987), 128.

3. Ibid., 127–28.

4. Ibid., 130.

5. Ibid., 138.

6. Qtd. in James C. Cobb, *Away Down South: A History of Southern Identity* (New York: Oxford University Press, 2005), 117. See also George Brown Tindall, *The Emergence of the New South, 1913–1945* (Baton Rouge: Louisiana State University Press, 1967), 576–82.

7. Twelve Southerners, *I'll Take My Stand: The South and the Agrarian Tradition*, 2nd ed. (Baton Rouge: Louisiana State University Press, 1977), xxxvii, xlvii.

8. W. J. Cash, *The Mind of the South*, 50th anniversary ed. (New York: Vintage Books, 1991), 182.

9. Ibid., 184.

10. C. Vann Woodward, *Origins of the New South, 1877–1913* (Baton Rouge: Louisiana State University Press, 1971), 124, 148.

11. James C. Cobb, "Beyond Planters and Industrialists: A New Perspective on the New South," *Journal of Southern History* 54, no. 1 (Feb. 1988): 66.

12. Edward L. Ayers, *The Promise of the New South: Life after Reconstruction* (1992; New York: Oxford, 2007), 20, 22.

13. Gavin Wright, *Old South, New South: Revolutions in the Southern Economy since the Civil War* (Baton Rouge: Louisiana State University Press, 1986), 157, 172. See also Ayers, *The Promise of the New South*, 104.

14. Corra Harris, qtd. in Ayers, *The Promise of the New South*, 105.

15. Ibid.

16. Don Doyle, *New Men, New Cities, New South: Atlanta, Nashville, Charleston, Mobile, 1860–1910* (Chapel Hill: University of North Carolina Press, 1990), 89–90, 109; Grady qtd. in Cash, *The Mind of the South*, 182.

17. Qtd. in Woodward, *Origins of the New South,* 153.

18. Ayers, *The Promise of the New South,* 20; Woodward, *Origins of the New South,* 147.

19. Doyle, *New Men, New Cities, New South,* 140–48, 148–49.

20. Woodward, *Origins of the New South,* 124; Doyle, *New Men, New Cities, New South,* 152–58.

21. Qtd. in Ayers, *The Promise of the New South,* 21. See also Paul M. Gaston, *The New South Creed: A Study in Southern Mythmaking* (1970; rpr. Baton Rouge: Louisiana State University Press, 1976), 87–90.

22. Ayers, *The Promise of the New South,* 21.

23. Qtd. in Cash, *The Mind of the South,* 184.

24. Ayers, *The Promise of the New South,* 59, 104; Tindall, *The Emergence of the New South,* 75–84.

25. Qtd. in Tindall, *The Emergence of the New South,* 98.

1. A LIVING MONUMENT TO THAT BROAD PRINCIPLE OF DEMOCRACY, 1915–1924

1. "Henry Ford Visits the Wilson Dam," *Florence Times,* June 17, 1921, 1.

2. *Congressional Record* (House), 67th Congress, 1st sess. (61:5), July 25, 1921, 4285–86; and "Henry Ford Backs Nitrate Project," *Christian Science Monitor,* July 15 1921, 2.

3. The story of Ford's interest in Muscle Shoals is detailed in a letter reprinted in the *Congressional Record* by Alabama Congressman Lister Hill. See *Congressional Record* (House), 69th Cong., 2nd sess., 1927, vol. 68, pt. 2: 1304–6.

4. "'I'll put the South on the Map,' Says Ford," *Wall Street Journal,* Nov. 18, 1921, 11; "Ford's Muscle Shoals Plans a National Benefit, Says Edison," *Wall Street Journal,* Nov. 23, 1921, 3.

5. "Ford Party Returns to Their Home," "Edison to Recommend Acceptance," "Ford Party Enjoys 'Cue," and "Ford Gives Message to the People," *Florence Times,* Dec. 9, 1921, 1. Richard C. Sheridan, a research chemist at TVA's National Fertilizer Development Center (located at the Muscle Shoals nitrate plant), reconstructed Ford and Edison's trip in "Thomas Alva Edison's Visit to Muscle Shoals," *Journal of Muscle Shoals History* 11 (1986): 127–33.

6. George Fort Milton, "The Tennessee Valley: An Experiment in a Way of Life," 85–94, in John Temple Graves II et al., eds., *A Book of the South* (Southern Editors Association, ca. 1940), 87.

7. In *The Formative Period of TVA: The Muscle Shoals Project, 1783–1916* (New York: Carlton Press, Inc., 1973), Adrian Daniel follows the efforts of promoters to convince the government of the need for regional development at Muscle Shoals from the "Tennessee River Frontier" in 1540 until the development's inception in 1916. Daniel provides an excellent overview of the plans to correct the navigational impediments of the river and utilize its resources. The only detailed account of the congressional fight over the development at Muscle Shoals between 1916 and 1933 is Preston J. Hubbard's *Origins of the TVA: The Muscle Shoals Controversy* (New York: W. W. Norton and Co., 1961). Hubbard's main interest is in following legislation from Ford's offer (in 1921) to the creation of the TVA (in 1933); however, in focusing on Washington, he fails to consider the ways in which the residents of the valley facilitated and directed development. While events in Washington proved crucial to the final outcome of the fight, the local debate was just as important.

8. Leah Rawls Atkins, *"Developed for the Service of Alabama": The Centennial History of the Alabama Power Company, 1906–2006* (Birmingham: Alabama Power Co., 2006), 21, 34, 56.

Atkins's official history of Alabama Power is an excellent source of information on the utility's early interest in and work on the Muscle Shoals site.

9. Charles H. Baker to John H. Bankhead Sr., July 24, 1909, box 41:8, John H. Bankhead Sr. Papers, Alabama Department of Archives and History, Montgomery (hereafter cited as ADAH).

10. Underwood, "The Water Power Bill," July 18, 1914, box 46:7, Oscar Underwood Papers, ADAH. According to Underwood's biographer, Evans Johnson, the senator was a "typical" southern Bourbon favoring the promotion of New South business through "generous" government concessions. Johnson argues that Underwood initially supported a more active governmental role at Muscle Shoals because of the national defense and fertilizer implications of the site. See Johnson, *Oscar W. Underwood: A Political Biography* (Tuscaloosa: University of Alabama Press, 2006), 452, 348–49.

11. *Congressional Record* (House), 63rd Cong., 3rd sess., 1915, vol. 53, pt. 2: 1866–70.

12. In the 1930s, the Tennessee Valley Authority's Legal Division, led by Judson King, produced two brief and informative summaries of the fight over Muscle Shoals. See Judson King, "A Brief Chronology of Muscle Shoals Legislation," Dec. 24, 1933, box 4: "010.12 Muscle Shoals Bibliography," David E. Lilienthal Correspondence, Records of the Tennessee Valley Authority, National Archives, Southeast Region, Morrow, Ga. (hereafter cited as NARASE); and King, *The Legislative History of Muscle Shoals* 1–4 (Knoxville: TVA, 1935), box 1: "Legislative History of Muscle Shoals by Judson King, Vol. 1 and 2," and "Legislative History of Muscle Shoals by Judson King, Vol. 3 and 4," Arthur E. Morgan Papers, 1933–58, Records of the Board of Directors (A. E. Morgan Papers), TVA Records, NARASE. See also Atkins, *"Developed for the Service of Alabama,"* 80, 606 n89.

13. Nashville Section Engineering Association of the South, *America's Gibraltar, Muscle Shoals* (Nashville, Tenn.: Muscle Shoals Association, 1916), 7, Hoole Special Collections Library, Tuscaloosa, Ala. (hereafter cited as Hoole).

14. Ibid., 48.

15. Ibid., 60.

16. U.S. Census Bureau, Thirteenth Census of the United States Taken in the Year 1910, vol. 2: Population (Washington, D.C.: GPO, 1913), 30, 50.

17. "Real Estate Very Active," *Florence Times*, Mar. 24, 1916, 1, 4.

18. "Muscle Shoals Meeting Held," *Florence Times*, Jan. 21, 1916, 1, 8; "Enthusiastic Meeting," *Florence Times*, Mar. 10, 1916, 1.

19. R. T. Simpson, "Big Muscle Shoals Meeting Friday Night at Court House," *Florence Times*, Aug. 4, 1916, 1.

20. "Will Soon Have Fine Quarters," *Florence Times*, Mar. 16, 1917, 1.

21. U.S. Census Bureau. Fourteenth Census of the United States Taken in the Year 1920, vol. 3: Population 1920, Composition and Characteristics of the Population by States (Washington, D.C.: GPO, 1922), 23, 30. Regional statistics are particularly high for Florence's surrounding counties and towns in the 1920 census, thanks to the economic boost resulting from construction on Wilson Dam.

22. Blaine A. Brownell, *The Urban Ethos in the South, 1920–1930* (Baton Rouge: Louisiana State University Press, 1975), xix.

23. Ibid., 66–79. In South Carolina, for instance, as early as the 1920s, cotton buyers, lien merchants, and retailers turned their agricultural profits into industrial start-up funds, encourag-

ing a kind of economic diversification that provided whites with an alternative to the farm, even as segregated hiring practices kept blacks tied to agriculture. See Peter A. Coclanis and Lacy K. Ford, "The South Carolina Economy Reconstructed and Reconsidered: Structure, Output, and Performance, 1670–1985," in *Developing Dixie: Modernization in a Traditional Society*, ed. Winfred B. Moore Jr., Joseph F. Trip, and Lyon G. Tyler Jr. (New York: Greenwood Press, 1988), 92–110.

24. Bankhead to Harris, Oct. 29, 1917, box 24:1, Bankhead Sr. Papers.

25. Wright, *Old South, New South*, 202–3; Charles S. Aiken, *The Cotton Plantation South since the Civil War* (Baltimore: Johns Hopkins University Press, 1998); Pete Daniel, *Breaking the Land: The Transformation of Cotton, Tobacco, and Rice Cultures since 1880* (Urbana: University of Illinois Press, 1985); and Gilbert C. Fite, *Cotton Fields No More: Southern Agriculture, 1865–1980* (Lexington: University Press of Kentucky, 1984). Conditions were particularly difficult for marginalized farm groups. See Wright, *Old South, New South*, 119–20, for a discussion of the effects on African American farmers. For farm women, see Melissa Walker, *All We Knew Was to Farm: Rural Women in the Upcountry South, 1919–1941* (Baltimore: Johns Hopkins University Press, 2000).

26. Fite, *Cotton Fields No More*, 102–4.

27. Particularly useful for understanding the economic conditions of agriculture in the valley is a report conducted by TVA's Social and Economic Research Division in 1939, investigating tenancy in the region. See Jasper B. Shannon, Social and Economic Research Division, Department of Regional Planning Studies, TVA, "Tenancy in the Big Bend of the Tennessee River: A Summary," 1 June 1939, 43–46, box 286: loose, [Harry] Curtis, [Arthur E.] Morgan, and [Harcourt A.] Morgan, Records of the Board of Directors, Office of the General Manager (hereafter cited as Curtis-Morgan-Morgan Papers), TVA Records.

28. Fite, *Cotton Fields No More*, 99–100; the quote is from Andrew Soule, president of Georgia College of Agriculture, found on page 118. Statistics are drawn from census records. See U.S. Census Bureau, Tenth Census of the United States Taken in the Year 1880, vol. 3: Report on the Productions of Agriculture (Washington, D.C.: GPO, 1883); Eleventh Census of the United States Taken in the Year 1890, vol. 5: Report of the Statistics of Agriculture of the United States (Washington, D.C.: GPO, 1895); Twelfth Census of the United States Taken in the Year 1900, vol. 5: Agriculture pt. 1, Farms, Livestock, and Animal Products (Washington, D.C.: GPO, 1902) and vol. 6: Agriculture pt. 2, Crops and Irrigation (Washington, D.C.: GPO, 1902); Thirteenth Census of the United States Taken in the Year 1910, vol. 6: Agriculture: Reports by States, Alabama-Montana (Washington, D.C.: GPO, 1913); Fourteenth Census of the United States Taken in the Year 1920, vol. 6: Agriculture, pt. 2, The Southern States (Washington, D.C.: GPO, 1922). Western Tennessee Valley counties are defined as Colbert, Lauderdale, Lawrence, Limestone, and Morgan.

29. Taken from census data. See previous note.

30. Stewart, "Report of the Work of the [Limestone] County Agent, Calendar Year [1915]," box 111: "1915, Limestone," Records of the Alabama Cooperative Extension Service, 1910–74, Auburn University Special Collections and Archives, Auburn, Ala. (hereafter cited as ACES). Agents from Colbert, Lauderdale, Lawrence, Limestone, and Morgan counties all provided similar advice to farmers, though Stewart's reports are especially descriptive.

31. Stewart, "Report of the Work of the [Limestone] County Agent, Calendar Year 1916," box 112: "Limestone, 1916," ACES.

32. Abernathy, "Report of the work of the [Colbert] County Agent, Calendar Year 1918," box 113: "Colbert 1918," ACES.

33. See, for instance, G. B. Phillips, Annual Narrative Report, Lauderdale County, 1932, box 147: "Lauderdale 1932," ACES.

34. Many farmers, too, distrusted the scientific agriculture of the Extension Service which, in Alabama, was headquartered at the Alabama Polytechnic Institute, now Auburn University. And, given that agents hoped to build support for the newly formed service, many were hesitant to prescribe more radical or severe changes to regional agriculture. See Fite, *Cotton Fields No More,* 11–16.

35. See, for instance, Phillips, "Report of the [Lauderdale] County Agent, Calendar Year 1916," box 112: "Lauderdale, 1916"; and Phillips, "Report of the [Lauderdale] County Agent, Calendar Year 1918," box 113: "Lauderdale 1918," ACES.

36. Phillips, "Report of the [Lauderdale] County Agent, Calendar Year 1923," box 119: "Lauderdale 1923," ACES.

37. Maxwell to Bankhead, Aug. 1, 1917, Bankhead Sr. Papers.

38. A. M. Tunstall to Bankhead, Oct. 1, 1917; Bankhead to Tunstall, Oct. 4, 1917, Bankhead Sr. Papers.

39. *Congressional Record* (Senate), 66th Cong., 3rd sess., 1921, vol. 60, pt. 2: 1213.

40. "Muscle Shoals Chemical Plants," *Wall Street Journal,* May 15, 1918, 10.

41. "Development in Fine Progress," *Florence Times,* Dec. 7, 1917, 1.

42. "Florence Growing by Leaps and Bounds," Jan. 18, 1918, *Florence Times,* 1.

43. William Warren Rogers, Robert David Ward, Leah Rawls Atkins, and Wayne Flynt, *Alabama: The History of a Deep South State* (Tuscaloosa: University of Alabama Press, 1994), 406.

44. "No Room for Dam 2 Forces," Apr. 12, 1918, *Florence Times,* 1; "U.S. Government Will Finance Florence Home Building," *Florence Times,* Apr. 26, 1918, 1.

45. "Government Cyanamid Plant at Muscle Shoals Affords Negro Labor Wonderful Opportunities," *Muscle Shoals Cyanamid News* 1, no. 1 [1918]: 1. The insert can be found in the bound collection of the *Florence Times,* 1918, ADAH.

46. Ibid.; "Uncle Sam's Call to the Negro," *Muscle Shoals Cyanamid News* 1, no. 1 [1918]: 1.

47. "Government Cyanamid Plant at Muscle Shoals Affords Negro Labor Wonderful Opportunities," 1; and "Large Theater at Cyanamid Plant for Negro Employees," *Muscle Shoals Cyanamid News* 1, no. 1 [1918]: 1, 2.

48. Rogers et al., *Alabama,* 406.

49. Ott, "From the Cotton Fields to the Great Waterway: African Americans and the Muscle Shoals Project during World War I," *Southern Historian* 22 (Spring 2001): 35–54. Ott's research has since been republished in *The Great War in the Heart of Dixie: Alabama during World War I,* ed. Martin T. Olliff (Tuscaloosa: University of Alabama Press, 2008): 101–20.

50. "Four Hundred Men at Work Building Quarters for Increased Force at Dam 2," *Florence Times,* June 6, 1919, 1.

51. In particular, black workers looked to the NAACP and the Urban League in attempts to correct discrimination on wartime projects. See Ott, "From the Cotton Fields," 49–52.

52. "Text of Platform Adopted by the Democratic Convention," *Washington Post,* July 3, 1920, 4.

53. *Congressional Record* (Senate), 66th Cong., 3rd sess., 1921, vol. 60, pt. 4: 4433.

54. "Bill Is Defeated, Dam Amendment Loses, Will Take Up Fight Next Congress," and "Fight Is Not Our Middle Name, It Is All the Name We've Got," *Florence Times,* Mar. 4, 1921, 1.

55. "Last Week of Real Work at Wilson Dam," *Florence Times,* Apr. 8, 1921, 1.

56. "Would Complete Project," *Florence Times*, Muscle Shoals sec., May 13, 1921, 1.

57. L. R. Collier, qtd. in Allan Nevins and Frank Ernest Hill, *Ford: Expansion and Challenge, 1915–1933* (New York: Charles Scribner's Sons, 1957), 301.

58. Qtd. in Nevins and Hill, *Ford*, 301–2.

59. Samuel Crowther and Henry Ford, *My Life and Work* (1922; rpr. Garden City, N.J.: Garden City Publishing Co., 1926), 273–74. Page numbers are from the 1926 edition.

60. Samuel Crowther and Henry Ford, *Today and Tomorrow* (Garden City, N.J.: Doubleday, Page and Co., 1926), 167.

61. Douglas Brinkley, *Wheels for the World: Henry Ford, His Company, and a Century of Progress, 1903–2003* (New York: Viking, 2003), 165–73.

62. Greg Grandin, *Fordlandia: The Rise and Fall of Henry Ford's Forgotten Jungle City* (New York: Metropolitan Books, 2009), 70.

63. "People Want Ford to Come"; and "They Want Mr. Ford," *Florence Times*, July 22, 1921, 1, 2.

64. ""Farmers Indorse Muscle Shoals Plan," *Christian Science Monitor*, July 22, 1921, 8; and untitled advertisement, Alabama–Muscle Shoals Association, *Florence Times*, Apr. 7, 1922, 3.

65. McKenzie, House Committee on Military Affairs, "Muscle Shoals Propositions," 67th Cong., 2nd sess. (Report 1084), June 9, 1922, box 44:4, Underwood Papers.

66. *Congressional Record* (House), 67th Cong., 2nd sess., 1922, vol. 61, pt. 8: 8685.

67. "Farmers Indorse Ford's Muscle Shoals Offer," *Washington Post*, June 12, 1922, 2.

68. William Jennings Bryan, "Bryan Sees Farmer Outstanding Problem," *New York Times*, 22 July 1923, XX3.

69. Littell McClung, "Nitrate Plant No. 2 Is Most Valuable Plant in the World," *Florence Times*, sec. 2, Dec. 15, 1922, 1.

70. Qtd. in Grandin, *Fordlandia*, 67–68. *Fordlandia* focuses on Ford's ultimately futile attempt to create a similar "industrial village" in the Amazon Basin.

71. "Ford Predicts 100,000 People," *Florence Times*, Aug. 5, 1921, 1.

72. "Ford Plans a City 75 Miles in Length," *New York Times*, Jan. 12, 1922, 1. Blaine A. Brownell notes that Ford's proposed city fit with claims of the advantages of urban-rural life that marked the increasing decentralization of southern urban areas (*The Urban Ethos in the South*, 67).

73. Nevins and Hill, *Ford*, 310.

74. Durham to Tyson, Jan. 13, 1922, box 32:1, Lister Hill Papers, Hoole.

75. C. C. Bailey, "Let Ford Have Muscle Shoals," *Florence Times*, sec. 2, Dec. 16, 1921, 1.

76. "Holland's Letter," *Wall Street Journal*, Sept. 8, 1921, 3; "South Sees in Ford a Good Organizer," *Wall Street Journal*, Nov. 15, 1922, 10.

77. Huntsville and Madison County Chamber of Commerce, *Happy Hustling Huntsville: The Undisputed Queen of the Tennessee Valley and the Biggest Town on Earth for It's [sic] Size* (Huntsville: Monroe Printing Co., 1919), 6, in Hoole.

78. "Present Condition of Wilson Dam in Muscle Shoals Power Project Which Alabama Is Eager to See in Henry Ford's Hands," *Christian Science Monitor*, Aug. 23, 1922, 5.

79. Littell McClung, "Resources and Advantages for Great Manufacturing Industries," *Florence Times*, Jan. 26, 1923, 2–3.

80. "Rush for Muscle Shoals," *New York Times*, Feb. 12, 1922, 69.

81. Advertisement, "Weeden Heights Subdivision," *Florence Times*, Feb. 10, 1922, 3. For average farmland prices, see 1920 Census, vol. 6: 489.

82. "C. of C. Says Investigate Land Offered," *Florence Times*, Feb. 3, 1922, 1; "Real Estate and Rentals the Subject," *Florence Times*, Nov. 11, 1921, 1; "City Zone Ordinance Considered," *Florence Times*, Oct. 28, 1921, 1.

83. "Muscle Shoals Values Soar as Boom Is Awaited," *Christian Science Monitor*, Feb. 9, 1922, 1.

84. Jackson Insurance and Real Estate Company, advertisement, "Henry Ford Has Put the Muscle in the Shoals," *Florence Times*, Aug. 26, 1921, 4.

85. Allen, *Only Yesterday: An Informal History of the 1920's* (New York: Harper & Row, 1931), 226–37, quote on 235.

86. Hubbard, *Origins of the TVA*, 109.

87. Qtd. in Marie Bankhead Owen, *The Story of Alabama: A History of the State* (New York: Lewis Historical Publishing Co., 1949), vol. 1: 326.

88. Thomas W. Martin, *The Story of Electricity in Alabama* (Birmingham, Ala.: Birmingham Publishing Co., 1952), 104.

89. Atkins, "*Developed for the Service of Alabama*," 84–85.

90. Bankhead Sr. to John H. Bankhead Jr., July 20, 1916, box 22:5, Bankhead Sr. Papers.

91. "Power Plant Leased," *Florence Times*, Nov. 11, 1921, 1.

92. "'It Would Be Most Unfortunate for the Alabama Power Co. to Get Muscle Shoals'—Gov. Kilby," *Florence Times*, Feb. 17, 1922; R. M. Jones, Secretary of the Gadsden Chamber of Commerce, to Hill, Feb. 18, 1922, box 32:1, Hill Papers.

93. Florence Chamber of Commerce, Florence Rotary Club, and Florence Exchange Club, "Resolutions," Feb. 20, 1922, box 32:1, Hill Papers.

94. Jordan A. Schwarz, *The New Dealers: Power Politics in the Age of Roosevelt* (New York: Knopf, 1993), 211.

95. In *A Fierce Discontent: The Rise and Fall of the Progressive Movement in America* (New York: Oxford University Press, 2003), 149, Michael McGerr explains the Progressive fear that trusts would deplete already limited natural resources with little concern for the public interest.

96. Qtd. in Sarah T. Phillips, *This Land, This Nation: Conservation, Rural America, and the New Deal* (New York: Cambridge University Press, 2007), 127.

97. Phillips, *This Land, This Nation*, 30–32.

98. Ibid., 141–48; Tindall, *The Emergence of the New South*, 73–74.

99. *Congressional Record*, 67th Cong., 2nd sess., 1922, vol. 61, pt. 4: 3698–3707.

100. Qtd. in John R. Hornady, *Soldiers of Progress and Industry* (New York: Dodd, Mead, and Co., 1930), 156–58.

101. Ibid., 166–67.

102. Johnson, "The New Industries Division of Alabama Power Company: Its Purpose and Functions," [ca. 1941–42] in Folder 5.1.1.98.237., Alabama Power Corporate Archives, Alabama Power Co., Birmingham.

103. Rpr. in *Powergrams* 4, no. 10 (Jan. 1924): 17–18, in Alabama Power Corporate Archives.

104. Atkins, "*Dedicated to the Service of Alabama*," 125–26.

105. V. O. Key. Jr., *Southern Politics in State and Nation* (New York: Vintage Books, 1949), 36–39.

106. Ibid., 55–56.

107. "Addresses by Mr. Logan Martin and Hon. W. B. Oliver before the League of Women Voters, Mar. 14, 1922," Folder 3.1.1.52.7, pp. 2–4, Alabama Power Corporate Archives.

108. Ibid., 21–22.

109. Ibid., 12–16, 21–25. Oliver's address is paginated separately from Martin's, although both are bound in a single volume.

110. George W. Norris, *Fighting Liberal: The Autobiography of George W. Norris* (Lincoln: University of Nebraska Press, 1992), 245; Norman L. Zucker, *George W. Norris: Gentle Knight of American Democracy* (Urbana: University of Illinois Press, 1966), 117.

111. Samuel P. Hays's *Conservation and the Gospel of Efficiency: The Progressive Conservation Movement, 1890–1920* (1959; Pittsburgh: University of Pittsburgh Press, 1999), 100–121, provides an excellent overview of the conservation movement in the years before Norris's rise to power in the Senate. While Hays stops short of the fight over Muscle Shoals, his discussion of the conservationist views on resource development, and particularly multipurpose waterways development, can easily be traced in the later writings of Norris, as well as Franklin D. Roosevelt.

112. Phillips, *This Land, This Nation*, 23.

113. Qtd. in Zucker, *George W. Norris*, 115–16.

114. Norris, *Fighting Liberal*, 162, 170.

115. Char Miller, *Gifford Pinchot and the Making of Modern Environmentalism* (Washington, D.C.: Island Press, 2001), 138–39.

116. Norris, *Fighting Liberal*, 248.

117. Norris, "Report of the Committee on Agriculture and Forestry (accompanying S.J. Res. 227)," 67th Cong., 2nd sess., Apr. 20, 1922, p. 12.

118. Hubbard, *Origins of the TVA*, 140.

119. Norris, *Fighting Liberal*, 256, 259. While Norris remained the driving force behind government ownership, he counted on support from other Progressives, including New York's Fiorella LaGuardia and Illinois's William Brown McKinley. See "Debate on Shoals Was Closed on Yesterday," *Florence Times*, Mar. 7, 1924, 1, 3; and *Congressional Record* (Senate), 68th Cong., 1st sess., 1924, vol. 65, pt. 6: 5747–49.

120. Ford was also angry about the status of a power plant, the "Gorgas" plant, owned by Alabama Power and leased to the government for the construction of the dam. Alabama Power refused to sell the plant to its competition, and Ford refused to accept a revised offer without Gorgas, which he claimed essential to his promise to produce nitrates. The incident provided a blow to Ford's plans and his ego, and it added to his growing frustration over Muscle Shoals. See Ford to Kahn, 31 May 1922, box 6:10, William B. Bankhead Papers, ADAH; "2 Ford Muscle Shoals Bills Are Introduced," *Florence Times*, June 6, 1922, 5; "Alabama Tells World Opinion of Power Co.," *Florence Times*, Mar. 3, 1922, 1, 4; and "Gorgas Plant Sold by the Government," *New York Times*, Sept. 25, 1923, 9.

121. John Temple Graves, "Opportunities before Henry Ford," *Washington Post*, May 31, 1924, 6.

122. Worthington to Hill, 5 Nov. 1924, box 32:5, Hill Papers.

123. "Ford Withdrawing Muscle Shoals Bid," *New York Times*, Oct. 14, 1924, 1.

124. Hill to Joseph H. Lyons, Oct. 17, 1924, 32:5, Hill Papers.

2. MUSCLE SHOALS SIGNIFIES POWER, 1924–1933

1. Untitled editorial, *Florence Times*, Dec. 12, 1924, 2.

2. "Company Acquires Tri-Cities Property," *Powergrams* 5, no. 9 (Jan. 1925): 3–5, in Alabama Power Corporate Archives.

3. "Unlimited Amount of Power Assured District Officers of Alabama Power Companies Say," *Florence Times*, Mar. 6, 1925; untitled editorial, *Florence Times*, June 5, 1925, 2; and "Factories Seeking Location in Florence," *Florence Times*, June 12, 1925, 1.

4. Johnson, "The New Industries Division of Alabama Power Company: Its Purpose and Functions," [ca. 1941–42], in Folder 5.1.1.98.237, Alabama Power Corporate Archives; Alabama Power, "New Industries Located in Service Area, 1925–1957, Inclusive," Apr. 9, 1953, in Folder 5.1.1.98.241, Alabama Power Corporate Archives.

5. "Power Company Makes Gift of Generous Amount toward Cost of Industrial Survey," *Florence Times*, Aug. 7, 1925, 1; "Barnwell Presents Report of Industrial Survey for Florence to Directors," *Florence Times*, Nov. 6, 1925, 1; "Industrial Survey Creates Real Foundation for Great Development to Occur Here," *Florence Times*, Nov. 20, 1925, 1, 7.

6. King, "A Brief Chronology of Muscle Shoals Legislation," Dec. 24, 1933, box 4: "010.12 Muscle Shoals Bibliography," David E. Lilienthal Correspondence, TVA Records, NARASE; "Norris Ridicules Shoals Commission," *New York Times*, Apr. 2, 1925, 23. The official name of the Coolidge commission was the "Muscle Shoals Commission of Inquiry."

7. Worthington to Underwood, July 23, 1925, box 40:4, Underwood Papers.

8. Coolidge, Address at the Meeting of the Business Organization of the Government, June 30, 1924, 1, 3, in the American Presidency Project, www.presidency.ucsb.edu/ws/print.php?pid=24174 (accessed Apr. 20, 2009).

9. Coolidge, Third Annual Message, Dec. 8, 1925, 8, in the American Presidency Project, www.presidency.ucsb.edu/ws/print.php?pid=29566 (accessed Apr. 20, 2009).

10. Hicks, *Republican Ascendancy, 1921–1933* (New York: Harper and Row, 1960), 81.

11. Ibid., 9. As his most recent biographer, Amity Shlaes, notes, Coolidge worried that, if he could not find a private company prepared to invest in the project at the Shoals, it "might stay forever in the public hands." See Shlaes, *Coolidge* (New York: Harper Collins, 2013), 239–40.

12. Martin to McKenzie, Oct. 27, 1925, box 40:4, Underwood Papers.

13. "Commission Split on Muscle Shoals," *New York Times*, Nov. 3, 1925, 44. See also Hubbard, *Origins of the TVA*, 171–76.

14. "President Asks Congress to Preserve Economy Program," *Washington Post*, Dec. 9, 1925, 10.

15. "Senate Passes Muscle Shoals Measure, 51–26," *Washington Post*, Mar. 9, 1926, 1; "Joint Committee Named to Receive Bids," *Florence Times*, Mar. 14, 1926, 1, 2.

16. "Ford May Submit Shoals Offer to Coolidge," *Florence Times*, Apr. 11, 1926, 1.

17. Bill S4106, Deneen, 69th Congress, 1st sess., Apr. 19. 1926, box 45:1, Underwood Papers.

18. James, Minority Report to Accompany HR 11602, 69th Cong., 1st sess., Apr. 26, 1926, 1.

19. Ibid., 4, 7–8, 23.

20. "Majority Accepts Power Companies Offer," *Florence Times*, Apr. 26, 1926, 1; "Mass Meeting Demands Power Co. Defeat," *Florence Times*, May 5, 1926, 1, 2.

21. "An Editorial," *Florence Times*, May 2, 1926, 1.

22. Thurlow to Thompson, Sept. 14, 1926, box SG21313:19, William G. Brandon Administration Papers [Brandon Papers], ADAH. Supporters of the utilities' offer rose to their defense. See *Congressional Record* (Senate), 69th Cong., 2nd sess., 1926, vol. 68, pt. 1: 354–57.

23. "Muscle Shoals, Comparison of Revised Bids of Air Nitrates Corporation and of Muscle Shoals Distributing Company and Muscle Shoals Fertilizer Company," [ca. 1926], box 45:2, Underwood Papers.

24. *Congressional Record* (Senate), 69th Cong., 1st sess., 1926, vol. 67, pt. 5: 5082.

25. Underwood's statement of support was included in the *Congressional Record* by W. B. Oliver. See *Congressional Record* (House), 69th Cong., 1st sess., 1926, vol. 67, pt. 9: 10245.

26. *Congressional Record* (House), 69th Cong., 1st sess., 1926, vol. 67, pt. 11: 11693–94.

27. Worthington to Hill, July 21, 1926; and Worthington to Hill, Sept. 21, 1926, box 32:18, Hill Papers.

28. Judson King, "A Brief Chronology of Muscle Shoals Legislation," Dec. 24, 1933, 6–7, box 4: "010.12 Muscle Shoals Bibliography," Lilienthal Correspondence, TVA Records.

29. Preston Hubbard comes to a similar conclusion. See his *Origins of the TVA*, 215.

30. *Congressional Record* (Senate), 68th Cong., 2nd sess., 1925, vol. 66, pt. 2: 1085.

31. *Congressional Record* (Senate), 69th Cong., 1st sess., 1926, vol. 67, pt. 5: 5213.

32. "Bonds for Sheffield-Tuscumbia Plant Taken," *Florence Times*, Jan. 3, 1926, 1; untitled editorial, *Florence Times*, Jan. 28, 1926, 2.

33. "Florence Men to Determine Progress Tonight," *Florence Times*, Apr. 26, 1926, 1, 7; "Very Desirable Location Is Secured for New Factory to Manufacture Underwear," *Florence Times*, June 13, 1926, 1. See also "Rogers, Thomas McLemore," in Graves et al., eds., *A Book of the South*, 442, 514.

34. Florence Industrial Corporation, "Our Dollars Will Be Divided Among Our New Neighbors," *Florence Times-Daily*, Feb. 20, 1927, 3; Florence Industrial Corporation, "Your Help Is Needed," *Florence Times-Daily*, Feb. 13, 1927, 2. Upon relocation, the company changed its name to J. T. Stagg. See William L. McDonald and L. D. Staggs Jr., *Remembering Sweetwater: The Museums, the Mills, the People* (Killen, Ala.: Bluewater Publications, 2002), 79–80.

35. "Realty Developers Organize Commercial Club," *Florence Times*, Sept. 12, 1926, 1, 7; "Two New Industries Secured Third Certain," *Florence Times*, Oct. 24, 1926, 1, 2.

36. Jacquelyn Dowd Hall et al., *Like a Family: The Making of a Southern Cotton Mill World* (New York: W. W. Norton and Co., 1987), 24–25.

37. Tindall, *The Emergence of the New South*, 75.

38. Whitney Adrienne Snow, "Cotton Mill City: The Huntsville Textile Industry, 1880–1989," *Alabama Review* 63, no. 4 (Oct. 2010): 248–49, 273.

39. George Tindall, "Business Progressivism: Southern Politics in the Twenties," *South Atlantic Quarterly* 62 (Winter 1963): 92–106. See also Cobb, "Beyond Planters and Industrialists."

40. Tindall, "Business Progressivism," 100.

41. "Federal Operation Now Looms," *Florence Times*, Oct. 14, 1927, 1.

42. Norris, "Politics and Muscle Shoals," *Congressional Record*, Dec. 19, 1927, 3, box 32:2, Hill Papers.

43. Ibid.

44. "Senate's Passage of Amended Norris Bill Biggest Step for Shoals Settlement Yet Taken," *Florence Times*, Mar. 14, 1928, 4.

45. "Don't Do It, Athens," *Florence Times*, Feb. 12, 1928, 2; *Congressional Record* (Senate), 70th Cong., 1st sess., 1928, vol. 69, pt. 3: 3435, 3437.

46. *Congressional Record* (Senate), 70th Cong., 1st sess., 1928, vol. 69, pt. 5: 4874–75.

47. Morin, Report, Committee on Military Affairs, House, 70th Cong., 1st sess., 30 Mar. 1928.

48. Hubert Baughn, "Hill Draws Up Minority Report," *Florence Times*, Apr. 14, 1928, 1.

49. *Congressional Record* (House), 70th Cong., 1st sess., 1928, vol. 69, pt. 7: 7682.

50. "Government Operation Offers Best Solution to Shoals Question," *Florence Times*, May 3, 1928, 1.

51. C. W. Bahr to Hill, May 15, 1928; Hill to "Friends," May 16, 1928, box 32:30, Hill Papers.

52. Hubert Baughn, "Shoals Measure Passed by Senate and House; Now Goes to Coolidge," *Florence Times*, May 25, 1928, 1, 8.

53. *Congressional Record* (House), 70th Cong., 1st sess., 1928, vol. 69, pt. 10: 10056.

54. Michael Hiltzik, *Colossus: Hoover Dam and the Making of the American Century* (New York: Free Press, 2010), 29–34, 61.

55. Ibid., 109–11.

56. Ibid., 144.

57. Robert Talley, "Talley Calls Big Nitrate Plant Here a Large 'Beehive without Any Bees,'" *Florence Times*, Nov. 23, 1928, 1, 8.

58. "Huge Crowd Hears Black and Endorses Shoals Views," *Florence Times*, July 18, 1928, 6. Black's views anticipated the perspective of the TVA's David E. Lilienthal.

59. Hill to W. Grady Clark, Sheffield, Dec. 18, 1929, box 33:38, Hill Papers.

60. Hill to E. B. Gaston, Fairhope, Jan. 30, 1929, box 33:38, Hill Papers.

61. *Congressional Record* (Senate), 71st Cong., 2nd sess., 1930, vol. 72, pt. 6: 6427.

62. "Let's Get Down to Earth," *Florence Times*, June 8, 1928, 1.

63. "A New Interest," *Florence Times*, Apr. 14, 1929, 2.

64. "An Industrial Campaign," *Florence Times*, July 28, 1929, 2; "Strength in Diversity," *Florence Times*, Sept. 9, 1929, 2.

65. U.S. Census Bureau, Fourteenth Census of the United States Taken in the Year 1920, vol. 8: Manufactures 1919, General Report and Analytical Tables (Washington, D.C.: GPO, 1923), 23–30, 60–68; U.S. Census Bureau, Fifteenth Census of the United States, Manufactures: 1929, vol. 1: General Report, Statistics by Subjects (Washington, D.C.: GPO, 1933), 252.

66. "Shoals Not Injured," *Florence Times*, Nov. 27, 1929.

67. Bragg, *Ava's Man* (New York: Vintage Books, 2001), 87–88.

68. "New Industries," *Florence Times*, Feb. 28, 1930, 4; "Prepare to Seek Factories," *Florence Times*, Sept. 2, 1930, 4.

69. Hubert Baughn, "Hill to Offer 6 Amendments to Shoals Bill," *Florence Times*, May 23, 1930, 1; *Congressional Record* (House), 71st Cong., 2nd sess., 1930, vol. 72, pt. 9: 9680–1.

70. "The Shoals Resolution," *Florence Times*, Feb. 13, 1931, 4.

71. "Will He Keep His Pledge on Muscle Shoals?" *Florence Times*, Feb. 24, 1931, 1.

72. Miller to Hoover, Feb. 24, 1931; Hoover to Miller, Feb. 24, 1931; and Miller to Hoover, Feb. 25, 1931, box SG19941:32, Benjamin M. Miller Administration Papers, ADAH.

73. *Congressional Record* (Senate), 71st Cong., 3rd sess., 1931, vol. 74, pt. 7: 7070–72.

74. Ibid., 7075.

75. Ibid., 7076–77, 7084.

76. *Congressional Record* (House), 71st Cong., 3rd sess., 1931, 74, pt. 7: 7357; and "Senate Fails to Override Shoals Veto," *Florence Times*, Mar. 4, 1931, 1.

77. "The Muscle Shoals Mass Meeting," *Florence Times*, Nov. 27, 1931, 1; "Private Lease Favored for Shoals Plant," *Florence Times*, Dec. 10, 1931, 1, 2.

78. "Agrees on Shoals Measure," *Florence Times*, Feb. 18, 1932, 1; *Congressional Record* (House), 72nd Cong., 1st sess., 1932, vol. 75, pt. 6: 6285. Hill's description came from a radio broadcast

on the CBS Dixie network on Mar. 15, 1932. His comparison referenced Germany's Ruhr Valley, the center of its industrial economy.

79. H.R. 10887, 72nd Cong., 1st sess., printed Mar. 28, 1932, box 33:56, Hill Papers.

80. "Hon. Lister Hill Adds another Laurel to His Crown," *Florence Times*, Apr. 1, 1932, 4; Hill, "The Hill Bill for the Utilization of Muscle Shoals," May 4, 1932 (Washington, D.C.: GPO, 1932), 2–3, 7, box 33:56, Hill Papers.

81. "Senator Black's Greatest Opportunity," *Florence Times*, May 6, 1932, 4.

82. Bankhead to Lee Glenn, May 12, 1932; Bankhead to Hill, May 17, 1932; and Hill to Bankhead, May 19, 1932, box 33:53, Hill Papers.

83. Democratic National Committee, *Campaign Book of the Democratic Party Candidates and Issues, 1932*, box 7:6, William B. Bankhead Papers.

84. Raymond Clapper, "Roosevelt Hopes Visit Shoals After Election," *Florence Times*, Oct. 24, 1932, 1.

85. "Roosevelt Promises to Put Muscle Shoals Back on the Map," *Florence Times*, Jan. 21, 1933, 1, 7.

86. Ibid.

87. "President-Elect Roosevelt's Speeches at Shoals Today," *Florence Times*, Jan. 21, 1933, 1.

88. "Congressional Leaders Declare for Tremendous Shoals Project," *Florence Times*, Jan. 26, 1933, 1, 6. Walsh's comments were included in the *Congressional Record* by Robert LaFollette. See *Congressional Record* (Senate), 72nd Cong., 2nd sess., 1933, vol. 76, pt. 4: 3708.

89. "G.O.P. Progressives Back Shoals Project," *Florence Times*, Feb. 3, 1933, 1, 5.

90. "Inaugural Speech of Franklin Delano Roosevelt," Mar. 4, 1933, www.hpol.org/fdr/inaug/ (accessed Sept. 18, 2008).

91. H.R. 1609, 73rd Cong., 1st sess., Mar. 9, 1933, 1–2, box 33:58, Hill Papers.

92. Ibid., 7–9, 10, 13.

93. Nathan to Roosevelt, Apr. 5, 1933, box 33:58, Hill Papers.

94. S.J.R. 4, 73rd Cong., 1st sess., Mar. 9, 1933, box 32:2, Hill Papers. Norris gives his views of Hill's Bill in the *Congressional Record* later on in the debate. See *Congressional Record* (Senate), 73rd Cong., 1st sess., 1933, vol. 77, pt. 3: 2635–39.

95. "A Suggestion for Legislation to Create the Tennessee Valley Authority," Apr. 10, 1933, in Roosevelt, *The Public Papers and Addresses of Franklin D. Roosevelt*, vol. 2: *The Year of Crisis, 1933* (New York: Random House, 1938), 122.

96. Ibid., 123.

97. For a more detailed discussion of the inner workings of the final debate over the TVA bill, see Hubbard, *Origins of the TVA*.

98. H.R. 5081, 73rd Cong., 1st sess., May 18, 1933, 223, in George McJimsey, ed., *Documentary History of the Franklin D. Roosevelt Presidency*, vol. 28: *Promulgation of the Tennessee Valley Authority* (LexisNexis, 2006), document 58: 213–27.

3. WE ARE TRYING TO MAKE A DIFFERENT TYPE OF CITIZEN OUT OF THEM, 1933–1938

1. TVA, Department of Regional Planning Studies, Land Planning Division, Harold V. Miller, "A Review of Economic Conditions in Waterloo, Alabama, Following Reservoir Construction,"

May 23, 1940, i–ii, box 219: "901.041–6 Guntersville," Curtis-Morgan-Morgan Papers, TVA Records.

2. TVA, Removal Information Form, J. Leonard Fisher, Sept. 9, 1936, box 79: "Folder 3 of 4," Family Removal and Population Readjustment Case Records, Reservoir Property Management Division, TVA Records; TVA, Removal Information Form, Wm. Wilson, Sept. 10, 1936, box 79: "Folder 4 of 4," Removal Records, TVA Records.

3. TVA, Removal Information Form, W. E. Haynes, Sept. 23, 1936, box 79: "Case Records, Special Survey, Wright, Ala., Waterloo, Ala., Folder 1 of 4 Folders," Removal Records, TVA Records.

4. TVA, Removal Information Form, J. C. Potts, undated, box 79: "Folder 3 of 4," Removal Records, TVA Records.

5. TVA, Removal Information Form, Panther Creek School, June 10, 1936, box 84: "Case Files—Northcutt, Laura thru Parrish, Will," Removal Records, TVA Records.

6. TVA, Removal Information Form, Wilson, Removal Records, TVA Records.

7. TVA, Removal Information Form, Fisher, Removal Records, TVA Records.

8. TVA, Removal Information Form, Culver, Removal Records, TVA Records; TVA, Removal Information Form, Sanford Higgins, Sept. 10, 1936, box 79: "Case Records, Special Survey, Wright, Ala., Waterloo, Ala., Folder 1 of 4 Folders," Removal Records, TVA Records.

9. TVA, Removal Information Form, Ben Lee, Sept. 25, 1936, box 79: "Folder 2 of 4," Removal Records, TVA Records.

10. Qtd. in TVA General Manager John B. Blandford Jr. to Sparkman, June 17, 1938, box 94: "032.11 Sparkman, John," Office of the General Manager, Records of the Board of Directors, Curtis-Morgan-Morgan Papers, TVA Records.

11. Miller, "A Review of Economic Conditions in Waterloo, Alabama, Following Reservoir Construction," i–ii, box 219: "901.041–6 Guntersville," Curtis-Morgan-Morgan Papers, TVA Records.

12. U.S. Census Bureau, Fifteenth Census of the United States: 1930, Agriculture, vol. 1: Farm Acreage and Farm Values by Townships or Other Minor Civil Divisions (Washington, D.C.: GPO, 1931), 23.

13. Miller, "A Review of Economic Conditions in Waterloo, Alabama, Following Reservoir Construction," 3, 6, box 219: "901.041–6 Guntersville," Curtis-Morgan-Morgan Papers, TVA Records.

14. Ibid., i–ii.

15. Ibid., 7–8.

16. Ibid., 10–12.

17. Ibid., 13–14.

18. Ibid., 4.

19. U.S. Census Bureau. Fifteenth Census of the United States Taken in the Year 1930, vol. 2: Agriculture, Part 2: The Southern States (Washington, D.C.: GPO, 1932).

20. G. B. Phillips, Annual Report, Limestone County, 1932, box 147: "Limestone 1932," ACES.

21. Amity Shlaes, *The Forgotten Man: A New History of the Great Depression* (New York: Harper Perennial, 2007), 177, 179.

22. "Morgan Visits Muscle Shoals," *Florence Times*, May 26, 1933, 1, 6.

23. "Authority Moves on Power," *Florence Times*, July 25, 1933, 1, 3.

24. Mark Winter, interview with Ernst Morgan, Apr. 6, 1983, 4, box 7: "Morgan, Ernst A.," Oral History Records, 1965–93 (Oral History Records), TVA Records.

25. Morgan, "The Valley Region Physical Characteristics," May 21, 1934, NBC Radio Address, box 2: "Social and Economic Planning," Records of the Chairmen and Members of the Board of Directors of TVA, Subject Index to Speeches, 1933–38 (A. E. Morgan Speech Files), TVA Records.

26. Morgan, "Self-Sufficiency," July 17, 1934, Knoxville, box 2: "Social Plan," A. E. Morgan Speech Files, TVA Records.

27. Tindall, *The Emergence of the New South,* 448. Tindall argues that Morgan's desire for social and physical engineering fit the early goals of TVA.

28. Roosevelt, "The Fourth 'Fireside Chat'—'We Are on Our Way, and We Are Headed in the Right Direction,'" Oct. 22, 1933, 420, in *The Public Papers and Addresses of Franklin D. Roosevelt,* vol. 2: *The Year of Crisis, 1933.*

29. Arthur E. Morgan, *The Making of the TVA* (Buffalo, N.Y.: Prometheus Books, 1974), 7.

30. "Press Conference #160," Nov. 23, 1934, 214, in Roosevelt, *Complete Presidential Press Conferences of Franklin D. Roosevelt,* vols. 3–4: 1934 (New York: Da Capo Press, 1972).

31. Historian Robert S. McElvaine suggested that Roosevelt's TVA was "a model of the best that could be accomplished largely under the planning philosophy espoused by many New Dealers." See McElvaine, *The Great Depression: America, 1929–1941* (New York: Times Books, 1984), 155.

32. For Roosevelt as an advocate of consumption, see Alan Brinkley, *The End of Reform: New Deal Liberalism in Recession and War* (New York: Vintage Books, 1995), 70–71.

33. Lilienthal, *The Journals of David E. Lilienthal,* vol. 1: *The TVA Years, 1939–1945* (New York: Harper & Row, 1964), 32–33, 36; William E. Leuchtenburg, *Franklin D. Roosevelt and the New Deal, 1932–1940* (New York: Harper & Row, 1967), 164–65.

34. "Authority Moves on Power," *Florence Times,* July 25, 1933, 1.

35. Schwarz, *The New Dealers,* 223–24. Municipalities contracting with TVA charged between 2 and 2.75 cents per kilowatt-hour, while Alabama Power charged 4.6 cents.

36. "Address of David E. Lilienthal, Director and General Counsel, Tennessee Valley Authority, Before the Rotary Club of Memphis, October 17, 1933," 302–3, in McJimsey, ed., *Documentary History* 28, document 92: 300–308.

37. Lilienthal to Col. Marvin H. McIntyre, Nov. 21, 1933, in McJimsey, ed., *Documentary History* 28, document 97: 327–30.

38. Schwarz, *The New Dealers,* 196.

39. Lilienthal, "The Future of Industry in the Tennessee Valley Region," Apr. 21, 1934, in *Congressional Record* (Senate), 73rd Cong., 2nd sess., 1934, vol. 78, pt. 7: 7110–12.

40. Lilienthal, "Project: Industrial Development Division," May 11, 1934, 1, box 218: "901.02 Industrial (surveys, statistics, studies, etc.)," Curtis-Morgan-Morgan Papers, TVA Records.

41. "TVA Ordered to Build Wheeler Dam," *Florence Times,* Oct. 14, 1933, 1.

42. Lawrence L. Durisch, Research Section, Social and Economic Division, "Preliminary and Confidential Report, Families of the Wheeler Reservoir Area," Sept. 12, 1935, 1–3, box 1: untitled folder, Removal Records, TVA Records.

43. Ibid., 3–5.

44. Ibid., 8, 10–12.

45. Ibid., 19–20. The central conflict of New Deal agricultural programs is well documented. See, for instance, Phillips, *This Land, This Nation,* 119–20.

46. In her history of the New Conservationists, Sarah Phillips notes that this situation was a central problem for New Deal–era conservationists, including those in TVA. In the name of encouraging resource conservation across the South as a means of correcting the failing economy, federal planners inadvertently raised the value of private property and forced farmers and nonfarmers to seek profits instead of sustainable agriculture (*This Land, This Nation*, 84).

47. Schedule 834, John Fuqua, Apr. 17, 1935, box 53: "White–male–separated–Wheeler"; and Family Case Record, John C. Fuqua, Oct. 24, 1935, box 64: "Fuqua, John, 834, Wheeler, Ala., Rt. 1," Removal Records, TVA Records. TVA hired case workers to interact with those living on the land needed for reservoir and dam construction. The workers interviewed residents and assessed their living conditions and the resources they could draw on for relocation. Case workers recommended how TVA, within its sphere of authority, might best facilitate resettlement. The workers became the face of TVA for many in the Tennessee Valley and, as such, received their share of complaints. The individual reports, drawn up by case workers for each family interviewed, provide interesting insight into the lives of residents and the difficulties encountered in relocation.

48. Schedule 368, Charly Hodges, Mar. 25, 1935, box 53: "Negro–male–separated–Wheeler," Removal Records, TVA Records.

49. Schedule 367, Charlie Webb, [1935], box 59: "Wheeler 970s, Snowden-Toney, various counties (28)," Removal Records, TVA Records.

50. Schedule 368, Hodges, Nov. 15, 1935, box 65: "Hodges, Charlie, 368, Decatur, Ala., Rt. 1," Removal Records, TVA Records.

51. Schedule 367, Webb, [1935–36], box 70: "Webb, Charlie, 367, Decatur, Alabama," Removal Records, TVA Records.

52. Reservoir Family Removal Section, "Activities of the Reservoir Family Removal Section, Wheeler Reservoir Area," undated, 2–3, box 71: "Wheeler-Final Report (First Draft)—Report of Family Removal Activities," Removal Records, TVA Records.

53. Reservoir Family Removal Division, "Manual," [ca. 1936], 2, box 1: "Norris Correspondence (manual, ca. 1936)," Removal Records, TVA Records.

54. See, for instance, Bob and Sara Jane Lokey, in Family Case Record, Schedule (Pickup), Lokey, [1935], box 66: "Lokey, Bob, Transient Pickup, Decatur, Ala.," Removal Records, TVA Records.

55. Schedule 642, R. F. "Buddy" Cole, [1935], box 56: "Wheeler 970s, Cauthers-Cowley, various counties (5)," Removal Records, TVA Records.

56. Ibid.

57. Family Case Record, Cole, Schedule 642, Nov. 25, 1935, box 63: "Cole, R. F. (Buddy), 642, Huntsville, Ala. Rt. 4," Removal Records, TVA Records.

58. Wallace qtd. in Fite, *Cotton Fields No More*, 143; see also 135–47; and Daniel, *Breaking the Land*, 92–108, 168–74.

59. Reservoir Property Management Division, "Population Readjustment, Wheeler Area," Feb. 1, 1937, 2–3, box 1: untitled folder, Removal Records, TVA Records.

60. Ibid., 12.

61. Ibid., 12–13.

62. Ibid., 2.

63. *Technical Report No. 3, The Pickwick Landing Project: A Comprehensive Report on the Planning, Design, Construction, and Initial Operations of the Pickwick Landing Project* (Knoxville, Tenn.:

TVA, 1941), box 335: "3–400, The Pickwick Landing Project," Office of Engineering, Design and Construction Files (EDC Files), TVA Records.

64. Mary Jane Lowe, interview with Mancil Milligan, July 7, 1988, 1–3, box 6: "Milligan, Mancil," Oral History Records, TVA Records.

65. Ibid., 11.

66. Steve Killingsworth, "Regional Planning on a Local Scale: The Brief Life of Pickwick Village," *West Tennessee Historical Society Papers* 51 (1997): 55. Killingsworth investigated life at both Pickwick Village and Slab Town, concluding optimistically that TVA "accomplished what its designers envisioned" and carried benefits that "extended far beyond the confines of the project area" (Killingsworth, "Regional Planning," 60).

67. Lowe, interview with Mancil Milligan, July 7, 1988, 8, 10, 6: "Milligan, Mancil," Oral History Records, TVA Records.

68. Research Division, Social and Economic Division, TVA, "The Guntersville Area and the Proposed Coles Bend Dam, Preliminary and Confidential Report," Nov. 23, 1935, 26, box 2: "Studies and Reports—Guntersville Area [2]," Removal Records, TVA Records.

69. Ibid., 27. Removal activities at Guntersville also affected more families than Wheeler and Pickwick (1,182 compared to 842 and 506, respectively) and required a larger outlay of funds ($36,000 compared to $29,000 and $34,000). See Reservoir Property Management Department, "Annual Report, Population Readjustment, 1938–39," [1939], 2, box 8: "Population Readjustment, Annual Reports, 1935–6 thru 1943–4," Removal Records, TVA Records.

70. Population Readjustment Division, Reservoir Property Management Department, "Population Readjustment: Guntersville Area," June 1940, 2–3, box 2: "Studies and Reports—Guntersville Area [1]," Removal Records, TVA Records.

71. Ibid., 8–9, 15.

72. Ibid., 16–17.

73. *Technical Report No. 2, The Wheeler Project: A Comprehensive Report on the Planning, Design, Construction, and Initial Operations of the Wheeler Project* (Knoxville, Tenn.: TVA, 1940), box 311: "3–400A The Wheeler Project"; *The Pickwick Landing Project,* box 335: "3–400A, The Pickwick Landing Project"; and *The Guntersville Project: A Comprehensive Report on the Planning, Design, Construction, and Initial Operations of the Guntersville Project* (Knoxville, Tenn.: TVA, 1941), box 387: "6–400 Guntersville Project," EDC Files, TVA Records.

74. Gus May, Assistant Secretary, Tennessee Valley Land Owners Protective Association, to Sparkman, Jan. 18, 1938, box 35, "TVA: Misc., 1938 (Jan.–Mar.)," John J. Sparkman Papers (Sparkman House Papers), Hoole; and untitled, *Florence Times,* June 4, 1937, 3.

75. Sparkman to R. C. Moore, May 26, 1937, box 35, "TVA: Misc., 1938 (Jan.–Mar.)," John J. Sparkman Papers (Sparkman House Papers), Hoole.

76. Rudder to Sparkman, Dec. 6, 1937, box 35: "Tennessee Valley Authority: Miscellaneous, 1937 (Jul.–Dec.), Sparkman House Papers, Hoole.

77. Knight to Hill, Apr. 10, 1935, 34: box 69, Hill Papers. See also Laura Beth Daws, "Overlooked: Dominant Ideology, Limestone County, Alabama, Newspapers, and TVA Family Relocation, 1934–1936," MA thesis, Auburn University, 2005.

78. As Michael J. McDonald and John Muldowny noted in their study of relocation activities at Norris, "socioeconomic planning for rural communities does not appear to have been [TVA's] primary goal. When work on the dam was begun, there had been little or no thought given to

translating the modernization process into realistic terms insofar as the removed populations were concerned." See McDonald and Muldowny, *TVA and the Dispossessed: The Resettlement of Population in the Norris Dam Area* (Knoxville: University of Tennessee Press, 1982), 266–67.

79. The Muscle Shoals plants shifted to phosphate production under the guidance of board member Harcourt Morgan, who argued that materials needed for the production of fertilizer from phosphates were closer in location and thus more widely available for the farmers of North Alabama. Morgan also hoped that the shift would allow TVA to continue with research and technical development at the facilities. See Gordon Clapp, *TVA: An Approach to the Development of a Region* (Chicago: University of Chicago Press, 1955), appendix A, 143–46.

80. *The Wheeler Project,* box 311: "3–400A The Wheeler Project," EDC Files, TVA Records.

81. Mary Jane Lowe, interview with Mancil Milligan, July 7, 1998, 3, box 6: "Milligan, Mancil," Oral History Records, TVA Records.

82. Ibid.

83. *The Pickwick Landing Project,* box 335: "3–400A the Pickwick Landing Project," EDC Files, TVA Records; Killingsworth, "Regional Planning on a Local Scale"; *The Guntersville Project,* box 387: "6–400 Guntersville Project," EDC Files, TVA Records. TVA built a separate black construction village at the Pickwick site and constructed a dorm for female workers at Guntersville.

84. Gordon Clapp to General Manager John B. Blandford Jr., "Analysis of Previous Experience of Major Personnel," Dec. 3, 1936, box 114: "210 Employee Relationship Policy, 1938," Lilienthal Correspondence, TVA Records.

85. Morgan, "Attitude of TVA Employees," Sept. 29, 1934, Knoxville, box 2: "Personnel," A. E. Morgan Speech Files, NARASE.

86. [Morgan], "Tennessee Valley Training Program, Muscle Shoals Area: A Tentative and Unofficial Statement of Work, Aims, and Objectives," Mar. 21, 1935, 2, box 9: "Training at Muscle Shoals," A. E. Morgan Papers, NARASE.

87. F. W. Reeves, Independent Consultant, to John B. Blandford, Mar. 27, 1936, box 222: "920.001 Training and Educational Programs in General," Curtis-Morgan-Morgan Papers, NARASE.

88. Ibid.

89. Training Division, "Summary Statement of Program, Training Division, Personnel Department," [1938], 6–7, box 159: "321-71-1-4 (2) Training Branch: Duties, Activities, Policy," Curtis-Morgan-Morgan Papers, TVA Records.

90. Morgan, "The Closed Shop on Public Works," Nov. 17, 1937, box 10: "Labor Policies—Addresses and Statements by TVA Officials," A. E. Morgan Papers, TVA Records. See chapter 4 for a larger discussion of TVA's efforts to encourage unionization in the region.

91. [Morgan], "Tennessee Valley Training Program, Muscle Shoals Area: A Tentative and Unofficial Statement of Work, Aims, and Objectives," Mar. 21, 1935, 1–2 [3–4], box 9: "Training at Muscle Shoals," A. E. Morgan Papers, TVA Records.

92. Davis and Prince E. Eggleston, Secretary, to Carmichael, Aug. 22, 1938; Clapp to Sparkman, Oct. 3, 1938, box 35: "TVA Misc., 1938 (Apr.–Dec.)," Sparkman House Papers, Hoole. Thomas later tried to get TVA to build parks in the valley for black residents. Again, TVA officials passed on the suggestion. See Thomas to Sparkman, Sept. 15, 1939; Amo B. Cammerer, Director of the National Park Service, to Sparkman, Oct. 3, 1939, box 35: "TVA Misc., 1939 (Jul.–Nov.), Sparkman House Papers, Hoole.

93. Clapp, "Board Management Item, #8, Review of the Negro Problems," May 15, 1939, box 68: "210.2221 Negroes or Colored," Records of the Chairman and the Members of the Board of Directors, 1939–1957, James P. Pope and Raymond R. Paty (Pope-Paty Papers), TVA Records.

94. Ibid.

95. Nancy L. Grant's *TVA and Black Americans: Planning for the Status Quo* (Philadelphia: Temple University Press, 1990) provides an engaging critique, illustrating the ways in which proportional representation preserved the "unique characteristics" of southern racial segregation by keeping black workers in temporary, low-paying jobs (xxvii, 23–24). See also Rogers et al., *Alabama,* 486. TVA's approach to race relations fits within a larger discussion of continuity in the South during the Great Depression. See, for instance, Roger Biles, "The Urban South in the Great Depression," *Journal of Southern History* 56, no. 1 (Feb. 1990): 71–100.

96. "Florence Ready to Welcome the Incoming Throngs," *Florence Times,* May 18, 1933, 8; "Florence Negotiates for Factories as Roosevelt's Name Put on Shoals Bill," *Florence Times,* May 26, 1933, 1.

97. Mary Jane Lowe, interview with George F. Davis, Nov. 21, 1990, box 2: "George F. Davis," Oral History Records, TVA Records.

98. For boom conditions at Muscle Shoals, see Frances Perkins to Roosevelt, June 7, 1933, in McJimsey, ed., *Documentary History* 28, document 74: 251. For telegrams to Governor Miller, see box SG19942:1, Miller Administration Files. G. E. Orley to Lister Hill, Sept. 21, 1933, and L. G. Chase, TVA, to Orley, Aug. 28, 1933, box 34:66, Hill Papers.

99. "Time to Organize Up-and-Doing, Go-Getting Chamber of Commerce," *Florence Times,* Dec. 9, 1933, 1.

100. Dixon, "The Utility Question," [ca. 1934], box 3:39, Frank W. Dixon Administration Files, ADAH.

101. Fifteenth Census, Manufactures: 1929, vol. 1 (1933): 292.

102. Ibid.

103. Shirley D. McCrary, interview with John A. Caddell, Feb. 27, 1989, tape AC-54, side A, Colonial Dames Oral History Collection (Colonial Dames), ADAH.

104. Shirey McCrary, interview with Rutledge Thomas, Feb. 23, 1989, SPR 521, tape AC-54, side A, Colonial Dames.

105. "Aluminum Plant for Decatur Looms with Signing of Act," *Decatur Daily,* July 11, 1935, 1, 2.

106. "Ingalls Iron Works to Put Permanent Plant in Decatur," *Decatur Daily,* Nov. 12, 1935, 1; "Varied Industry," *Decatur Daily,* Dec. 5, 1935, 4.

107. Shelton to Sparkman, Mar. 2, 1937, 35: "TVA: Misc., 1937," Sparkman House Papers, NARASE. For a brief biography of Shelton, see "Barrett Shelton," Alabama Academy of Honor, ADAH, www.archives.state.al.us/famous/academy/b_shelto.html (accessed 11 Feb. 2013).

108. Shelton to Lilienthal, Sept. 15, 1937; J. Haden Aldridge, Principal Transportation Economist, to Lilienthal, Sept. 23, 1937; and Shelton to Lilienthal, Sept. 23, 1937, box 58: "095, Decatur, Alabama, thru 1937," Lilienthal Correspondence, TVA Records.

109. "Second Development," *Decatur Daily,* Apr. 10, 1939, 4.

110. Shelton, qtd. in "Oral History of the Tennessee Valley Authority: Interview with Barrett Shelton, Sr., June 18, 1970," box 11, Charles W. Crawford, Oral History Research Office, Memphis State University, archive.org/stream/oralhistoryofteooshel/oralhistoryofteooshel_djvu.txt.

111. Lilienthal, *Journals* 1: 37, 39 (June 22, 1933). As with any entry from Lilienthal's published journal, this statement must be considered critically. While his hostility towards A. E. Morgan undoubtedly colored his remembrance of their earlier interactions, the journal is valuable as proof that, at least for Lilienthal, the disagreements that erupted in the late 1930s came from earlier differences in opinion.

112. Marguerite Owen, *The Tennessee Valley Authority* (New York: Praeger Publishers, 1973), 46–47. Owen served as head of TVA's Washington office, giving her unprecedented access to internal documents. Her history provides a detailed account of the agency's policy-making process.

113. Ibid., 42–43.

114. Owen, *The Tennessee Valley Authority*, 51.

115. Harold Ickes, *The Secret Diary of Harold Ickes: The First Thousand Days, 1933–1936* (New York: Simon and Schuster, 1953), 566 (Apr. 30, 1936).

116. Morgan, *The Making of the TVA*, 26–27.

117. Lilienthal, *Journals* 1: 62 (May 12, 1936).

118. "Morgan Not Present for Meeting," *Decatur Daily*, July 15, 1936, 1.

119. Morgan, *The Making of the TVA*, 137–38.

120. See Schwarz, *The New Dealers*, 217–19.

121. Lilienthal to Roosevelt, Sept. 9, 1936, box 14: "031 White House, 1936," Lilienthal Correspondence, TVA Records.

122. Roosevelt, "White House Statement on a Conference to Establish a Southeastern Power Pool," Sept. 19, 1936, in *The Public Papers and Addresses of Franklin D. Roosevelt*, vol. 5: *The People Approve, 1936* (New York: Random House, 1938), 372.

123. Lilienthal, *Journals* 1: 63–64 (Sept. 12, 1936); "New TVA Policy to End Fight with Utilities Is Considered," *Decatur Daily*, Sept. 11, 1936, 1.

124. Morgan, "Memorandum on a Proposed TVA and Commonwealth and Southern Corporation Power Transmission Pool," Sept. 28, 1936, 2–5, box 218: "951.04 Power Pool of TVA with Private Utilities and Municipalities," Curtis-Morgan-Morgan Papers, TVA Records.

125. Ibid., 7–8.

126. Lilienthal to Norris, Nov. 4, 1936, box 224: "951.04 Power Pool of TVA with Private Utilities and Municipalities," Curtis-Morgan-Morgan Papers, TVA Records. This extended letter provides Lilienthal's account of the negotiations over the pool and gives a fairly clear picture of how the discussions exacerbated the conflict between him and Morgan.

127. Ibid.

128. Roosevelt, "Conferences to Establish a Southeastern Power Pool Are Discontinued," 25 Jan. 1937, in *The Public Papers and Addresses of Franklin D. Roosevelt*, vol. 6: *The Constitution Prevails, 1937* (New York: Macmillan Co., 1941), 16. For a more detailed discussion of TVA's relationship with private power, see Thomas K. McCraw's *TVA and the Power Fight, 1933–1939* (Philadelphia: J. P. Lippincott Co., 1971).

129. "TVA Chief Is Hit by Colleagues," *Decatur Daily*, Dec. 22, 1937, 1; "Norris Seeks Senate Probe of TVA Today," *Decatur Daily*, Jan. 3, 1938, 1, 2.

130. "Morgan Hints He Will Not Quit," *Decatur Daily*, Mar. 7, 1938, 1, 2; Morgan to Roosevelt, Mar. 9, 1938, box 3: "White House Correspondence, 1938," A. E. Morgan Papers, TVA Records.

131. Roosevelt to Morgan, Mar. 22, 1938, box 3: "White House Correspondence, 1938," A. E. Morgan Papers, TVA Records.

132. Morgan, rough draft, "Statement of My Relations with the President," July 1, 1938, box 3: "Statement of My Relations with the President, 1 July 1938," A. E. Morgan Papers, TVA Records.

133. Clipping, *Congressional Record*, 76th Cong., 1st sess., 1939, in box 91: "Complete Summary of the Majority Report," A. E. Morgan Papers, TVA Records.

4. PULLING TOGETHER IN THE SAME DIRECTION, 1938–1945

1. Qtd. in William E. Leuchtenburg, *The White House Looks South: Franklin D. Roosevelt, Harry S. Truman, Lyndon B. Johnson* (Baton Rouge: Louisiana State University Press, 2005), 102.

2. Qtd. in David L. Carlton and Peter A. Coclanis, eds., *Confronting Southern Poverty in the Great Depression: The Report on Economic Conditions of the South with Related Documents* (Boston: Bedford/St. Martin's, 1996), 14. Carlton and Coclanis's brief introduction provides a succinct history of the decision to produce the pamphlet.

3. Carlton and Coclanis, eds., *Confronting Southern Poverty in the Great Depression*, 15, 21.

4. Ibid., 42.

5. Ibid., 47.

6. Ibid., 78.

7. Ibid.

8. "Summary Statement, TVA Cognizance of the Economic Conditions of the South and Its Contribution Toward Their Improvement," [1938], box 111: "901.04 thru 1948," Pope-Paty Papers, TVA Records.

9. "Number 1 Opportunity," *Decatur Daily*, Oct. 31, 1938, 4.

10. "Definite Objectives," *Decatur Daily*, Sept. 11, 1939, 4.

11. Carlton and Coclanis, eds., *Confronting Southern Poverty in the Great Depression*, 64, 70.

12. Ibid., 48, 70, 78.

13. Fifteenth Census (1930 census), vol. 2, pt. 2 (1932); U.S. Census Bureau, Sixteenth Census of the United States: 1940, Agriculture, vol. 1, pt. 4 (Washington, D.C.: GPO, 1942).

14. Jackson, "To the Citizenship of Florence, Sheffield and Tuscumbia," *Florence Times*, June 1, 1933, 5.

15. "Cities Seek Cheap Power," *Florence Times*, May 18, 1933, 2; "Power Plant Approved in Sheffield," *Florence Times*, June 6, 1933, 1.

16. "Municipal Ownership Is a Golden Opportunity—and a Real Test of the People of Florence," *Florence Times*, June 27, 1933, 1; and "Florence Votes Municipal Power," *Florence Times*, July 1, 1933, 1, 3.

17. "Memorandum of Meeting Held on Friday, February 2, 1934, in Decatur City Hall," box 41: "095, Alabama Power Co., thru June 1934," Lilienthal Correspondence, TVA Records.

18. *Congressional Record* (House), 73rd Cong., 2nd sess., 1934, vol. 78, pt. 2: 2124.

19. Llewellyn Evans, TVA, to Lilienthal, Mar. 7, 1934, box 41: "095, Alabama Power Co., thru June 1934," Lilienthal Correspondence, TVA Records; "TVA Power Contract Is Signed by Decatur," *Decatur Daily*, Mar. 15, 1934, 1.

20. "Decatur Accepts TVA Plan," *Decatur Daily*, July 6, 1934, 1, 4.

21. Owen, *The Tennessee Valley Authority*, 36.

22. "Suit Attacks TVA Program," *Decatur Daily*, Sept. 13, 1934, 1; *Ashwander v. Tennessee Valley Authority*, 297 U.S. 288 (1936), FindLaw, laws.findlaw.com/us/297/288.html (accessed May 30, 2013).

23. Lilienthal, *Journals* 1: appendix, 711–14.

24. Lilienthal to Marvin H. McIntyre, Secretary to the President, Jan. 1, 1935, box 13: "031 White House 1935," Lilienthal Correspondence, TVA Records; Charles E. Hoffman, Assistant Secretary, TVA, to Alabama Power Company, Jan. 25, 1935, box 41: "095, Alabama Power Co., 1935," Lilienthal Correspondence, TVA Records; "TVA's Purchase Contracts Held Invalid by Grubb," *Decatur Daily*, Mar. 4, 1935, 1, 2; and *Ashwander v. TVA*.

25. "Fate of TVA before High Court," *Decatur Daily*, Dec. 19, 1935, 1, 2.

26. The sole dissenter, Justice James Clark McReynolds, argued that, under the "thin mask of disposing of property of the United States," TVA was setting a dangerous precedent, operating beyond its constitutional limitations and adversely affecting a legitimate private enterprise, Alabama Power. See *Ashwander v. TVA*.

27. *Congressional Record* (Senate), 74th Cong., 2nd sess., 1936, vol. 80, pt. 3: 2416.

28. "TVA Advocates Hail Davis Edict," *Decatur Daily*, Apr. 16, 1937, 1; "Power Company Appeal Denied," *Decatur Daily*, May 10, 1937, 1; and "Sweeping Victory Is Won by TVA," *Decatur Daily*, May 14, 1937, 1.

29. TVA's legal victories combined with the stream of challenges from Commonwealth & Southern to squash all discussions of a "power pool" agreement with private utilities. See chapter 3.

30. "Lilienthal Avers TVA Willing to Talk Over Power Line Purchase," *Decatur Daily*, Jan. 18, 1938, 1, 2.

31. J. A. Krug, Chief Power Engineer, to Gordon Clapp, General Manager, Dec. 20, 1939, box 232: "951.3113 Alabama Power Co.," Curtis-Morgan-Morgan Papers, TVA Records. Alabama Power was particularly afraid that TVA would expand into the lucrative Birmingham market. See "TVA, APC Parley Next Week," *Decatur Daily*, Feb. 7, 1939, 1.

32. TVA Press Release, "Alabama Purchase," Feb. 24, 1940, box 41: "095, Alabama Power Co., 1937–1941," Lilienthal Correspondence, TVA Records.

33. Lilienthal, *Journals* 1: 106–7 (Apr. 16, 1939), 110 (June 9, 1939).

34. Lilienthal's speech, "New Industries for the New South," Mar. 20, 1941, was included in the *Congressional Record* by John Sparkman. See *Congressional Record* (appendix), 77th Cong., 1st sess., 1941, vol. 87, pt. 11: A1280–1.

35. Lilienthal's desire to cooperate with local leadership in the pursuit of private development is part of a larger critique of the agency's increased privatization, a development discussed further in chapter 5. This trend has also been noted by historians, particularly Philip Selznick in *TVA and the Grass Roots: A Study in the Sociology of Formal Organization* (Berkeley: University of California Press, 1949) and David Whisnant in *Modernizing the Mountaineer: People, Power, and Planning in Appalachia* (1980; rev. ed., Knoxville: University of Tennessee Press, 1994). Both Whisnant and Selznick decry the movement by the agency away from a focus on the "grass roots" and the needs of underdeveloped communities, bypassed by industrialization and left out of economic growth.

36. Carlton and Coclanis, eds., *Confronting Southern Poverty in the Great Depression*, 65.

37. The New Deal was a time of remarkable labor activism in the South, given government protection for unionization and the economic impact of the Great Depression. See, for instance, Robert J. Norrell, "Labor at the Ballot Box: Alabama Politics from the New Deal to the Dixiecrat

Movement," *Journal of Southern History* 57, no. 2 (May 1991): 201–234, and Robin D. G. Kelley, *Hammer and Hoe: Alabama Communists during the Great Depression* (Chapel Hill: University of North Carolina Press, 1990).

38. Lilienthal, *Journals* 1: 461 (Mar. 31, 1942).

39. Ibid., 462.

40. The council included the following unions: the Brotherhood of Painters, Decorators and Paperhangers of America; the International Brotherhood of Boiler Makers, Iron Ship Builders, and Helpers of America; the International Brotherhood of Blacksmiths, Drop Forgers and Helpers; the International Association of Machinists; the International Brotherhood of Electrical Workers; the International Hod Carriers', Building and Common Laborers' Union of America; the International Union of Operating Engineers; the Sheet Metal Workers' International Association; the International Union of Wood, Wire and Metal Lathers; the Operative Plasterers' and Cement Finishers' International Association; the United Association of Journeymen and Apprentices of the Plumbing and Pipefitting Industry of the United States and Canada; the United Brotherhood of Carpenters and Joiners of America; the Bricklayers', Masons', and Plasterers' International Union of America; and the International Brotherhood of Teamsters, Chauffeurs, Warehousemen and Helpers of America. See "General Agreement between the Tennessee Valley Authority and the Tennessee Valley Trades and Labor Council," 6 Aug. 1940 (rev. June 26, 1949), box 135: "254.1 Union Management Cooperative Plans, 1949–1955," Curtis-Morgan-Morgan Papers, TVA Records.

41. "General Agreement between the Tennessee Valley Authority and the Tennessee Valley Trades and Labor Council," Aug. 6, 1940 (rev. June 26, 1949), 2–8, box 135: "254.1 Union Management Cooperative Plans, 1949–1955," Curtis-Morgan-Morgan Papers, TVA Records. Salaried workers could join the "TVA Annual Employees," though TVA struggled to develop a relationship on par with that of TVA and the council. See Clapp to Board, May 30, 1942, box 135: "254.1 Union Management Cooperative Plans thru 1946," Curtis-Morgan-Morgan Papers, TVA Records.

42. Lilienthal, *Journals* 1: 617 (Nov. 24, 1943).

43. Clapp to Board, May 12, 1942, box 113: "Training and Educational Programs in General thru 1949," Pope-Paty Papers, TVA Records.

44. Ibid.

45. Lilienthal to McSherry, May 11, 1942, box 68: "210.2221 Negroes or Colored," Pope-Paty Papers, TVA Records.

46. Lilienthal, *Journals* 1: 516 (July 14, 1942).

47. Departmental Committee on Race Relations, "Placement Opportunities for Negroes," Aug. 25, 1941, 2–3, box 68: "210.2221 Negroes or Colored," Pope-Paty Papers, TVA Records.

48. John Morton Blum, *V Was for Victory: Politics and American Culture during World War II* (San Diego: Harcourt Brace, 1976), 187–88.

49. Bruce Nelson, "Organized Labor and the Struggle for Black Equality in Mobile during World War II," *Journal of American History* 80, no. 3 (Dec. 1993): 954.

50. Ibid., 960.

51. Ibid., 978–82.

52. Clapp to White, Sept. 24, 1945, box 96: "622.1 Houses," Pope-Paty Papers, TVA Records.

53. Pounders to Sparkman, Apr. 3, 1943; Sparkman to Pounders, Apr. 6, 1943; Sparkman to Lilienthal, Apr. 8, 1943; and Lilienthal to Sparkman, Apr. 23, 1943, box 35: "TVA: Misc., 1943," Sparkman House Papers, Hoole.

54. Lilienthal to Roosevelt, Oct. 4, 1939, box 88: "095, National Defense—General," Lilienthal Correspondence, TVA Records.

55. Bruce J. Schulman, *From Cotton Belt to Sunbelt: Federal Policy, Economic Development, and the Transformation of the South, 1938–1980* (Durham, N.C.: Duke University Press, 1994), 91–92, 95, 110–11. For the economic impact of the war, see also Wright, *Old South, New South.*

56. Ralph C. Hon, "The South in a War Economy," *Southern Economic Journal* 8, no. 3 (Jan. 1942): 308.

57. Bartley's *The New South;* John Egerton's *Speak Now against the Day: The Generation before the Civil Rights Movement in the South* (Chapel Hill: University of North Carolina Press, 1995); and Neil McMillen's edited work, *Remaking Dixie: The Impact of World War II on the American South* (Oxford: University Press of Mississippi, 2007), provide excellent overviews of the impact of World War II on the South. For Alabama, see Allen Cronenberg, *Forth to the Mighty Conflict: Alabama and World War II* (Tuscaloosa: University of Alabama Press, 1995), and Wayne Flynt, *Alabama in the Twentieth Century* (Tuscaloosa: University of Alabama Press, 2006).

58. Lilienthal, *Journals* 1: 166–68 (May 28, 1940).

59. Menhinick to Clapp, "Analysis of TVA Program in Relation to National Defense and Post-Emergency Adjustment," Apr. 28, 1941, box 88: "095 National Defense—Post-War," Lilienthal Correspondence, TVA Records.

60. "Valley Future," *Decatur Daily,* June 21, 1940, 4; and Don Whitehead, "World at War Rapidly Is Reshaping Economic Scenery in Tennessee Valley," *Decatur Daily,* Aug. 14, 1940, 3.

61. "The Tennessee Valley Authority and National Defense," Apr. 22, 1941, *Congressional Record* (appendix), 77th Cong., 1st sess., 1941, vol. 87, pt. 11: A1832–33.

62. Hon, "The South in a War Economy," 301.

63. "TVA Ready to Help Defense," *Decatur Daily,* June 14, 1940, 1; "TVA Will Get Defense Role Solon Is Told," *Decatur Daily,* June 18, 1940, 1; and "Defense Board to Ask TVA Power to Be Materially Hiked," *Decatur Daily,* June 20, 1940, 1.

64. Sparkman to Morgan, Dec. 20, 1940; Clapp to Sparkman, Jan. 3, 1941; and Sparkman to Clapp, Jan. 6, 1941, box 52: "032.11 Sparkman, John," Pope-Paty Papers, TVA Records.

65. Lilienthal, *Journals* 1: 315 (May 19, 1941).

66. Sparkman to Lilienthal, Aug. 27, 1941; Clapp to Sparkman, Sept. 12, 1941; and Lilienthal to Sparkman, Sept. 16, 1941, box 17: "032.1 Sparkman, John J.," Lilienthal Correspondence, TVA Records.

67. Memo, "Covering Conference Held at Knoxville, Tennessee, with Officials of T.V.A. in Connection with Service to Chemical Warfare Arsenal, Huntsville, September 8, 1941," box 9: "Huntsville Projects," Sparkman House Papers, Hoole.

68. "A Message to the People of the Tennessee Valley Region," *Huntsville Times,* Nov. 1, 1941, 3.

69. Sparkman to Lilienthal, Nov. 3, 1941, box 52: "032.11 Sparkman, John," Pope-Paty Papers, TVA Records.

70. TVA, Press Release, Nov. 4, 1941, box 52: "032.11 Sparkman, John," Pope-Paty Papers, TVA Records.

71. Sparkman to Undersecretary of War Robert P. Patterson, Dec. 2, 1941; Patterson to Sparkman, Dec. 20, 1941, box 9: "Madison County: Huntsville Projects, 1939–43," Sparkman House Papers, Hoole.

72. Woltersdorf to Sparkman, Dec. 5, 1941; Woltersdorf to Sparkman, Dec. 24, 1941, box 52: "032.11 Sparkman, John," Pope-Paty Papers, TVA Records.

73. Lilienthal to Lister Hill, Dec. 9, 1941, box 95: "032.21 Hill, Lister, 1940–1947," Curtis-Morgan-Morgan Papers, TVA Records

74. "Aluminum Plant to Be Built in North Alabama by Virginia Firm," Aug. 2, 1940, *Decatur Daily*, 1; Allen J. Roulhac to Hill, June 30, 1940, box 162:3, Hill Papers. Virginia Van der Veer Hamilton's *Lister Hill: Statesman from the South* (Chapel Hill: University of North Carolina Press, 1987) is an excellent introduction to the life and career of the congressman.

75. T. M. Rogers to Sparkman, Aug. 5, 1940; Roulhac to Sparkman, Aug. 12, 1940; Rogers to Sparkman, Aug. 17, 1940; Harold T. Pounders, Secretary, to Rogers, Aug. 19, 1940; Rogers to Sparkman, Aug. 27, 1940; and Rogers to Sparkman, Sept. 3, 1940, box 22: "House Miscellaneous: Reynolds Aluminum," Sparkman House Papers, Hoole.

76. Sparkman to Rogers, Sept. 2, 1940, box 22: "House Miscellaneous: Reynolds Aluminum," Sparkman House Papers, Hoole.

77. Krug to Hill, Aug. 24, 1940; Krug to Reynolds, Aug. 30, 1940; and Hill to Krug, Sept. 11, 1940, box 162:7, Hill Papers.

78. Pounders to Rogers, Sept. 20, 1940, 22: "House Miscellaneous: Reynolds Aluminum," Sparkman House Papers, Hoole; "Valley Gets Huge Plant," *Decatur Daily*, Oct. 7, 1940, 1; and "Aluminum Plant Is Expected to Be Completed Within Next Six Months," *Decatur Daily*, Oct. 17, 1940, 1.

79. John M. Nelson, Secretary, Decatur Chamber of Commerce, Sept. 17, 1941; Sparkman to Nelson, Oct. 2, 1941, box 11: "Morgan County: Decatur Projects, 1940–1," Sparkman House Papers, Hoole; Pounders to Barrett Shelton, Sept. 1941, box 12: "Morgan County: Reynolds Metals Company, 1941," Sparkman House Papers, Hoole. See also Hon, "The South in a War Economy," 299–300.

80. Wessenauer and Solicitor J. C. Swidler to Clapp, Feb. 10, 1942, box 234: "951.3113 Reynolds Metals Co. 1943–1945," Curtis-Morgan-Morgan Papers, TVA Records.

81. Pope to Lilienthal, Harcourt Morgan, and Clapp, Feb. 20, 1942, box 234: "951.3113 Reynolds Metals Co. 1943–1945," Curtis-Morgan-Morgan Papers, TVA Records.

82. Lilienthal to Board, Mar. 10, 1942, box 234: "951.3113 Reynolds Metals Co. 1943–1945," Curtis-Morgan-Morgan Papers, TVA Records.

83. Clipping, Hill, "The Reynolds Metals Co.," in *Congressional Record*, 77th Cong., 2nd sess., May 18, 1942, in Robert E. Jones Papers, M. Louis Salmon Library and Special Collections, University of Alabama, Huntsville (hereafter cited as Bob Jones Papers).

84. "Bombers from Reynolds Aluminum Blast the Axis," in *Alabama: Today and Tomorrow* 5, no. 8 (July 1942): 7, box 37: "092, Alabama, State of," Lilienthal Correspondence, TVA Records.

85. See Marion Caskie to Hill, June 12, 1942, box 120:340, Hill Papers; Caskie to Sparkman, June 30, 1942, and "The Facts," box 22: "House Miscellaneous: Reynolds Metals," Sparkman House Papers, Hoole; and Lilienthal to Caskie, Aug. 15, 1942, and Caskie to Lilienthal, Sept. 1, 1942, box 130:341, Hill Papers; Reynolds to Hill, Oct. 9, 1945, box 130:341, Hill Papers. By way of comparison, during the early years of the war, ALCOA produced six times the amount of aluminum that Reynolds Metals did. See Hon, "The South in a War Economy," 300.

86. Qtd. in Hubbard, *Origins of the TVA*, 314. Hubbard's study of the congressional debate over the Muscle Shoals site provides a more in-depth look at the complicated nature of McKellar's support.

87. Owen, *The Tennessee Valley Authority*, 87.

88. "McKellar and TVA," *Huntsville Times*, Apr. 17, 1942, 4.

89. *Congressional Record* (Senate), 77th Cong., 2nd sess., 1942, vol. 88, pt. 3: 3877–79.

90. Ibid., 3895–96.

91. Lilienthal, *Journals* 1: 487 (May 5, 1942).

92. "House Defeats TVA Amendment," June 9, 1942, *Huntsville Times*, 1; "McKellar and the TVA," Feb. 24, 1943, *Huntsville Times*, 2.

93. Shelton to Sparks, Feb. 24, 1943, box SG12412:8, Chauncey Sparks Administration Papers, ADAH; Hill to Muscle Shoals City Commissioners, Feb. 26, 1943, box 270:2, Hill Papers; and "An Important Message," Feb. 28, 1943, *Huntsville Times*, 3.

94. "TVA Record Cited by Senator Hill," *Huntsville Times*, Mar. 4, 1943, 2.

95. *Congressional Record* (Senate), 78th Cong., 1st sess. 1943, vol. 89, pt. 4: 5798–800.

96. "Double-Barreled Fire Laid on TVA," Mar. 9, 1944, *Huntsville Times*, 3; "McKellar Fights Alone," *Huntsville Times*, Mar. 15, 1944, 4; and *Congressional Record* (Senate), 78th Cong., 1st sess., 1943, vol. 89, pt. 4: 5801.

97. *Congressional Record* (Senate), 78th Cong., 2nd sess., 1944, vol. 90, pt. 3: 2884–86.

98. "McKellar Threat to TVA Is Beaten," June 15, 1944, *Huntsville Times*, 2; "McKellar to Ask TVA Fund Change," Mar. 11, 1945, *Huntsville Times*, 2.

99. See James C. Cobb, *The Selling of the South: The Southern Crusade for Industrial Development, 1936–1980* (Baton Rouge: Louisiana State University Press, 1982); Connie L. Lester, "Balancing Agriculture with Industry: Capital, Labor, and the Public Good in Mississippi's Home-Grown New Deal," *Journal of Mississippi History* 70 (Fall 2008): 235–63.

100. "Alabama Planning and Local Planning in Six North Alabama Towns, Part I, Alabama Planning," [1940s], 10–11, box 38: "092, Alabama (A–Z)," Lilienthal Correspondence, TVA Records.

101. Rogers et al., *Alabama*, 471.

102. "Dixon Pleads South's Case in New York," *Decatur Daily*, Nov. 20, 1940, 1, 2.

103. Alabama State Planning Commission Annual Report, "Alabama Planning," Dec. 14, 1942, 1, box 1: "095 Alabama A–Z," Pope-Paty Papers, TVA Records.

104. W. O. Dobbins to Governor Chauncey Sparks, July 14, 1943, box SG12411:3(B), Sparks Administration Papers. In fact, the State Planning Commission served as the de facto postwar planning commission for Alabama.

105. "Alabama Planning and Local Planning in Six North Alabama Towns, Part I, Alabama Planning," [1940s], 12, box 38: "092, Alabama (A–Z)," Lilienthal Correspondence, TVA Records.

106. Menhinick to Clapp, Sept. 9, 1943, box 110: "092 Alabama, Folder 1," Curtis-Morgan-Morgan Papers, TVA Records.

107. Lilienthal to Dixon, Sept. 25, 1941, box 110: "092 Alabama, A–Z," Curtis-Morgan-Morgan Papers, TVA Records.

108. Alabama State Planning Board, "Progress Report on Local Planning in North Alabama, July 1, 1942-June 30, 1943," Aug. 1943, 1, 3–9, box 110: "092 Alabama, A–Z," Curtis-Morgan-Morgan Papers, TVA Records.

109. Menhinick, "A Suggested Program for the Alabama State Planning Board: A Statement Prepared at the Request of the Governor of Alabama," Aug. 10, 1944, 1–3, box 59: "092 Alabama A–Z," Pope-Paty Papers, TVA Records.

110. Ibid., 9.

111. The preeminent scholar of regionalism, Howard Odum, noted the possibilities that TVA, and by extension the agency's relationship with local organizations, suggested for the notion of

regional planning: "The Tennessee Valley now represents no mere river basin, but the skill and planning of a nation, the imagination of the people many times divided, and the on-goings of engineers, planners, educators, economists, sociologists, critics and patrons, politicians, manufacturers, dreamers and schemers, reformers and statesmen, common folks in the South and out." By the late 1940s, TVA directed such regionalism almost exclusively in the direction of regional cooperation for economic growth and development. See Odum and Harry Estill Moore, *American Regionalism: A Cultural-Historical Approach to National Integration* (New York: Henry Holt and Co., 1938), 105. Clarence Hodge agreed, suggesting that, in working with various agencies, TVA was able to achieve "active consent and participation in a program of regional reconstruction." See Hodge, *The Tennessee Valley Authority: A National Experiment in Regionalism* (New York: Russell & Russell, 1968), 243.

112. Shelton to Hill, Sept. 20, 1939; Hill to Shelton, Sept. 23, 1939, box 162:9, Hill Papers.

113. Shelton to Morgan, May 13, 1940, Shelton to Morgan, May 18, 1940, box 33: "095 Shelton, Barrett," Pope-Paty Papers, TVA Records.

114. Clapp to Shelton, May 22, 1940, box 33: "095 Shelton, Barrett," Pope-Paty Papers, TVA Records.

115. "Nebraska Consolidated Mills to Put Big Flour Plant Here," *Decatur Daily*, Aug. 28, 1940, 1. Nebraska Consolidated Mills eventually changed its name to ConAgra.

116. Nelson to Sparkman, July 9, 1941, box 11: "Morgan County: Decatur Projects, 1940–1," Sparkman House Papers, Hoole. The school is now the site of Pryor (Air) Field and Calhoun Community College.

117. Lilienthal, *Journals* 1: 215 (Sept. 15, 1940).

118. U.S. Census Bureau, Sixteenth Census of the United States: 1940, Population, vol. 2: Characteristics of the Population, pt. 1: United States Summary and Alabama—District of Columbia (Washington, D.C.: GPO, 1943), 321; Fifteenth Census (1933), Manufactures: 1929, vol. 1: 292.

119. Lilienthal, *Journals* 1: 215 (Sept. 15, 1940).

120. "Boom Towns," *Decatur Daily*, Dec. 2, 1940, 4; "Building Facts," *Decatur Daily*, Sept. 30, 1940, 4.

121. "Triple City-Building Plan Begun," *Decatur Daily*, Aug. 8, 1940, 1.

122. Alabama State Planning Commission, Annual Report, "Alabama Planning," Dec. 14, 1942, 2, box 1: "095 Alabama A–Z," Pope-Paty Papers, TVA Records. The use of waterfront land to attract industry was an important part of TVA's postwar development efforts. See chapter 5.

123. Alabama State Planning Board, "Progress Report on Local Planning in North Alabama, July 1, 1942–June 30, 1943," Aug. 1943, 17–21, box 110: "092 Alabama, A–Z," Curtis-Morgan-Morgan Papers, TVA Records.

124. "Ten Year Appraisal," *Decatur Daily*, May 18, 1943, rpr. in *Congressional Record* (Appendix), 78th Cong., 1st sess., 1943, vol. 89, pt. 10: A2619.

125. "Post-War Planning," *Huntsville Times*, Aug. 3, 1943, 4.

126. "Lilienthal Views on Reconversion," *Huntsville Times*, Sept. 12, 1944, 4.

127. Commerce Department Service Committee, "The Authority's Relationships to the Region's Business Community," Feb. 1945, 1, box 146: loose, Pope-Paty Papers, TVA Records.

128. Ibid., 2–9.

129. "Report of Conference between Representatives of State Planning Commissions and the TVA," Knoxville, Dec. 12–13, 1945, 2, box 112: "913 Regional Planning, Social Planning, Economic Planning, National Planning, Etc.," Pope-Paty Papers, TVA Records.

130. Ibid., 2–3.

131. Ibid., 4–5.

132. Ibid., 13–4.

133. Lilienthal, *TVA: Democracy on the March* (New York: Harper & Brothers Publishers, 1944), 3. Lilienthal's is one of the first in a line of celebratory works written by current and former workers for the agency. See also Willson Whitman's *God's Valley: People and Power along the Tennessee River* (New York: Viking Press, 1939); Gordon Clapp's *TVA: An Approach to the Development of the Region* (1955); Marguerite Owen's *Tennessee Valley Authority* (1973); and North Callahan, *TVA: Bridge over Troubled Waters* (South Brunswick, N.J.: A. S. Barnes, 1980). A. E. Morgan's *The Making of the TVA* (1974) continues in the vein of former employees commenting on the agency, though his, written decades after leaving TVA, is more complex and critical in its conclusions. When read together, these works provide a fascinating insight into the mind of the TVA as it developed a plan for the region.

134. Morgan, *The Making of the TVA*, 182.

5. AN AGENCY OF ITS OWN CREATION, 1945–1960

1. Qtd. in Brinkley, *The End of Reform*, 144. Brinkley is the quintessential study of the decline of the New Dealers.

2. Ibid., 168–9.

3. Ibid., 134–34, 138.

4. John Ferris, "Industrial-Business Development in the Tennessee Valley Region," Meeting of Directors of Valley States Planning and Development Agencies and Other Organizations Interested in Industrial-Business Development, July 9, 1947, 2–4, 218: "901.02 Industrial 1944–1957," Curtis-Morgan-Morgan Papers, TVA Records.

5. Ferris, "Industrial-Business Development in the Tennessee Valley Region," 11.

6. State Planning Board Minutes, Jan. 17, 1947 and June 26, 1947, box SG13419:3, James E. Folsom Administration Papers (1947–51) (First Folsom Administration Papers), ADAH. This was particularly true in Mobile, where Dobbins and the State Planning Board worked to use the expanded state docks to accommodate the needs of private industry.

7. The volumes are scattered throughout the ADAH collection. For pertinent examples, see *Alabama's Industrial Opportunities*, vol. 7: *Stone, Clay, and Glass Products* (Montgomery, 1947), box SG13419:4(4), First Folsom Administration Papers; and *Alabama's Industrial Opportunities*, vol. 9: *Electrical Machinery*, and vol. 10: *Automobiles and Automobile Equipment* (Montgomery, 1947), box SG13437:13, First Folsom Administration Papers.

8. Dobbins, "Summary Industrial Opportunities in Alabama (Preliminary Draft), 4, 12, box SG13437:15, First Folsom Administration Papers.

9. Memo, Aelred J. Gray, Apr. 29, 1955, box 7: "092, Alabama A–Z," Government Relations and Economic Staff, General Correspondence, 1953–57, Office of the General Manager (GRES Files), TVA Records.

10. See Peter K. Eisinger, *The Rise of the Entrepreneurial State: State and Local Economic Development Policy in the United States* (Madison: University of Wisconsin Press, 1988), 25–26. Eisinger argues that, in the United States, the "state" became an "entrepreneur," seeking out opportunities for investment and mobilizing the resources necessary to realize them.

11. Albert Lepawsky, *State Planning and Economic Development in the South* (Kingsport, Tenn.: Kingsport Press, Inc., 1949), 72. See also Cobb, *The Selling of the South*, and Lester, "Balancing Agriculture with Industry."

12. Lepawsky, *State Planning and Economic Development in the South*, 62–77.

13. Lacy K. Ford and R. Phillip Stone, "Economic Development and Globalization in South Carolina," *Southern Cultures* (Spring 2007): 24–25. Philip Stone's "Making a Modern State" recounts the maturation of South Carolina's state development efforts and provides an excellent comparison for Alabama's own program. See Richard Philip Stone II, "Making a Modern State: The Politics of Economic Development in South Carolina, 1938–1962," PhD diss., University of South Carolina, 2003. David Carlton suggests that state action helped to "unclump" localized economic growth and spread industrial competition across the state. See Carlton, "Unbalanced Growth and Industrialization: The Case of South Carolina," and "The South Carolina Economy Reconstructed and Reconsidered: Structure, Output, and Performance, 1670–1985," in *Developing Dixie*, ed. Moore, Trip, and Tyler, 92–110.

14. Anne Permaloff and Carl Grafton, *Political Power in Alabama: The More Things Change* (Athens: University of Georgia Press, 2008), 65.

15. Charles M. Stephenson, *Industrial Sites: A Community Problem* (Knoxville: Bureau of Public Administration, University of Tennessee, 1961), 6–7, box 48: loose, Division of Navigation Development Volume Files, 1954–68, Office of the General Manager (Navigation Files), TVA Records. For a succinct account of Alabama's development program, with special attention to incentives and concessions, see Permaloff and Grafton, *Political Power in Alabama*, 57–61.

16. Government Relations and Economics Staff, "Industrial Development on the Tennessee River," Jan. 1955, 3, box 15: "901.2 Industrial, 1955," GRES Papers, TVA Records.

17. Ibid., 6–8, 17–18.

18. Ibid., 20.

19. Ibid., 28–29.

20. TVA did protect some land along the river for preservation as a wildlife refuge, but even then the agency was willing to shift that land to industrial purposes if needed.

21. Gray, untitled memo, Apr. 29, 1955, box 7: "092: Alabama A–Z," GRES Papers, TVA Records.

22. Gray to Robert B. Nichols, Navigation Engineering Section, Mar. 2, 1956, box 15: "902.2 Industrial, 1956–57"; Gray, untitled memo, Dec. 30, 1955, box 8: "092.1 Counties A–L," GRES Papers, TVA Records.

23. Stephenson, *Industrial Sites*, 1–2.

24. Ibid., 16–17.

25. Commerce Dept., "Physical Problems Relating to Industrial Waterfront Development at Decatur, Alabama," Jan. 1948, box 57: loose, Navigation Files, TVA Records.

26. Campbell to General Manager John Oliver, May 26, 1954, box 15: "901.2 Industrial, 1955," GRES Papers, TVA Records.

27. Decatur City Planning Commission and Alabama State Planning Board, "Preliminary Decatur Waterfront Development Report," June 1948, 14–18, box SG13438:1, First Folsom Administration Papers.

28. "Industrial Variety Makes Decatur Grow," *Huntsville Times*, Aug. 18, 1959, 15.

29. Richard J. Ricard, Manager, Guntersville-Wheeler Branch, Division of Reservoir Properties to Director Raymond J. Paty, July 16, 1953; E. J. Schwanhausser, Executive Vice President,

Worthington, to Paty, July 29, 1953, box 12: "095 Decatur, Alabama," Pope-Paty Papers, TVA Records. See also "New Plant to Be Operating by December 1," *Decatur Daily*, July 24, 1953, clipping courtesy of North Alabama Industrial Development Association, Decatur (NAIDA).

30. Stephenson, *Industrial Sites*, 15.

31. Listing of Morgan County Industries, 1947–61, from Alabama Manufacturing Directory, courtesy of NAIDA.

32. "Wolverine Picked Decatur Because of River Location," *Huntsville Times*, July 16, 1959, 8.

33. Clapp to Shelton, Dec. 10, 1948, box 111: "901.04 1949," Pope-Paty Papers, TVA Records.

34. "Organization of a North Alabama Development Council," Dec. 1948, box 111: "901.04 1949," Pope-Paty Papers, TVA Records.

35. Huntsville left NAA after forming its own industrial development group, an act discussed more fully in chapter 7. See "Area Organizations for Industrial Development," June 1961, box 48: "620 Industrial and Commercial Development, Jan.–Jun. 1961," EDC Papers, TVA Records.

36. Ferris to Gant, Jan. 10, 1949, box 48: "620 Industrial and Commercial Development, Jan.–Jun. 1961," EDC Papers, TVA Records.

37. Johnson, Meeting of Cullman Rotary Club, Aug. 8, 1950, 2–3, courtesy of NAIDA.

38. Johnson, untitled speech, [ca. Jan.–Feb. 1952], 3, courtesy of NAIDA.

39. Johnson to Sparkman, July 17, 1950, box 119: "A, Reactivation, Retention, or Expansion of Army Facilities, #1"; Sparkman to Wilson, July 24, 1950, box 119: "4G, Hydrogen Bomb Site," John J. Sparkman Papers [Senate] (Sparkman Senate Papers), Hoole.

40. "Air Engineering Development Center: Adaptability of Sites in the TVA Area," May 1949, 6, box 19: "044.42 V.F.," GRES Papers, TVA Records.

41. Ibid., 2–3. Again, TVA proved willing to sacrifice the needs of the few for the benefits to the many. The agency assumed that, with an improved local economy, those two hundred families would undoubtedly lead a much better life, even if it meant leaving the land.

42. "Looking Back on the Wind Tunnel Project," *Huntsville Times*, Nov. 9, 1949, 4.

43. Johnson, untitled speech, [ca. Jan.–Feb. 1952], 5, courtesy of NAIDA.

44. Ibid.

45. Ibid., 6.

46. Johnson, Annual Meeting of Chamber of Commerce, Hartselle, Ala., Feb. 28, 1952, courtesy of NAIDA.

47. Johnson, untitled speech, [ca. Jan.–Feb. 1952], 7, courtesy of NAIDA.

48. Ibid., 7–10.

49. Ibid., 10.

50. John Washburn, Executive Director, NAIDA, "'Success Story' Chronicles Industrial Growth," *Decatur Daily*, June 20, 1976, B1; "New Plant to Be Operating by December 1," *Decatur Daily*, July 24, 1953; and "3M Announces New 4 1/2 Million Plant in Decatur," *Hartselle Enquirer*, July 23, 1959, 1, clippings courtesy of NAIDA.

51. U.S. Census Bureau, Census of Population: 1950, vol. 2: Characteristics of the Population, pt. 2: Alabama (Washington, D.C.: GPO, 1952), 2–8.

52. Ibid., 1960, vol. 1: Characteristics of the Population, pt. 2: Alabama (Washington, D.C.: GPO, 1961), 157.

53. Ibid., 1950, vol. 2, pt. 2: 95; Census of Population: 1960, vol. 1, pt. 2: 206, 212.

54. Shelton, "The Decatur Story," Dec. 1949, box 152: 2528, Bob Jones Papers, UAH. Shelton's speech was printed by TVA as well. See Shelton, *The Decatur Story* (Knoxville, Tenn.: Tennessee Valley Authority, 1950). For the venue of Shelton's speech, see G. H. Aull, L. P. Gabbard, and John F. Timmons, "United Nations Scientific Conference on the Conservation and Utilization of Resources," *Journal of Farm Economics* 32, no. 1 (Feb. 1950): 95–111.

55. Shelton, "Unity in the Valley," *Huntsville Times*, Aug. 4, 1950, 4; Shelton, "The Decatur Story," box 152:2528, Bob Jones Papers, UAH.

56. Shelton, "The Decatur Story," 152:2528, Bob Jones Papers, UAH.

57. Lepawsky, *State Planning and Economic Development in the South*, 72; Calvin B. Hoover and B. U. Ratchford, *Economic Resources and Policies of the South* (New York: MacMillan Co., 1951), 381–84, 387–89.

58. The consequences of Sunbelt development practices are well documented. See William D. Ross, "Industrial Promotion by Southern States," PhD diss., Duke University, 1951; Cobb, *The Selling of the South*; Eisinger, *The Rise of the Entrepreneurial State*, 224; and Schulman, *From Cotton Belt to Sunbelt*. Wanda Rushing's study of Memphis provides insight into the long-term problems of development strategy in a particular southern city. See Rushing, *Memphis and the Paradox of Place: Globalization in the American South* (Chapel Hill: University of North Carolina Press, 2009), 98–118.

59. Stefan H. Robock, "Industrialization and Economic Progress in the Southeast," *Southern Economic Journal* 20, no. 4 (Apr. 1954): 327.

60. *Childersburg Pilot Study: A Survey of the Impact of Rapid Industrial Development on a Southern Community* (Auburn Research Foundation, 1953), 3–5, box 21: "901.02 (VFs)," GRES Files, TVA Records.

61. Ibid., 6.

62. Ibid., 6–13. The lack of trained and skilled labor was a serious problem across the Sunbelt South. In the Tennessee Valley, Huntsville struggled to bring in workers proficient in aerospace technology (see chapter 7).

63. *Childersburg Pilot Study*, 23–24, 27.

64. Students were divided into two groups: those who had lived in Childersburg for more than eleven years (before the rapid growth) and those whose families came to the area during and after the war. Using the "Family Adjustment Test," researchers determined that the "native" children expressed "homey" feelings, defined as a positive sense of their home and community life. The "foreign" children, however, tended towards feelings of "homelessness": "negative, cold, hateful, and loveless" emotions usually expressed when a subject "feels himself moving away from the family group or its members [or] feels that his family group or its members are desirous of moving away from or repelling him" (*Childersburg Pilot Study*, 44).

65. "Auburn Research Foundation: Conference on Problems of Rapid Industrialization of the South, December 9–10, 1953"; Vernon W. Ruttan and Hershel Macon to L. L. Durisch and Stefan H. Robock, Jan. 8, 1954, box 16: "901.2 Industrial, 1954," GRES Files, TVA Records.

66. "Second Conference on the Impact of Rapid Industrialization, Feb. 17, 1954," 1–3, box 16: "901.2 Industrial, 1954," GRES Files, TVA Records.

67. Robock to Edward A. Ackerman, Assistant General Manager, Feb. 23, 1954, box 16: "901.2 Industrial, 1954," GRES Files, TVA Records.

68. Franklin D. Roosevelt, "A Suggestion for Legislation to Create the Tennessee Valley Authority," 10 Apr. 1933, in Roosevelt, *The Public Papers and Addresses of Franklin D. Roosevelt*, vol. 2: *The Year of Crisis, 1933* (New York: Random House, 1938), 128.

69. *Congressional Record* (Senate), 76th Cong., 3rd sess., 1940, vol. 86, pt. 1: 325–26.

70. E. S. Draper, "Recreational Opportunities in the Tennessee Valley," May 2, 1940, *Congressional Record* (Appendix), 76th Cong., 3rd sess., 1940, vol. 86, pt. 15: 2607–8; "Vast Increase in Recreation Pointed Out in TVA Report," *Huntsville Times*, 6 Jan. 1952, 2.

71. "Growth of Recreation Industry," *Huntsville Times*, June 11, 1950, 4; "Amazing Growth of River Recreation," *Huntsville Times*, July 1, 1951, 5.

72. A. C. Howard to Morgan, Aug. 18, 1933, in McJimsey, ed., *Documentary History* 28, document 84: 277–79.

73. "Waterfowl 'Refuge' Is Set Up in Valley," *Decatur Daily*, July 12, 1938, 1.

74. Roy Spangler to Bob Jones, Aug. 22, 1947; Gant to Bob Jones, Sept. 29, 1947, box 236:3443, Bob Jones Papers, UAH. A great example of the give-and-take between the State of Alabama and TVA on recreational oversight can be found in Gov. Chauncey Sparks to Lilienthal, Dec. 3, 1945; Ben C. Morgan to H. A. Smith, Dec. 4, 1945; and Harcourt Morgan to Sparks, Feb. 8, 1946, box 110: "092 Alabama," Curtis-Morgan-Morgan Papers, TVA Records.

75. Huntsville City Planning Commission, "Long Range Parks and Recreation Plan for Huntsville, Alabama," Sept. 1952, 1, 5–7, 16–17, box SG12625:6, Gordon Persons Administration Papers, ADAH.

76. Draper, "Recreational Opportunities in the Tennessee Valley," Apr. 22, 1940, in *Congressional Record* (Appendix), 76th Cong., 3rd sess., 1940, vol. 86, pt. 15: 2608.

77. Hutchens, "Guntersville State Park to Feature Water Sports," *Huntsville Times*, Nov. 4, 1945, 1, 8.

78. Mayor T. E. Martin to Vogel, Curtis, and Paty, Nov. 27, 1956; Vogel to Martin, Dec. 21, 1956, box 18: "095 Guntersville, Alabama," Pope-Paty Papers, TVA Records.

79. Bartmess to Jones, July 6, 1967; Wagner to Jones, July 21, 1967, box 150:2507, Bob Jones Papers, UAH.

80. TVA, "Outdoor Recreation for a Growing Nation: TVA's Experience with Man-made Reservoirs," Sept. 1961, box 57: loose, Navigation Files, TVA Records.

81. Jones has only one biography, a fifty-one-page booklet written in 1960, sixteen years before he retired from public service. See William Wray Eckl, *The Story of an Alabama Congressman: Bob Jones* (1960), 2.

82. Eckl, *The Story of an Alabama Congressman*, 4.

83. Clipping, *Congressional Record* (House), 82nd Cong., 2nd sess., June 28, 1952, 8538, box 138:2327, Bob Jones Papers, UAH; Jones, untitled speech, Apr. 10, 1952, box 152:2529, Bob Jones Papers, UAH.

84. Lister Hill, qtd. in Eckl, *The Story of an Alabama Congressman*, 13.

85. Qtd. in Eckl, *The Story of an Alabama Congressman*, 25.

86. *Congressional Record* (House), 82nd Cong., 2nd sess., 1952, vol. 98, pt. 3: 3988–89.

87. TVA tried to rebut claims that the region "stole" industry. In 1953, Stefan Robock argued that, of 7,000 new plants in the region, only 8 relocated from other areas, and none came from New England ("Industrialization and Economic Progress in the Southeast," 319).

88. "Stalled Steam Plant Program for TVA Seen," *Huntsville Times,* Dec. 5, 1952, 1; "'Choking to Death' the TVA," *Huntsville Times,* Dec. 14, 1952, 4.

89. "Gen. Eisenhower and TVA," *Huntsville Times,* Oct. 16, 1952, 4; Owen, *The Tennessee Valley Authority,* 97.

90. Dwight D. Eisenhower, *Mandate for Change, 1953–1956* (Garden City, N.Y.: Doubleday & Co., 1963), 380–81.

91. Ibid., 378–79.

92. For Eisenhower's views on the Dixon-Yates scandal, see Eisenhower, *Mandate for Change,* 378–85. The best account from TVA's perspective is Owen's *Tennessee Valley Authority,* 102–11.

93. Owen, *The Tennessee Valley Authority,* 106; Eisenhower, *Mandate for Change,* 376.

94. Jones to Brownell Jr., July 13, 1954, 152: box 2535, Bob Jones Papers, UAH.

95. Hill to Louis A. Eckl, July 21, 1954, box 272:54, Hill Papers. Hill's papers, particularly folders 54 and 55, contain numerous telegrams from across the valley calling for action against the Dixon-Yates contract.

96. Eisenhower, *Mandate for Change,* 382–84.

97. Dempster to Sparkman, Nov. 26, 1954; Sparkman to Dempster, Nov. 29, 1954, box 207: "26, TVA," Sparkman Senate Papers, Hoole. Dempster also worked to dispel the myth that the valley stole industry from New England, producing a pamphlet that used statistical evidence to show that only 10 of the 1,600 manufacturing plants that located in the area since 1933 came from the Northeast. See Eisenhower, *Mandate for Change,* and Joseph Marshall to Tennessee Valley Congressmen and Senators, May 29, 1956, box 273:79, Hill Papers.

98. Owen, *The Tennessee Valley Authority,* 109–10.

99. Ibid., 111–14; Eisenhower, *Mandate for Change,* 384.

100. Eisenhower, *Mandate for Change,* 384, 394.

101. Qtd. in Eckl, *Story of an Alabama Congressman,* 15.

102. G. R. Scott and S. L. Jones, *Studies of the Pollution of the Tennessee River System, II: Detailed Discussion of Types and Sources of Pollution and Their Effects on the River System with Results of Studies of the Major Tributaries, 1937–1939* (TVA, 1945), 2, 5–7, 9–10, box 142: loose, Pope-Paty Papers, TVA Records.

103. Ibid., 11.

104. Ibid., 14.

105. "Tennessee River Pollution Worse," *Huntsville Times,* Jan. 22, 1953, 16; R. A. Haden to Bob Jones, Nov. 3, 1953, and Oliver to Jones, Nov. 21, 1953, box 152:2529, Bob Jones Papers, UAH.

106. Jones, "Remarks of Rep. Bob Jones to the Kiwanis Club of Decatur, Alabama," Nov. 30, 1967, 1–2, box 138:2325, Bob Jones Papers, UAH.

107. Ibid., 2–4.

108. Ibid., 4–5.

109. Orvis Collins, "Industrial Democracy on the TVA—the Authority and the Council: A Pilot Report," Feb. 26, 1948, 2, box 72: "254.1 Union Management Cooperative Plans, R. R. Paty and J. P. Pope, 1948–49," Pope-Paty Papers, TVA Records.

110. Ibid., 12–13.

111. A. J. Hayes, President, International Association of Machinists, to General Manager John Oliver and Director of Personnel Harry L. Case, June 17, 1951, box 210: "1404 Strikes and Strikebreakers," Pope-Paty Papers, TVA Records.

112. Oliver to Hayes, July 26, 1951, box 210: "1404 Strikes and Strikebreakers," Pope-Paty Papers, TVA Records; Case, "Notice to All Employees," July 17, 1951, box 210: "1404 Strikers and Strike Breakers," Curtis-Morgan-Morgan Papers, TVA Records.

113. TVA, "Statement of TVA Concerning Machinists' Picket Lines," Sept. 14, 1951, box 210: "1404 Strikes and Strikebreakers," Pope-Paty Papers, TVA Records.

114. Clapp to Edward H. Rees, Chairman, Committee on Post Office and Civil Service, Nov. 24, 1953; Personnel Division, "Promotion Policy and Methods and Programs of Supervisory Training and Selection in the Tennessee Valley Authority," Nov. 1953, box 92: "032.03 Congressional Committees and Reports on, 1951–1960," Curtis-Morgan-Morgan Papers, TVA Records.

115. Gordon Clapp to James L. Houghteling, Chairman, Fair Employment Board, Nov. 29, 1950, box 127: "210.14 Hire of Employees thru 1950," Curtis-Morgan-Morgan Papers, TVA Records.

116. May to H. Alexander Smith, Chairman of Committee on Labor and Public Welfare, Nov. 23, 1953, box 68: "210.2221 Negroes or Colored," Pope-Paty Papers, TVA Records.

117. Clapp to Roy E. Jones, Staff Director, Committee on Labor and Public Welfare, Dec. 21, 1953, box 68: "210.2221 Negroes or Colored," Pope-Paty Papers, TVA Records.

118. Campbell to Wagner, Apr. 24, 1957, 2–3, 9, box 68: "210.2221 Negroes or Colored," Pope-Paty Papers, TVA Records.

119. Ibid., 12.

120. William L. Sturdevant Jr. to Folsom, June 7, 1955, box SG13857: 12, James E. Folsom Administration (1955–59) (Second Folsom Administration Papers), ADAH.

121. Clipping, Jones, *Congressional Record* (House), Mar. 20, 1956, 4614, box 213:3296, Bob Jones Papers, UAH.

122. Ibid., 4615.

123. "Statement of Hon. Robert E. Jones, Representative of Eighth District, Alabama, Opening the Hearings on TVA Financing Bill," [ca. 1957], 1, box 148:2467, Bob Jones Papers, UAH.

124. Eckl, untitled statement, [ca. Mar.–Apr. 1957], 1–2, box 215:3322, Bob Jones Papers, UAH. Valley chambers of commerce backed Jones legislation. See for instance, C. H. Jackson, Manager, Florence Chamber of Commerce, to Jones, May 13, 1957; and Jimmy Walker, Secretary-Manager, Huntsville Chamber of Commerce, to Jones, May 21, 1957, box 148:2466, Bob Jones Papers, UAH.

125. Jones, untitled speech, [ca. 1958], box 148:2471, Bob Jones Papers, UAH.

126. "Rep. Jones Raps Utility Attack upon TVA Bill," *Huntsville Times*, July 31, 1958, 1, 2.

127. "TVA Self-Finance Plan Given Okay," *Huntsville Times*, July 30, 1958, 1; "Self-Finance TVA Program Chance Goes," *Huntsville Times*, Aug. 6, 1958; and J. Wiley Bowers, Executive Secretary, Tennessee Valley Public Power Association, to Eckl, Aug. 18, 1958, box 148:2465, Bob Jones Papers, UAH.

128. Sparkman to Robert S. Gellerstedt, May 22, 1959, box 333: "Fed. Gov. 1–2, TVA," Sparkman Senate Papers, Hoole.

129. Gordon Brown, "TVA Self-Finance Plan Given Senate Okay," *Huntsville Times*, July 10, 1959, 1; Atkins, *"Developed for the Service of Alabama,"* 360–61.

130. Eisenhower, *Mandate for Change*, 385, 394.

131. Owen, *The Tennessee Valley Authority*, 123. See also Clapp, *TVA*, 89–90.

132. Owen, *The Tennessee Valley Authority*, 123–25.

133. Criley, Minutes of Elk River Development Association Meeting, May 20, 1959, box 39: "220 Elk River, 1958–1961," EDC Papers, TVA Records.

134. Weldon Payne, "Tennessee Valley Area Bands to Boost Growth," *Huntsville Times*, Feb. 3, 1960, 1; Clayton Braddock, "TVA Leader Surveys Area of Elk River," *Huntsville Times*, 1, 2.

135. Vogel to Hill, Feb. 14, 1961, box 129:2175, Bob Jones Papers, UAH.

136. Vogel to Sir, Apr. 3, 1961; Sir to Vogel, Apr. 17, 1961, box 39: "220 Elk River, 1958–1961," EDC Papers, TVA Records.

137. Water Control Planning Division, "Water Supply and Use in the Elk River Basin," Feb. 1962, 3; ERDA Business and Industry Committee, "Preliminary Report," Mar. 1962, 14, 15, box 39: "220 Elk River, Jan.–Feb. 1962," EDC Papers, TVA Records.

138. Wendell Russell, "Meeting on Training Project Possibilities: Elk River Watershed," Sept. 1, 1964; Robert E. Lowery, Assistant to Director of Tributary Area Development, "Progress of Southern Rural Training Project," Sept. 3, 1964, box 39: "220 Elk River, 1963," EDC Papers, TVA Records.

6. HUNTSVILLE HAS WHAT IT TAKES, 1940–1949

1. Whitman, *God's Valley*, 165–67. Huntsville was the temporary capital of Alabama in 1819.

2. Huntsville and Madison County Chamber of Commerce, *Happy Hustling Huntsville*, 1, 4, Hoole.

3. See Wayne Flynt, *Poor but Proud: Alabama's Poor Whites* (Tuscaloosa: University of Alabama Press, 1989), 93–94, 99, 112.

4. Snow, "Cotton Mill City," 273; U.S. Census Bureau, Fourteenth Census of the United States Taken in the Year 1920, vol. 3: Population 1920, Composition and Characteristics of the Population by States (Washington, D.C.: GPO, 1922), 67. Madison County's recorded population in 1920 was 51,000, with 42,000 residents over the age of seven.

5. Rogers et al., *Alabama*, 470.

6. Snow, "Cotton Mill City," 275–76.

7. Cronenberg, *Forth to the Mighty Conflict*, 49.

8. Nelson to Sparkman, May 20, 1940; Sparkman to Nelson, May 22, 1940, box 9: "Madison County: Huntsville Projects, 1939–43," Sparkman House Papers, Hoole.

9. Nelson to Sparkman, Aug. 9, 1940; Sparkman to Nelson, Aug. 12, 1940, box 22: "House Matters: Reynolds Aluminum," Sparkman House Papers, Hoole.

10. Cronenberg, *Forth to the Mighty Conflict*, 49.

11. C. H. Pipes to Sparkman, Jan. 16, 1941; Sparkman to Pipes, Jan. 17, 1941; Van Valkenburgh to Sparkman, 8 Jan. 1941; and Sparkman to Van Valkenburgh, Jan. 10, 1941, box 9: "Madison County: Huntsville Projects, 1939–43," Sparkman House Papers, Hoole.

12. Clipping, "An Editorial," *The Mercury* (Huntsville), Jan. 17, 1941, 1, box 9: "Madison County: Huntsville Projects, 1939–43," Sparkman House Papers, Hoole.

13. Circuit Court Clerk H. M. Hughes to Sparkman, Mar. 14, 1941, box 9: "Madison County: Huntsville Projects, 1939–43," Sparkman House Papers, Hoole.

14. Hill to Malone, Jan. 13, 1941, box 113:111, Hill Papers.

15. Sparkman to Rogers, Mar. 18, 1938; Sparkman to W. T. Archer, Jan. 17, 1939, box 36: "TVA: Arsenal, 1938–9," Sparkman House Papers, Hoole.

16. Goldsmith to Sparkman, June 9, 1941; Sparkman to Goldsmith, 11 June 1941; and Goldsmith to Sparkman, June 12, 1941, box 9: "Madison County: Huntsville Projects, 1939–43," Sparkman House Papers, Hoole.

17. Hill to Goldsmith, June 14, 1941, box 113:81, Hill Papers; Sparkman to Amis, June 14, 1941, box 34: "Appointments: CWA, Letters Not Filed (2)," Sparkman House Papers, Hoole.

18. Hill to A. McAllister, June 20, 1941, June 23, 1941, box 113:81, Hill Papers.

19. Goldsmith to Sparkman, June 16, 1941; Sparkman to Goldsmith, June 19, 1941, box 34: "Appointments: Chemical Warfare Arsenal, Letters Not Filed (2)," Sparkman House Papers, Hoole.

20. Press Release, "New Chemical Warfare Arsenal," [undated]; Sparkman to Goldsmith, July 3, 1941, box 34: "Appointments: Chemical Warfare Arsenal, Letters Not Filed (2)," Sparkman House Papers, Hoole. See also "Huntsville Given $41,293,000 Chemical War Service Plant," *Huntsville Times*, July 3, 1941, 1; and "Redstone Ordnance Plant to Open Operations Soon," *Huntsville Times*, Feb. 1, 1942, 2.

21. "Huntsville Given $41,293,000 Chemical War Service Plant," *Huntsville Times*, July 3, 1941, 1; "It's a Great Day," *Huntsville Times*, July 3, 1941, 4.

22. Reese Amis to Sparkman, [July 2, 1941] and [July 3, 1941], box 34: "Appointments: Chemical Warfare Arsenal, Letters Not Filed (2)," Sparkman House Papers, Hoole.

23. Ibid.; Mary Jane Lowe interview with George F. Davis, Nov. 21, 1990, box 2: "George F. Davis," Oral History Records, 1965–93, TVA Records.

24. "Progress Seen Upon Barracks in Plant Area," *Huntsville Times*, Aug. 21, 1941, 1.

25. "Views of Chemical Arsenal Site," *Huntsville Times*, July 22, 1941, 3.

26. "Initial Tract of Land Taken for War Plant," *Huntsville Times*, July 27, 1941, 1; "3 Farms Vacated on Arsenal Site," *Huntsville Times*, Aug. 4, 1941, 2; "Arsenal Residents Given Until Nov. 30th to Move," *Huntsville Times*, Oct. 15, 1941, 1.

27. "Relocation Office Continues Moving," *Huntsville Times*, Dec. 21, 1941, 10; "Arsenal Families Moved from Area," *Huntsville Times*, Jan. 25, 1942, 3.

28. "FSA to Relocate Farm Families," *Huntsville Times*, July 23, 1941, 1; and "Appraisers Seek Good Farm Land," *Huntsville Times*, Oct. 28, 1941, 2.

29. "Ousted Farmers Being Relocated," *Huntsville Times*, Sept. 29, 1941, 2.

30. "FSA Explains How Help Can Be Given Families," *Huntsville Times*, Nov. 3, 1941, 2.

31. "Labor Shortage Sure to Exist," *Huntsville Times*, Mar. 9, 1942, Farm and Home sec., 1, 3; "Labor on Farms Said Improved," *Huntsville Times*, May 3, 1943, 1.

32. Wall to Sparkman, July 7, 1941, box 34: "Appointments: Chemical Warfare Arsenal, Letters Not Filed (2)"; Jones to Sparkman, July 25, 1941, box 9: "Madison County: J, 1937–41," Sparkman House Papers, Hoole.

33. "Labor Shortage Sure to Exist," *Huntsville Times*, Mar. 9, 1942, Farm and Home sec., 1, 3.

34. Mary Jane Lowe, Interview with George F. Davis, Nov. 21, 1990, box 2: "George F. Davis," Oral History Records, TVA Records.

35. Hudson to Sparkman, July 7, 1941; Hudson to Sparkman, Aug. 16, 1941; and Hudson to Sparkman, Nov. 7, 1941, box 33: "Appointments: Chemical Warfare Arsenal, H's," Sparkman House Papers, Hoole. Sparkman's House Papers include a series of folders full of employment requests and correspondence detailing his efforts to find employment for certain constituents.

36. Fowler's actual fate is unrecorded. Fowler to Sparkman, Aug. 26, 1941, box 33: "Appointments: Chemical Warfare Arsenal, F's," Sparkman House Papers, Hoole.

37. "1,029 Persons Now Working on Big Plant," *Huntsville Times*, Aug. 25, 1941, 1; "Payrolls Rise as More Speed Seen on Plant," *Huntsville Times*, Nov. 8, 1941, 1.

38. "Chemical Plant Jobs Announced," *Huntsville Times*, Nov. 30, 1941, 3; "6,500 Will Be Added on Arsenal," *Huntsville Times*, Dec. 14, 1941, 1, 13; and "10,000 Persons Now at Work on War Plant," *Huntsville Times*, Dec. 17, 1941, 1. See also Cronenberg, *Forth to the Mighty Conflict*, 49.

39. Brooks to Sparkman, Dec. 20, 1941; W. C. Brown, Kershaw, Butler Engineers, Ltd., Dec. 26, 1941, box 33: "Appointments: Chemical Warfare Arsenal, B's," Sparkman House Papers, Hoole.

40. "Defense Training Classes Opened," *Huntsville Times*, Sept. 9, 1941, 1; "Defense Classes Now Registering," *Huntsville Times*, Dec. 11, 1941, 18; and "Training Urged for Arsenal Jobs," *Huntsville Times*, Jan. 16, 1942, 2.

41. Lowe, Interview with Davis, Nov. 21, 1990, box 2: "George F. Davis," Oral History Records, TVA Records.

42. The lack of skilled labor was a problem for much of the South in the war, and particularly for African Americans. Black workers unprepared for more technical employment were more likely to leave the South for unskilled jobs in northern factories, a continuation of the Great Migration. See Schulman, *Cotton Belt to Sunbelt*, 72.

43. Flynt, *Alabama in the Twentieth Century*, 140–41.

44. In *From Cotton Belt to Sunbelt*, 73–81, Bruce Schulman provides an excellent discussion of the operations and limitations of the NWLB in the South.

45. "Men Required to Join Union to Land Jobs," *Huntsville Times*, Sept. 3, 1941, 1; and "Demand Congressional Investigation," *Huntsville Times*, Sept. 7, 1941, 4.

46. "Crowd around Labor Union's Offices Drops," *Huntsville Times*, Sept. 10, 1941, 1.

47. "Some Figures," *Huntsville Times*, Sept. 14, 1941, 4; "Big Shakeups in High Jobs at War Plant," *Huntsville Times*, Oct. 5, 1941, 1. Such hostility to unionization was unsurprising, even as the city modernized its economy. As Marko Maunula noted in his study of Spartanburg, South Carolina, southern civic elites wanted economic prosperity without fundamental changes to the community power structure. New industries were "fresh elephants" that "had to be trained to dance to the music of the old circus." See Maunula, *Guten Tag, Y'All: Globalization and the South Carolina Piedmont, 1950–2000* (Athens: University of Georgia Press, 2009), 77.

48. "Plumbers Leave Job on Arsenal, Other Labor Trouble Disclosed," and "Stop This Foolishness," *Huntsville Times*, Dec. 5, 1941, 1, 4.

49. "Jap Ships Flee U.S. Fleet; $4,000,000 More for Arsenal," *Huntsville Times*, Dec. 12, 1941, 1; "Change Slated to Ban Racket in Jobs Here," *Huntsville Times*, Dec. 28, 1941, 1, 6.

50. "Electricians Quit One Day at War Plant," *Huntsville Times*, Jan. 2, 1942, 1, 2; "The Electricians," *Huntsville Times*, Jan. 2, 1942, 4; "Work, not Squabble," *Huntsville Times*, Jan. 8, 1942, 4; and "Lincoln Pledges All-Out War Production Efforts," *Huntsville Times*, Jan. 13, 1942, 1, 3.

51. "Sparkman Lauds Southern Labor," *Huntsville Times*, July 25, 1943, 1, 3.

52. Hall et al., *Like a Family*, 67.

53. Burleson to Sparkman, Feb. 23, 1942; Pounders to Burleson, Feb. 27, 1942, box 33: "Appointments: Chemical Warfare Arsenal, B's," Sparkman House Papers, Hoole.

54. McCurry to Sparkman, [mid-Mar. 1942], box 33: "Appointments: Chemical Warfare Arsenal, B's," Sparkman House Papers, Hoole.

55. Sparkman to Ditto, Mar. 27, 1942; Ditto to McCurry, Mar. 28, 1942; McCurry to Sparkman, [mid-Apr. 1942]; and Sparkman to McCurry, Apr. 16, 1942, box 33: "Appointments: Chemical Warfare Arsenal, B's," Sparkman House Papers, Hoole.

56. Elise Hopkins Stephens, *Historic Huntsville: A City of New Beginnings* (Woodland Hills, Calif.: Windsor Publications, 1984), 107.

57. "Ordnance Plant to Hire Women," *Huntsville Times*, Jan. 22, 1942, 2.

58. Mary Martha Thomas, *Riveting and Rationing in Dixie: Alabama Women and the Second World War* (Tuscaloosa: University of Alabama Press, 1987), 50.

59. "Industrial Amazons," *Huntsville Times*, Aug. 30, 1942, 4.

60. Qtd. in Thomas, *Riveting and Rationing in Dixie*, 116.

61. Kaylene Hughes, *Women at War: Redstone's WWII Female "Production Soldiers"* (Redstone Arsenal Historical Office, [ca. 1991]), 7–8, in Heritage Room, Huntsville (Ala.) Public Library (HPL). Some women were able to find positions as skilled technicians, though such occurrences were rare enough to merit special attention. See "Huntsville Girl 'Arsenal Chemist,'" *Huntsville Times*, Dec. 24, 1943, 14.

62. Geraldine R. Byrd, interviewed by Mary Jane Lowe, Sept. 16, 1992, 4, 6, box 2: "Byrd Geraldine," Oral History Records, TVA Records.

63. Ibid., 7, 15.

64. Johnson to Sparkman, Nov. 30, 1941; Sparkman to Johnson, Dec. 9, 1941, box 34: "Appointments: Chemical Warfare Arsenal, Letters Not Filed (1)," Sparkman House Papers, Hoole.

65. "Negro Housing Site Considered," *Huntsville Times*, Jan. 29, 1943, 1.

66. Enoc P. Waters, "Jim Crow Still in Business . . . but Slipping," *Chicago Defender*, Aug. 18, 1945, 11.

67. Hughes, *Women at War*, 2, 8.

68. Ibid., 10.

69. Waters, "Jim Crow Still in Business . . . but Slipping," 11.

70. Dunn to Dixon, June 10, 1941, box 1:6, Frank W. Dixon Papers (Dixon Papers), ADAH.

71. Stephens, *Historic Huntsville*, 109.

72. "Influx of Destitute Men Creates Serious Problem," *Huntsville Times*, Sept. 17, 1941, 1.

73. U.S. Census Bureau, Sixteenth Census of the United States: 1940, Population, vol. 2: Characteristics of the Population, pt. 1: United States Summary and Alabama—District of Columbia (Washington, D.C.: GPO, 1943), 322.

74. "Serious Traffic Problem Seen on Roads to Arsenal," *Huntsville Times*, Aug. 22, 1941, 1; "Extensive Road Work Planned," *Huntsville Times*, Mar. 6, 1942, 1.

75. "Transportation Problem," *Huntsville Times*, Mar. 31, 1942, 4; "Arsenal and Local People Alike Try 'Share-A-Ride,'" *Huntsville Times*, Apr. 6, 1942, 3.

76. N. M. Payne, Clerk-Treasurer, City of Huntsville, to Sparkman, Nov. 27, 1941, box 9: "Huntsville Projects," Sparkman House Papers, Hoole; Karl Woltersdorf to Sparkman, Dec. 5, 1941, box 9: "Madison County: Huntsville Projects, 1939–43," Sparkman House Papers, Hoole.

77. Dr. Carl Grote to Federal Works Agency, Jan. 23, 1942; Dr. E. V. Caldwell to Sparkman, Jan. 23, 1942; Hudson to Col. W. B. Persons, June 13, 1942; and Brig. Gen. R. C. Ditto to Federal Works Agency, June 15, 1942, box 9: "Huntsville Projects," Sparkman House Papers, Hoole.

78. Jackie McCullough, "Huntsville Public Library Has Place in War Effort," *Huntsville Times*, Apr. 2, 1942, 7.

79. Isom to Hill, July 5, 1941, box 113:81, Hill Papers.

80. Lowe, Interview with Davis, Nov. 21, 1990, box 2: "George F. Davis," Oral History Records, TVA Records.

81. Stephens, *Historic Huntsville*, 108.

82. Collier to Sparkman, Sept. 24, 1943; Colonel Marshall to Sparkman, Oct. 8, 1943, box 17: "Huntsville Matters: Huntsville Arsenal, 1943–5," Sparkman House Papers, Hoole.

83. "Saving Fish in Arsenal Creeks No Simple Task," *Huntsville Times*, June 22, 1947, 14.

84. Tom Schlesinger, with John Gaventa and Juliet Merrifield, *Our Own Worst Enemy: The Impact of Military Production on the Upper South* (New Market, Tenn.: Highlander Research and Education Center, 1983), 42–44.

85. "Word of Caution," *Huntsville Times*, July 6, 1941, 4; "City to File Plea for Aid on New Needs," *Huntsville Times*, July 16, 1941, 1; and "Millions Asked for Expansion in Huntsville," *Huntsville Times*, July 18, 1941, 1.

86. "Sparkman Warns to Be Sensible," *Huntsville Times*, July 20, 1941, 2.

87. Pipes to Sparkman, Sept. 19, 1941, box 9: "Huntsville Projects," Sparkman House Papers, Hoole.

88. Dixon, "The States and National Defense," [ca. 1942], box 4:3, Dixon Papers.

89. "Agency Speeds Housing Plans," *Huntsville Times*, Feb. 17, 1942; "Early Relief upon Housing Problem Seen," *Huntsville Times*, Mar. 20, 1942, 1; and "Rent Committee Promises Action," *Huntsville Times*, Apr. 30, 1942, 1.

90. Jacqueline McCullough, "Facts Placed Before House Group Today," *Huntsville Times*, May 7, 1942, 1, 4; "Tolan Praises Huntsville for Defense Conditions," *Huntsville Times*, May 10, 1942, 1.

91. "The Rent Situation," *Huntsville Times*, May 17, 1942, 4.

92. Ibid., July 1, 1942, 4.

93. "Housing Problem Acute Once More," *Huntsville Times*, Sept. 8, 1942, 1, 8.

94. Telegram, A. L. Essman to Sparkman, June 1, 1943, box 9: "Huntsville Projects," Sparkman House Papers, Hoole.

95. Gormley to Sparkman, Jan. 16, 1945; Robert K. Creighton to Sparkman, Jan. 24, 1945; and Gormley to Sparkman, Jan. 26, 1945, box 9: "Madison County: Madison County Housing Authority," Sparkman House Papers, Hoole.

96. "4.2 Mortar Shell, Smoke Pots of Arsenal Praised," *Huntsville Times*, Oct. 21, 1943, 3; "Arsenal's Great Part," *Huntsville Times*, July 8, 1945, 4; "Arsenal Products Win Praise from Patterson," *Huntsville Times*, Apr. 14, 1946, 14; and "Redstone Output Totals Revealed at Anniversary," *Huntsville Times*, Mar. 29, 1945, 3. Patterson, who had been under secretary of war under Roosevelt, was promoted to secretary of war by Truman in 1945.

97. "Postwar Objectives," *Huntsville Times*, Oct. 24, 1943, 4.

98. U.S. Department of Labor, Bureau of Labor Statistics, "Impact of the War on the Huntsville Area," July 1943, 1, in Hoole.

99. Ibid., 20.

100. Ibid., 3.

101. Alabama State Planning Board, "Alabama Postwar Employment Prospects," Sept. 1944, 2–4, box SG12500:1, Sparks Administration Papers. Childersburg's experience inspired TVA to action. See chapter 5.

102. Senter to Sparkman, Nov. 3, 1943, box 15: "House Miscellaneous, Decentralization of Industry," Sparkman House Papers, Hoole.

103. "Speakers Offer Post-War Plans," *Huntsville Times*, Aug. 5, 1943, 1. In some ways, the Concan negotiations exhibited the convoluted nature of wartime bureaucracy. While Huntsville

Arsenal answered to the Chemical Warfare Service, Redstone fell under the jurisdiction of the Ordnance Department. While there seem to be no recorded conflicts between the two organizations at the Huntsville facility, correspondence necessarily followed a convoluted path during times of crisis, as the Concan incident showed.

104. Sparkman to Patterson, Aug. 24, 1943; Howard C. Peterson to Sparkman, Aug. 28, 1943; and Campbell to Sparkman, Sept. 2, 1943, box 17: "House Miscellaneous: Huntsville Arsenal and Redstone Arsenal," Sparkman House Papers, Hoole.

105. "Private Firm to Take Over at Redstone," *Huntsville Times*, Sept. 3, 1943, 1; "Matter of Policy," *Huntsville Times*, Sept. 5, 1943, 4.

106. Amis to Sparkman, [early Nov. 1943]; Sparkman to Amis, Nov. 8, 1943; Amis to Sparkman, [mid-Nov. 1943]; and Sparkman to Amis, Nov. 19, 1943, box 17: "House Miscellaneous: Huntsville Arsenal and Redstone Arsenal," Sparkman House Papers, Hoole.

107. "Several Firms Seeking Sites in Huntsville," *Huntsville Times*, Feb. 17, 1946, 1, 10; Schlesinger et al., *Our Own Worst Enemy*, 25. The best documented southern civic-development group is probably the Louisville Industrial Foundation, formed in 1916 to bring business to the Kentucky city and its environs. Like state and regional groups, the foundation advertised to potential clients, extended loans, and provided general assistance to incoming companies. By 1945, the LIF attracted over seventy industries to the city, including two wartime developments. See E. J. Hopkins, *The Louisville Industrial Foundation: A Study in Community Capitalization of Local Industries* (Federal Reserve Bank of Atlanta, 1945), 55.

108. H. Y. Bassett, General Manager, Wolverine Tube Division, to Sparkman, Oct. 14, 1946; Sparkman to W. R. Hudspeth, Apr. 13, 1946, box 9: Madison County, Huntsville Projects, 1944–46, Sparkman House Papers, Hoole.

109. T. D. (Tom) Johnson, North Alabama Associates, to Jones, Mar. 30, 1949, box 42:760, Bob Jones Papers, UAH.

110. "Huntsville Has What It Takes," Huntsville Industrial Expansion Committee, 1946, 4, Hoole.

111. Ibid., 17.

112. "Both Arsenals Cut Contracts for Materials," *Huntsville Times*, Aug. 16, 1945, 1; 1,850 Workers to Be Granted Furlough Soon," *Huntsville Times*, Aug. 22, 1945, 1; "Local Arsenal Cancellation is $97,000,000," *Huntsville Times*, Sept. 2, 1945, 1.

113. "4,000 Unemployed around Huntsville," *Huntsville Times*, Oct. 3, 1946, 1.

114. "The Arsenal's Passing—Gain or Loss?" *Huntsville Times*, Dec. 21, 1947, 4. Some scholars have pointed to such demobilization to suggest that wartime growth was not as transformative as historians have suggested. In particular, geographer Robert Lewis argued that "[few] southern places received any substantial contributions from the defense industry." See Lewis, "World War II Manufacturing and the Postwar Southern Economy," *Journal of Southern History* 73, no. 4 (Nov. 2007): 854–56.

115. "Arsenal Gas Mask Plant Will Close," *Huntsville Times*, Sept. 10, 1946, 1.

116. "Redstone Arsenal Given Standby Status Order," *Huntsville Times*, Feb. 24, 1947, 1; "Rubber Firm Starts Line 6 Production," *Huntsville Times*, May 11, 1947, 1; "Keller Corp. Taking Over Arsenal Site," *Huntsville Times*, Oct. 7, 1947, 1, 3; "Arsenal to Become Surplus," *Huntsville Times*, Dec. 17, 1947, 1, 4.

117. "Standby Use of Arsenal Is Ordered," *Huntsville Times*, May 29, 1947, 1, 4.

118. Press Release, "Sparkman Urges Hold-up in Disposal of Surplus War Plants," Apr. 2, 1948, box 66A677–23:31, Sparkman Senate Papers, Hoole; "Mayor, Cummings to Push Arsenal," *Huntsville Times*, Oct. 10, 1947, 2; "Redstone Due on Permanent, Reduced Basis," *Huntsville Times*, Sept. 21, 1947, 1. For voter petitions, see box 187:168, Hill Papers.

119. "The Arsenal's Passing—Gain or Loss?" *Huntsville Times*, Dec. 21, 1947, 4. Huntsville's experience in the postwar period mirrors the challenges that faced defense-dependent cities experiencing later, Cold War–era funding cuts. For example, when Schilling Air Force Base closed in Salina, Kansas, in 1964, the community experienced a loss of 13,000 employees and staff members and an annual payroll of $35 million. As in Huntsville, leaders remained optimistic, even as they worked to repurpose the facilities. They formed the Salina Development Council, dedicated their efforts to industrial expansion, and began to attract business to the region. See Darwin W. Daicoff, Marston M. McCluggage, Charles K. Warriner, and Ronald R. Olsen, *Economic Impact of Military Base Closings*, vol. 1: *Adjustments by Communities and Workers* (United States Arms Control and Disarmament Agency, Apr. 1970), 63, 78–80, 89–92.

120. Huntsville City Council, "Resolution No. 4-H," Jan. 8, 1948, box 187:169, Hill Papers.

121. John E. Lynch, "Defense Spending in the Economy," 16, in Lynch, ed., *Economic Adjustment and Conversion of Defense Industries* (Boulder, Colo.: Westview Press, 1987).

122. "Keller Corp. Taking Over Arsenal Site," *Huntsville Times*, Oct. 7, 1947, 1, 3. For a detailed history of the Keller Motor Corporation, see Ken Gross and Rich Taylor, "America's Most Needed Car: The Story of the Keller Super Chief," *Special Interest Autos* (Sept.–Oct. 1975): 31–40, 59, rpr. in www.redstone.army.mil/history/auto/auto.html.

123. "Group to Visit Arsenal for TB Hospital Study," *Huntsville Times*, Jan. 4, 1948, 2.

124. Crow to Jones, Jan. 12, 1948, box 236:3443, Bob Jones Papers, UAH; Hamm to Hill, Jan. 17, 1948; and Pinkston to Hill, [ca. 1948], box 187:169, Hill Papers.

7. HOLD ONTO WHAT YOU HAVE WORKED SO HARD TO GET IN, 1949–1960

1. "Redstone Made Rocket Center for Research," *Huntsville Times*, Dec. 2, 1948, 1; "News Just Two Months Old," *Huntsville Times*, Feb. 8, 1949, 4.

2. "Redstone Arsenal Being Converted," *Huntsville Times*, Apr. 10, 1949, 1, 4; Martha Witt Smith, "Full Use of Redstone Arsenal Now in Sight," *Huntsville Times*, May 29, 1949, 1, 2.

3. "Sale of Arsenal Again Called Off," *Huntsville Times*, Oct. 30, 1949, 1; "The Greater Redstone Arsenal Installation," *Huntsville Times*, Nov. 4, 1949, 4.

4. Rees's recollections were included in "Clearly Huntsville," a pamphlet created in conjunction with the city's 1976 bicentennial celebration. See "Clearly Huntsville," [ca. 1976], 11, Hoole.

5. Erik Bergaust, *Wernher von Braun* (Washington, D.C.: National Space Institute, 1976), 152–53.

6. Qtd. in Michael J. Neufield, *Von Braun: Dreamer of Space, Engineer of War* (New York: Alfred A Knopf, 2007), 4.

7. While every biography of Wernher von Braun carries some version of this story, the best remains von Braun and Frederick I. Ordnay III, *History of Rocketry and Space Travel* (New York: Thomas Y. Cromwell Co., 1969), 114–18.

8. Bergaust, *Wernher von Braun*, 124–29.

9. Stephens, *Historic Huntsville*, 116–17.

10. Erik Bergaust, *Rocket City, U.S.A.: From Huntsville, Alabama, to the Moon* (New York: Macmillan Co., 1963), 111.

11. Neufield, *Von Braun*, 247, 251.

12. Ann Markusen, Peter Hall, Scott Campbell, and Sabina Deitrick, *The Rise of the Gunbelt: The Military Remapping of Industrial America* (New York: Oxford University Press, 1991), 25.

13. Thomas A. Scott, "Winning World War II in an Atlanta Suburb: Local Boosters and the Recruitment of the Bell Bomber," in *The Second Wave: Southern Industrialization from the 1940s to the 1970s*, ed. Philip Scranton (Athens: University of Georgia Press, 2001), 1–23; Richard S. Combes, "Aircraft Manufacturing in Georgia: A Case Study of Federal Industrial Investment," in *The Second Wave*, ed. Scranton, 33.

14. "GE May Have Laboratories at Redstone," *Huntsville Times*, Nov. 13, 1949, 1; "GE Move Getting Well Under Way," *Huntsville Times*, May 21, 1950, 1.

15. "Redstone Contract Signed by Thiokol," *Huntsville Times*, Apr. 17, 1949, 1, 2; "Rohm, Haas Co. to Establish Redstone Labs," *Huntsville Times*, May 19, 1949, 1.

16. Neufield, *Von Braun*, 251.

17. "Chance for Small Business," *Huntsville Times*, July 8, 1951, 4; "Redstone Lets Outside Contracts for $671,485," *Huntsville Times*, July 29, 1951, 1; and "Small Firms Get Arsenal Contracts," *Huntsville Times*, Dec. 7, 1951, 5.

18. Ivadell Bowser (Jones's Secretary), to Eigenbrod, Oct. 2, 1950; Eigenbrod to Jones, Sept. 28, 1950, box 26:507, Bob Jones Papers, UAH; and Maxwell Caskie to Hugh M. Manley, Oct. 25, 1950, box 42:759, Bob Jones Papers, UAH.

19. L. H. Shelley, Decatur Iron and Steel, to Major General Lewis A. Pick, Chief of Engineers, Mar. 1, 1951; Shelley to Hill, Mar. 2, 1951; and Hill to Shelley, Mar. 6, 1951, box 180:9, Hill Papers.

20. "Redstone's Total Payroll for 1955 Near $40,000,000," *Huntsville Times*, Jan. 1, 1956, 1.

21. Charles Black et al. to Jones, May 5, 1956; Jones, Hill, and Sparkman to Toftoy, May 9, 1956; and Toftoy to Hill, May 11, 1956, box 188:201, Hill Papers; and Black and Hartselle to Jones, May 21, 1956, box 267: "43-H, Industrial Relations," Sparkman Senate Papers, Hoole.

22. "1,150 Jobs to Be Added at Redstone," *Huntsville Times*, Mar. 27, 1958, 1, 2.

23. U.S. Census Bureau, Census of Population: 1960, vol. 1: Characteristics of the Population, pt. 2: Alabama (Washington, D.C.: GPO, 1961), 163.

24. "Local Center Is Authorized by University," *Huntsville Times*, Nov. 16, 1949, 1; "Graduate Study Institute Established for Arsenal," *Huntsville Times*, Sept. 30, 1951, 1.

25. "First Step to Center Building," *Huntsville Times*, June 7, 1957, 4; "A Major, Forward Step," *Huntsville Times*, Apr. 14, 1958, 4; "Construction of $750,000 U of A Branch Okayed Here," *Huntsville Times*, Sept. 11, 1958, 1; and "4-Year College Here Proposed by Medaris," *Huntsville Times*, June 23, 1959, 1, 2.

26. Von Braun to Hill, June 19, 1961, box 188:206, Hill Papers; Cummings qtd. in "Huntsville, Research Center," *Huntsville Times*, June 28, 1961, 4; Weldon Payne, "Von Braun Asks Legislature for Rocket Institute Here," *Huntsville Times*, June 20, 1961, 1, 3. See also "Public Meeting Scheduled on Research Institute," *Marshall Star* 1, no. 50 (Sept. 13, 1961): 7, box 1: bound, Office of Strategic Communications, Internal Communications Office, Marshall Space Flight Center, Huntsville, Ala., National Aeronautics and Space Administration Records (MSFC Papers), NARASE.

27. Von Braun, "Educating Engineers in the Space Age," address to the University of Alabama, College of Engineering, Oct. 11, 1962, 4, 7, box 3: "Dr. von Braun Speeches, 1962," Office of the Director, Speech Files, 1954–68, NASA Records, NARASE.

28. "Alabama Ratifies Space Center Bonds," *Christian Science Monitor*, Dec. 6, 1961, 8; Bob Ward, "NASA Grants $600,000 to Research Institute," *Huntsville Times*, Mar. 5, 1963, 1.

29. U.S. Census Bureau, Census of Population: 1950, vol. 2: Characteristics of the Population, pt. 2: Alabama (Washington, D.C.: GPO, 1952), 8; U.S. Census Bureau. Census of Population: 1960, vol. 1: Characteristics of the Population, pt. 2: Alabama (Washington, D.C.: GPO, 1961), 155, 157; Huntsville City Council, "Huntsville . . . Reports to Its Citizens," [1958], 7, in Hoole.

30. "Civic Housing Group Formed at Redstone," *Huntsville Times*, Nov. 6, 1949, 1; "Group Formed to Construct 50 New Homes," *Huntsville Times*, Feb. 22, 1950, 1; "$23,500 Raised for Redstone Home Building," *Huntsville Times*, Feb. 28, 1950, 1; and "A 'Must' if Huntsville Is to Expand," *Huntsville Times*, Feb. 28, 1950, 4.

31. "Arsenal Housing Appeal Made City, Nearby Town," *Huntsville Times*, July 2, 1951, 1; "250 More Low Rent Housing Units Okayed," *Huntsville Times*, Aug. 26, 1951, 1.

32. "Medaris Sees 100,000 City for Huntsville," *Huntsville Times*, Feb. 24, 1956, 1, 14; "FHA Will Start Housing Survey Here Tomorrow, Home Shortage Could Stymie Army Mission," *Huntsville Times*, Feb. 5, 1956, 1.

33. See, for instance, "Put First Things First," *Huntsville Times*, July 18, 1950, 4; "The Growing Traffic Problem," *Huntsville Times*, June 1, 1951, 4; and "Necessity for Forward Planning," *Huntsville Times*, June 20, 1951, 4.

34. Beamguard, Director of the Regional Library Service, Huntsville Public Library, to Sparkman, Jan. 22, 1952, box 167: "1952-43-Misc. (2)," Sparkman Senate Papers, Hoole.

35. "Problems of a Growing City," *Huntsville Times*, Mar. 3, 1952, 4.

36. $8,500,000 in Bonds for Expanding City Services Proposed," *Huntsville Times*, Apr. 11, 1952, 1, 9; "The Morrow Survey of Huntsville," *Huntsville Times*, May 18, 1952, 4.

37. "Annexation of Suburbs without Vote Agreed," *Huntsville Times*, Mar. 4, 1956, 1, 18.

38. Brockway to Secretary of Defense, Apr. 4, 1956, box 267: "43-M, Miscellaneous," Sparkman Senate Papers, Hoole.

39. Matthew D. Lassiter notes the importance of metropolitan annexation in *The Silent Majority: Suburban Politics in the Sunbelt South* (Princeton, N.J.: Princeton University Press, 2006), 276–77. He argues that southern city leaders sponsored annexation programs as a means of controlling the sprawling growth of suburbs and maintaining white municipal rule as white voters fled city centers. In Huntsville, annexation allowed city leaders to reserve economic control as well, providing the local government with the ability to spread city services to an expanding population.

40. Alex Thomas, "City to Buy More Property for Expansion," *Huntsville Times*, Aug. 9, 1957, 1; Joe Hochstein, "Huntsville Okays Plan to Expand City Limits," *Huntsville Times*, Nov. 25, 1958, 1; and "Vote in Three Areas Favors Joining City," *Huntsville Times*, Apr. 1, 1959, 1, 3.

41. "Rockets, Fame, Expansion Marked Area's Best Decade," *Huntsville Times*, Jan. 1, 1960, 1; Jerry Wilkerson, "$790,000 Grant Won by Huntsville Hospital," *Huntsville Times*, Sept. 29, 1960, 1.

42. Bergaust, *Rocket City, U.S.A.*, 59.

43. Hannes Luehrsen, "Luehrsen Gives City Center Plan," *Huntsville Times*, Jan. 13, 1957, 1, 2.

44. "Space Capital Drive Urged at Huntsville," *Huntsville Times*, May 5, 1959, 1, 2.

45. "Huntsville Has Neglected to Plan, Luehrsen Says," *Huntsville Times*, Dec. 11, 1959, 15.

46. "Clearly Huntsville" [1976], Hoole.

47. On Florida's growing "Space Coast," civic leaders worked with NASA to accommodate rapid growth that mirrored that happening in Huntsville. See Sallie Middleton, "Space Rush: Local Impact of Federal Aerospace Programs on Brevard and Surrounding Counties," *Florida Historical Quarterly* 87 (Fall 2008): 258–89. For a larger history of Kennedy Space Center, with a comparative discussion on the impact the center had on the economy of central Florida, see Kenneth Lipartito and Orville R. Burton, *A History of the Kennedy Space Center* (Gainesville: University Press of Florida, 2007).

48. Wiesman to Sparkman, July 19, 1957; Jones to Wiesman, July 24, 1957, box 119:199, Bob Jones Papers, UAH.

49. "How Mississippi Attracts Industry," *Huntsville Times*, Dec. 19, 1950, 4. Cobb's *The Selling of the South* is the quintessential account of the importance of Mississippi's Balance Agriculture with Industry program to the modernization of the southern economy, though Lester's "Balancing Agriculture with Industry" is equally informative.

50. "One Way to Attract Plants," *Huntsville Times*, Feb. 26, 1952, 4.

51. Charles MacArthur Wilson, "The Impact of Industrial Development on Lawrence County, Tennessee," MS thesis, University of Tennessee, 1965, 102.

52. Johnson, untitled speech, [ca. Jan.–Feb. 1952], courtesy NAIDA.

53. "One Big New Industry for 1953," *Huntsville Times*, Jan. 1, 1953, 4.

54. "Industrial Sites Funds Are Sought," *Huntsville Times*, Jan. 8, 1956, 1; "New Metals Industry Will Be Located Here Soon," *Huntsville Times*, Jan. 26, 1956, 1, 24.

55. "2 Years of Effort Required to 'Land' Green Mountain," *Huntsville Times*, June 4, 1956, 1, 6.

56. Amis to Folsom, June 4, 1956; Folsom to Amis, June 8, 1956, box SG13958:11, Second Folsom Administration Papers.

57. "Opportunity for New Effort," *Huntsville Times*, July 15, 1956, 4.

58. "Large Liquid Oxygen, Nitrogen Plant to Be Erected in Madison County," *Huntsville Times*, Feb. 18, 1959, 1, 8.

59. North Alabama Associates, "A Study of Huntsville, Alabama," [1952–53], 47, in Hoole.

60. "Industry Outlook Bright for City," Alex Thomas, *Huntsville Times*, Apr. 30, 1958, 1, 8; "Brown Engineering Co. Leases Lincoln Site," *Huntsville Times*, Feb. 9, 1958, 2; and "Chrysler Sets Consolidation at Lincoln Site, *Huntsville Times*, July 1, 1958, 1.

61. Alan Gergerman and R. Leo Penne, "Community Economic Adjustment to Defense Industrial Cutbacks," in Lynch, ed., *Economic Adjustment and Conversion of Defense Industries*, 69.

62. Albert N. Link, *From Seed to Harvest: The Growth of Research Triangle Park* (Chapel Hill: University of North Carolina Press, 2002), 5.

63. Ibid. Link includes an example of the park's promotional material in appendix C: 135–42.

64. "Teamwork for Industry Missing," *Huntsville Times*, Nov. 30, 1958, 4.

65. Ibid.

66. "New Industrial Development Formula Deserves Support," *Huntsville Times*, Oct. 4, 1959, 4.

67. Alex Thomas, "Frustration Is Reaction to News Here," *Huntsville Times*, Oct. 6, 1957, 1; "Committees Hamper Him, Says Medaris," *Huntsville Times*, Dec. 15, 1957, 1.

68. Walter A. McDougall's *The Heavens and the Earth: A Political History of the Space Age* (New York: Basic Books, 1985), remains the seminal work on the development of the American space program.

69. "President Says He Alone Will Decide Whether Army Gives Up Scientists," *Huntsville Times*, Oct. 15, 1958, 1; "The NASA Proposal," *Huntsville Times*, Oct. 15, 1958, 4; and memo, Charles Mitchell to Hill, Oct. 27, 1958, box 188:203, Hill Papers.

70. McDougall, *The Heavens and the Earth*, 198.

71. "Air Force Wins Control of Space Work; Saturn Will Continue Here," *Huntsville Times*, Sept. 23, 1959, 2; "No Change Predicted in ABMA's Personnel," *Huntsville Times*, Sept. 24, 1959, 2.

72. Sparkman to Eisenhower, Oct. 9, 1959, box 332: "Fed. Gov. 1–1, RSA," Sparkman Senate Papers, Hoole; "Remarks by Representative Robert E. Jones (D Ala.) Concerning Proposed ABMA Transfer," undated [ca. 1959], 2–4, box 118:1979, Bob Jones Papers, UAH.

73. Qtd. in "Transfer of ABMA to NASA Will Be Requested by President," *Huntsville Times*, Oct. 21, 1959, 1, 2.

74. "Army-NASA Transfer Plan," Dec. 11, 1959, 1–3, box 355: "Mili. 4, Redstone Arsenal, 1960," Sparkman Senate Papers, Hoole.

75. "Gen. Medaris Makes Report to Huntsville," *Huntsville Times*, Dec. 9, 1959, 16, 17.

76. "Arsenal Gets Bulk of NASA Budget," *Huntsville Times*, Mar. 10, 1960, 1; Jerry Wilkerson, "Stability to Rule NASA Plan Here," *Huntsville Times*, Mar. 27, 1960, A1, A6.

77. "NASA's Redstone Unit Named for Marshall," *Huntsville Times*, Mar. 15, 1960, 1; Weldon Payne, "NASA Transfer Progresses Here," *Huntsville Times*, May 5, 1960, 1, 2.

78. Lewis Odom to Sparkman, May 12, 1960, box 355: "4, Redstone Arsenal, 1960," Sparkman Senate Papers, Hoole; Wernher von Braun, transcript of telephone call to Lister Hill, June 29, 1960, box 299:1, Hill Papers.

79. Qtd. in "Here Is the Text of Ike's Talk," *Huntsville Times*, Sept. 4, 1960, 2.

80. John G. Norris, "New Weapons Question . . . ," *Washington Post, Times Herald*, July 5, 1957, A15.

81. "Redstone Big Shot of Health for Business across Nation," *Huntsville Times*, May 4, 1958, 11; Bob Ward, "4,200 from Industry Aid Redstone Projects," *Huntsville Times*, Apr. 19, 1959, 22.

82. Gen. Orval R. Cook, President of Aircraft Industries Association, qtd. in Norris, "New Weapons Question. . . ," A15.

83. Sparkman to Medaris, Mar. 5, 1959; Hayes Aircraft Workers to Sparkman, Mar. 5, 1959, box 332: "Fed. Gov. 1–1, Redstone," Sparkman Senate Papers, Hoole.

84. D. M. Morris for von Braun, to Sparkman, Aug. 30, 1960, box 355: "Mili. 4, Redstone Arsenal, 1960," Sparkman Senate Papers, Hoole; "Industry's Role at MSFC Told," *Huntsville Times*, Sept. 27, 1960, 1.

85. "400 Attending Industry Conference at Marshall," *Marshall Star* 1, no. 1 (Sept. 28, 1960): 1, 2; "Tour of MSFC Facilities Ends Industry Meeting," *Marshall Star* 1, no. 2 (Oct. 5, 1960): 3, box 1, Office of Strategic Communications, Internal Communications Office, "Marshall Star," MSFC Papers.

86. McDougall (*The Heavens and the Earth*, 196) notes Glennan's reliance on private industry.

87. Jules Witcover, "Redstone's Key Losses Explained," *Huntsville Times*, Apr. 17, 1960, AI, A3; "Space Agency Group Forms Private Firm," *Huntsville Times*, June 18, 1961, B10. See also Neufield, *Von Braun*, 339.

88. "September Awards Total $45 Million," *Marshall Star* 3, no. 5 (Oct. 24, 1962): 1; "$, Manpower, Construction Show Growth," *Marshall Star* 3, no. 14 (Jan. 2, 1963): 1, 6, box 1, Office of Strategic Communications, Internal Communications Office, "Marshall Star," MSFC Papers.

89. "Lockheed Buys Tract for New Plant Here," *Huntsville Times,* Sept. 21, 1962, 1; "Lockheed and Our Future," *Huntsville Times,* Sept. 23, 1962, 4; and Bob Ward, "West Coast Firm to Employ 200 in Plant Here," *Huntsville Times,* Sept. 25, 1962, 1.

90. Schomburg to Jeffers, May 3, 1961; Jeffers to Schomburg, May 10, 1961, box 64A577-13: "Mili. 12, Hayes Aircraft Co.," Sparkman Senate Papers, Hoole.

91. "Marshall Contracts Total $82 Million during January," *Marshall Star* 2, no. 22 (Feb. 28, 1962): 1, 7; "Nine MSFC Contracts Net Local Firms $27,588,482," *Marshall Star* 3, no. 35 (May 29, 1963): 6, box 1, Office of Strategic Communications, Internal Communications Office, "Marshall Star," MSFC Papers.

92. Von Braun, "Huntsville in the Space Age," Dec. 8, 1964, 29–35, box 1: "Dr. von Braun's Speeches 1964," Office of the Director, Speech Files, 1954–64, Speeches Given by Wernher von Braun, MSFC Papers.

93. Von Braun, "Alabama's Future with the Space Program," June 1965, box 1: "Dr. von Braun's Speeches 1965," Office of the Director, Speech Files, 1954–64, Speeches Given by Wernher von Braun, MSFC Papers; Gergerman and Penne, "Community Economic Adjustment to Defense Industrial Cutbacks," 68.

94. Von Braun, "Alabama's Future with the Space Program," June 1965, 1: "Dr. von Braun's Speeches 1965," Office of the Director, Speech Files, 1954–64, Speeches Given by Wernher von Braun, MSFC Papers.

95. Stephens, *Historic Huntsville,* 184–85. In 1967, Brown merged with California-based Teledyne, Inc., and began expanding into larger defense projects for the U.S. government as well as foreign defense agencies.

96. "Nine Firms Win Support Contracts; $58.5 Million," *Marshall Star* 5, no. 23 (Mar. 10, 1965), 1, box 2, Office of Strategic Communications, Internal Communications Office, "Marshall Star," MSFC Papers; and Cummings to J. C. McCall, Assistant to the Director, Sept. 29, 1961, box 1: "6. Brown Engineering Company, 1961–66," Office of the Director, 1958–68, Upper Management Files, #17 Series, Contract Corp. Records, MSFC Papers.

97. Vice-President William A. Giardini to Space Craft, Inc. (SCI), May 31, 1961, box 1: "6. Brown Engineering Company, 1961–66," Office of the Director, 1958–68, Upper Management Files, #17 Series, Contract Corp. Records, MSFC Papers.

98. Bob Ward, "Space Employment Spiraling," *Huntsville Times,* Jan. 2, 1966, 1, 2. For a general discussion of the history of Cummings Research Park, see Melinda Gorham Joiner and Peter Coburn, *Huntsville: Where Technology Meets Tradition* (Huntsville, Ala.: Community Communications, 1993).

99. Cummings to Assistant to the Director J. C. McCall, Apr. 26, 1961, box 1: "6. Brown Engineering Company, 1961–66," Office of the Director, 1958–68, Upper Management Files, #17 Series, Contract Corp. Records, MSFC Papers.

100. Sparkman to Joseph Sabias, Bay City (Michigan), July 2, 1956; Sparkman to Sampson R. Bilyen, Taylorville (Illinois), Sept. 24, 1956, box 277: "54—Segregation from June," Sparkman Senate Papers, Hoole.

101. Qtd. in "U.S. May Penalize South for Stand on Race Issue," *Huntsville Times,* Dec. 10, 1958, 1.

102. William H. Murray to Sparkman, Oct. 23, 1964; H. O. Ragland to Sparkman, Oct. 24, 1964, box 66A677-7: "Fed. Gov't, NASA," Sparkman Senate Papers, Hoole; and John W. Finney, "NASA May Leave Its Alabama Base," *New York Times,* Oct. 24, 1964, 12.

103. Sparkman to Representative Frank Boykin, Oct. 29, 1964, box 66A677-7: "Fed. Gov't, NASA," Sparkman Senate Papers, Hoole.

104. Von Braun, "Alabama's Future with the Space Program," June 1965, 1: "Dr. von Braun Speeches 1965," MSFC Papers. Von Braun made a similar plea to Huntsville business leaders. See von Braun, "Huntsville in the Space Age," Dec. 8, 1964, 1: "Dr. von Braun's Speeches 1964," "Dr. von Braun Speeches 1965," MSFC Papers.

105. "Segregation Aid Charged to Military," *Washington Post, Times Herald,* Mar. 4, 1959, B3.

106. "City Officials Here Say Plan to Integrate Was Surprise," *Huntsville Times,* Nov. 10, 1959, 1, 2. See also Warren Trest, *Nobody but the People: The Life and Times of Alabama's Youngest Governor* (Montgomery, Ala.: New South Books, 2008), 304.

107. "A Time for Caution and Wisdom," *Huntsville Times,* Nov. 11, 1959, 4.

108. "U.S. Aid Said to Curb School Integration," *New York Times,* Mar. 8, 1962, 12; Robert E. Baker, "Rights Movement Stabs into Depths of Dixie," *Washington Post, Times Herald,* Sept. 9, 1962, E1.

109. Bill Austin, "U.S. Sues to Integrate City-County Schools for Army's Children," *Huntsville Times,* Jan. 18, 1963, 1; "4 Areas in South Are Sued to End Pupil Separation," *New York Times,* Jan. 19, 1963, 1.

110. "Alabama Drops 6-Week Seminar after Negro Enrolls for Course," *Chicago Daily Defender,* Jan. 28, 1963, 6.

111. Claude Sitton, "Racial Test Due over Alabama U.," *New York Times,* Mar. 25, 1963, 7.

112. "Negro Scientists File Suit to Enter Alabama U. Unit," *Chicago Daily Defender,* May 10, 1963, 14; Hedrick Smith, "Showdown Near at U. of Alabama," *Chicago Daily Defender,* May 17, 1963, 14.

113. "U.S. School Suit Rejected by Alabama Federal Court," *Chicago Daily Defender,* May 30, 1963, 1; "Wallace Sends Guard to Area of University," *Washington Post, Times Herald,* June 9, 1963, A6.

114. Laurence Stern, "Policies of Gov. Wallace Unpopular in Huntsville," *Washington Post,* June 10, 1963, A1.

115. S. W. Ellis to Sparkman, May 18, 1960, box 355: "Mili. 4, Redstone Arsenal, 1960," Sparkman Senate Papers, Hoole; Stern, "Policies of Gov. Wallace Unpopular in Huntsville."

116. "Third Student Admitted to Alabama U. at Huntsville," *Chicago Defender,* June 15, 1963, 1; "In Brighter Alabama," *Washington Post, Times Herald,* June 16, 1963, E6.

117. Robert E. Baker, "Now Wallace Faces a Homegrown Challenge," *Washington Post, Times Herald,* Sept. 8, 1963, E1; "Huntsville, Ala., Schools Admit 10 More Negroes," *Washington Post, Times Herald,* Jan. 28, 1964, A2.

118. Elizabeth Jacoway and David R. Colburn, eds., *Southern Businessmen and Desegregation* (Baton Rouge: Louisiana State University Press, 1982), 3. James Cobb's "Yesterday's Liberalism: Business Boosters and Civil Rights in Augusta, Georgia," 151–69, in the same volume, provides an excellent comparison for integration in Huntsville.

119. Permaloff and Grafton, *Political Power in Alabama,* 156, 207–8.

120. "Hunt for Industry Charted by Study," *Huntsville Times,* June 22, 1960, 1, 3.

121. "Industry Job Just Beginning," *Huntsville Times,* Aug. 15, 1960, 4; "HIEC Hires Industrial Specialist," *Huntsville Times,* Dec. 4, 1960, 1.

122. "Parker Aircraft to Locate Rocket-Parts Plant in City," *Huntsville Times,* May 23, 1961, 1.

123. Halsey to Patterson, June 19, 1961, box SG14009:2, John Patterson Administration Papers, ADAH; "Bill to Aid HIEC Plan Now Pending," *Huntsville Times,* June 30, 1961, 1, 2.

124. "Huntsville, Ala., Is Flourishing on Boom Created by Space Age," *New York Times*, Nov. 26, 1961, F7.

125. Halsey Jr. to Sparkman, Feb. 26, 1963; "Itinerary for West Coast Trip, 17–22 February 1963," undated, HIEC; Sparkman to Lawson, Mar. 15, 1963; and Burns to Sparkman, Apr. 1, 1963, box 66A89-4: "Econ. 2, Industry," Sparkman Senate Papers, Hoole.

126. "Huntsville Industrial Expansion Committee Meeting," Dec. 5, 1968, box 140:2341, Bob Jones Papers, UAH.

127. Untitled address, James E. Webb, Administrator, NASA, May 15, 1965, 9–12, 18, box 299:15, Hill Papers.

128. Edward C. Burgs, "U.S. Business: Industry Mushrooms in North Alabama," *New York Times*, May 30, 1965, F13.

CONCLUSION: A GREAT PLACE TO DO BUSINESS

1. See, for instance, the "Saturn Project Factsheet," published by the Public Affairs Office at Marshall Space Flight Center on Aug. 5, 1965, available via the MSFC History Office, history.msfc.nasa.gov/.

2. R. J. Richey, "MSFC Work Peaks with Apollo in '68," *Huntsville Times*, Jan. 1, 1969, 6.

3. "Change Was Key to the Science Element in '70," *Huntsville Times*, Jan. 3, 1971, 7.

4. "Goals for the '70s—V," *Huntsville Times*, Jan. 6, 1970, 5.

5. "Change Was Key to Science Element in '70," *Huntsville Times*, Jan. 3, 1971, 7.

6. Gergerman and Penne, "Community Economic Adjustment to Defense Industrial Cutbacks," 68. Gergerman and Penne use Huntsville as an example of a reconversion success story (67–72).

7. "A Base for Building," *Huntsville Times*, Jan. 1, 1974, 7.

8. Don Chapin, "Progress in Economy Shown for Huntsville," *Huntsville Times*, Jan. 2, 1972, A1, A10.

9. Randy Quarles, "1978 a Year of Steady Growth in Area," *Huntsville Times*, Jan. 1, 1979, 37.

10. Stephens, *Historic Huntsville*, 184–86.

11. Gergerman and Penne, "Community Economic Adjustment to Defense Industrial Cutbacks," 72; Joiner and Coburn, *Huntsville*, 35.

12. Joiner and Coburn, *Huntsville*, 37, 48.

13. Ibid., 50–53.

14. Spires, "'This Is the Biggest Step,'" *Huntsville Times*, May 14, 2005, A1, A6.

15. Mike Marshall, "Leaders Predict More Huntsville Growth with BRAC-type Actions," *Huntsville Times*, Feb. 13, 2011, www.al.com (accessed Aug. 2, 2011).

16. Spires, "'This Is the Biggest Step,'" A1, A6.

17. Gina Hannah, "Defense Contractors Focus on Growth," *Huntsville Times*, Apr. 20, 2008, www.al.com (accessed June 12, 2009).

18. Marshall, "Leaders Predict More Huntsville Growth with BRAC-type Actions," *Huntsville Times*, Feb. 13, 2011, www.al.com (accessed Aug. 2, 2011).

19. Spires, "'This Is the Biggest Step,'" *Huntsville Times*, 14 May 2005, A6.

20. Lee Roop, "More than Half of BRAC Hires Are New to Huntsville," *Huntsville Times*, June 13, 2011, www.al.com (accessed Aug. 2, 2011).

21. Erin Musland, "BRAC Brings Boost to Service Industry," *Huntsville Times*, Apr. 20, 2008, www.al.com (accessed June 12, 2009).

22. Wendy Reeves, "Madison Striving to Meet Needs of BRAC"; Steve Doyle, "From Cotton Fields to 'Fields of Homes,'" *Huntsville Times*, Apr. 20, 2008, www.al.com (accessed June 12, 2009).

23. Steve Campbell, "3 School Systems Face Tough Decisions," *Huntsville Times*, Apr. 20, 2008, www.al.com (accessed June 12, 2009).

24. William David Baker, "Slow the Growth," Letter to the Editor, *Huntsville Times*, Mar. 15, 2011, www.al.com (accessed Aug. 2, 2011).

25. Dustin Mansfield, "VW, Toyota Latest to Buy TVA Megasites," [July 2008], tvaed.com/news/2008/vw_ap.htm (accessed June 12, 2009).

26. William Williams, "Marketing the Megasite," *Business TN* (Mar.–Apr. 2009), businesstn.com (accessed Aug. 2, 2011).

27. "Volkswagen Picks Tennessee for New U.S. Plant," July 15, 2008, www.tvaed.com/news/2008/volkswagen.htm (accessed June 12, 2009).

28. NAIDA, "Aerospace and Defense Companies in North Alabama," northalabamausa.com/site_pages/is_aerospace_defense.cfm (accessed June 12, 2009); NAIDA, "Automotive Suppliers in North Alabama," northalabamausa.com/stie_pages/is_automotive.cfm (accessed June 12, 2009); and NAIDA, "North Alabama Chemical Companies," www.northalabamausa.com/site_pages/is_chemicals.cfm (accessed June 12, 2009).

29. NAIDA, "Labor Force," northalabamausa.com/site_pages/dr_labor_force.cfm (accessed June 12, 2009); and NAIDA, "Taxes & Incentives," northalabamausa.com/site_pages/dr_taxes_incentives.cfm (accessed June 12, 2009).

30. U.S. Census Bureau, Thirteenth Census of the United States Taken in the Year 1910, vol. 6: Agriculture: Reports by States, Alabama–Montana (Washington, D.C.: GPO, 1913); U.S. Census Bureau, Sixteenth Census of the United States: 1940, Population, vol. 2: Characteristics of the Population, pt. 1: United States Summary and Alabama—District of Columbia (Washington, D.C.: GPO, 1943); U.S. Census Bureau, Census of Population: 1960, vol. 1: Characteristics of the Population, pt. 2: Alabama (Washington, D.C.: GPO, 1961).

31. Ibid.; U.S. Census Bureau, Fourteenth Census of the United States Taken in the Year 1920, vol. 2: Population 1920, Composition and Characteristics of the Population by States (Washington, D.C.: GPO, 1922); U.S. Census Bureau, Fifteenth Census of the United States, Manufactures: 1929, vol. 1: General Report, Statistics by Subjects (Washington, D.C.: GPO, 1933); U.S. Census Bureau, Fifteenth Census of the United States Taken in the Year 1930, vol. 2: Agriculture, pt. 2: The Southern States (Washington, D.C.: GPO, 1932); and U.S. Census Bureau, Census of Population: 1950, vol. 2: Characteristics of the Population, pt. 2: Alabama (Washington, D.C.: GPO, 1952).

32. Ibid.

33. "Interview with Holland Greer," clips 2 and 3, conducted by Patti Hannah and Rhonda Haygood, Nov. 6, 2007, in Florence-Lauderdale Public Library Digital Archive, archive.flpl.org (accessed Sept. 20, 2012).

34. "Interview with Huston Cobb," clip 1 of 9, conducted by Clint Alley and Patti Hannah, May 27, 2009, in Florence-Lauderdale Public Library Digital Archive, archive.flpl.org (accessed Sept. 20, 2012).

35. Mary Jane Lowe, "Interview with George F. Davis," Nov. 21, 1990, box 2: "George F. Davis," RG 142, TVA Administrative Services, Oral History Records, 1965–93.

36. Shirley McCrary, assisted by Toby Sewell, "Interview with John Caddell," Feb. 27, 1989, tape AC-54, side A, Colonial Dames.

BIBLIOGRAPHY

MANUSCRIPT COLLECTIONS

Alabama Department of Archives and History. Montgomery (ADAH).

Bankhead, John H., Sr. Papers.

Bankhead, William B. Papers.

Brandon, William G. Papers of the Brandon Administration.

Colonial Dames Oral History Collection. Audio.

Dixon, Frank W. Papers of the Dixon Administration.

———. Papers (Personal).

Folsom, James E. Papers of the First Folsom Administration (1947–51).

———. Papers of the Second Folsom Administration (1955–59).

Miller, Benjamin M. Papers of the Miller Administration.

Patterson, John. Papers of the Patterson Administration.

Persons, Gordon. Papers of the Persons Administration.

Sparks, Chauncey. Papers of the Sparks Administration.

Underwood, Oscar. Papers.

Alabama Power Co. Alabama Power Corporate Archives. Birmingham.

Auburn University Special Collections and Archives. Auburn.

Alabama Cooperative Extension Service Records (ACES), 1910–1974.

Florence-Lauderdale Public Library. Digital Archive. Florence, Ala. archive.flpl.org.

W. S. Hoole Special Collections Library. University of Alabama. Tuscaloosa (Hoole).

Hill, Lister. Papers.

Sparkman, John J. Papers [House of Representatives].

———. Papers [Senate].

Huntsville, Ala., Public Library. Heritage Room. Clippings Collections (HPL).

National Archives, Southeast Region, Morrow, Georgia (NARASE).

Records of the National Aeronautics and Space Administration (MSFC Papers).

Contract Corporation Records. Upper Management Files. #17 Series. Office of the Director, 1958–68.

Marshall Star. Office of Strategic Communications, Internal Communications Office, Marshall Space Flight Center, Huntsville, Ala.

Von Braun, Wernher. Speech Files, 1954–68. Office of the Director.

Records of the Tennessee Valley Authority (TVA Records).

Curtis, [Harry], [Arthur E.] Morgan, and [Harcourt] Morgan. Records of the Board of Directors. Office of the General Manager.

Division of Navigation Development Volume Files. 1954–68. Office of the General Manager.

Family Removal and Population Readjustment Case Records. Reservoir Property Management Division.

Government Relations and Economic Staff, General Correspondence. 1953–57. Office of the General Manager.

Lilienthal, David E. Correspondence Files.

Morgan, Arthur E. Records of the Board of Directors. 1933–58.

———. Records of the Chairmen and Members of the Board of Directors of TVA. Subject Index to Speeches. 1933–38.

Office of Engineering, Design and Construction Files.

Oral History Records. 1965–93.

Pope, James P., and Raymond R. Paty. Records of the Chairman and the Members of the Board of Directors. 1939–57.

North Alabama Industrial Development Association, Records. Decatur (NAIDA).

M. Louis Salmon Library and Special Collections. University of Alabama, Huntsville (UAH).

Jones, Robert E. Papers.

PUBLISHED PRIMARY SOURCES

Congressional Record. Washington, D.C., 1873–.

Coolidge, Calvin. Addresses. The American Presidency Project. www.presidency.ucsb.edu. Accessed Apr. 20, 2009.

Crawford, Charles W. *Oral History of the Tennessee Valley Authority: Interview with Barrett Shelton, Sr., June 18, 1970*. archive.org/stream/oralhistoryofteooshel/oralhistoryofteooshel_djvu.txt. Accessed Aug. 2, 2013.

McJimsey, George, ed. *Documentary History of the Franklin D. Roosevelt Presidency*, vol. 28: *Promulgation of the Tennessee Valley Authority*. LexisNexis, 2006.

Roosevelt, Franklin D. *Complete Presidential Press Conferences of Franklin D. Roosevelt*. 25 vols. New York: Da Capo Press, 1972.

———. "Inaugural Speech of Franklin Delano Roosevelt." Mar. 4, 1933. www.hpol.org/fdr/inaug/. Accessed Sept. 18, 2008.

———. *The Public Papers and Addresses of Franklin D. Roosevelt.* 13 vols. New York: Random House, 1938 (vols. 1–5); New York: Macmillan Co., 1941 (vols. 6–9); New York: Harper Brothers, [ca. 1950] (vols. 10–13).

U.S. Census, 1880–1960.

U.S. Supreme Court. *Ashwander v. Tennessee Valley Authority.* 297 U.S. 288 (1936). FindLaw. laws.findlaw.com/us/297/288.htm. Accessed May 30, 2013.

NEWSPAPERS

Chicago Defender
Christian Science Monitor
Decatur (Ala.) Daily
Florence (Ala.) Times
Huntsville (Ala.) Times
New York Times
Wall Street Journal
Washington Post

THESES AND DISSERTATIONS

Daws, Laura Beth. "Overlooked: Dominant Ideology, Limestone County, Alabama, Newspapers, and TVA Family Relocation, 1934–1936." MA thesis. Auburn University, 2005.

Ross, William D. "Industrial Promotion by Southern States." PhD diss., Duke University, 1951.

Stone, Richard Philip, II. "Making a Modern State: The Politics of Economic Development in South Carolina, 1938–1962." PhD diss., University of South Carolina, 2003.

Wilson, Charles MacArthur Wilson, "The Impact of Industrial Development on Lawrence County, Tennessee." MS thesis, University of Tennessee, 1965.

ARTICLES

Aull, G. H., L. P. Gabbard, and John F. Timmons. "United Nations Scientific Conference on the Conservation and Utilization of Resources." *Journal of Farm Economics* 32, no. 1 (Feb. 1950): 95–111.

Biles, Roger. "The Urban South in the Great Depression." *Journal of Southern History* 56, no. 1 (Feb. 1990): 71–100.

Cobb, James C. "Beyond Planters and Industrialists: A New Perspective on the New South." *Journal of Southern History* 54, no. 1 (Feb. 1988): 45–68.

Ford, Lacy K., and R. Phillip Stone, "Economic Development and Globalization in South Carolina." *Southern Cultures* (Spring 2007): 18–50.

Hon, Ralph C. "The South in a War Economy," *Southern Economic Journal* 8, no. 3 (Jan. 1942): 291–308.

Killingsworth, Steve. "Regional Planning on a Local Scale: The Brief Life of Pickwick Village." *West Tennessee Historical Society Papers* 51 (1997): 48–63.

Lester, Connie L. "Balancing Agriculture with Industry: Capital, Labor, and the Public Good in Mississippi's Home-Grown New Deal." *Journal of Mississippi History* 70 (Fall 2008): 235–63.

Lewis, Robert. "World War II Manufacturing and the Postwar Southern Economy." *Journal of Southern History* 73, no. 4 (Nov. 2007): 837–66.

Middleton, Sallie. "Space Rush: Local Impact of Federal Aerospace Programs on Brevard and Surrounding Counties." *Florida Historical Quarterly* 87 (Fall 2008): 258–89.

Nelson, Bruce. "Organized Labor and the Struggle for Black Equality in Mobile during World War II." *Journal of American History* 80, no. 3 (Dec. 1993): 952–88.

Norrell, Robert J. "Labor at the Ballot Box: Alabama Politics from the New Deal to the Dixiecrat Movement," *Journal of Southern History* 57, no. 2 (May 1991): 201–234.

Ott, Victoria. "From the Cotton Fields to the Great Waterway: African Americans and the Muscle Shoals Project during World War I." *Southern Historian* 22 (Spring 2001): 35–54.

Robock, Stefan H. "Industrialization and Economic Progress in the Southeast." *Southern Economic Journal* 20, no. 4 (Apr. 1954): 307–27.

Sheridan, Richard C. "Thomas Alva Edison's Visit to Muscle Shoals." *Journal of Muscle Shoals History* 11 (1986): 127–33.

Snow, Whitney Adrienne, "Cotton Mill City: The Huntsville Textile Industry, 1880–1989," *Alabama Review* 63, no. 4 (Oct. 2010): 243–81.

Tindall, George B. "Business Progressivism: Southern Politics in the Twenties." *South Atlantic Quarterly* 62 (Winter 1963): 92–106.

Williams, William. "Marketing the Megasite." *BusinessTN* (Mar./Apr. 2009). businesstn.com. Accessed Aug. 2, 2011.

BOOKS AND ESSAYS

Aiken, Charles S. *The Cotton Plantation South since the Civil War.* Baltimore: Johns Hopkins University Press, 1998.

Allen, Frederick Lewis. *Only Yesterday: An Informal History of the 1920's.* New York: Harper & Row, 1931.

Atkins, Leah Rawls. *"Developed for the Service of Alabama": The Centennial History of the Alabama Power Company, 1906–2006.* Birmingham: Alabama Power Co., 2006.

Ayers, Edward L. *The Promise of the New South: Life after Reconstruction.* 1992. New York: Oxford University Press, 2007.

Bartley, Numan V. *The New South, 1945–1980.* Baton Rouge: Louisiana State University Press, 1995.

Bergaust, Erik. *Rocket City, U.S.A.: From Huntsville, Alabama, to the Moon.* New York: Macmillan Co., 1963.

———. *Wernher von Braun.* Washington, D.C.: National Space Institute, 1976.

Blum, John Morton. *V Was for Victory: Politics and American Culture during World War II.* San Diego: Harcourt Brace, 1976.

Bragg, Rick. *Ava's Man.* New York: Vintage Books, 2001.

Brinkley, Alan. *The End of Reform: New Deal Liberalism in Recession and War.* New York: Vintage, 1995.

Brinkley, Douglas. *Wheels for the World: Henry Ford, His Company, and a Century of Progress, 1903–2003.* New York: Viking, 2003

Brownell, Blaine A. *The Urban Ethos in the South, 1920–1930.* Baton Rouge: Louisiana State University Press, 1975.

Callahan, North. *TVA: Bridge over Troubled Waters.* South Brunswick, N.J.: A. S. Barnes, 1980.

Carlton, David L. "Unbalanced Growth and Industrialization: The Case of South Carolina." In *Developing Dixie: Modernization in a Traditional Society,* ed. Winfred B. Moore Jr., Joseph F. Tripp, and Lyon G. Tyler Jr., 111–30. New York: Greenwood Press, 1988.

Carlton, David L., and Peter A. Coclanis, eds. *Confronting Southern Poverty in the Great Depression: The Report on Economic Conditions of the South with Related Documents.* Boston: Bedford/St. Martin's, 1996.

Cash, W. J. *The Mind of the South.* 50th anniversary ed. New York: Vintage Books, 1991.

Clapp, Gordon. *TVA: An Approach to the Development of a Region.* Chicago: University of Chicago Press, 1955.

Cobb, James C. *Away Down South: A History of Southern Identity.* New York: Oxford University Press, 2005.

———. *The Selling of the South: The Southern Crusade for Industrial Development, 1936–1980.* Baton Rouge: Louisiana State University Press, 1982.

Coclanis, Peter A. and Lacy K. Ford. "The South Carolina Economy Reconstructed and Reconsidered: Structure, Output, and Performance, 1670–1985." In *Developing Dixie: Modernization in a Traditional Society,* ed. Winfred B. Moore Jr., Joseph F. Tripp, and Lyon G. Tyler Jr., 92–110. New York: Greenwood Press, 1988.

Combes, Richard S. "Aircraft Manufacturing in Georgia: A Case Study of Federal Industrial Investment." In *The Second Wave: Southern Industrialization from the 1940s to the 1970s,* ed. Philip Scranton, 24–42. Athens: University of Georgia Press, 2001.

Cronenberg, Allen. *Forth to the Mighty Conflict: Alabama and World War II.* Tuscaloosa: University of Alabama Press, 1995.

Crowther Samuel, and Henry Ford. *My Life and Work.* 1922. Rpr. Garden City, N.J.: Garden City Publishing Co., 1926.

———. *Today and Tomorrow.* Garden City, N.J.: Doubleday, Page and Co., 1926.

Daicoff, Darwin W., Marston M. McCluggage, Charles K. Warriner, and Ronald R. Olsen. *Economic Impact of Military Base Closings*, vol. 1: *Adjustments by Communities and Workers.* United States Arms Control and Disarmament Agency, Apr. 1970.

Daniel, Adrian G. *The Formative Period of TVA: The Muscle Shoals Project, 1783–1916.* New York: Carlton Press, 1973.

Daniel, Pete. *Breaking the Land: The Transformation of Cotton, Tobacco, and Rice Cultures since 1880.* Urbana: University of Illinois Press, 1985.

Doyle, Don. *New Men, New Cities, New South: Atlanta, Nashville, Charleston, Mobile, 1860–1910.* Chapel Hill: University of North Carolina Press, 1990.

Eckl, William Wray. *The Story of an Alabama Congressman: Bob Jones* [1960].

Egerton, John. *Speak Now against the Day: The Generation before the Civil Rights Movement in the South* (Chapel Hill: University of North Carolina Press, 1995.

Eisenhower, Dwight D. *Mandate for Change, 1953–1956.* Garden City, N.Y.: Doubleday & Co., 1963.

Eisinger, Peter K. *The Rise of the Entrepreneurial State: State and Local Economic Development Policy in the United States.* Madison: University of Wisconsin Press, 1988.

Fite, Gilbert C. *Cotton Fields No More: Southern Agriculture, 1865–1980.* Lexington: University Press of Kentucky, 1984.

Flynt, Wayne. *Alabama in the Twentieth Century.* Tuscaloosa: University of Alabama Press, 2004.

———. *Poor but Proud: Alabama's Poor Whites.* Tuscaloosa: University of Alabama Press, 1989.

Gaston, Paul M. *The New South Creed: A Study in Southern Mythmaking.* 1970. Rpr. Baton Rouge: Louisiana State University Press, 1976.

Gergerman, Alan, and R. Leo Penne. "Community Economic Adjustment to Defense Industrial Cutbacks." In *Economic Adjustment and Conversion of Defense Industries*, ed. John E. Lynch, 59–80. Boulder, Colo.: Westview Press, 1987.

Grandin, Greg. *Fordlandia: The Rise and Fall of Henry Ford's Forgotten Jungle City.* New York: Metropolitan Books, 2009.

Grant, Nancy L. *TVA and Black Americans: Planning for the Status Quo.* Philadelphia: Temple University Press, 1990.

Hall, Jacqueline Dowd, et al. *Like a Family: The Making of a Southern Cotton Mill World.* New York: W. W. Norton, 1987.

Hamilton, Virginia Van der Veer. *Lister Hill: Statesman from the South.* Chapel Hill: University of North Carolina Press, 1987.

Hays, Samuel P. *Conservation and the Gospel of Efficiency: The Progressive Conservation Movement, 1890–1920.* 1959. Rpr. Pittsburgh, Pa.: University of Pittsburgh Press, 1999.

Hicks, John D. *Republican Ascendancy, 1921–1933.* New York: Harper and Row, 1960.

Hiltzik, Michael. *Colossus: Hoover Dam and the Making of the American Century.* New York: Free Press, 2010.

Hodge, Clarence. *The Tennessee Valley Authority: A National Experiment in Regionalism.* New York: Russell & Russell, 1968.

Hoover, Calvin B., and B. U. Ratchford. *Economic Resources and Policies in the South.* New York: MacMillan Co., 1951.

Hopkins, E. J. *The Louisville Industrial Foundation: A Study in Community Capitalization of Local Industries.* Federal Reserve Bank of Atlanta, 1945.

Hornady, John R. *Soldiers of Progress and Industry.* New York: Dodd, Mead, and Co., 1930.

Hubbard, Preston J. *Origins of the TVA: The Muscle Shoals Controversy, 1920–1932.* New York: W. W. Norton and Co., 1961.

Ickes, Harold. *The Secret Diary of Harold Ickes: The First Thousand Days, 1933–1936.* New York: Simon and Schuster, 1953.

Jacoway, Elizabeth, and David R. Colburn, eds. *Southern Businessmen and Desegregation.* Baton Rouge: Louisiana State University Press, 1982.

Johnson, Evans. *Oscar W. Underwood: A Political Biography.* Tuscaloosa: University of Alabama Press, 2006.

Joiner, Melinda Gorham, and Peter Coburn. *Huntsville: Where Technology Meets Tradition.* Huntsville, Ala.: Community Communications, 1993.

Kelley, Robin D. G. *Hammer and Hoe: Alabama Communists during the Great Depression.* Chapel Hill: University of North Carolina Press, 1990.

Key, V. O., Jr., *Southern Politics in State and Nation.* New York: Vintage Books, 1949.

Lassiter, Matthew D. *The Silent Majority: Suburban Politics in the Sunbelt South.* Princeton, N.J.: Princeton University Press, 2006.

Lepawsky, Albert. *State Planning and Economic Development in the South.* Kingsport, Tennessee: Kingsport Press, Inc., 1949.

Leuchtenburg, William E. *Franklin D. Roosevelt and the New Deal, 1932–1940.* New York: Harper & Row, 1967.

———. *The White House Looks South: Franklin D. Roosevelt, Harry S. Truman, Lyndon B. Johnson.* Baton Rouge: Louisiana State University Press, 2005.

Lilienthal, David E. *The Journals of David E. Lilienthal.* Vol. 1: *The TVA Years, 1939–1945.* New York: Harper & Row, 1964.

———. *TVA: Democracy on the March.* New York: Harper & Brothers Publishers, 1944.

Link, Albert N. *From Seed to Harvest: The Growth of Research Triangle Park.* Chapel Hill: University of North Carolina Press, 2002.

Lipartito, Kenneth, and Orville R. Burton. *A History of Kennedy Space Center.* Gainesville: University Press of Florida, 2007.

Lynch, John E. "Defense Spending in the Economy." In *Economic Adjustment and Conversion of Defense Industries*, ed. John E. Lynch, 13–28. Boulder, Colo.: Westview Press, 1987.

Markusen, Ann, Peter Hall, Scott Campbell, and Sabina Deitrick. *The Rise of the Gunbelt: The Military Remapping of Industrial America*. New York: Oxford University Press, 1991.

Martin, Thomas W. *The Story of Electricity in Alabama*. Birmingham, Ala.: Birmingham Publishing Co., 1952.

Maunula, Marko. *Guten Tag, Y'All: Globalization and the South Carolina Piedmont, 1950–2000*. Athens: University of Georgia Press, 2009.

McCraw, Thomas K. *TVA and the Power Fight, 1933–1939*. Philadelphia: J. P. Lippincott Co., 1971.

McDonald, Michael J., and John Muldowny. *TVA and the Dispossessed: The Resettlement of Population in the Norris Dam Area*. Knoxville: University of Tennessee Press, 1982.

McDonald, William L., and L. D. Staggs Jr. *Remembering Sweetwater: The Museums, the Mills, the People*. Killen, Ala.: Bluewater Publications, 2002.

McDougall, Walter A. *The Heavens and the Earth: A Political History of the Space Age*. New York: Basic Books, 1985.

McElvaine, Robert S. *The Great Depression: America, 1929–1941*. New York: Times Books, 1984.

McGerr, Michael. *A Fierce Discontent: The Rise and Fall of the Progressive Movement in America*. New York: Oxford University Press, 2003.

McMillen, Neil R. *Remaking Dixie: The Impact of World War II on the American South*. Oxford: University Press of Mississippi, 1997.

Miller, Char. *Gifford Pinchot and the Making of Modern Environmentalism*. Washington, D.C.: Island Press, 2001.

Milton, George Fort. "The Tennessee Valley: An Experiment in a Way of Life." In *A Book of the South*, ed. John Temple Graves II et al., 85–94. Southern Editors Association, ca. 1940.

Morgan, Arthur E. *The Making of the TVA*. Buffalo, N.Y.: Prometheus Books, 1974.

Neufield, Michael H. *Von Braun: Dreamer of Space, Engineer of War*. New York: Alfred A Knopf, 2007.

Nevins, Allan, and Frank Ernest Hill. *Ford: Expansion and Challenge, 1915–1933*. New York: Charles Scribner's Sons, 1957.

Norris, George W. *Fighting Liberal: The Autobiography of George W. Norris*. Lincoln: University of Nebraska Press, 1992.

Odum, Howard, and Harry Estill Moore. *American Regionalism: A Cultural-Historical Approach to National Integration*. New York: Henry Holt and Co., 1938.

Olliff. Martin T., ed. *The Great War in the Heart of Dixie: Alabama during World War I*. Tuscaloosa: University of Alabama Press, 2008.

Owen, Marguerite. *The Tennessee Valley Authority.* New York: Praeger Publishers, 1973.

Owen, Marie Bankhead. *The Story of Alabama: A History of the State.* Vol. 1. New York: Lewis Historical Publishing Co., 1949.

Permaloff, Anne, and Carl Grafton. *Political Power in Alabama: The More Things Change.* Athens: University of Georgia Press, 2008.

Phillips, Sarah T. *This Land, This Nation: Conservation, Rural America, and the New Deal.* New York: Cambridge University Press, 2007.

Rogers, William Warren, Robert David Ward, Leah Rawls Atkins, and Wayne Flynt. *Alabama: The History of a Deep South State.* Tuscaloosa: University of Alabama Press, 1994.

Rushing, Wanda. *Memphis and the Paradox of Place: Globalization in the American South.* Chapel Hill: University of North Carolina Press, 2009.

Schlesinger, Tom, with John Gaventa and Juliet Merrifield. *Our Own Worst Enemy: The Impact of Military Production on the Upper South.* Highland Research and Education Center, 1983.

Schulman, Bruce J. *From Cotton Belt to Sunbelt: Federal Policy, Economic Development, and the Transformation of the South, 1938–1980.* Durham, N.C.: Duke University Press, 1994.

Schwarz, Jordan A. *The New Dealers: Power Politics in the Age of Roosevelt.* New York: Knopf, 1993.

Scott, Thomas A. "Winning World War II in an Atlanta Suburb: Local Boosters and the Recruitment of the Bell Bomber." In *The Second Wave: Southern Industrialization from the 1940s to the 1970s*, ed. Philip Scranton, 1–23. Athens: University of Georgia Press, 2001.

Selznick, Philip. *TVA and the Grass Roots: A Study in the Sociology of Formal Organization.* Berkeley: University of California Press, 1949.

Shelton, Barrett. *The Decatur Story.* Knoxville, Tenn.: Tennessee Valley Authority, 1950.

Shlaes, Amity. *Coolidge.* New York: Harper Collins, 2013.

———. *The Forgotten Man: A New History of the Great Depression.* New York: Harper Perennial, 2007.

Stephens, Elise Hopkins. *Historic Huntsville: A City of New Beginnings.* Woodland Hills, Calif.: Windsor Publications, 1984.

Thomas, Mary Martha. *Riveting and Rationing in Dixie: Alabama Women and the Second World War.* Tuscaloosa: University of Alabama Press, 1987.

Tindall, George Brown. *The Emergence of the New South, 1913–1945.* Baton Rouge: Louisiana State University Press, 1967.

Trest, Warren. *Nobody but the People: The Life and Times of Alabama's Youngest Governor.* Montgomery, Ala.: New South Books, 2008.

Twelve Southerners. *I'll Take My Stand: The South and the Agrarian Tradition.* 2nd ed. Baton Rouge: Louisiana State University Press, 1977.

Von Braun, Wernher, and Frederick I. Ordnay III. *History of Rocketry and Space Travel.* New York: Thomas Y. Cromwell Co., 1969.

Walker, Melissa. *All We Knew Was to Farm: Rural Women in the Upcountry South, 1919–1941.* Baltimore: Johns Hopkins University Press, 2000.

Whisnant, David E. *Modernizing the Mountaineer: People, Power, and Planning in Appalachia,* 1980. Rev. ed. Knoxville: University of Tennessee Press, 1994. Page references are to the 1994 edition.

Whitman, Willson. *God's Valley: People and Power along the Tennessee River.* New York: Viking Press, 1939.

Woodward, C. Vann. *Origins of the New South, 1877–1913.* 1951. Baton Rouge: Louisiana State University Press, 1971.

Wolfe, Thomas. "Boom Town." In *The Complete Short Stories of Thomas Wolfe,* ed. Francis E. Skipp, 120–41. New York: Charles Scribner's Sons, 1987.

Wright, Gavin. *Old South, New South: Revolutions in the Southern Economy since the Civil War.* Baton Rouge: Louisiana State University Press, 1986.

Zucker, Norman L. *George W. Norris: Gentle Knight of American Democracy.* Urbana: University of Illinois Press, 1966.

INDEX